Microsoft Official Academic Course
MICROSOFT POWERPOINT 2013

WILEY

Editor	Bryan Gambrel
Publisher	Don Fowley
Director of Sales	Mitchell Beaton
Technical Editor	Joyce Nielsen
Executive Marketing Manager	Chris Ruel
Assistant Marketing Manager	Debbie Martin
Microsoft Strategic Relationships Manager	Gene Longo of Microsoft Learning
Editorial Program Assistant	Allison Winkle
Project Coordinator	Ashley Barth
Content Manager	Kevin Holm
Production Editor	James Metzger
Creative Director	Harry Nolan
Cover Designer	Tom Nery
Product Designer	Jennifer Welter
Content Editor	Wendy Ashenberg

This book was set in Garamond by Aptara®, Inc., and printed and bound by Courier/Kendallville. The covers were printed by Courier/Kendallville.

ISBN 978-0-470-13309-5

Printed in the United States of America

10 9 8 7 6 5 4 3 2 1

Foreword from the Publisher

Wiley's publishing vision for the Microsoft Official Academic Course series is to provide students and instructors with the skills and knowledge they need to use Microsoft technology effectively in all aspects of their personal and professional lives. Quality instruction is required to help both educators and students get the most from Microsoft's software tools and to become more productive. Thus our mission is to make our instructional programs trusted educational companions for life.

To accomplish this mission, Wiley and Microsoft have partnered to develop the highest quality educational programs for Information Workers, IT Professionals, and Developers. Materials created by this partnership carry the brand name "Microsoft Official Academic Course," assuring instructors and students alike that the content of these textbooks is fully endorsed by Microsoft, and that they provide the highest quality information and instruction on Microsoft products. The Microsoft Official Academic Course textbooks are "Official" in still one more way—they are the officially sanctioned courseware for Microsoft IT Academy members.

The Microsoft Official Academic Course series focuses on workforce development. These programs are aimed at those students seeking to enter the workforce, change jobs, or embark on new careers as information workers, IT professionals, and developers. Microsoft Official Academic Course programs address their needs by emphasizing authentic workplace scenarios with an abundance of projects, exercises, cases, and assessments.

The Microsoft Official Academic Courses are mapped to Microsoft's extensive research and job-task analysis, the same research and analysis used to create the Microsoft Office Specialist (MOS) exams. The textbooks focus on real skills for real jobs. As students work through the projects and exercises in the textbooks they enhance their level of knowledge and their ability to apply the latest Microsoft technology to everyday tasks. These students also gain resume-building credentials that can assist them in finding a job, keeping their current job, or in furthering their education.

The concept of life-long learning is today an utmost necessity. Job roles, and even whole job categories, are changing so quickly that none of us can stay competitive and productive without continuously updating our skills and capabilities. The Microsoft Official Academic Course offerings, and their focus on Microsoft certification exam preparation, provide a means for people to acquire and effectively update their skills and knowledge. Wiley supports students in this endeavor through the development and distribution of these courses as Microsoft's official academic publisher.

Joe Heider
Senior Vice President, Wiley Global Education

Illustrated Book Tour

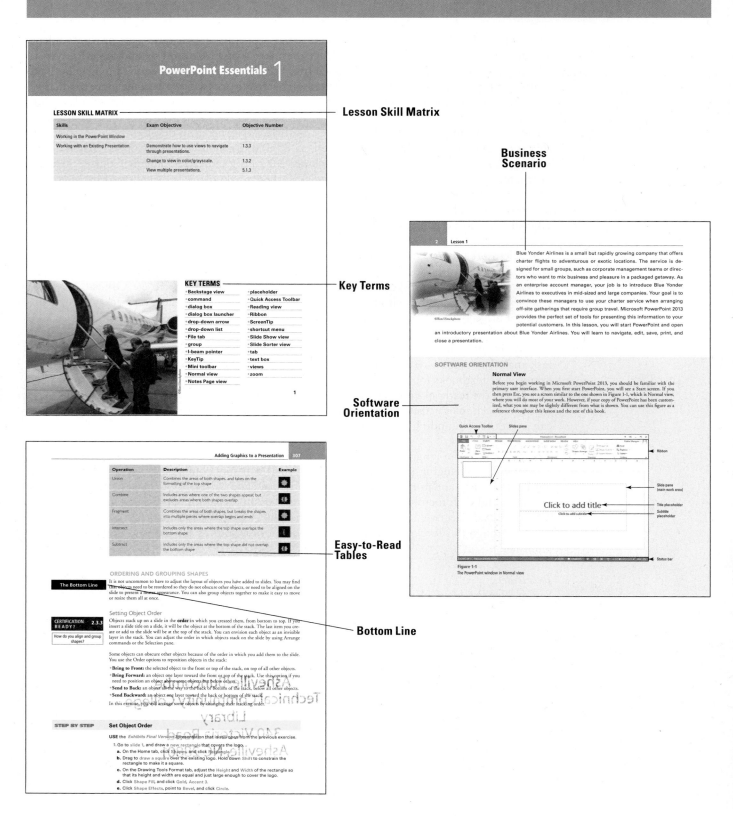

Lesson Skill Matrix

Business Scenario

Key Terms

Software Orientation

Easy-to-Read Tables

Bottom Line

Illustrated Book Tour

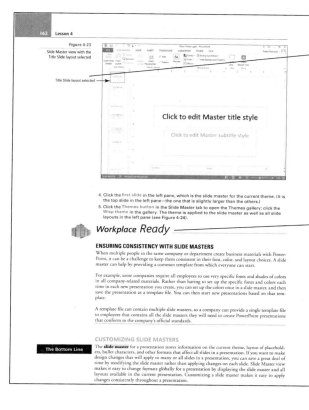

Screen Images with Callouts

Take Note
Reader Aids

Workplace Ready

Step by Step Exercises

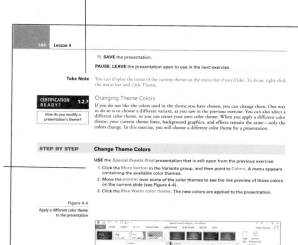

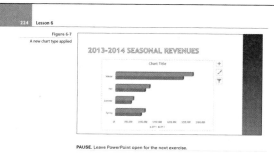

Troubleshooting
Reader Aids

Another Way
Reader Aids

Illustrated Book Tour

Microsoft Office
Specialist Certification
Objective Alert

Data Files Icon

Cross Reference
Reader Aid

Skill Summary

Knowledge
Assessment
Questions

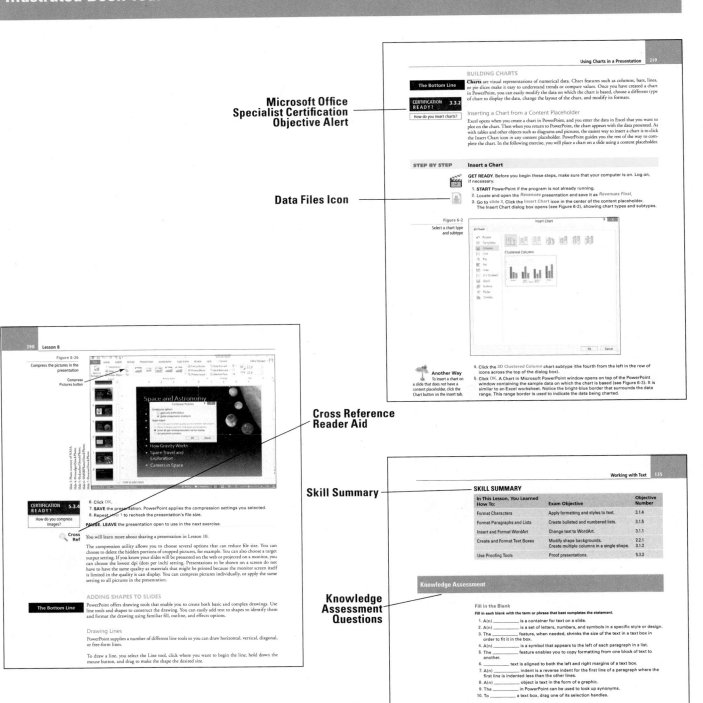

Illustrated Book Tour

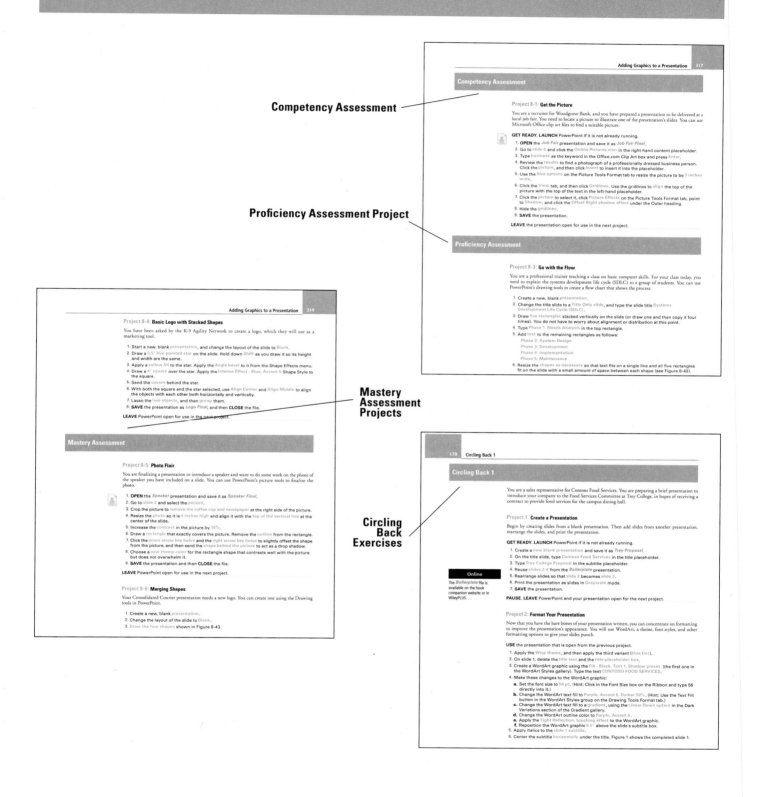

Competency Assessment

Proficiency Assessment Project

Mastery Assessment Projects

Circling Back Exercises

Preface

Welcome to the Microsoft Official Academic Course (MOAC) program for Microsoft Office 2013. MOAC represents the collaboration between Microsoft Learning and John Wiley & Sons, Inc., publishing company. Microsoft and Wiley teamed up to produce a series of textbooks that deliver compelling and innovative teaching solutions to instructors and superior learning experiences for students. Infused and informed by in-depth knowledge from the creators of Microsoft Office and Windows, and crafted by a publisher known worldwide for the pedagogical quality of its products, these textbooks maximize skills transfer in minimum time. Students are challenged to reach their potential by using their new technical skills as highly productive members of the workforce.

Because this knowledgebase comes directly from Microsoft, architect of the Office 2013 system and creator of the Microsoft Office Specialist (MOS) exams (www.microsoft.com/learning/mcp/mcts), you are sure to receive the topical coverage that is most relevant to students' personal and professional success. Microsoft's direct participation not only assures you that MOAC textbook content is accurate and current; it also means that students will receive the best instruction possible to enable their success on certification exams and in the workplace.

THE MICROSOFT OFFICIAL ACADEMIC COURSE PROGRAM

The Microsoft Official Academic Course series is a complete program for instructors and institutions to prepare and deliver great courses on Microsoft software technologies. With MOAC, we recognize that, because of the rapid pace of change in the technology and curriculum developed by Microsoft, there is an ongoing set of needs beyond classroom instruction tools for an instructor to be ready to teach the course. The MOAC program endeavors to provide solutions for all these needs in a systematic manner in order to ensure a successful and rewarding course experience for both instructor and student—technical and curriculum training for instructor readiness with new software releases; the software itself for student use at home for building hands-on skills, assessment, and validation of skill development; and a great set of tools for delivering instruction in the classroom and lab. All are important to the smooth delivery of an interesting course on Microsoft software, and all are provided with the MOAC program. We think about the model below as a gauge for ensuring that we completely support you in your goal of teaching a great course. As you evaluate your instructional materials options, you may wish to use the model for comparison purposes with available products.

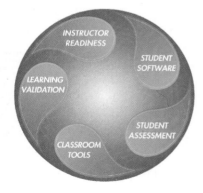

Illustrated Book Tour

PEDAGOGICAL FEATURES

The MOAC courseware for *Microsoft Office 2013 system* are designed to cover all the learning objectives for that MOS exam, which is referred to as its "objective domain." The Microsoft Office Specialist (MOS) exam objectives are highlighted throughout the textbooks. Many pedagogical features have been developed specifically for *Microsoft Official Academic Course* programs. Unique features of our task-based approach include a Lesson Skills Matrix that correlates skills taught in each lesson to the MOS objectives; Certification, and three levels of increasingly rigorous lesson-ending activities: Competency, Proficiency, and Mastery Assessment.

Presenting the extensive procedural information and technical concepts woven throughout the textbook raises challenges for the student and instructor alike. The Illustrated Book Tour that follows provides a guide to the rich features contributing to *Microsoft Official Academic Course* program's pedagogical plan. Following is a list of key features in each lesson designed to prepare students for success on the certification exams and in the workplace:

- Each lesson begins with a **Lesson Skill Matrix**. More than a standard list of learning objectives, the skill matrix correlates each software skill covered in the lesson to the specific MOS exam objective domain.

- Each lesson features a real-world **Business Case** scenario that places the software skills and knowledge to be acquired in a real-world setting.

- Every lesson opens with a **Software Orientation**. This feature provides an overview of the software features students will be working with in the lesson. The orientation will detail the general properties of the software or specific features, such as a ribbon or dialog box; and it includes a large, labeled screen image.

- Concise and frequent **Step-by-Step** instructions teach students new features and provide an opportunity for hands-on practice. Numbered steps give detailed, step-by-step instructions to help students learn software skills. The steps also show results and screen images to match what students should see on their computer screens.

- **Illustrations**: Screen images provide visual feedback as students work through the exercises. The images reinforce key concepts, provide visual clues about the steps, and allow students to check their progress.

- **Key Terms**: Important technical vocabulary is listed at the beginning of the lesson. When these terms are used later in the lesson, they appear in bold italic type with yellow highlighter and are defined. The Glossary contains all of the key terms and their definitions.

- Engaging point-of-use **Reader aids**, located throughout the lessons, tell students why this topic is relevant (*The Bottom Line*), provide students with helpful hints (*Take Note*), or show alternate ways to accomplish tasks (*Another Way*), or point out things to watch out for or avoid (*Troubleshooting*). Reader aids also provide additional relevant or background information that adds value to the lesson.

- **Certification Ready?** features throughout the text signal students where a specific certification objective is covered. They provide students with a chance to check their understanding of that particular MOS exam objective and, if necessary, review the section of the lesson where it is covered. MOAC provides complete preparation for MOS certification.

- **Workplace Ready.** These new features preview how the Microsoft Office 2013 system applications are used in real-world situations.

- Each lesson ends with a **Skill Summary** recapping the topics and MOS exam skills covered in the lesson.

- **Knowledge Assessment:** Provides a total of 20 questions from a mix of True/False, Fill-in-the-Blank, Matching or Multiple Choice testing students on concepts learned in the lesson.

- **Competency, Proficiency, and Mastery Assessment:** Provides three progressively more challenging lesson-ending activities.

- **Circling Back:** These integrated projects provide students with an opportunity to renew and practice skills learned in previous lessons.

- **Online files:** The student companion website contains the data files needed for each lesson. These files are indicated by the file download icon in the margin of the textbook.

Conventions and Features Used in This Book

This book uses particular fonts, symbols, and heading conventions to highlight important information or to call your attention to special steps. For more information about the features in each lesson, refer to the Illustrated Book Tour section.

Convention	Meaning
Bottom Line	This feature provides a brief summary of the material to be covered in the section that follows.
CLOSE	Words in all capital letters indicate instructions for opening, saving, or closing files or programs. They also point out items you should check or actions you should take.
CERTIFICATION READY?	This feature signals the point in the text where a specific certification objective is covered. It provides you with a chance to check your understanding of that particular MOS objective and, if necessary, review the section of the lesson where it is covered.
Take Note	Reader aids appear in shaded boxes found in your text. Take Note provides helpful hints related to particular tasks or topics.
Another Way	Another Way provides an alternative procedure for accomplishing a particular task.
Cross Ref	These notes provide pointers to information discussed elsewhere in the textbook or describe interesting features that are not directly addressed in the current topic or exercise.
ALT + Tab	A plus sign (+) between two key names means that you must press both keys at the same time. Keys that you are instructed to press in an exercise will appear in the font shown here.
A **shared printer** can be used by many individuals on a network.	Key terms appear in bold italic.
Key My Name is	Any text you are asked to key appears in color.
Click OK	Any button on the screen you are supposed to click on or select will also appear in color.
	The names of data files will appear in bold, italic and red for easy identification. These data files are available for download from the Student Companion Site (www.Wiley.com/college/Microsoft).
	Step-by-step tutorial videos are available for many of the activities throughout this course. For information on how to access these videos, see the Student Companion Site (www.Wiley.com/college/Microsoft).
OPEN *BudgetWorksheet1*	The names of data files will appear in bold, italic, and red for easy identification.

Instructor Support Program

The *Microsoft Official Academic Course* programs are accompanied by a rich array of resources that incorporate the extensive textbook visuals to form a pedagogically cohesive package. These resources provide all the materials instructors need to deploy and deliver their courses. Resources available online for download include:

• The **Instructor's Guide** contains Solutions to all the textbook exercises as well as chapter summaries and lecture notes. The Instructor's Guide and Syllabi for various term lengths are available from the Instructor's Book Companion site (www.wiley.com/college/microsoft).

• The **Solution Files** for all the projects in the book are available online from our Instructor's Book Companion site (www.wiley.com/college/microsoft).

• The **Test Bank** contains hundreds of questions organized by lesson in multiple-choice, true-false, short answer, and essay formats and is available to download from the Instructor's Book Companion site (www.wiley.com/college/microsoft). A complete answer key is provided.

 This title's test bank is available for use in Respondus' easy-to-use software. You can download the test bank for free using your Respondus, Respondus LE, or StudyMate Author software.

 Respondus is a powerful tool for creating and managing exams that can be printed to paper or published directly to Blackboard, WebCT, Desire2Learn, eCollege, ANGEL, and other eLearning systems.

• **Test Bank Projects.** Two projects for each lesson are provided on the Instructor's Book Companion Site as well as solution files suitable for grading with OfficeGrader. These projects cover topics from within one specific lesson.

• **Comprehensive Projects:** Two comprehensive projects are provided on the Instructor's Book Companion Site for each Circling Back. These projects cover topics from all lessons in the book up to that point. Solution files suitable for grading with OfficeGrader are also provided.

• **Capstone Projects:** Two capstone projects are provided with the final Circling Back on the Instructor's Book Companion Site. These projects are suitable for a final exam or final project for the course. These projects cover a range of topics from throughout the entire book. Solution files suitable for grading with OfficeGrader are also provided.

• **PowerPoint Presentations and Images**. A complete set of PowerPoint presentations is available on the Instructor's Book Companion site (www.wiley.com/college/microsoft) to enhance classroom presentations. Tailored to the text's topical coverage and Skills Matrix, these presentations are designed to convey key Microsoft .NET Framework concepts addressed in the text.

 All figures from the text are on the Instructor's Book Companion site (www.wiley.com/college/microsoft). You can incorporate them into your PowerPoint presentations, or create your own overhead transparencies and handouts.

 By using these visuals in class discussions, you can help focus students' attention on key elements of Windows Server and help them understand how to use it effectively in the workplace.

- **Office Grader** automated grading system allows you to easily grade student data files in Word, Excel, PowerPoint or Access format, against solution files. Save tens or hundreds of hours each semester with automated grading. More information on OfficeGrader is available from the Instructor's Book Companion site (www.wiley.com/college/microsoft).

- The **Student Data Files** are available online on both the Instructor's Book Companion Site and for students on the Student Book Companion Site.

- Wiley **Faculty Network:** When it comes to improving the classroom experience, there is no better source of ideas and inspiration than your fellow colleagues. The Wiley Faculty Network connects teachers with technology, facilitates the exchange of best practices, and helps to enhance instructional efficiency and effectiveness. Faculty Network activities include technology training and tutorials, virtual seminars, peer-to-peer exchanges of experiences and ideas, personal consulting, and sharing of resources. For details visit www.WhereFacultyConnect.com.

IMPORTANT WEB ADDRESSES AND PHONE NUMBERS

To locate the Wiley Higher Education Rep in your area, go to the following Web address and click on the "*Contact Us*" link at the top of the page.

www.wiley.com/college

Or Call the MOAC Toll Free Number: 1 + (888) 764-7001 (U.S. & Canada only).

To learn more about becoming a Microsoft Certified Professional and exam availability, visit **www.microsoft.com/learning/mcp.**

DREAMSPARK PREMIUM
Free 3-Year Membership available to Qualified Adopters

DreamSpark Premium is designed to provide the easiest and most inexpensive way for schools to make the latest Microsoft developer tools, products, and technologies available in labs, classrooms, and on student PCs. DreamSpark Premium is an annual membership program for departments teaching Science, Technology, Engineering, and Mathematics (STEM) courses. The membership provides a complete solution to keep academic labs, faculty, and students on the leading edge of technology.

Software available through the DreamSpark Premium program is provided at no charge to adopting departments through the Wiley and Microsoft publishing partnership.

Contact your Wiley rep for details.

For more information about the DreamSpark Premium program, go to Microsoft's DreamSpark website.

Visit Microsoft.com for more information.

BOOK COMPANION WEBSITE
(WWW.WILEY.COM/COLLEGE/MICROSOFT)

The students' book companion site for the MOAC series includes any resources, exercise files, and web links that will be used in conjunction with this course.

WILEY E-TEXT: POWERED BY VITALSOURCE

When you choose a Wiley E-Text you not only save money; you benefit from being able to access course materials and content anytime, anywhere through a user experience that makes learning rewarding.

With the Wiley E-Text you will be able to easily:
* Search
* Take notes
* Highlight key materials
* Have all your work in one place for more efficient studying

In addition, the Wiley E-Text is fully portable. Students can access it online and download to their computer for off line access and access read and study on their device of preference—computer, tablet, or smartphone.

WHY MOS CERTIFICATION?

Microsoft Office Specialist (MOS) 2013 is a valuable credential that recognizes the desktop computing skills needed to use the full features and functionality of the Microsoft Office 2013 suite.

In the worldwide job market, Microsoft Office Specialist is the primary tool companies use to validate the proficiency of their employees in the latest productivity tools and technology, helping them select job candidates based on globally recognized standards for verifying skills. The results of an independent research study show that businesses with certified employees are more productive compared to non-certified employees and that certified employees bring immediate value to their jobs.

In academia, as in the business world, institutions upgrading to Office 2013 may seek ways to protect and maximize their technology investment. By offering certification, they validate that decision—because powerful Office 2013 applications such as Word, Excel, and PowerPoint can be effectively used to demonstrate increases in academic preparedness and workforce readiness.

Individuals seek certification to increase their own personal sense of accomplishment and to create advancement opportunities by establishing a leadership position in their school or department, thereby differentiating their skill sets in a competitive college admissions and job market.

PREPARING TO TAKE THE MICROSOFT OFFICE SPECIALIST
(MOS) EXAM

The Microsoft Office Specialist credential has been upgraded to validate skills with the Microsoft Office 2013 system. The MOS certifications target information workers and cover the most popular business applications such as Word 2013, Excel 2013, PowerPoint 2013, Outlook 2013, and Access 2013.

By becoming certified, you demonstrate to employers that you have achieved a predictable level of skill in the use of a particular Office application. Employers often require certification either as a condition of employment or as a condition of advancement within the company or other organization. The certification examinations are sponsored by Microsoft but administered through exam delivery partners like Certiport.

To learn more about becoming a Microsoft Office Specialist and exam availability, visit http://www.microsoft.com/learning/en/us/mos-certification.aspx.

Preparing to Take an Exam

Unless you are a very experienced user, you will need to use a test preparation course to prepare to complete the test correctly and within the time allowed. The *Microsoft Official Academic Course* series is designed to prepare you with a strong knowledge of all exam topics, and with some additional review and practice on your own. You should feel confident in your ability to pass the appropriate exam.

After you decide which exam to take, review the list of objectives for the exam. This list can be found in the MOS Objectives Appendix at the back of this book. You can also easily identify tasks that are included in the objective list by locating the Lesson Skill Matrix at the start of each lesson and the Certification Ready sidebars in the margin of the lessons in this book.

To take the MOS test, visit http://www.microsoft.com/learning/en/us/mos-certification.aspx to locate your nearest testing center. Then call the testing center directly to schedule your test. The amount of advance notice you should provide will vary for different testing centers, and it typically depends on the number of computers available at the testing center, the number of other testers who have already been scheduled for the day on which you want to take the test, and the number of times per week that the testing center offers MOS testing. In general, you should call to schedule your test at least two weeks prior to the date on which you want to take the test.

When you arrive at the testing center, you might be asked for proof of identity. A driver's license or passport is an acceptable form of identification. If you do not have either of these items of documentation, call your testing center and ask what alternative forms of identification will be accepted. If you are retaking a test, bring your MOS identification number, which will have been given to you when you previously took the test. If you have not prepaid or if your organization has not already arranged to make payment for you, you will need to pay the test-taking fee when you arrive.

Test Format

MOS exams are Exams are primarily performance-based and conducted in a "live," or simulated, environment. Exam candidates taking exams for MOS 2007 or 2010 are asked to perform a series of tasks to clearly demonstrate their skills. For example, a Word exam might ask a user to balance newspaper column lengths or keep text together in columns. The new MOS 2013 exam format presents a short project the candidate must complete, using the specifications provided. This creates a real-world testing experience for candidates. All MOS exams must be completed in 90 minutes or less.

Student Data Files

All of the practice files that you will use as you perform the exercises in the book are available for download on our student companion site. By using the practice files, you will not waste time creating the samples used in the lessons, and you can concentrate on learning how to use Microsoft Office 2013. With the files and the step-by-step instructions in the lessons, you will learn by doing, which is an easy and effective way to acquire and remember new skills.

COPYING THE PRACTICE FILES

Your instructor might already have copied the practice files before you arrive in class. However, your instructor might ask you to copy the practice files on your own at the start of class. Also, if you want to work through any of the exercises in this book on your own at home or at your place of business after class, you may want to copy the practice files.

1. OPEN Internet Explorer.
2. In Internet Explorer, go to the student companion site: **www.wiley.com**
3. Search for your book title in the upper right hand corner.
4. On the Search Results page, locate your book and click on the **Visit the Companion Sites** link.
5. Select **Student Companion Site** from the pop-up box.
6. From the menu, select the **arrow** next to Browse By Resource and select **Student Data Files** from the menu.
7. A new screen will appear.
8. On the Student Data Files page, you can select to download files for just one lesson or for all lessons. Click on the file of your choice.
9. On the File Download dialog box, select **Save As** to save the data files to your external drive (often called a ZIP drive or a USB drive or a thumb drive) or a local drive.
10. In the Save As dialog box, select a local drive in the left-hand panel that you'd like to save your files to; again, this should be an external drive or a local drive. Remember the drive name that you saved it to.

Acknowledgments

We would like to thank the many instructors and reviewers who pored over the Microsoft Official Academic Course series design, outlines and manuscript, providing invaluable feedback in the service of quality instructional materials.

Erik Amerikaner, *Oak Park Unified*
Connie Aragon, *Seattle Central Community College*
Sue Bajt, *Harper College*
Gregory Ballinger, *Miami-Dade College*
Catherine Bradfield, *DeVry University*
DeAnnia Clements, *Wiregrass Georgia Technical College*
Mary Corcoran, *Bellevue College*
Andrea Cluff, *Freemont High School*
Caroline de Gruchy, *Conestoga College*
Janis DeHaven, *Central Community College*
Rob Durrance, *East Lee County High School*
Janet Flusche, *Frenship High School*
Greg Gardiner, *SIAST*
Debi Griggs, *Bellevue College*
Phil Hanney, *Orem Junior High School*
Portia Hatfield, *Tennessee Technology Center-Jacksboro*
Dee Hobson, *Richland College*
Terri Holly, *Indian River State College*
Kim Hopkins, *Weatherford College*
Sandra Jolley, *Tarrant County College*
Keith Hoell, *Briarcliffe College*
Joe LaMontagne, *Davenport University*
Tanya MacNeil, *American InterContinental University*
Donna Madsen, *Kirkwood Community College*
Lynn Mancini, *Delaware Technical Community College*
Edward Martin, *Kingsborough Community College-City University of New York*
Lisa Mears, *Palm Beach State College*
Denise Merrell, *Jefferson Community and Technical College*
Diane Mickey, *Northern Virginia Community College*
Robert Mike, *Alaska Career College*
Cynthia Miller, *Harper College*
Sandra Miller, *Wenatchee Valley College*
Mustafa Muflehi, *The Sheffield College*
Aditi Mukherjee, *University of Florida—Gainesville*
Linda Nutter, *Peninsula College*
Diana Pack, *Big Sandy Community & Technical College*
Bettye Parham, *Daytona State College*
Tatyana Pashnyak, *Bainbridge State College*
Kari Phillips, *Davis Applied Technical College*

Michelle Poertner, *Northwestern Michigan College*

Barbara Purvis, *Centura College*

Dave Rotherham, *Sheffield Hallam University*

Theresa Savarese, *San Diego City College*

Janet Sebesy, *Cuyahoga Community College-Western*

Lourdes Sevilla, *Southwestern College*

Elizabeth Snow, *Southwest Florida College*

Denise Spence, *Dunbar High School*

Amy Stolte, *Lincoln Land Community College*

Linda Silva, *El Paso Community College*

Dorothy Weiner, *Manchester Community College*

Faithe Wempen, *Indiana University/Purdue University at Indianapolis*

We would also like to thank the team at Microsoft Learning Xperiences (LeX), including Alison Cunard, Tim Sneath, Zubair Murtaza, Keith Loeber, Rob Linsky, Anne Hamilton, Wendy Johnson, Gene Longo, Julia Stasio, and Josh Barnhill for their encouragement and support in making the Microsoft Official Academic Course programs the finest academic materials for mastering the newest Microsoft technologies for both students and instructors. Finally we would like to thank Jeff Riley and his team at Box Twelve Communications, Laura Town and her team at WilliamsTown Communications, Debbie Collins and Sandy DuBose for their editorial and technical assistance.

We would like to thank the following instructors for their contributions to particular titles in the series as well:

ACCESS 2013

Catherine Bradfield, *DeVry University*

Mary Corcoran, *Bellevue College*

Cynthia Miller, *Harper College*

Aditi Mukherjee, *University of Florida—Gainesville*

Elizabeth Snow, *Southwest Florida College*

EXCEL 2013

Catherine Bradfield, *DeVry University*

DeAnnia Clements, *Wiregrass Georgia Technical College*

Dee Hobson, *Richland College*

Sandra Jolley, *Tarrant County College*

Joe Lamontagne, *Davenport University*

Edward Martin, *Kingsborough Community College-City University of New York*

Aditi Mukherjee, *University of Florida—Gainesville*

Linda Nutter, *Peninsula College*

Dave Rotherham, *Sheffield Hallam University*

POWERPOINT 2013

Mary Corcoran, *Bellevue College*

Rob Durrance, *East Lee County High School*

Phil Hanney, *Orem Junior High School*

Terri Holly, *Indian River State College*

Kim Hopkins, *Weatherford College*

Tatyana Pashnyak, *Bainbridge State College*

Michelle Poertner, *Northwestern Michigan College*

Theresa Savarese, *San Diego City College*

WORD 2013

Erik Amerikaner, *Oak Park Unified*

Sue Bajt, *Harper College*

Gregory Ballinger, *Miami-Dade College*

Andrea Cluff, *Freemont High School*

Caroline de Gruchy, *Conestoga College*

Donna Madsen, *Kirkwood Community College*

Author Credits

FAITHE WEMPEN

Faithe Wempen, M.A., is a Microsoft Office Master Instructor, an A+ certified PC technician, and the author of over 140 books on computer hardware and software, including "PowerPoint 2013 Bible" and "Office 2013 eLearning Kit for Dummies." She is an adjunct instructor of Computer Information Technology at Indiana University/Purdue University at Indianapolis, and in her spare time runs a small bed and breakfast in central Indiana.

Brief Contents

Contents

Lesson 1: PowerPoint Essentials

©Bim/iStockphoto

Lesson 2: Presentation Basics

©thinair28/iStockphoto

Lesson 3: Working with Text

©marcomayer/iStockphoto

Lesson 4: Designing a Presentation

©bjones27/iStockphoto

Lesson 5: Adding Tables to Slides

©rramirez125/iStockphoto

Lesson 6: Using Charts in a Presentation

©Tongshan/iStockphoto

Lesson 7: Creating SmartArt Graphics

©mediaphotos/iStockphoto

Lesson 8: Adding Graphics to a Presentation

©FrankyDeMeyer/iStockphoto

Lesson 9: Using Animation and Multimedia

©CowboyRoy/iStockphoto

Lesson 10: Securing and Sharing a Presentation

©choja/iStockphoto

Lesson 11: Delivering a Presentation

©graemenicholson/iStockphoto

LESSON SKILL MATRIX

Skills	Exam Objective	Objective Number
Working in the PowerPoint Window		
Working with an Existing Presentation	Demonstrate how to use views to navigate through presentations.	1.3.3
	Change to view in color/grayscale.	1.3.2
	View multiple presentations.	5.1.3

©Bim/iStockphoto

KEY TERMS

- Backstage view
- command
- dialog box
- dialog box launcher
- drop-down arrow
- drop-down list
- File tab
- group
- I-beam pointer
- KeyTip
- Mini toolbar
- Normal view
- Notes Page view
- placeholder
- Quick Access Toolbar
- Reading view
- Ribbon
- ScreenTip
- shortcut menu
- Slide Show view
- Slide Sorter view
- tab
- text box
- views
- zoom

©Bim/iStockphoto

Blue Yonder Airlines is a small but rapidly growing company that offers charter flights to adventurous or exotic locations. The service is designed for small groups, such as corporate management teams or directors who want to mix business and pleasure in a packaged getaway. As an enterprise account manager, your job is to introduce Blue Yonder Airlines to executives in mid-sized and large companies. Your goal is to convince these managers to use your charter service when arranging off-site gatherings that require group travel. Microsoft PowerPoint 2013 provides the perfect set of tools for presenting this information to your potential customers. In this lesson, you will start PowerPoint and open an introductory presentation about Blue Yonder Airlines. You will learn to navigate, edit, save, print, and close a presentation.

SOFTWARE ORIENTATION

Normal View

Before you begin working in Microsoft PowerPoint 2013, you should be familiar with the primary user interface. When you first start PowerPoint, you will see a Start screen. If you then press Esc, you see a screen similar to the one shown in Figure 1-1, which is Normal view, where you will do most of your work. However, if your copy of PowerPoint has been customized, what you see may be slightly different from what is shown. You can use this figure as a reference throughout this lesson and the rest of this book.

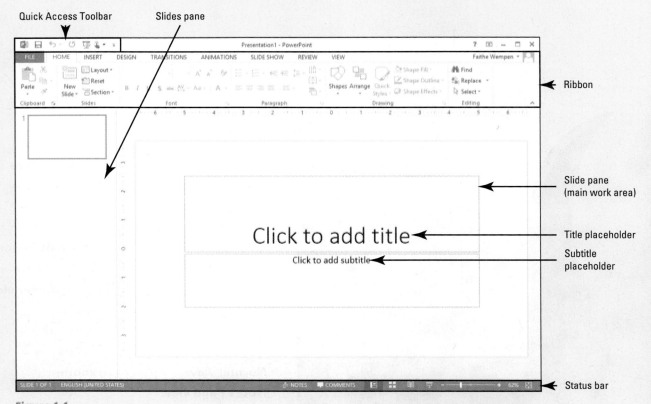

Figure 1-1

The PowerPoint window in Normal view

The Ribbon across the top of the window contains a set of tabs; each tab has a different collection of groups and buttons on it. Additional contextual tabs appear when you select certain types of content, such as graphics or tables.

WORKING IN THE POWERPOINT WINDOW

The Bottom Line

To use PowerPoint 2013 efficiently, you need to learn how to navigate in the PowerPoint application window.

Starting PowerPoint

Before you can use PowerPoint, you need to start the program. In this exercise, you learn to start PowerPoint using the Start screen or Start button. The steps for starting PowerPoint depend on which version of Windows you have on your PC. PowerPoint 2013 runs on either Windows 7 or Windows 8.

STEP BY STEP　　**Start PowerPoint (Windows 8)**

GET READY. Before you begin these steps, make sure that your computer is on. Sign on, if necessary.

1. If the Start screen does not already appear, press the Windows key on the keyboard to display it.
2. If needed, scroll to the right to locate the PowerPoint 2013 tile (see Figure 1-2).

Figure 1-2

Starting PowerPoint

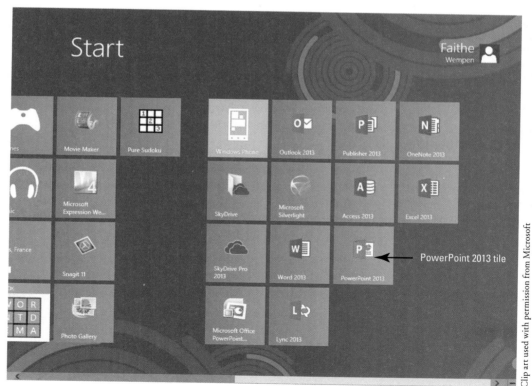

PowerPoint 2013 tile

Clip art used with permission from Microsoft

Another Way
Instead of locating the PowerPoint 2013 tile by scrolling, you can type the first few letters to filter the displayed tiles to show only the one you want.

Another Way
From the Start screen, you can right-click the PowerPoint 2013 tile and choose Pin to taskbar. This places a shortcut to PowerPoint on the desktop's taskbar, and you can click that shortcut to start PowerPoint.

3. Click PowerPoint 2013. PowerPoint starts and its Start screen appears.
4. Press Esc or click Blank Presentation. A new, blank presentation appears in the PowerPoint window.

PAUSE. LEAVE the blank presentation open to use in the next exercise.

GET READY. Before you begin these steps, make sure that your computer is on. Log on, if necessary.

1. On the Windows taskbar at the bottom of your screen, click the Start button, and then click All Programs. A menu of installed programs appears.
2. Click Microsoft Office. A submenu opens, listing the available programs in your installation of Microsoft Office.
3. Click Microsoft PowerPoint 2013. PowerPoint starts and its Start screen appears.
4. Press Esc or click Blank Presentation. A new, blank presentation appears in the PowerPoint window.

PAUSE. LEAVE the blank presentation open to use in the next exercise.

SELECTING TOOLS AND COMMANDS

A **command** is a tool (such as an icon, a button, or a list) that tells PowerPoint to perform a specific task. Each tab provides commands that are relevant to the kind of task you are performing—whether you are formatting a slide, adding animations to a presentation, or setting up a slide show for display. Most of the tools and commands for working with PowerPoint are accessible through the PowerPoint Ribbon. In addition to the Ribbon, PowerPoint also offers tools and commands on the File menu (also known as **Backstage view**), a Quick Access toolbar, a floating mini-toolbar, and a status bar.

Using the Ribbon

In this exercise, you learn how to select commands from the **Ribbon**, which is the tabbed toolbar at the top of the window. The Ribbon is divided into **tabs**, and each tab contains several **groups** of related commands.

On the Ribbon, some command groups feature a tool called a **dialog box launcher**—a small arrow in the group's lower-right corner. You can click the arrow to open a **dialog box**, which provides tools and options related to a specific task. To close a dialog box without accepting any changes you may have made to it, click the Cancel button.

Some of the Ribbon's tools have small, downward-pointing arrows next to them. These arrows are called **drop-down arrows**; when you click one, a **drop-down list** opens, displaying options you can choose (such as a list of fonts). You can choose the option you want by clicking it.

If you need more space on your screen, you can minimize (hide) the Ribbon by double-clicking the active tab. To restore the Ribbon, double-click the active tab again.

Another Way
If PowerPoint has recently been used on your computer, it may appear on the top level of the Start menu, when you first click the Start button. If it appears there, you can click that shortcut to start the program, rather than clicking All Programs and Microsoft Office to find it.

Another Way
You can also click the Start button and then begin typing PowerPoint; after you have typed the first few letters, PowerPoint should appear above the Start button; click on it there to start the program.

USE the new, blank presentation that is still open from the previous exercise.

1. Look at the Ribbon, which appears in Figure 1-3. Note that each tab contains several groups of related commands. By default, the Home tab is active.

Figure 1-3

The Ribbon

Home tab (active)

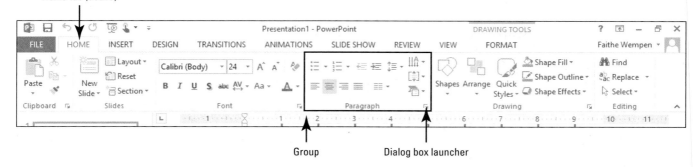

Group   Dialog box launcher

2. Click the Design tab to make it active. The groups of commands change.

3. Click the Home tab.

4. On the slide, click anywhere in the text Click to add title. The text disappears and a blinking insertion point appears.

Cross Ref

You will learn about adding and editing text later in this lesson.

5. In the lower-right corner of the Font group, click the dialog box launcher (the small box with a diagonal, downward-pointing arrow, see Figure 1-3). Clicking this button opens the Font dialog box. Click Cancel to close the dialog box.

6. In the Font group, click the Font list drop-down arrow. A drop-down list appears (see Figure 1-4). This list shows all the fonts that are currently available for use. The default font for headings is Calibri Light.

Another Way

You can also open the Font dialog box by pressing Ctrl+Shift+F. Many common commands have keyboard shortcuts; the PowerPoint Help system (covered later in this lesson) can help you identify them.

Figure 1-4

The Font list

Another Way

You can also collapse the Ribbon by right-clicking one of its tabs and clicking Collapse the Ribbon. Repeat that procedure to redisplay the Ribbon. You can also use the arrow at the far right end of the Ribbon to collapse the Ribbon. To reopen it, click any of the tabs and then click the pushpin icon at the far right end of the Ribbon to pin the Ribbon open again.

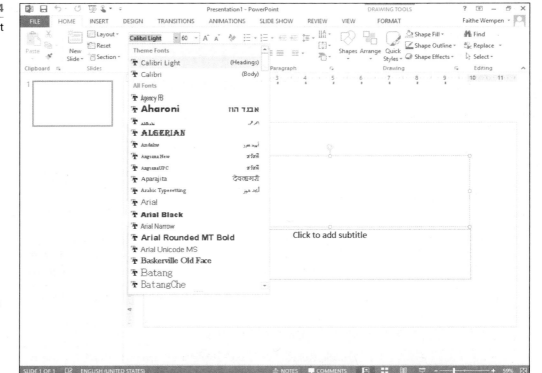

7. Click the drop-down arrow again to close the list.
8. Double-click the Home tab. This action collapses the Ribbon, hiding the groups of commands but leaving the tabs' names visible on the screen.
9. Double-click the Home tab again to redisplay the Ribbon.

PAUSE. LEAVE the presentation open to use in the next exercise.

Take Note If you aren't sure what a command does, just point to it. When the mouse pointer rests on a tool, a ScreenTip appears. A basic **ScreenTip** displays the tool's name and shortcut key (if a shortcut exists for that tool). Some of the Ribbon's tools have enhanced ScreenTips that also provide a brief description of the tool.

Using the Mini Toolbar

In this exercise, you practice using the **Mini toolbar**, a small toolbar that appears when you point to text that has been selected (highlighted). The Mini toolbar displays tools for formatting text appearance and alignment. The Mini toolbar is faint and semi-transparent until you point to it; then it becomes bright and opaque, indicating that the toolbar is active. If you right-click selected text, PowerPoint displays both the Mini toolbar and a **shortcut menu**, which displays additional commands.

STEP BY STEP **Use the Mini Toolbar**

USE the presentation that is still on the screen from the preceding exercise.

1. On the slide, double-click at the insertion point's location. Because you double-clicked, the insertion point is highlighted. The Mini toolbar appears (see Figure 1-5).

Figure 1-5

The Mini toolbar appears by the highlighted insertion point

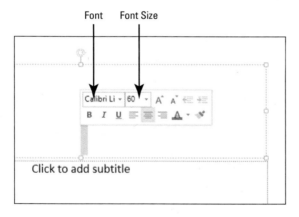

2. Click the Font drop-down arrow in the Mini toolbar. The list of available fonts opens.
3. Click the Font drop-down arrow again to close the list.

Another Way
You can also press Esc to close an open drop-down list.

4. Move the mouse pointer back to the highlighted insertion point, then right-click. A shortcut menu with commonly used commands appears along with the Mini toolbar.
5. Move the mouse pointer to a blank area of the slide (such as the upper-left corner), and then click twice. The first click removes the Mini toolbar and shortcut menu from the screen; the second click restores the slide to its original state.

PAUSE. LEAVE the presentation open to use in the next exercise.

Using the Quick Access Toolbar

The **Quick Access Toolbar** displays commands that you use frequently. By default, the Save, Undo, and Redo commands appear on the toolbar. You can add any commands to the Quick Access Toolbar for easy access to the commands you use most frequently. You can also choose where the Quick Access Toolbar appears via the Customize Quick Access Toolbar button's menu. In this exercise, you learn to use and customize the Quick Access Toolbar.

The Save command quickly saves an existing presentation while you are working on it or when you are finished with it. If you have not yet given the presentation a file name, PowerPoint will prompt you for a name by launching the Save As dialog box. If you have previously saved the file, the dialog box does not reopen.

The Undo command lets you reverse ("undo") the action of your last command. The Redo button lets you reverse an undo action. If either the Undo or Redo command is gray, then you cannot undo or redo.

STEP BY STEP   ## Use the Quick Access Toolbar

USE the presentation that is still open from the previous exercise.

1. Look for the Quick Access Toolbar in the upper-left corner of the PowerPoint window. The Quick Access Toolbar appears in Figure 1-6. Yours may look different if it has been customized.

Figure 1-6

The Quick Access Toolbar

Another Way
You can also click the left-pointing arrow button in the top left corner of Backstage view to return to Normal view.

2. Click the Save button on the Quick Access Toolbar. The Save As tab of Backstage view appears.

3. Press Esc to return to Normal view.

4. Click the Customize Quick Access Toolbar button. A menu appears (see Figure 1-7). This menu lets you choose the tools you want to appear on the Quick Access Toolbar.

Figure 1-7

Customizing the Quick Access Toolbar

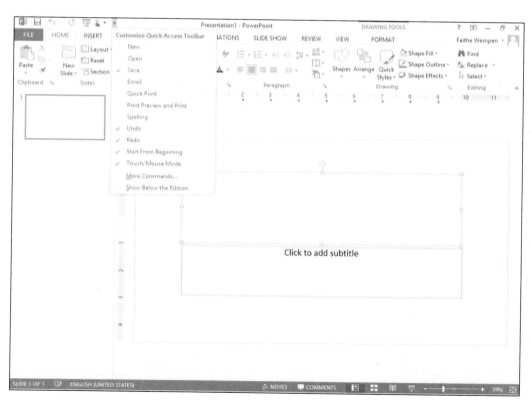

5. Click **Show Below the Ribbon**. The toolbar moves down and appears directly beneath the Ribbon.

6. Click the **Customize Quick Access Toolbar button** again. Click **Show Above the Ribbon**. The toolbar moves back to its original location.

7. On the Home tab, right-click the **Bold button**. A shortcut menu appears (see Figure 1-8).

Figure 1-8

Adding a button to the Quick Access Toolbar

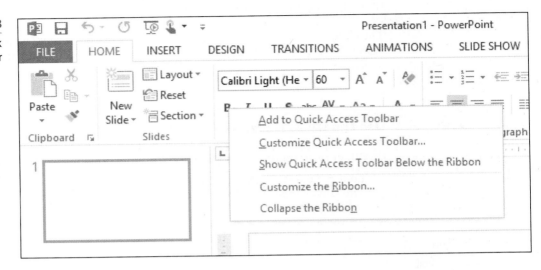

8. Click **Add to Quick Access Toolbar**. A copy of the Bold button appears on the toolbar.

9. On the Quick Access Toolbar, right-click the **Bold button**. A shortcut menu appears.

10. Click **Remove from Quick Access Toolbar**. The copy of the Bold button is removed.

PAUSE. LEAVE the presentation open to use in the next exercise.

Using KeyTips

When you press the Alt key, small letters and numbers—called **KeyTips**—appear on the Ribbon. To issue a command by using its KeyTip, press the Alt key, and then press the key or keys that correspond to the command you want to use. Every command on the Ribbon has a KeyTip.

STEP BY STEP　　**Use KeyTips**

USE the presentation that is still open from the previous exercise.

1. Press **Alt**. Letters and numbers appear on the Ribbon and the Quick Access Toolbar (see Figure 1-9). These characters show you which keyboard keys you can press to access the tabs or the items on the Quick Access Toolbar.

Figure 1-9

KeyTips

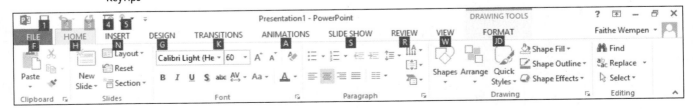

2. Press **N** to activate the Insert tab. When the Insert tab opens, notice that a new set of letters appears. These characters show you which keys to use to insert different kinds of objects in the current slide.
3. Press **P** to open the Insert Picture dialog box.
4. Click **Cancel** to close the dialog box and remove KeyTips from the display.

PAUSE. LEAVE the presentation open to use in the next exercise.

KeyTips are one type of a keyboard shortcut. In addition to the KeyTips, there are also many other key combinations you can press to issue common commands that open dialog boxes, select and manipulate text, save, print, and much more. For example, Ctrl+S saves the current presentation, and Ctrl+Z reverses the last action taken. The PowerPoint Help system, covered later in this lesson, provides a complete list of keyboard shortcuts available.

Keyboard shortcuts let you issue commands without using the mouse. This is handy for experienced users who prefer to keep their hands on the keyboard as much as possible. In fact, if you master keyboard shortcuts, you may find that you use the mouse less often over time.

Take Note   You must press Alt each time you want to see a tab's KeyTips. If you issue one command by a keyboard shortcut, you have to press Alt again to redisplay the tab's KeyTips before you can issue another one.

Using Backstage View

The **File tab** is not a regular tab; instead of displaying Ribbon commands, it displays a full-screen menu called Backstage view. Each command you select along the left side of the Backstage view, screen displays a different dialog box or page of options and commands in the right panel.

Commands on the menu in Backstage view include the following:

- **Info:** Shows information about the active presentation and provides commands that control permissions, sharing, and version management.
- **New:** Lists available templates from which you can create a new presentation.
- **Open:** Opens an existing presentation stored on a disk, either on your computer's disk or a network drive.
- **Save:** Saves the current presentation in your choice of locations.
- **Save As:** Lets you re-save a previously saved presentation with a different name, type, or location than before.
- **Print:** Provides settings and options for printing a presentation in a variety of formats.
- **Share:** Provides options for sending the presentation via email, inviting others to view it online, and publishing slides to a slide library.
- **Export:** Offers a variety of options for saving a presentation in different formats, and publishing it to video, CD, or other media.
- **Close:** Closes the currently open presentation.
- **Account:** Enables you to choose which account you are signed into Office with, manage connected services like Facebook and YouTube, and get activation information.
- **Options:** Opens the PowerPoint Options dialog box, from which you can configure many aspects of program operation.

Take Note   In PowerPoint 2010 there was an Exit command on the File menu. There is not in PowerPoint 2013, but you can exit the application by closing its window, which you can do by clicking the X button in the upper right corner or pressing Alt+F4.

STEP BY STEP   **Use Backstage View**

USE the presentation you used in the previous exercise.

1. Click the File tab on the Ribbon. Backstage view opens.
2. Click Share. Four options appear: Invite People, Email, Present Online, and Publish Slides.
3. Click Email. Buttons appear on the right pane for sending various email versions (see Figure 1-10).

Figure 1-10

The Share tab in Backstage view

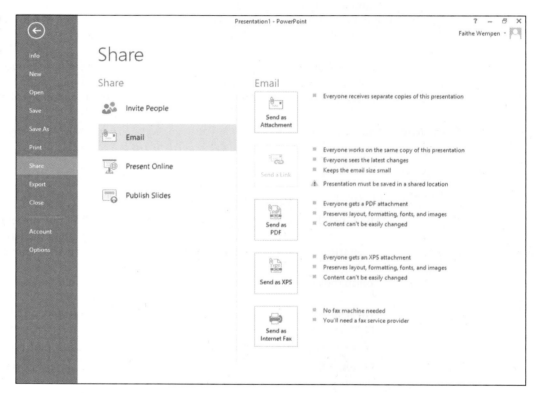

4. Click Export on the left pane. A list of export-related activities appears.
5. Click Create a Video. Options and commands for completing that activity appear at the right (see Figure 1-11).

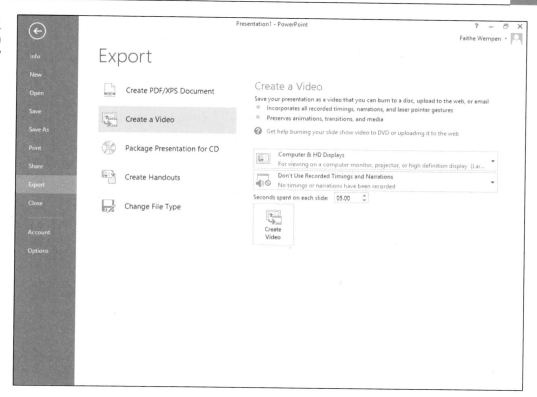

Another Way
You can also press Esc to close Backstage view.

Another Way
To open the File menu by using KeyTips, press Alt, and then press F.

6. Click Open in the left pane. A list of activities related to opening files appears. Recent Presentations is selected in the center pane, and a list of recently opened files appears in the right pane.

7. Click New. A list of templates appears.

8. Click the Back arrow button in the upper left corner to leave Backstage view.

PAUSE. LEAVE the presentation open to use in the next exercise.

Working with PowerPoint's Help System

PowerPoint's Help system is rich in information, illustrations, and tips that can help you complete any task as you create a presentation. Some of PowerPoint's help information is stored on your computer, and much more is available via the Internet. Finding the right information is easy: you can pick a topic from the Help system's table of contents, browse a directory of help topics, or perform keyword searches by entering terms that best describe the task you want to complete. In this exercise, you learn to access and use PowerPoint's Help system.

STEP BY STEP   **Use the Help System**

USE the presentation that is open from the previous exercise.

Another Way
You can also open the Help window by pressing F1.

1. Click the Microsoft Office PowerPoint Help button ? in the upper right corner of the PowerPoint window. The PowerPoint Help window appears (see Figure 1-12).

Figure 1-12

The PowerPoint Help window.

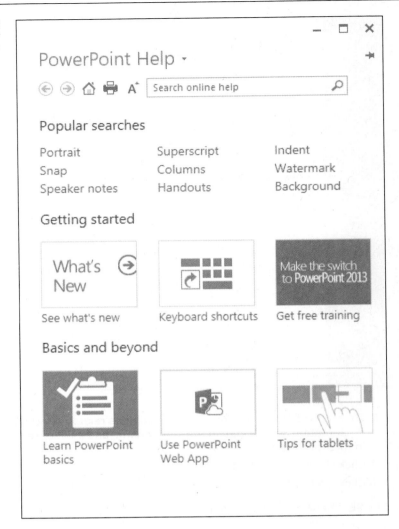

2. Click the **Search box**, type **Ribbon**, and then click the **Search button** or press **Enter**. A list of help topics appears (see Figure 1-13).

Figure 1-13

Searching for help articles about the Ribbon

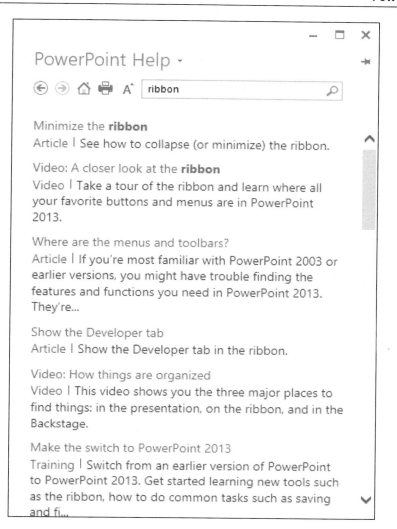

3. Click the Home button in the PowerPoint Help window. ⌂ The main Help topics reappear (see Figure 1-12).

4. Click Learn PowerPoint basics. The corresponding article appears. Read the article if you wish.

5. Click the Back button. ⟵ The main PowerPoint Help window reappears.

6. Click the Use Large Text button. A⁺ The text in the PowerPoint Help window becomes larger.

7. Click the Use Large Text button again. The text becomes smaller again.

8. Click See what's new. The help topic appears in the window (see Figure 1-14). This help topic contains a video clip, which you can click to watch if you like. If you do so, a new window opens; close that window when you are finished watching.

9. Click the Close button to close the Help window.

Figure 1-14

Article explaining the new
features in PowerPoint 2013

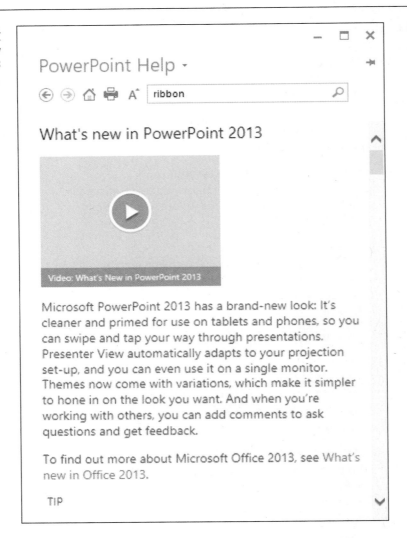

PAUSE. LEAVE the presentation open to use in the next exercise.

PowerPoint's Help window gives you access to many different help topics. A help topic is an article about a specific PowerPoint feature. Help topics can assist you with virtually any task or problem you encounter while working with PowerPoint.

The Help window is set up like a browser window and features some of the same tools you will find in your Web browser, plus some additional buttons unique to the Help system. From left to right, the buttons across the top of the PowerPoint Help window are:

- **Back:** Jumps to the previously opened Help topic.
- **Forward:** Jumps to the next opened Help topic.
- **Home:** Returns to the initial Help window.
- **Print:** Prints the currently open Help topic.
- **Use Large Text:** Toggles between normal-sized text and large text in the PowerPoint Help window.

Take Note   Many PowerPoint dialog boxes contain a Help button. When you click it, a Help window opens with information about the dialog box.

You can find help in several ways. For example, you can type a word or phrase into the Search box and then click the Search button. A list of related help topics appears in the Help window.

Closing a Presentation

When you close a presentation, PowerPoint removes it from the screen. PowerPoint continues running so you can work with other files. You should always save and close any open presentations before you exit PowerPoint or shut down your computer. In this exercise, you will practice closing an open presentation.

STEP BY STEP **Close a Presentation**

USE the presentation that is open from the previous exercise.

1. Click the File tab; Backstage view appears.
2. Click Close. PowerPoint clears the presentation from the screen.

PAUSE. LEAVE PowerPoint open to use in the next exercise.

WORKING WITH AN EXISTING PRESENTATION

The Bottom Line

If you want to work with an existing presentation, you need to open it. After opening a presentation, you can use PowerPoint's View commands to change the way the presentation is displayed onscreen; different views are suitable for different types of presentation editing and management tasks. You can also use PowerPoint's Zoom tools to make slides look larger or smaller on the screen. The following exercises show you how to view your slides in different ways, and how to add, edit, and delete text on your slides. You will then learn how to print a presentation and to save it to a disk.

Opening an Existing Presentation

PowerPoint makes it easy to work on a presentation over time. If you can't finish a slide show today, you can reopen it later and resume working on it. The Open dialog box lets you open a presentation that has already been saved on a disk. Presentations can be stored on any disk on your PC or network or on removable media (such as a flash drive). You can also store presentations on your SkyDrive, which is a free online cloud storage location provided by Microsoft. You can use the Look In box to navigate to the file's location, and then click the file to select it. This exercise shows you how to use the Open command to open an existing presentation—one that has already been created and saved as a file on a disk.

STEP BY STEP **Open an Existing Presentation**

GET READY. To open an existing presentation, do the following.

1. Click the File tab to open Backstage view.
2. Click Open. The Open tab of Backstage view appears.
3. Click one of the following, depending on where the data files for this lesson are stored (see Figure 1-15):
   * Click [username's] SkyDrive where [username] is the logged-in Office user.
   * Click Computer to access the drives on the local PC.
4. Click the Browse button. The general location you selected in step 3 appears.

Another Way
You can also open the Open tab of Backstage view by pressing Ctrl+O.

Figure 1-15

The Open tab of
Backstage view.

Figure 1-15

The Open tab of
Backstage view.

5. Browse to locate the data files for this lesson, and select *Blue Yonder Overview* (see Figure 1-16).

Figure 1-16

Browse the data files for
this lesson.

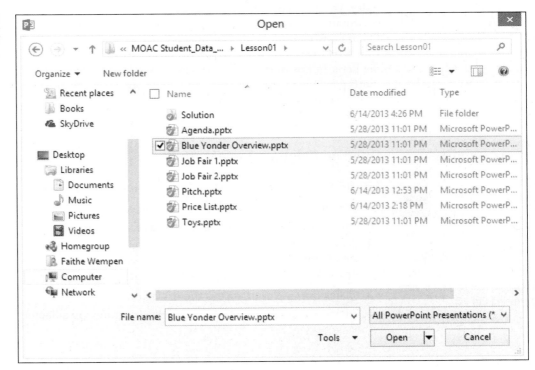

Another Way
Instead of clicking the file's name in the Open dialog box and then clicking the Open button, you can double-click the file's name to open the presentation.

6. Click **Open**. The presentation appears on your screen (see Figure 1-17).

Figure 1-17

The Blue Yonder Overview presentation

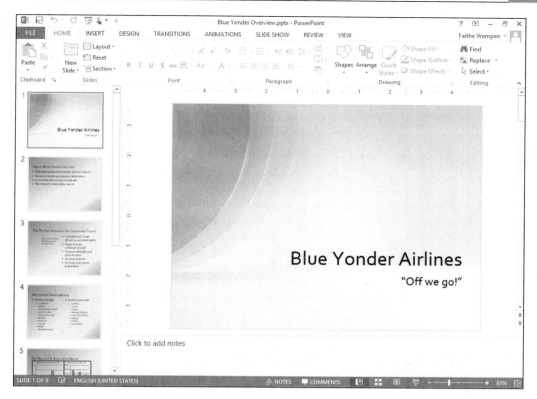

PAUSE. LEAVE the presentation open to use in the next exercise.

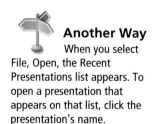

Another Way
When you select File, Open, the Recent Presentations list appears. To open a presentation that appears on that list, click the presentation's name.

When you click Open, you can choose whether to browse your SkyDrive or your Computer (local drives). SkyDrive is a cloud-based private storage system that Microsoft provides at no charge. Storing your files there makes them available to you no matter what computer you are using at the moment. However, accessing your SkyDrive requires Internet access, so if you do not always have Internet access available, storing files on your local hard drive may be a better option. If you decide to store the data files for this book locally, you might want to put them in your Documents library for easy access.

Viewing a Presentation in Different Ways

PowerPoint's various **views** enable you to see your presentation in a variety of ways. For example, in Normal view, you can work with just one slide at a time, which is helpful when you are adding text or graphics to a slide. Alternately, in Slide Sorter view, you can view all the slides in a presentation at the same time, which makes it easy to rearrange the slides. The following exercise shows you how to change PowerPoint views.

PowerPoint provides these **views**:

- **Normal view** is the default view that lets you focus on an individual slide. The slide you are currently editing is called the **current slide**. The current slide appears in the Slide pane, which is the largest of the view's three panes. Below the Slide pane is the Notes pane, where you can add and edit notes you want to associate with the current slide. The Notes pane is optional; you can toggle it on and off with the Notes button on the View tab. In the left pane—called the Slides pane—you can click the thumbnail images of the slides to jump from one slide to another, as you will see later in this lesson.

- **Outline view** is the same as Normal view except instead of thumbnail images of the slides, a text outline of the presentation appears in the left pane. Only text from placeholders appears in the outline; any text from manually created text boxes does not. Text from graphical objects such as SmartArt also does not appear in the outline.

- **Slide Sorter view** displays all the slides in a presentation on a single screen. (If there are more slides than can fit in one screen, you can use scroll bars to move slides in and out of view.) In Slide Show view, you can reorganize a slide show by dragging slides to different positions. You can also duplicate and delete slides in this view.

- **Notes Page view** shows one slide at a time, along with any notes that are associated with the slide. This view lets you create and edit notes. You may find it easier to work with notes in this view than in Normal view. You can also print notes pages for your presentation; they are printed as they appear in Notes Page view.

CERTIFICATION READY?   **1.3.3**

How can you use views to navigate through a presentation?

- **Slide Show view** lets you preview your presentation on the screen, so you can see it the way your audience will see it.

- **Reading view** is like Slide Show view except it is in a window rather than filling the entire screen. Displaying the presentation in a window enables you to also work in other windows at the same time.

STEP BY STEP   **Change PowerPoint Views**

USE the presentation that you opened during the previous exercise.

1. Click the View tab (see Figure 1-18). Notice that the Normal button is highlighted on both the Ribbon and the Views toolbar in the bottom-right corner of the PowerPoint window.

Figure 1-18

Normal view, with the View tab selected

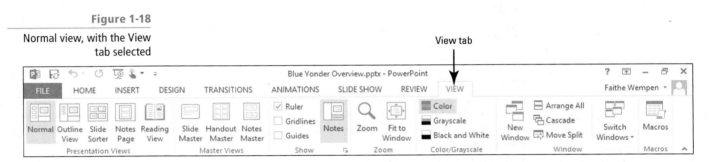

2. Click the Slide Sorter View button to change to Slide Sorter view (see Figure 1-19).

Another Way
Instead of using the Ribbon to change views, you can use the Views toolbar in the lower-right corner of the PowerPoint window. The Normal button there toggles between Normal and Outline views each time you click it.

Figure 1-19

Slide Sorter view

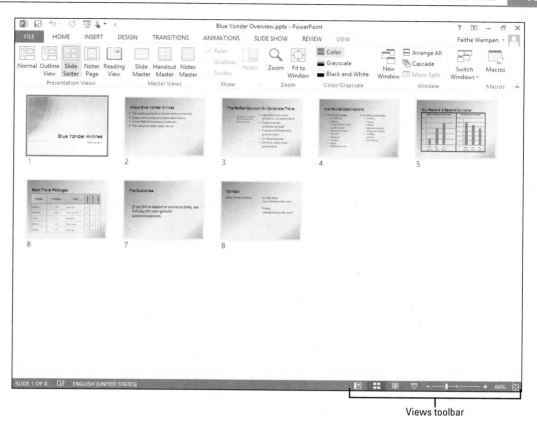

Views toolbar

Take Note   If formatted slides are hard to read in Slide Sorter view, press Alt and click a slide to see its heading clearly.

3. Click **slide 2**, and then click the **Notes Page View button**. PowerPoint switches to Notes Page view (see Figure 1-20).

Figure 1-20

Notes Page view

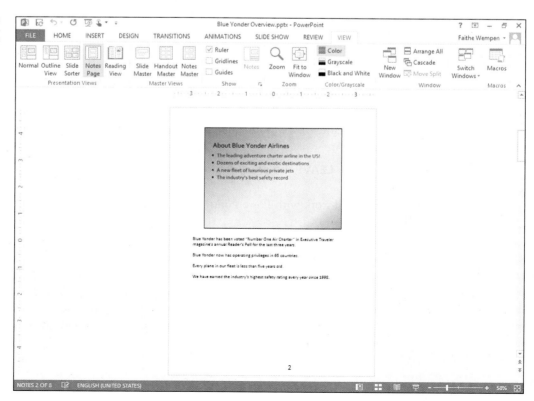

Take Note   There is no button for Notes Page view on the Views toolbar at the bottom of the PowerPoint window; you must access it via the Ribbon.

Take Note   If you have stored the data files on your SkyDrive, you may see a message at step 3 warning you that edits made in this view will be lost when saved to the server. That is not a concern at this point, so click View to continue.

Another Way
You can also switch to Slide Show view by pressing F5 or by clicking the Slide Show icon in the bottom right corner.

4. Click the Slide Show tab, and click From Beginning. The first slide of the presentation fills the screen (see Figure 1-21).

Figure 1-21

Slide Show view

Take Note   If you have a widescreen monitor (16:9 height/width ratio), black panels appear to the left and right of the slide because this particular presentation is set up for 4:3 monitors.

5. Press Esc to exit Slide Show view and return to Notes Page view.
6. Click the View tab, and click the Reading View button. The first slide appears in a reading window. It looks just like Figure 1-21 except it does not fill the screen.
7. Close the reading window by pressing Esc.
8. On the Views toolbar, click the Normal button. PowerPoint switches back to Normal view.

PAUSE. LEAVE the presentation open to use in the next exercise.

Cross Ref   You will work with PowerPoint's printing options and practice previewing a presentation later in this lesson.

Using Zoom

PowerPoint's **zoom** tools let you change the magnification of slides on the screen. By zooming out, you can see an entire slide; by zooming in, you can inspect one area of the slide. Both views have advantages: higher magnifications make it easier to position objects on the slide, and lower magnifications enable you to see how all the parts of a slide look as a whole. In this exercise, you practice using the zoom tools.

STEP BY STEP   **Use Zoom**

USE the presentation that is open from the previous exercise.

1. Click the slide in the Slide pane to ensure that the Slide pane is active. As a reminder, the Slide pane is the large pane on the right side of Normal view, in which one slide appears at a time.

2. On the View tab, click the Zoom button. The Zoom dialog box appears (see Figure 1-22).

Figure 1-22

The Zoom dialog box

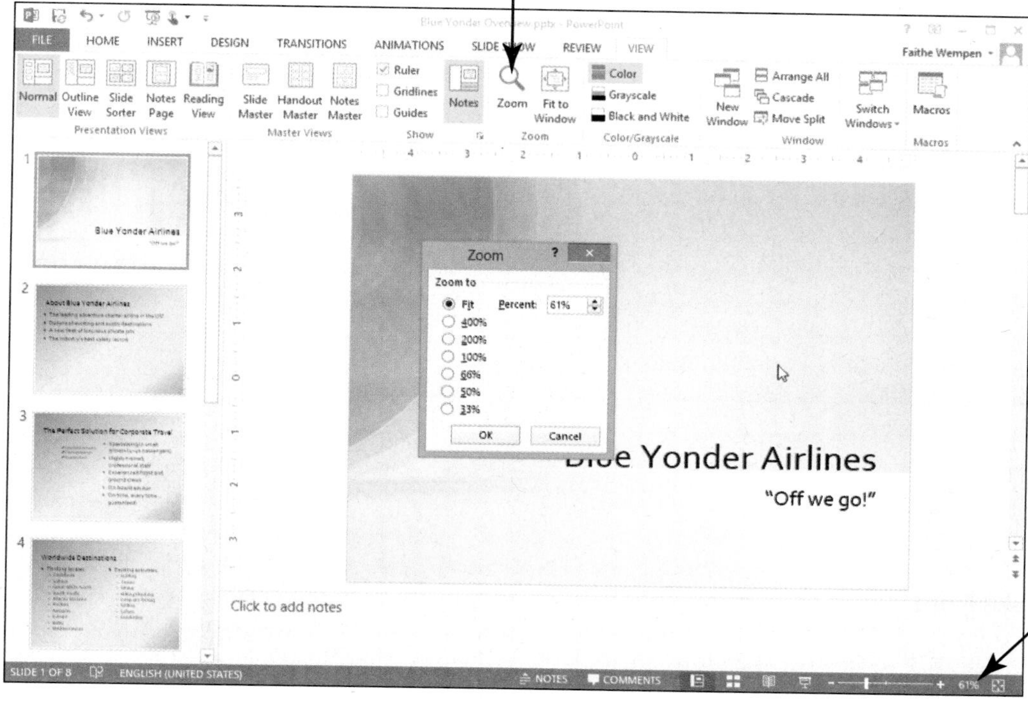

You can also click here to display the Zoom dialog box

Another Way
You can click the Zoom level indicator at the far right of the Zoom control (located on the right end of the status bar) to display the Zoom dialog box.

Another Way
You can drag the Zoom control's slider bar to the right or left to change the zoom level. However, in Normal view, dragging the Zoom slider changes the zoom only in the Slide pane. If you want to change the zoom for a different pane, you must use the dialog box.

3. Click the 200% option button, then click OK. In the Slide pane, the slide is magnified by 200%. Notice that you can no longer see the entire slide.

4. Click the Zoom Out button at the left end of the Zoom control, at the lower-right of the screen (see Figure 1-23). Continue clicking the button until the zoom level drops to 100%. Notice that, even at 100% magnification, the slide is too large for the Slide pane.

Figure 1-23

Using the Zoom controls

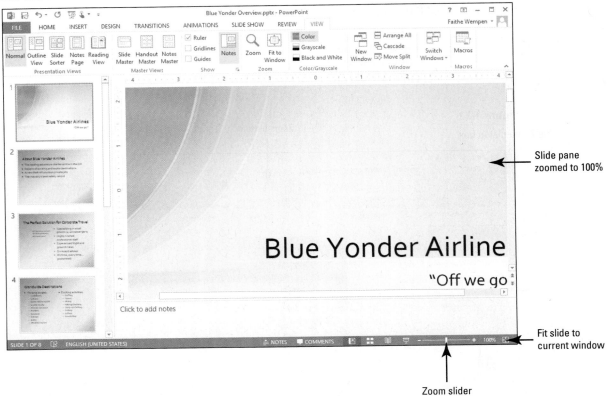

Slide pane
zoomed to 100%

Fit slide to
current window

Zoom slider

Take Note   You can resize the Slide pane by dragging its bottom border up or down, or by dragging its left-hand border to the right or left. The Slides pane (or Outline pane) and Notes pane also change size when you drag the borders.

> 5. Click the **Fit slide to current window** button at the far right end of the Zoom control. PowerPoint zooms out to fit the entire slide in the Slide pane.
>
> **PAUSE. LEAVE** the presentation open to use in the next exercise.

You can use either the Zoom dialog box or the Zoom control to change magnification levels. In the Zoom dialog box, you can zoom in or out by choosing one of seven preset magnification levels, or you can use the Percent spin control to set the zoom level precisely. All zoom options are available in Normal view. In Slide Sorter view, some zoom options are available, but the Fit slide to current window tool is not.

Viewing in Color or Grayscale

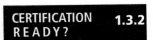

CERTIFICATION READY?   **1.3.2**

How can you view the presentation in grayscale mode?

Grayscale is a viewing mode in which there are no colors, only shades of gray. When you distribute a presentation using some low-tech methods, such as printing slides on a black-and-white printer, your slides might look different than they do in full-color on your screen. Therefore, it is sometimes useful to look at your slides in Grayscale mode on the screen so you can identify any potential problems that might occur when slides are printed without color. There is also a Black and White viewing mode that can check how slides will look with only black and white (no gray shades). Some fax machines transmit only in black and white, for example, if you faxed your slides, you might need to know how the recipient will see them.

STEP BY STEP **Switch Between Color and Grayscale Modes**

USE the presentation that is open from the previous exercise.

1. On the View tab, click Grayscale. The presentation slides appear in grayscale mode, and a Grayscale tab appears on the Ribbon (see Figure 1-24).

Figure 1-24

The Grayscale tab

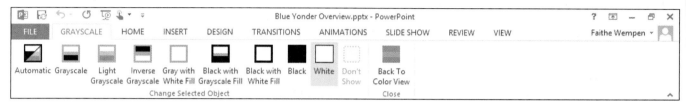

2. Click several of the buttons on the Grayscale tab and observe the difference in the slide appearance.
3. Click Back To Color View. The presentation returns to color mode.
4. On the View tab, click Black and White. The presentation appears in Black and White mode, and a Black and White tab appears on the Ribbon.
5. Click Back to Color View. The presentation returns to color mode.

PAUSE. LEAVE the presentation open to use in the next exercise.

CERTIFICATION READY? **5.1.3**

How can you view multiple presentations?

Viewing Multiple Presentations at Once

You can have multiple presentations open at the same time in PowerPoint, and you can arrange their windows so that they are all visible at once. This makes it easy to drag-and-drop content between windows, and also to compare different versions of a presentation. In the following exercise you will open two presentations and arrange them.

STEP BY STEP **Arrange Multiple Presentation Windows**

USE the presentation that is open from the previous exercise. You will also be opening a second presentation in this exercise so that multiple presentation windows are available to arrange.

1. Click the File tab.
2. Click Open. The Open tab of Backstage view appears.
3. Navigate to the location containing the data files for this lesson.

4. Locate and open *Job Fair 1*. The presentation appears on your screen.
5. Click the View tab.
6. Click Arrange All in the Window group. The presentations appear side-by-side (see Figure 1-25).

Figure 1-25

Two presentations open
side-by-side

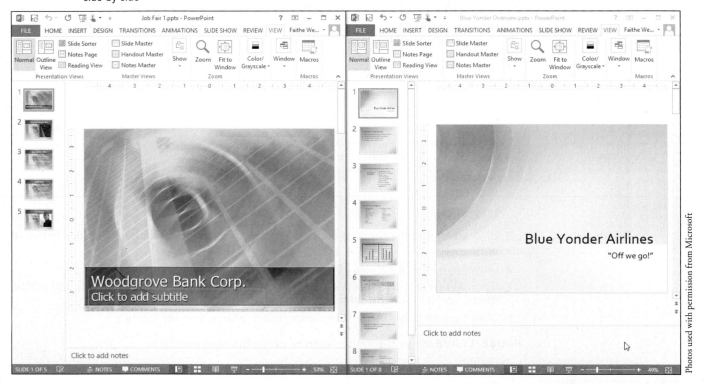

7. Use the Close button on the Job Fair 1 window ☒ to close the Job Fair 1 presentation, as you learned in "Closing a Presentation" earlier in this lesson.

8. In the Blue Yonder Overview window, click the **Maximize button** ☐ in the upper-right corner. The PowerPoint window fills the screen.

PAUSE. LEAVE the presentation open for the next exercise. If you don't wish to work with the maximized PowerPoint window, you can restore the window and then manually resize it to the size you prefer.

Moving Between Slides

PowerPoint provides a number of methods for moving through a presentation in different views. You can move from one slide to another with either the mouse or the keyboard. You can specify that a certain slide should be displayed, or you can browse the available slides to identify the one you want based on its content.

Using the Mouse to Scroll Through a Presentation

PowerPoint's scroll bars let you move up and down through your presentation. When you drag the scroll box in the Slide pane, PowerPoint displays a ScreenTip with the slide number and slide title to show which slide will appear on screen when you release the mouse button. Click the scroll buttons to move up or down one line or one slide at a time, depending on the current zoom level. Click and hold a scroll button to move more quickly or drag a scroll box to move even more quickly. In this exercise, you use the mouse to scroll through a PowerPoint presentation.

STEP BY STEP   ### Scroll Through a Presentation Using the Mouse

USE the presentation that is open and maximized from the previous exercise.

1. Click the scroll down button on the right side of the Slide pane (see Figure 1-26). Because the zoom level is set at Fit Slide to Current Window, slide 2 appears on the screen.

Figure 1-26

Scroll tools

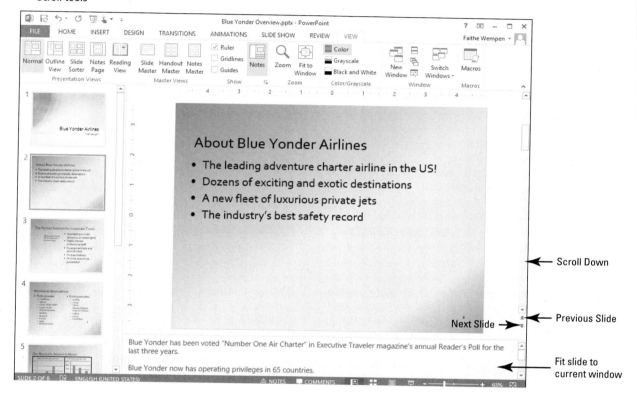

2. Use the zoom control to change the zoom level to 100%, then click the scroll down button twice. Because the slide is now larger than the Slide pane, the scroll button scrolls the slide down in small increments instead of jumping to the next slide.

3. Click the Fit to Window button in the Zoom command group on the View tab of the **Ribbon**. The Fit to Window button does the same thing as the Fit Slide to Current Window button on the status bar.

4. At the bottom of the scroll bar, click the Next Slide button twice. Slide 3 appears, and then slide 4 appears.

5. In the Slides pane on the left, scroll down to locate slide 5, and click it. The selected slide appears in the Slide pane (see Figure 1-27).

Figure 1-27

Click a slide's thumbnail image
in the Slides pane to jump to
that slide.

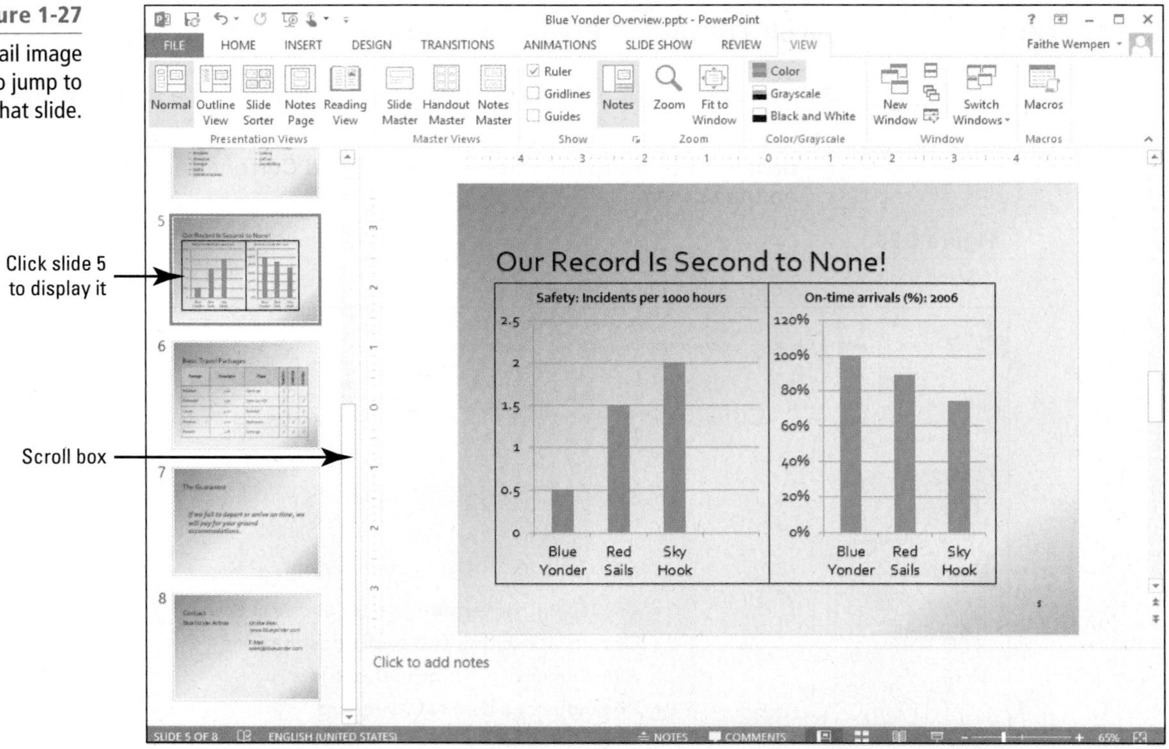

Click slide 5
to display it

Scroll box

Take Note   The current slide's number always appears in the lower-left corner of the status bar.

6. Point to the scroll box that appears to the right of the Slides pane, and then drag the scroll box all the way down to the bottom of the scroll bar. The last slide (slide 8) appears on the Slides pane, but slide 5 remains visible in the Slide pane.

7. Click the Previous Slide button (at the bottom right of the Slide pane, see Figure 1-26). Slide 4 appears in the Slide pane; notice that the slide also appears highlighted on the Slides pane.

8. Click the scroll box that appears to the right of the Slide pane, and then drag the scroll box all the way up to the top of the scroll bar. You return to the beginning of the presentation.

PAUSE. LEAVE the presentation open for the next exercise.

In Normal view, both the Slide pane and the Slides pane have scroll bars, buttons, and boxes. If there is text in the Notes pane, scroll tools will appear there to let you move up and down through the text, if necessary. In Slide Sorter view and Notes Page view, scroll tools will appear on the right side of the window if they are needed.

In **Normal view**, you can click the Previous Slide button to move up to the previous slide and click the Next Slide button to move to the following slide.

Using the Keyboard to Move Through a Presentation

Your keyboard's cursor control keys let you jump from one slide to another, as long as no text or object is selected on a slide. If text is selected, the arrow keys move the insertion point within the text; however, the Page Up, Page Down, Home, and End keys will still let you move from slide to slide. In this exercise, you practice using the keyboard to navigate through presentations.

STEP BY STEP | **Move Through a Presentation Using the Keyboard**

USE the presentation that is open from the previous exercise.

1. With slide 1 visible in Normal view in the Slide pane, press Page Down on your keyboard. Slide 2 appears.
2. Press Page Down to jump to slide 3.
3. Press Page Down to jump to slide 4.
4. Press Page Up to go back to slide 3.
5. Press Page Up to move up to slide 2.
6. Press Page Up to view slide 1.
7. Press End to jump to slide 8, the last slide in the presentation.
8. Press Home to return to slide 1.

PAUSE. LEAVE the presentation open to use in the next exercise.

Working with Text

Text is not typed directly onto a slide in PowerPoint, but instead is placed in text boxes. A **text box** is, as the name implies, a box that holds text that you type into it. Most of the available slide layouts have one or more placeholders that become text boxes when you type text into them, and you can also add more text boxes manually to slides, as you will learn in Lesson 3. Text can be placed on a slide either by typing it directly into a text box or placeholder, or by typing in the Outline pane in Normal view. In the following exercises, you will practice adding text to a placeholder; adding text to the Outline pane in Outline view; selecting, replacing, and deleting text on a slide; and copying and moving text from one slide to another.

Adding Text to a Placeholder

In this exercise, you practice entering text in a **placeholder**, which is a box that can hold either text or a graphic object. The placeholders available depend on the slide layout. In the Blue Yonder presentation, slide 1 is an example of a Title Slide layout; it contains two placeholders—one for the title and one for the subtitle. Placeholders make it easy to add text—just click in the placeholder, and then type the text.

STEP BY STEP | **Add Text to a Text Placeholder**

USE the presentation that is open from the previous exercise.

1. Click the Home tab. On slide 1, click at the beginning of the slide's title (Blue Yonder Airlines). The borders of the title's placeholder appear (see Figure 1-28), and a blinking insertion point appears before the word *Blue*.

Figure 1-28

The title placeholder

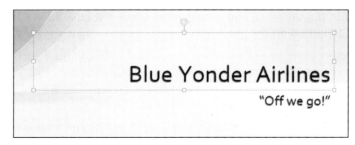

2. Click the slide's subtitle, which is the second line of text. The subtitle's placeholder appears, as does the insertion point.
3. Go to slide 4 by clicking the slide in the Slides pane, or by pressing Page Down until it appears.

4. Click after the word *Snorkeling* in the second column. The insertion point appears.

5. Press **Enter** to start a new line, and type **Scuba**.

6. Press **Enter**, and then type **Sightseeing**. Your slide should look like the one shown in Figure 1-29.

Figure 1-29

Slide 4 with added text

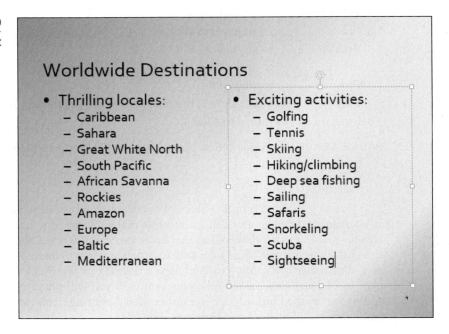

PAUSE. LEAVE the presentation open for the next exercise.

Adding Text in Outline View

Working in Outline view is like working in a word processor. PowerPoint displays the text from each slide on the Outline pane, without any backgrounds, placeholders, or anything else that might distract you from your writing. You can navigate a presentation in the Outline pane the same way you use the Slides pane—scroll to the desired slide's outline, and then click it. Here, you practice adding text on the Outline tab.

STEP BY STEP   **Add Text in Outline View**

USE the presentation that is open from the previous exercise.

1. Go to slide 8. This slide is supposed to contain contact information, but the mailing address and telephone number are missing.

2. Click the **View tab** and click **Outline View**. Because slide 8 is the current slide, its text is highlighted on the tab.

Take Note   Remember that you can adjust the Zoom level for the Outline pane, or any other pane, as needed if the content is not shown at a convenient size for working with it. Click in the Outline pane and then on the View tab, click Zoom to open the Zoom dialog box, and choose a lower percentage, such as 50% or 33%, to shrink the text to a readable size.

3. In the Outline pane, click after the word *Airlines* on slide 8 to place the insertion point there.

4. Press **Enter** to start a new line.

5. On the new line, type **12 Ferris Street**, and then press **Enter**. As you type the new text in the Outline pane, notice that it appears on the slide.

6. Type **Diehard, TN 34567**, and then press Enter.

7. Type (707) 555-AWAY. Your slide should look like the one shown in Figure 1-30.

Figure 1-30

Text added to the Outline pane appears on the slide

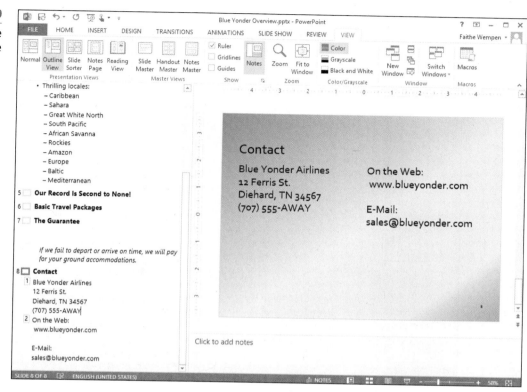

8. Switch to Normal view.

PAUSE. LEAVE the presentation open for the next exercise.

Selecting, Replacing, and Deleting Text

You can edit, replace, and delete text directly on a slide. First, you must select the text to let PowerPoint know you want to edit it. You can select any amount of text by dragging the mouse pointer across it. When you move the mouse pointer over text, it changes to an **I-beam pointer**, a vertically oriented pointer that resembles the letter I. This pointer makes it easy to select text precisely. In this exercise, you practice editing text in PowerPoint.

STEP BY STEP	**Select, Replace, and Delete Text**

USE the presentation that is open from the previous exercise. Switch back to Normal view before starting the exercise.

1. Go to slide 3, and in the fourth item of the bulleted list on the right, double-click the word advisor to select it (see Figure 1-31).

Figure 1-31

Selected text

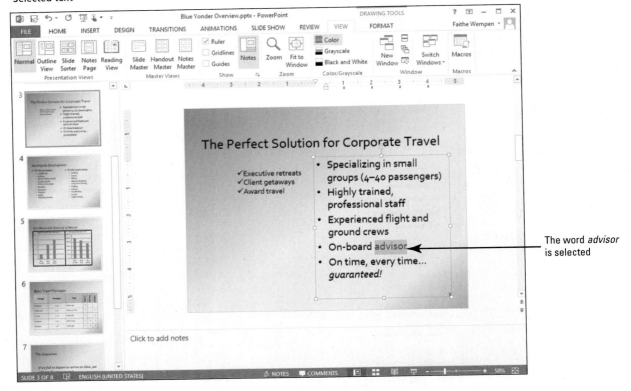

The word *advisor* is selected

2. While the text is selected, type **concierge**. The new text replaces the selected text.

3. Go to slide 7, and select the word **ground** by dragging the mouse pointer over it. (The mouse pointer changes from an arrow to an I-beam whenever it is in a text placeholder, as shown in Figure 1-32.)

Figure 1-32

Selecting text and the I-beam pointer

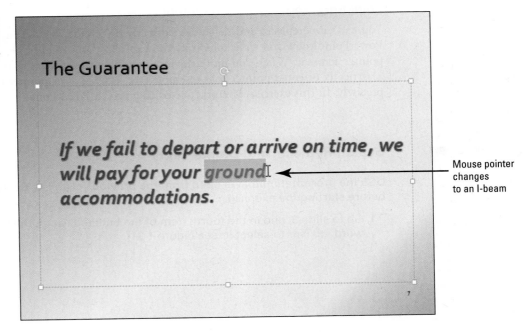

Mouse pointer changes to an I-beam

4. Press **Delete** to delete the word from the slide.

PAUSE. LEAVE the presentation open for the next exercise.

Whenever you select text in PowerPoint—whether it is a single character or all the text on a slide—it is highlighted with a colored background. Once the text is selected, you can type new text in its place or delete it.

Take Note   Only text from text-based placeholders appears in the Outline pane; text from manually created text boxes (see Lesson 2) and from graphics and charts does not appear.

Copying and Moving Text from One Slide to Another

In this exercise, you practice copying and moving text from one slide to another, using the Copy, Cut, and Paste commands. You can use these commands on many kinds of objects in PowerPoint, including pictures, charts, and placeholders. Don't be surprised if these commands become your most frequently used tools, because they can save you a great deal of typing.

STEP BY STEP   **Copy and Move Text from One Slide to Another**

USE the presentation that is open from the previous exercise.

1. Go to slide 2, and in the slide's title placeholder, select Blue Yonder Airlines by dragging the mouse pointer across the text.
2. On the Home tab, click the Copy button (see Figure 1-33).

Figure 1-33

Clipboard tools

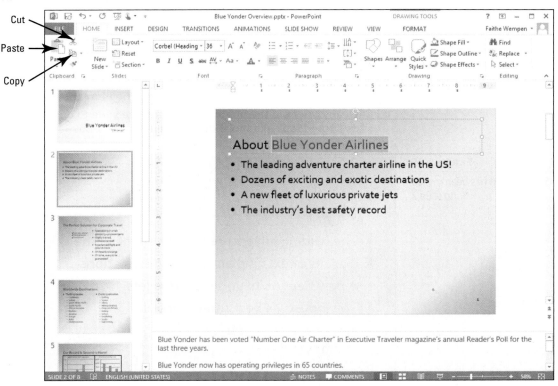

3. Go to slide 7.
4. Click between the two words of the title to place the insertion point before the word *Guarantee*.
5. On the Home tab, click the Paste button. PowerPoint inserts the copied text at the insertion point's position (see Figure 1-34). Press the Spacebar if necessary to insert a space before the word *Guarantee*.

Another Way
You can issue the Copy command by pressing Ctrl+C or by right-clicking and choosing Copy.

Take Note   The Paste Options icon that appears near the pasted text in Figure 1-33 opens a menu when clicked; from that menu you can choose pasting options. In this case you will ignore the icon, accepting the default pasting options.

Figure 1-34

The selected text has been copied to slide 7

Another Way
You can issue the Paste command by pressing Ctrl+V or by right-clicking and choosing Paste.

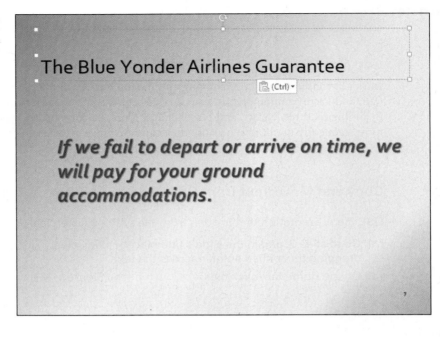

6. Go to slide 3.
7. Select the last item of the bulleted list on the right side of the slide.
8. On the Home tab, click the **Cut button**. The selected item is removed from the list.
9. Go to slide 2.
10. Click below the last item of the bulleted list.
11. On the Home tab, click the **Paste button**. The item appears at the bottom of the list.
12. Click anywhere in the blank area around the slide to deselect the placeholder. Your slide should look like the slide shown in Figure 1-35.

Another Way
You can issue the Cut command by pressing Ctrl+X or by right-clicking and choosing Cut.

Figure 1-35

Selected text has been moved to slide 2

About Blue Yonder Airlines
- The leading adventure charter airline in the US!
- Dozens of exciting and exotic destinations
- A new fleet of luxurious private jets
- The industry's best safety record
- On time, every time...
  guaranteed!

PAUSE. LEAVE the presentation open for the next exercise.

Printing a Presentation

The PowerPoint Print command sends the currently open presentation to the printer. The default settings produce a printout of the entire presentation, one slide per page, on whatever printer is set up in Windows as the default.

STEP BY STEP | **Print a Presentation with the Default Settings**

Another Way
You can press Ctrl+P instead of steps 1 and 2.

USE the presentation that is open from the previous exercise.

1. Click the File tab.
2. Click Print. Print options appear. You will learn about them in Lesson 2; leave the defaults set for now. Check with your instructor before completing the next step; to save paper, he or she may ask you not to print.
3. Click the Print button. PowerPoint prints the entire presentation, using the default print settings, assuming your PC has at least one printer set up.

Cross Ref Printing options are discussed in Lesson 2.

PAUSE. LEAVE the document open to use in the next exercise.

Saving an Edited Presentation

Whenever you work on a presentation, you should save it to a disk—especially if you have made changes that you want to keep. In this exercise, you will practice saving a presentation with a different file name, in native PowerPoint 2013 format.

Cross Ref In Lesson 10, you will learn how to save a presentation in other formats for sharing with people who might not have PowerPoint 2013 installed.

STEP BY STEP | **Save an Edited Presentation**

USE the presentation that is open from the previous exercise.

1. Click the File tab to open Backstage view.
2. Click Save As. The Save As tab of Backstage view appears (see Figure 1-36). It is like the Open tab in that it allows you to choose between your SkyDrive and Computer as a starting point for browsing.

Figure 1-36

Save As tab of Backstage view

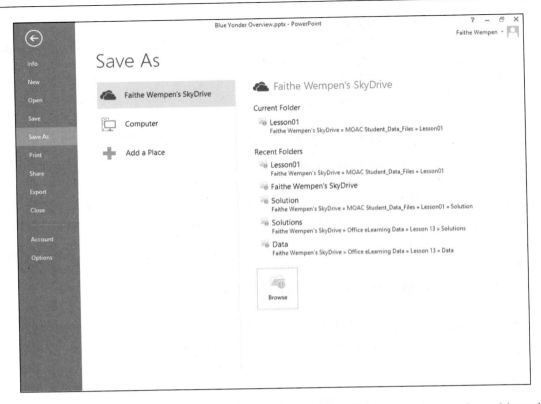

3. Select the location where you want to save your files (ask your instructor for guidance), and then type *Blue Yonder Introduction* in the File name box (see Figure 1-37).

Figure 1-37

Save As dialog box

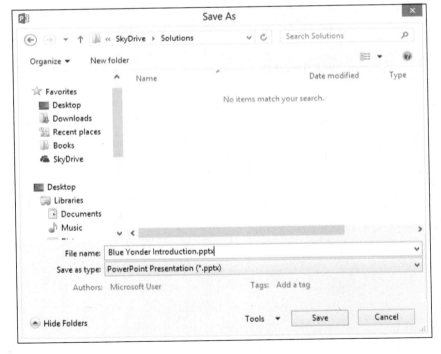

Take Note   Ask your instructor if you should append your initials to the end of each file name for the exercises in this book, to keep your files separate from those of other students.

4. Click **Save**.
5. Click **File** and click **Close** to close the presentation.

PAUSE. LEAVE PowerPoint open to use in the next exercise.

Cross Ref Presentations created in PowerPoint 2007 and higher are incompatible with earlier versions of PowerPoint. However, you can save in an earlier format for backward compatibility; that skill is covered in Lesson 2.

When you need to save an existing presentation in a new location or with a different file name, use the Save As command. In the Save As dialog box, you can specify a different disk drive and folder to store the file; you can also give the file a different name in the File name box. After the presentation is saved in the new location and with its new file name, you can click the Save button on the Quick Access Toolbar when you need to resave the file.

Take Note You can also download a free conversion utility from the Microsoft website for earlier versions of PowerPoint that will allow those users to open files in PowerPoint 2007/2013 format.

Exiting PowerPoint

When you exit PowerPoint, the program closes and is removed from your computer's memory. In this exercise, you will practice exiting PowerPoint.

STEP BY STEP **Exit PowerPoint**

GET READY. In order to exit PowerPoint, do the following.

1. Click the Close button on the PowerPoint window.

SKILL SUMMARY

In This Lesson, You Learned How To:	Exam Objective	Objective Number
Work in the PowerPoint Window		
Work with an Existing Presentation	Demonstrate how to use views to navigate through presentations.	1.3.3
	Change to view in color/grayscale.	1.3.2
	View multiple presentations.	5.1.3

Knowledge Assessment

Matching

Match the term in Column 1 to its description in Column 2.

Column 1	Column 2
1. Tab	a. Includes the Slide, Notes, and Slides panes
2. Ribbon	b. A small toolbar that appears when you point to selected text
3. Normal view	c. Shows the keyboard key that will issue a command
4. Current slide	d. To highlight text for editing
5. Backstage view	e. A set of related tools on the Ribbon
6. Mini toolbar	f. Displays commands for managing files
7. Placeholder	g. The slide you are editing
8. KeyTip	h. A Ribbon tool that opens a dialog box
9. Dialog box launcher	i. A large toolbar that presents tools in related groups
10. Select	j. A box, built into many slides, that holds text or an object

True/False

Circle T if the statement is true or F if the statement is false.

T F 1. If you need more room on the screen, you can hide the Ribbon.

T F 2. When you start PowerPoint, the last presentation you worked on appears on the screen.

T F 3. When you save a presentation that has been previously saved, clicking the Save button on the Quick Access Toolbar reopens the Save As tab of Backstage view.

T F 4. The Quick Access Toolbar contains no buttons by default.

T F 5. To close a dialog box without accepting any changes you may have made to it, click the Cancel button.

T F 6. You can use the Undo command to reverse the last action you took.

T F 7. To print a presentation, open Backstage view and click Print.

T F 8. Backstage view gives you access to all of the PowerPoint design tools.

T F 9. You can use the Cut and Paste commands to move text from one slide to another slide.

T F 10. In Normal view, PowerPoint displays five different panes for viewing different aspects of your slides.

Competency Assessment

Project 1-1: The Central City Job Fair

As personnel manager for Woodgrove Bank, you have accepted an invitation to give a presentation at a local job fair. Your goal is to recruit applicants for positions as bank tellers. You have created the presentation but need to finish it.

GET READY. LAUNCH PowerPoint if it is not already running.

1. Click the **File tab** and open the presentation named *Job Fair 1* from the data files for this lesson.

2. Save the presentation as *Central City Job Fair*.

3. On slide 1, click in the subtitle box to place the insertion point there, and then type Central City Job Fair. Go to slide 2.

4. In the title of slide 2, select the words Woodgrove Bank by dragging the mouse pointer over them, and then replace the selected text by typing Us.

5. In the bulleted list, click after the word *assets* to place the insertion point there.

6. Press Enter to move the insertion point down to a new, blank line.

7. Type Voted "Best Local Bank" by City Magazine. The new text will wrap to fit in the box.

8. Display slide 3, and switch to Outline view.

9. In the outline, select the words Help Wanted (do not select the colon), and then press Delete to delete the text.

10. Type Now Hiring.

11. Click at the end of the first item in the bulleted list, and then press Enter to create a new line in the list.

12. Type Responsible for cash drawer and station bookkeeping.

13. Switch to Normal view, and then press Page Down to go to slide 4.

14. Select the last item in the bulleted list by dragging the mouse pointer across it.

15. On the Ribbon, click the Home tab, if necessary, and then click the Cut button. In the Slides pane, click slide 5.

16. Click at the end of the last item in the bulleted list to place the insertion point there, and then press Enter.

17. On the Ribbon, click the Paste button. The item you cut from slide 4 is pasted into slide 5.

18. **SAVE** the presentation and **CLOSE** the file.

LEAVE PowerPoint open for the next project.

Project 1-2: **Messenger Service**

Consolidated Messenger is a new company offering in-town courier service to corporate and private customers. As the company's owner, you want to tell as many people as possible about your new service, and a presentation can help you do it. You need to review your presentation, make some minor changes, and print it.

GET READY. LAUNCH PowerPoint if it is not already running.

1. Click the File tab and open the presentation named *Pitch* from the data files for this lesson, and save it as *Messenger Pitch*.

2. Read slide 1. In the Slides pane, click slide 2 and read it.

3. Click the scroll down button to go to slide 3, and then read it.

4. Click the Next Slide button to go to slide 4, and then read it.

5. Press Page Down to go to slide 5, and then read it.

6. Press Home to return to the beginning of the presentation.

7. On slide 1, select the words and Delivery by dragging the mouse pointer over them.

8. Press Delete to delete the selected text from the subtitle. Go to slide 2.

9. On slide 2, select the word *delayed* and type scheduled in its place.

10. Select the third item in the bulleted list (24-hour emergency service) by dragging the mouse pointer over it.

11. On the Home tab of the Ribbon, click the Copy button. Go to slide 4.

12. On slide 4, click at the end of the last item in the bulleted list to place the insertion point there.

13. Press Enter to move the insertion point down to a new, blank line. On the Ribbon, click the Paste button.

14. Click at the end of the newly pasted line to move the insertion point there. Type a colon and then type $250. Go to slide 5.

15. On slide 5, click at the end of the last line of text in the left-hand column, and then press Enter.
16. Type 555-1087 (daytime), and then press Enter.
17. Type 555-1088 (emergency), and then press Enter.
18. Type 555-1089 (fax).
19. Go to slide 1. Click the File tab.
20. When Backstage view opens, click Print. Then click the Print button to print with the default settings. (Check with your instructor; to save paper, he or she may ask you to not to print.)
21. **SAVE** the presentation and **CLOSE** the file.

LEAVE PowerPoint open for the next project.

Proficiency Assessment

Project 1-3: The Big Meeting

You are the director of documentation at Litware, Inc., which develops software for use in elementary schools. You have scheduled a conference with the writing staff and are working on an agenda for the meeting. Because the agenda is a single PowerPoint slide, you can display it on a projection screen for reference during the meeting.

1. **OPEN** the *Agenda* file from the data files for this lesson and save it as *Final Agenda*.
2. Copy the second line of the bulleted list and paste the copy below the original as a new bullet point.
3. In the newly pasted line, replace the word *Upcoming* with Revised.
4. In Outline view, add a new line to the end of the agenda. On the new line, type Adjourn.
5. Print the presentation. (Check with your instructor; to save paper, he or she may ask you not to print.)
6. **SAVE** the presentation, then **CLOSE** the file.

LEAVE PowerPoint open for the next project.

Project 1-4: Job Fair, Part 2

You have decided to make some last-minute changes to your presentation before going to the job fair.

1. **OPEN** *Job Fair 2* from the data files for this lesson and save it as *Final Job Fair*.
2. Copy the word Woodgrove on slide 1. In the title of slide 2, delete the word Us and paste the copied word in its place.
3. On slide 2, change the word *owned* to managed.
4. On slide 4, add the line References a must to the bottom of the bulleted list.
5. Print the presentation. (Check with your instructor; to save paper, he or she may ask you not to print.)
6. **SAVE** the presentation, then **CLOSE** the file.

LEAVE PowerPoint open for the next project.

Mastery Assessment

Project 1-5: **Price Fixing**

You are the general manager of Alpine Ski House. It's time to update the staff on the store's new prices, and a slide show is a good way to give everyone the details. An easy way to handle this job is to open last season's presentation and update it with new prices.

1. **OPEN** *Price List* from the data files for this lesson and save it as *New Price List*.
2. Move Black Ice Armageddon Skis - $692.50 from slide 3 to the bottom of slide 2.
3. On slides 2 and 3, increase the price of every item by ten dollars.
4. Print the presentation. (Check with your instructor; to save paper, he or she may ask you not to print.)
5. **SAVE** the presentation, then **CLOSE** the file.

LEAVE PowerPoint open for the next project.

Project 1-6: **A Trip to Toyland**

As the general manager for Tailspin Toys, you introduce new products to many other people in the company, such as the marketing and sales staff. You need to finalize a presentation about several new toys.

1. **OPEN** *Toys* from the data files for this lesson and save it as *New Toys*.
2. Copy List Price: $14.99 on slide 2 and paste it at the bottom of the bulleted lists on slides 3 and 4.
3. On slide 3, change the teddy bear's name from *Rory* to George.
4. On slide 4, change the top speed from *800* to 1,200.
5. Print the presentation. (Check with your instructor; to save paper, he or she may ask you not to print.)
6. **SAVE** the presentation and **CLOSE** the file.

EXIT PowerPoint.

LESSON SKILL MATRIX

Skill	Exam Objective	Objective Number
Creating a New Blank Presentation	Create a blank presentation.	1.1.1
Saving a Presentation	Embed fonts.	5.3.5
Creating a Presentation from a Template	Create presentations using templates.	1.1.2
Adding, Deleting, and Organizing Slides	Duplicate existing slides.	2.1.2
	Modify slide order.	2.3.2
	Delete slides.	2.1.4
Creating a Presentation from Existing Content	Apply styles to create slides.	2.1.6
	Reuse slides from other presentations.	5.1.2
	Import text files into presentations.	1.1.3
	Import Word document outlines into presentations.	1.1.4
Adding Notes to Your Slides		
Printing a Presentation	Print speaker notes.	1.4.6
	Print selections from presentations.	1.4.2
	Print presentations in grayscale.	1.4.5

KEY TERMS

- **contiguous**
- **handout**
- **indent level**
- **layout**
- **non-contiguous**
- **note**
- **Presenter view**
- **slide library**
- **template**
- **themes**
- **thumbnails**

©thinair28/iStockphoto

©thinair28/iStockphoto

Northwind Traders is a retailer of high-quality outdoor apparel and accessories for men, women, and children. The company has six stores in the Minneapolis–St. Paul area and a thriving online presence. As an assistant general manager, you help oversee the company's daily operations, hire and train new employees, and develop strategic plans. You also perform day-to-day functions assigned by the general manager. Your job frequently requires you to present information to an audience—for example, when training new workers on company policies or when providing executives with information about revenue or expenses. These duties often require you to create presentations from scratch, and PowerPoint lets you do that in several ways. In this lesson, you will learn different methods for creating presentations. You will also learn how to organize the slides in a presentation, add notes to your slides, select printing options, preview a slide show, and save a presentation for the first time.

SOFTWARE ORIENTATION

Selecting a Template

PowerPoint's New tab in Backstage view enables you to create a new presentation from a template. You can choose templates from Office.com or browse templates stored on your own hard drive (see Figure 2-1).

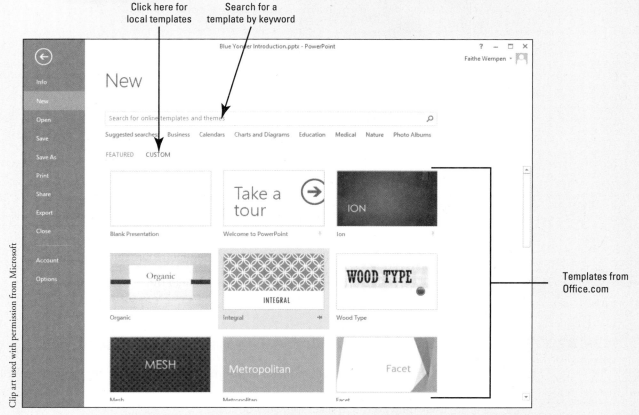

Figure 2-1
New tab in Backstage view

CREATING A NEW BLANK PRESENTATION

The Bottom Line

When you start PowerPoint, its Start screen appears. If you click Blank Presentation at that point, or press the Esc key, a new, blank presentation appears, containing a single slide. The fastest and simplest way to create a new presentation is to start with a blank presentation. You can add text to the presentation and then format the slides later.

CERTIFICATION READY?   **1.1.1**

How do you create a new blank presentation?

Creating a Blank Presentation

You can use the single slide that opens with a new, blank presentation to begin creating your new presentation. In this exercise, you will learn how to open a blank presentation.

STEP BY STEP   **Create a Blank Presentation at Startup**

GET READY. Before you begin these steps, make sure that your computer is on. Sign in to Windows, if necessary.

1. **START** PowerPoint. PowerPoint's Start screen appears (see Figure 2-2).

Figure 2-2

The Start screen in PowerPoint 2013

Clip art used with permission from Microsoft

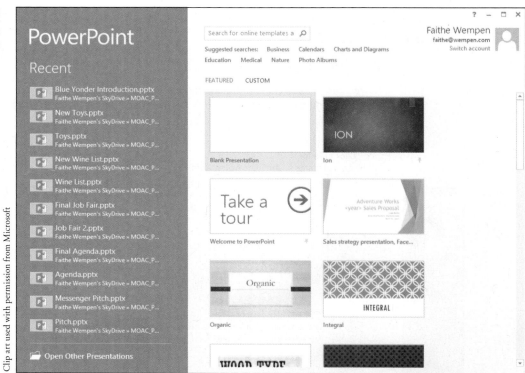

2. Click **Blank Presentation**, or press **Esc**. A new blank presentation appears.

PAUSE. LEAVE the blank presentation open to use in the next exercise.

STEP BY STEP   **Create a Blank Presentation (PowerPoint Already Open)**

GET READY. Before you begin these steps, make sure that your computer is on. Sign in to Windows, if necessary, and start PowerPoint.

1. Click the **File tab**. Backstage view opens.

2. Click **New**. The New tab of Backstage view opens (see Figure 2-1).

3. Click Blank Presentation. A new, blank presentation appears in Normal view (see Figure 2-3).

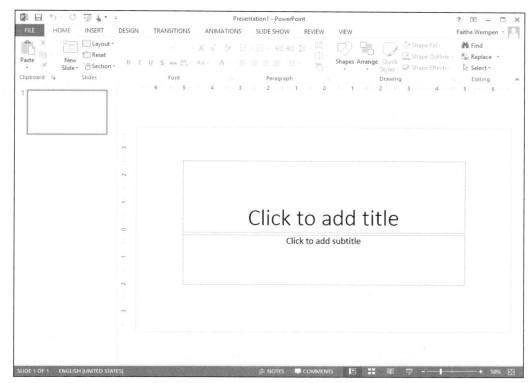

Figure 2-3

A blank presentation begins with a title slide

Another Way
Press Ctrl+N to open a new, blank presentation without using Backstage view. If another presentation is already open, the blank presentation opens in a separate window.

PAUSE. LEAVE the blank presentation open to use in the next exercise.

There are two advantages to using a blank presentation to start a slide show. First, PowerPoint creates a blank presentation every time the program starts, so you always have immediate access to the first slide of a new presentation by just pressing Esc at startup. Second, because the presentation is not formatted (meaning there are no backgrounds, colors, or pictures), you can focus on writing your text. Many experienced PowerPoint users prefer to start with a blank presentation because they know they can format their slides after the text is finished.

Changing a Slide's Layout

Most slides have a **layout**—a predefined arrangement of placeholders for text or objects (such as charts or pictures). PowerPoint has a variety of built-in layouts that you can use at any time. Layouts are shown in the Layout gallery as **thumbnails**—small pictures showing each available layout. (A gallery is a collection of thumbnail images.) Choose the layout that is best suited to display the text or objects you want to place on the slide. You can change a slide's layout at any time to arrange text or objects on the slide exactly the way you want. The following exercise shows you how to apply a different layout to the current slide.

STEP BY STEP   **Choose a Different Layout**

USE the new, blank presentation that is still open from the previous exercise.

1. Click the Home tab to make it active, if necessary, and then click Layout. A drop-down menu (called a *gallery*) appears, displaying PowerPoint's default layouts (see Figure 2-4). The title of the gallery is Office Theme, indicating that all these layouts come from the default theme (named Office).

Figure 2-4

Choosing a new layout

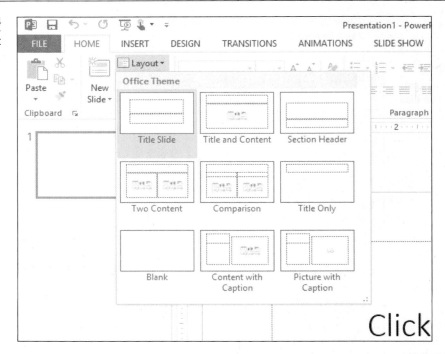

Figure 2-4

Choosing a new layout

2. Click the **Title and Content thumbnail** in the gallery. The gallery closes and PowerPoint applies the chosen layout to the current slide (see Figure 2-5).

Figure 2-5

The new layout applied to the current slide

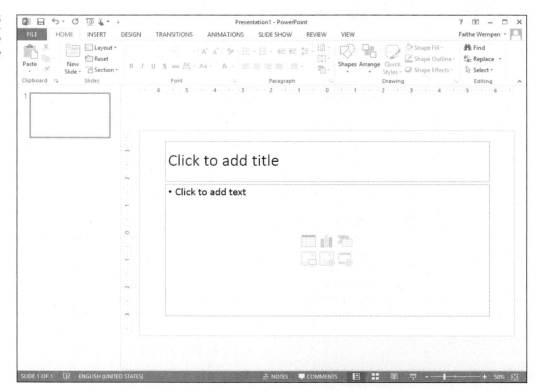

Another Way
To change a slide's layout, right-click a blank area of the slide outside a placeholder. When the shortcut menu opens, point to Layout, and then click a layout.

PAUSE. LEAVE the presentation open to use in the next exercise.

In this exercise, you chose the Title and Content layout, which contains a placeholder for the slide's title and a second placeholder that can display text, a picture, a table, or some other kind of object.

Cross Ref You will work with other slide layouts in Lesson 4.

You can change a slide's layout whether the slide is blank or contains text. If the slide already has text, PowerPoint will fit the text into the new layout's placeholders. If the new layout does not have an appropriate placeholder for the existing content, the existing content remains on the slide, but it is not part of the layout.

Adding Text to a Blank Slide

If a blank slide has one or more text placeholders, you can easily add text to the slide. To enter text, just click the sample text in the placeholder, and then type your text. In this exercise, you will enter text into a blank slide's placeholders to create a set of discussion points for a meeting of store managers. The slide you work with in this exercise has a title placeholder and a content placeholder that can hold text and other types of content.

STEP BY STEP **Add Text to a Blank Slide**

USE the slide that is still on the screen from the preceding exercise.

1. Click the title placeholder at the top of the slide. The text *Click to add title* disappears and a blinking insertion point appears in the placeholder.
2. Type Discussion Points.
3. Click the text at the top of the lower placeholder. The words *Click to add text* disappear and the insertion point appears.
4. Type Customer surveys, and then press Enter to move the insertion point down to a new line.
5. Type Inventory tracking and press Enter.
6. Type Absenteeism policy and press Enter.
7. Type Break and press Enter.
8. Type Store security and press Enter.
9. Type Store closing procedures and press Enter.
10. Type Cash drawer management, then click anywhere in the blank area outside the placeholder to clear its borders from the screen. Your slide should look like the one shown in Figure 2-6.

Figure 2-6

The completed slide

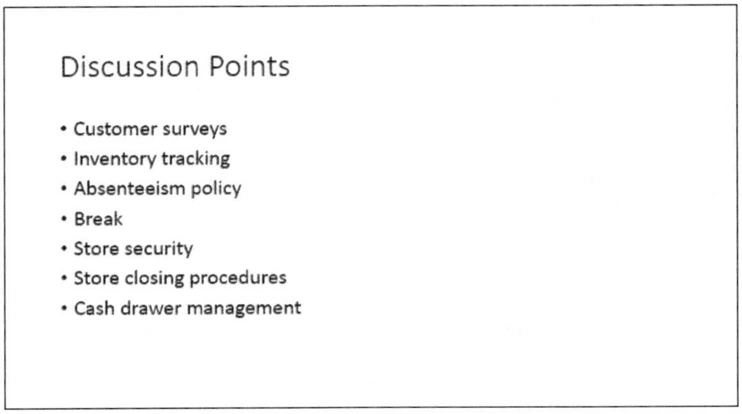

Discussion Points

- Customer surveys
- Inventory tracking
- Absenteeism policy
- Break
- Store security
- Store closing procedures
- Cash drawer management

PAUSE. LEAVE the presentation open to use in the next exercise.

Take Note If you click any of the icons in the lower placeholder, PowerPoint will display tools for adding non-text content, such as a table or chart. These types of content are covered in later lessons. The icons disappear after you insert content into the placeholder.

Even when a multiple-slide presentation is not needed at a meeting, displaying an agenda, a list of discussion points, or a list of breakout rooms can be helpful for the group.

SAVING A PRESENTATION

When you create a new presentation, it exists only in your computer's memory. If you want to keep the presentation, you must save it on a disk or to a network location or flash drive. After you save a file, you can close it, then reopen it again later and resume working on it. The following exercises show you how to save a new presentation to a disk, how to save the presentation in a different file format, and how to work with PowerPoint's Save options.

Saving a New Presentation for the First Time

When you save a presentation for the first time, PowerPoint displays the Save As dialog box so you can give the presentation a name before saving it. In this exercise, you will name and save the presentation you created earlier.

STEP BY STEP   **Save a New Presentation**

Another Way
When saving a presentation for the first time, you can display the Save As tab of Backstage view by pressing Ctrl+S.

USE the presentation that is still on the screen from the preceding exercise.

1. On the Quick Access Toolbar, click Save. The Save As tab of Backstage view appears.
2. Navigate to the folder where you want to save your file. To do so, click either SkyDrive or Computer, and then click Browse. Then use the Save As dialog box to change the location as needed.
3. Select the text in the File name box by dragging the mouse pointer over it, and then press Delete to delete it.
4. Type Managers Meeting (see Figure 2-7).

Figure 2-7

Saving the presentation for the first time

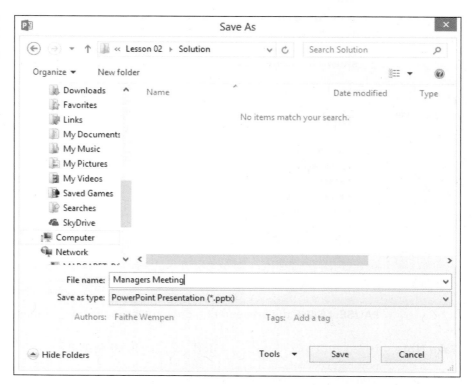

5. Click Save. PowerPoint saves the presentation in the folder you chose, under the name you have given it.

PAUSE. LEAVE the presentation open to use in the next exercise.

When you save a presentation (or any type of document), be sure to give it a name that describes its contents. Giving the presentation a name that describes its contents will help you identify your presentations more easily when you are trying to find the right one.

Choosing a Different File Format

PowerPoint can save presentations in several different file formats. In this exercise, you will save your presentation in a format that is compatible with earlier versions of PowerPoint.

STEP BY STEP **Choose a Different File Format**

USE the *Managers Meeting* presentation that is still open from the previous exercise.

1. Click the File tab, and then click the Save As command. The Save As tab of Backstage View reappears.
2. Navigate to the folder where you want to save your file. To do so, click either SkyDrive or Computer, and then click Browse. Then use the Save As dialog box to change the location as needed.
3. In the Save As dialog box, next to Save as Type, click the current type: PowerPoint Presentation. A menu of file types opens.
4. Click PowerPoint 97-2003 Presentation. The file type changes (see Figure 2-8).

Figure 2-8

Saving with a different file format

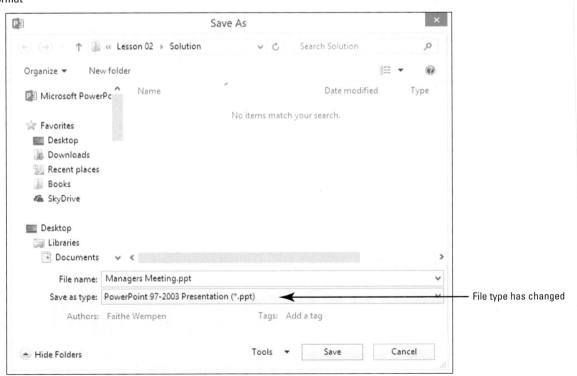

File type has changed

Take Note Because you are saving the presentation in a different file format, it is not necessary to give it a new name. Files of different formats can have the same file name. This exercise renames it anyway.

5. Select the file's name in the File name box, delete the name, and then type Old Format Discussion Points.
6. Click Save, and then close the presentation.

PAUSE. LEAVE PowerPoint open to use in the next exercise.

By default, PowerPoint 2013 saves presentations in a type of XML format, which is not compatible with versions of PowerPoint prior to 2007. If you want to be able to use a presentation with an older version of PowerPoint, you can save it by using the PowerPoint 97-2003 Presentation file format. (PowerPoint 2007 and 2010 use the same XML-based format as PowerPoint 2013, so no special version is necessary to share with users of PowerPoint 2007 or 2010.)

You can save a presentation in other formats as well. For example, if you select the PowerPoint Show format, the presentation will always open in Slide Show view, rather than in Normal view. You can also save a presentation as a template, or as a series of graphics, or in a macro-enabled format.

 Cross Ref Lesson 10 covers the details of saving in many different formats, including saving slides as pictures and saving presentations in PDF or XPS format.

Changing the Default File Format

PowerPoint has settings that control the default file location, the default file format, and more. If you find yourself frequently changing the file location or file type when you save a presentation, it may be worth your time to change the settings in PowerPoint that specify the defaults. In the following exercise, you learn how to modify the application's save settings.

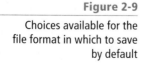

STEP BY STEP **Set the Save Options**

Take Note No presentation is open as you begin this exercise, but that is not important. These steps can be completed without having a presentation open.

GET READY. To set the save options, do the following:

1. Click the File tab and then click Options. The PowerPoint Options dialog box opens.
2. Click the Save category in the left panel of the dialog box. The Save options appear in the right panel.
3. Click on the Save files in this format drop-down list and examine the available file types (see Figure 2-9). Do not change the current setting (PowerPoint Presentation).

Figure 2-9

Choices available for the file format in which to save by default

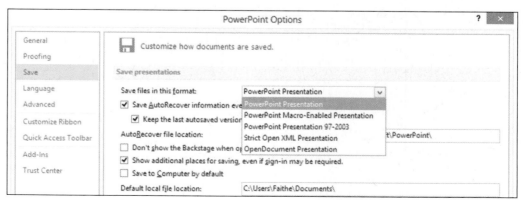

4. In the Default local file location text box, take note of the location referenced.

Take Note   By default, files are stored in the Documents (or My Documents) folder for the current user. In Windows Vista and Windows 7, this is the C:\Users*username*\Documents folder, where username is the current user. That is what appears as the default in Figure 2-9, for example.

5. (Optional) Change the location in the Default local file location text box to the location where you are storing your completed work for this course. If you do this, you will not have to change the location for saving and opening files every time you want to save or open files for class exercises and projects.

6. Click OK to close the dialog box.

7. Click Save, then close the presentation.

PAUSE. LEAVE PowerPoint open to use in the next exercise.

You can choose to create regular PowerPoint 2013 presentations, PowerPoint 97-2003 presentations, macro-enabled presentations, Strict Open XML presentations, or OpenDocument presentations by default. OpenDocument is a widely accepted generic format for presentation files, useful for sharing files with people who use OpenOffice and other freeware office suites. Strict Open XML is a variation of that.

You can set a default save location of any accessible drive, including not only folders on your hard disk, but also network locations and removable drives. (It is not usually a good idea to set the default location to a drive that is not always available, however.) The location you specify will appear in both the Save As and Open dialog boxes by default.

Also in the Save options, you can set an interval at which PowerPoint autosaves your work. Autosaving helps PowerPoint recover any work that would otherwise be lost if your PC shuts off or crashes while there are unsaved changes to a presentation. The default interval is 10 minutes.

Embedding Fonts

CERTIFICATION READY?   5.3.5

How can you embed fonts when saving a presentation?

When you create a presentation, you can choose any of the fonts installed on that computer. When you present the presentation on another computer that does not have the same font installed that you used in the presentation, PowerPoint substitutes a different font, which may or may not be acceptable to you. To ensure that the correct font is always available no matter what computer you open the presentation on, you can embed the fonts in the presentation file. The disadvantage in embedding fonts is that it makes the presentation file larger.

STEP BY STEP   **Embed Fonts When Saving**

Take Note   Some fonts cannot be embedded because of their licensing restrictions.

GET READY. To set the embed fonts while saving, do the following:

1. Click the File tab, and then click Save As.

2. Browse to the location where you want to save.

3. In the Save As dialog box, click Tools. A menu opens.

4. Click Save Options. The PowerPoint Options dialog box opens.

5. Mark the Embed fonts in the file check box. This check box is located under the Preserve fidelity when sharing this presentation heading (see Figure 2-10).

Figure 2-10

Choose to embed fonts

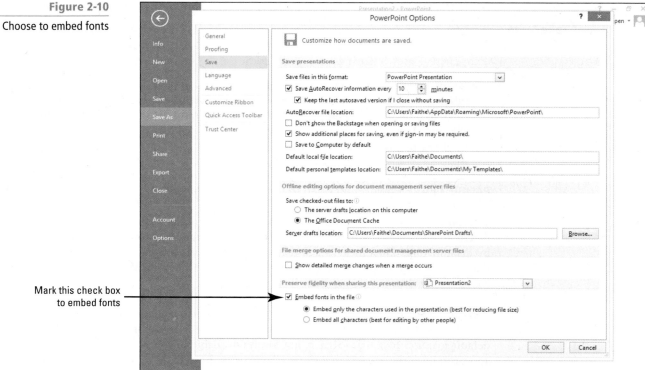

Figure 2-10

Choose to embed fonts

Mark this check box
to embed fonts

6. Click OK.

7. Continue saving normally.

When you mark the Embed fonts in the file check box, two option buttons become available. Click the one that best fits your needs:

* Embed only the characters used in the presentation (best for reducing file size): Choose this option if the presentation text is final, if you do not anticipate making any changes to it, and if small file size is important.

* Embed all characters (best for editing by other people): Choose this option if the presentation text is not final, or if file size is not important (for example, if there is plenty of space on the drive where it is being stored).

CREATING A PRESENTATION FROM A TEMPLATE

The Bottom Line

PowerPoint's templates give you a jump start in creating complete presentations. A **template** is a reusable sample file that includes a background, layouts, coordinating fonts, and other design elements that work together to create an attractive, finished slide show. Templates may (but are not required to) contain sample content, too.

Using a Template as the Basis for a Presentation

CERTIFICATION READY? 1.1.2

How can you create a new presentation using an existing template?

Each template employs one or more **themes**. A theme is a collection of settings including colors, fonts, background graphics, bullet graphics, and margin and placement settings. You can create your own templates or download new ones from Office.com. In this exercise, you will use a downloaded template to start a presentation that, when finished, will help you show pictures and descriptions of new products to a group of store managers.

STEP BY STEP   **Create a Presentation from a Template**

GET READY. To create a presentation from a template, do the following:

1. Click the File tab.
2. Click New to open the New tab.
3. Under the Search box, click the Photo Albums hyperlink. Clicking the hyperlink will take you to Thumbnail images of the photo album templates.
4. Scroll down to locate and click the Classic Photo Album thumbnail, then click Create in the Preview pane, which appears in the middle of the screen (see Figure 2-11). PowerPoint opens a new presentation based on the selected template. It contains several sample slides with text and graphics.

Figure 2-11

Selecting a sample template

5. On slide 1, select Classic Photo Album and type Northwind Traders to replace it.
6. Click the text in the subtitle placeholder to place the insertion point there, and then type New Product Preview (see Figure 2-12).

Figure 2-12

Customizing the text on the first slide

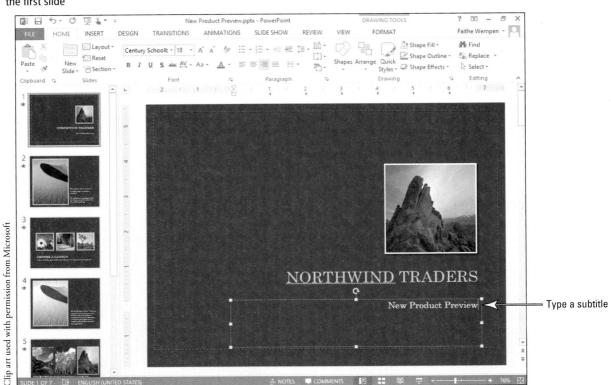

Take Note   In Figure 2-12, and perhaps on your screen too, NORTHWIND has a wavy red underline, indicating that the word is not in PowerPoint's dictionary. You can ignore that for now. Lesson 3 covers using the spellcheck feature.

7. On the Quick Access Toolbar, click Save. The Save As tab of Backstage view appears.

8. Navigate to the folder where you want to save your files, and then save the presentation with the file name *New Product Preview*.

PAUSE. LEAVE the presentation open to use in the next exercise.

Take Note   You can change a presentation's theme from the Design tab; you do not have to create a new presentation based on a template just to get a new look. You will learn how to change themes in Lesson 4.

It is important to choose a template that is appropriate for your audience and your message. If you need to deliver business information to a group of managers, for example, choose a template that looks professional and does not have elements that will distract the audience from getting your message. Conversely, a whimsical template might work better for a group of young people.

Besides the Microsoft-supplied templates, you can also store and use your own templates. Click the Custom (or Personal) heading beneath the Suggested Searches line on the New tab of Backstage view, and then browse to locate the template you want to use from your own template collection.

Take Note   In Figure 2-1 there are two headings below the Suggested Searches line: Featured and Custom. If you do not see those, you need to specify a default personal template location. To do so, choose File, Options, and click Save. In the Default Personal Templates Location text box, enter a path to a location that you want to be able to access quickly from the New tab. Then click OK. At that point you will see Featured and either Custom or Personal headings on the New tab. (Custom headings appear if a workgroup template location is set up for Office 2013 applications, and Personal headings appear if it is not.)

ADDING, DELETING, AND ORGANIZING SLIDES

The Bottom Line   A template's sample slides can provide a basic structure as a starting point, but you will probably want to make some changes. In PowerPoint it is easy to add, delete, and reorder the slides in a presentation to suit your unique needs.

Adding a New Slide to a Presentation

You can add as many new slides as you want to a presentation. The following exercise shows you how to insert a new slide into the current presentation in two different ways: using the New Slide command on the Ribbon, and using the Slides pane.

STEP BY STEP   **Add a New Slide**

USE the *New Product Preview* presentation that is still open from the previous exercise.

1. On the Home tab in the Slides group, click the New Slide button drop-down arrow. A gallery opens, showing thumbnail images of the slide layouts that are available for this template (see Figure 2-13).

Figure 2-13

New Slide gallery

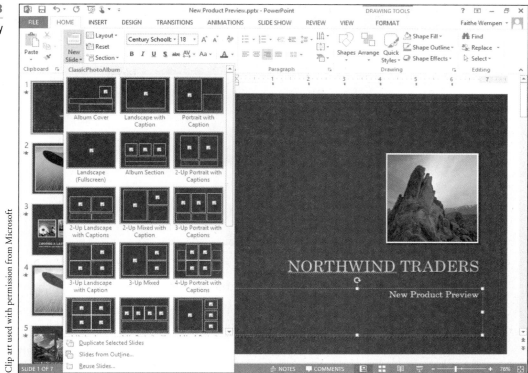

2. Scroll down to the bottom of the gallery, and then click Title and Content.

Take Note To view the New Slide gallery, you must click the New Slide button's drop-down arrow. If you click the face of the New Slide button, PowerPoint will insert the default new slide for the current template.

3. On the new slide, click the title placeholder and type This Year's New Products.

4. Click the sample text at the top of the second placeholder, and then type the following items, placing each item on its own line:

Women's jackets

Men's jackets

Boots

Backpacks

Flannel shirts

Fleece

Turtlenecks

Underwear

Socks

5. Click in the area surrounding the slide to clear the placeholder's border. When you are done, your slide should look like the one shown in Figure 2-14.

Figure 2-14

The inserted slide

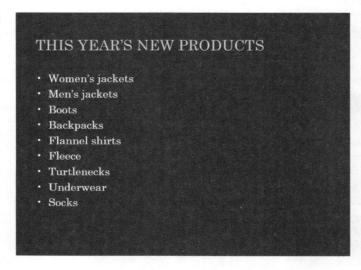

6. On the View tab, click the Outline View button to switch to Outline view.

Take Note   Some of the slides in the Outline pane show no text in their Title placeholder; that is because this presentation is based on a photo album template.

7. In the Outline pane, click to place the text insertion point after the word *Socks* in slide 2 and press Enter, creating a new paragraph. At this point the new paragraph is a bullet on slide 2.

8. Press Shift+Tab. The new paragraph is promoted into a new slide title. The orange rectangle to the left of the line indicates it is a new slide.

9. Type Clearance Items and press Enter. A new slide appears. Because the previous paragraph was a slide title, the new one is too.

10. Press Tab. The new paragraph is indented so that it is a bullet on the Clearance Items slide.

11. Type the following items, pressing Enter after each one except the last item to place it in its own paragraph:

    Biking accessories

    Camping supplies

    Spelunking gear

12. After all the text is typed in for the new slide, it appears in the Outline (see Figure 2-15).

Figure 2-15

A slide added via the Outline

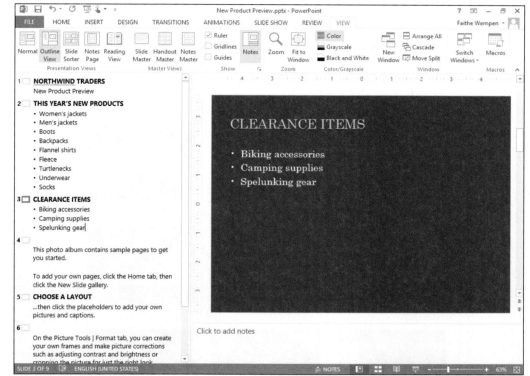

Another Way

In Normal view, you can click in the Outline pane to place a flashing horizontal line after an existing slide, and then press Enter to create a new blank slide that uses the same layout as the one before it.

PAUSE. LEAVE the presentation open to use in the next exercise.

Duplicating Selected Slides

If you want several similar slides in a presentation, you may be able to save some time by duplicating some of the slides and then modifying the copies. The following exercise shows how to select the slides you want to duplicate, even when they are non-contiguous (not adjacent), and make copies of them. You will also learn how to use the Duplicate Selected Slides command to make duplicates of slides.

STEP BY STEP   **Duplicate Non-Contiguous Slides**

USE the *New Product Preview* presentation that is still open from the previous exercise.

1. Click the Slide Sorter button on the View tab to switch to Slide Sorter view. The presentation's slides appear together in a single pane.
2. Change the Zoom level to 90% for the Slide Sorter pane by clicking the minus sign . button at the left end of the Zoom slider located in the far right of the status bar in the bottom right corner (see Figure 2-16).

Figure 2-16

Slide Sorter view at 90% Zoom

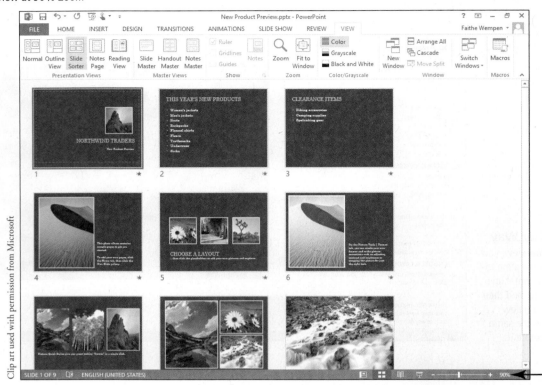

Zoom level of 90%

Another Way
You can also press Ctrl+C to copy, and Ctrl+V to paste.

3. Click slide 4. An orange outline appears around it, indicating that it is selected.
4. Hold down Ctrl and click slide 7. An orange outline appears around it too.
5. Click the Home tab and click Copy. The two slides are copied to the Clipboard.
6. Click to the right of slide 9. A vertical line appears there.
7. On the Home tab, click Paste. The copied slides are pasted after slide 9 (see Figure 2-17).

Figure 2-17

Copied slides are pasted

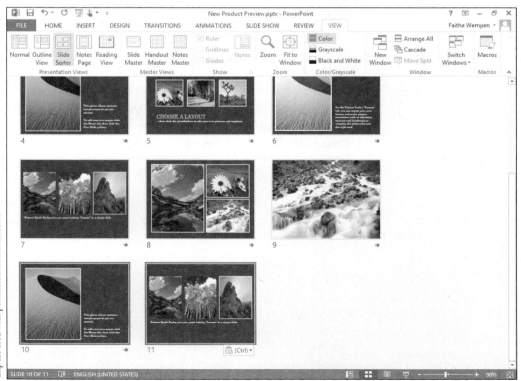

8. Click slide 2 *(This Year's New Products)* to select it.

9. On the Home tab, open the New Slide button's drop-down list.

10. Click Duplicate Selected Slides. A copy of slide 2 is pasted directly following the original slide 2.

11. **SAVE** the presentation file and **CLOSE** it.

PAUSE. LEAVE PowerPoint open for the next exercise.

Contiguous means "together," so **non-contiguous** slides are not adjacent to one another in the presentation. As you just learned, to select non-contiguous slides hold down Ctrl as you click each one you want. To select contiguous slides, you can use the Shift key. Click the first slide in the group, and then hold down the Shift key as you click the last slide in the group. All the intervening slides are selected also.

You can also select slides from the Slides pane in Normal or Outline view. On the Slides pane in Normal view, select slide thumbnails just as in Slide Sorter view. On the Outline pane in Outline view, click the small rectangle (the Slide icon) to the left of the slide title to select everything on that slide (see Figure 2-18).

Figure 2-18

To select a slide in the Outline pane, click its Slide icon to the left of its title

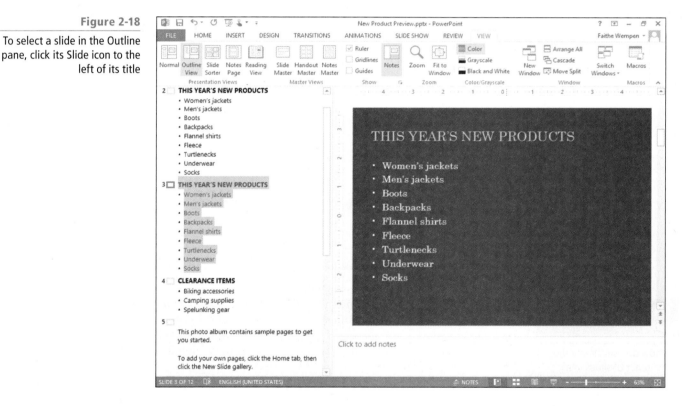

Rearranging the Slides in a Presentation

It is important to organize your slides so they best support your message. In PowerPoint, reorganizing slides is a simple drag-and-drop procedure. In Slide Sorter view (or in the Outline pane in Normal view), you can click a slide and drag it to a new location in the presentation. A line shows you where the slide will be placed when you drop it. Moving a slide is a simple procedure, as you will learn in the following exercise.

STEP BY STEP   **Rearrange the Slides in a Presentation**

GET READY. To rearrange the slides in a presentation, do the following:

1. **OPEN** the *Management Values* presentation, and then save it as *Management Values Final*.
2. Click the View tab, and then click the Slide Sorter button to switch to Slide Sorter view. The presentation's slides appear together in a single window.
3. Use the Zoom control in the status bar to set the Zoom to 70% if it is not already so.
4. Click slide 5 *(Our extended family)* and drag it to the left of slide 4 *(Our customers)* (see Figure 2-19). The moved slide is now slide 4.

Figure 2-19

Moving a slide in Slide Sorter view

Drag the slide to a new position ⟶

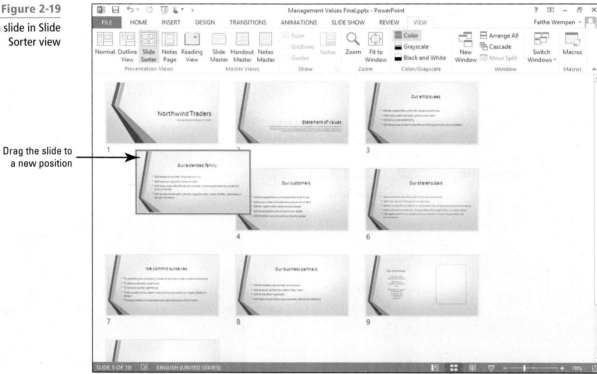

CERTIFICATION READY?   **2.3.2**

How do you change the order of slides in a presentation?

5. Switch to Outline view, and in the Outline pane, click the icon to the left of slide 7's title *(We commit ourselves)*. All the text from slide 7 is selected.
6. Drag slide 7's icon downward. When a vertical line appears between slides 8 and 9, release the mouse button. The moved slide is now slide 8 (see Figure 2-20).

Figure 2-20

Moving a slide in Outline view

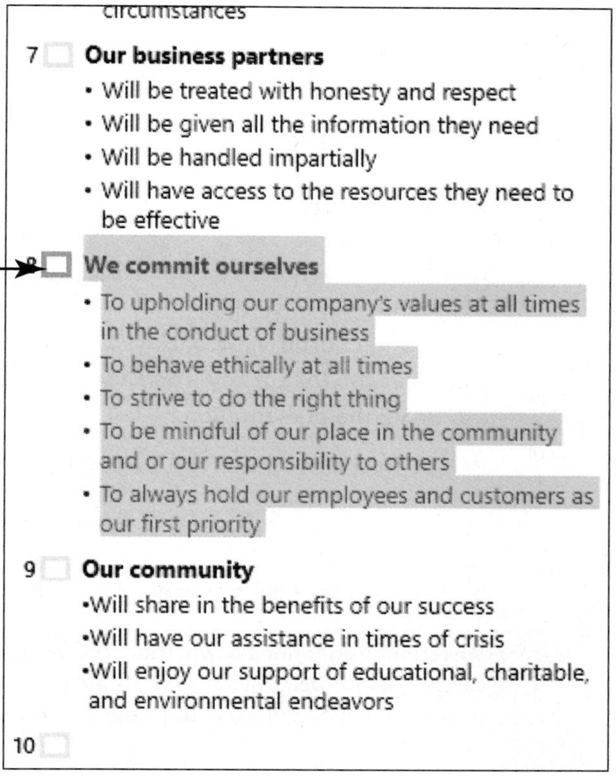

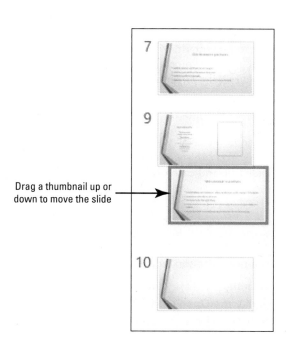

Drag the slide icon up or
down to move the slide

Figure 2-20

Moving a slide in Outline view

circumstances

7 ☐ **Our business partners**
- Will be treated with honesty and respect
- Will be given all the information they need
- Will be handled impartially
- Will have access to the resources they need to be effective

8 ☐ **We commit ourselves**
- To upholding our company's values at all times in the conduct of business
- To behave ethically at all times
- To strive to do the right thing
- To be mindful of our place in the community and or our responsibility to others
- To always hold our employees and customers as our first priority

9 ☐ **Our community**
- Will share in the benefits of our success
- Will have our assistance in times of crisis
- Will enjoy our support of educational, charitable, and environmental endeavors

10 ☐

7. Switch to Normal view and select slide 8 *(We commit ourselves)*.

8. Drag slide 8 downward and drop it between slides 9 and 10 (see Figure 2-21), and then release the mouse button. The moved slide is now slide 9.

Figure 2-21

Moving a slide in the Slides pane in Normal view

Another Way
You can also use the Clipboard to move slides: select a slide and use the Cut command (Ctrl+X) to move it to the Clipboard, and then position the insertion point and use the Paste command (Ctrl+V) to paste it from the Clipboard.

Drag a thumbnail up or down to move the slide

9. **SAVE** the presentation.

PAUSE. LEAVE the presentation open to use in the next exercise.

CERTIFICATION READY? 2.1.4

How can you delete a slide from a presentation?

Deleting a Slide

When you do not want to keep a slide in a presentation, you can delete it. The following exercise shows you how.

STEP BY STEP **Delete a Slide**

Another Way
You can also delete a selected slide by clicking the Cut button on the Home tab of the Ribbon.

USE the *Management Values Final* presentation that is still open from the previous exercise.

1. In Slide Sorter view, click slide 10 (the blank slide).
2. Press the Delete key. The slide is removed from the presentation.
3. **SAVE** the presentation.

CLOSE the presentation file. **LEAVE** PowerPoint open for the next exercise.

To select more than one slide at a time for deletion, hold down the Ctrl key and click each slide you want to delete. (If you change your mind, you can deselect the selected slides by clicking in a blank area of the PowerPoint window.) You can then delete all the selected slides at the same time.

PowerPoint does not ask whether you are sure if you want to delete a slide, so it is important to be careful before deleting. If you accidentally delete a slide, click the Undo button on the Quick Access Toolbar right away to bring the slide back (see Figure 2-22).

Figure 2-22

Undo an accidental deletion

Undo button

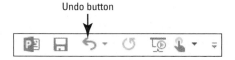

CREATING A PRESENTATION FROM EXISTING CONTENT

The Bottom Line

If the content you want to present already exists in another form, it makes sense to reuse it rather than starting from scratch. PowerPoint imports content easily from a variety of formats, including Word outlines, other PowerPoint presentations, and slide libraries.

Using Content from Word

Microsoft Word's Outline view enables you to create a well-structured hierarchical outline consisting of multiple heading levels. You can then open such outlines in PowerPoint, where each of the major headings becomes a slide title and each of the minor headings becomes a bullet of body text.

STEP BY STEP **Start a Presentation from a Word Outline**

GET READY. To start a presentation from a Word outline, do the following:

1. In PowerPoint, click the File tab.
2. Click Open to display the Open tab of Backstage view
3. Navigate to the folder that contains the data files for this lesson.
4. Open the File type drop-down list by clicking the All PowerPoint Presentations button.
5. In the File type list, click All Outlines. The file listing in the dialog box changes to show outlines (including Word documents). The file location is the same; the only thing that's changed is the filter that determines which file types are displayed (see Figure 2-23).

Figure 2-23

Open a Word outline file

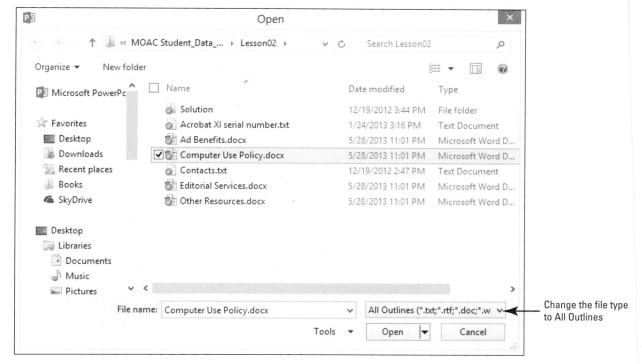

Change the file type
to All Outlines

6. Click *Computer Use Policy.docx*.

7. Click the Open button. The outline opens as a new presentation.

8. **SAVE** the new presentation as *Computer Use Policy Final.pptx*.

Take Note Even though you used the Open command and not the New command, PowerPoint still started a new presentation. Look at the file name in the title bar of the application prior to step 8; it is a generic name such as Presentation5, not the name of the original Word document. That's why you have to save it in step 8.

PAUSE. LEAVE the presentation open to use in the next exercise.

How do you apply styles to
create slides?

If you create an outline in Microsoft Word, you can import it into PowerPoint and generate slides from it. Before you can create slides from a Word outline, the outline must be formatted correctly. Paragraphs formatted with Word's Heading 1 style become slide titles. Paragraphs formatted with subheading styles (such as Heading 2 or Heading 3) are converted into bulleted lists in the slides' subtitle placeholders. Any Word document may be opened in PowerPoint and converted to a presentation, but documents that are not structured as outlines may require quite a bit of cleanup in PowerPoint after importing.

Promoting or Demoting Outline Content

After importing data from a Word outline or other external source, you may find that the outline levels are not set as you would like them for some text. You can promote a paragraph to make it a higher level in the outline, or demote it to make it a lower level.

STEP BY STEP **Promote and Demote Content**

USE the *Computer Use Policy Final* presentation that is still open from the previous exercise.

1. Select slide 2 *(Ownership)* and click at the beginning of the second line of the bulleted list *(Desktops, laptops and handheld systems)*.

2. Press Tab. The second bulleted list item is demoted, making it subordinate to the preceding item in the list *(Computers:)*.

3. Click at the beginning of the third line of the bulleted list *(Network servers and hardware)* and press Tab. The item is demoted.

4. Select the last two bullets on the slide and press Tab. They are both demoted to a lower outline level. (See Figure 2-24.)

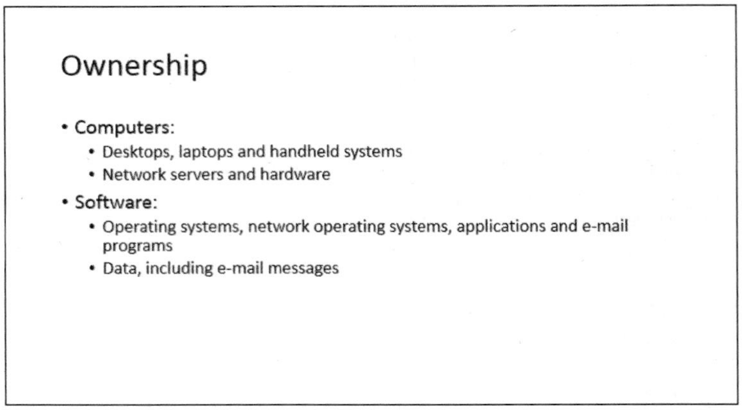

Figure 2-24

Several paragraphs have been demoted, creating a multilevel list

Ownership

- Computers:
  - Desktops, laptops and handheld systems
  - Network servers and hardware
- Software:
  - Operating systems, network operating systems, applications and e-mail programs
  - Data, including e-mail messages

5. Switch to Outline view.

6. In the Outline pane, select the last three paragraphs on slide 2 (the *Software* heading and both of its subordinate bullet points).

7. Press Shift+Tab. The Software heading is promoted to its own slide, and the two bullet points beneath it are promoted to first-level bullet points.

8. Delete the colon (:) following *Software* on the slide title (see Figure 2-25).

Figure 2-25

Software has been moved to its own slide by promotion

Software has been promoted →

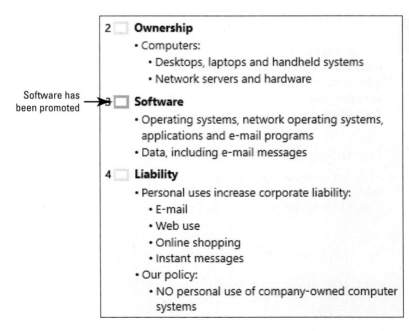

2 Ownership
- Computers:
  - Desktops, laptops and handheld systems
  - Network servers and hardware
3 Software
- Operating systems, network operating systems, applications and e-mail programs
- Data, including e-mail messages
4 Liability
- Personal uses increase corporate liability:
  - E-mail
  - Web use
  - Online shopping
  - Instant messages
- Our policy:
  - NO personal use of company-owned computer systems

9. In the Outline pane, select the slide 2 title *(Ownership)* and press Delete to remove it. The bullets that were subordinate to it move to slide 1.

10. On slide 1, select the bullets that were previously subordinate to Ownership (Computers: and the two bullet points subordinate to it) and press Shift+Tab. The selected text is promoted to its own slide.

11. Select the Computers: title on the slide layout and type Hardware to replace it. (See Figure 2-26.)

Figure 2-26

Hardware (previously Computers) has been moved to its own slide by promotion

Hardware has been promoted →

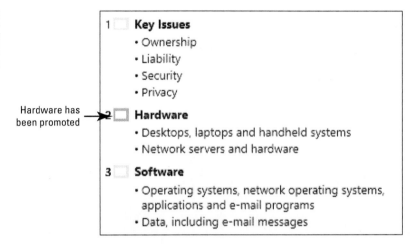

1   **Key Issues**
- Ownership
- Liability
- Security
- Privacy

2   **Hardware**
- Desktops, laptops and handheld systems
- Network servers and hardware

3   **Software**
- Operating systems, network operating systems, applications and e-mail programs
- Data, including e-mail messages

12. **SAVE** the presentation and then close the file.

PAUSE. LEAVE PowerPoint open to use in the next exercise.

Just like the headings in a book's outline, some of the items in a list are superior while others are subordinate. In a PowerPoint slide, the relationship between items in a list is shown by indent level. An item's **indent level** is the distance it is indented from the placeholder's left border. Superior items are indented less than subordinate ones. You can change the indent level of an item in a list by pressing Shift+Tab or Tab, or by right-clicking the paragraph and choosing Promote or Demote. You can also use the Decrease List Level or Increase List Level buttons on the Home tab of the Ribbon. Promoting a paragraph to the top level makes it into the title of its own slide, and everything subordinate to it becomes the slide's content.

Reusing Slides from Presentations and Libraries

CERTIFICATION READY?   5.1.2

How can you reuse slides from other presentations in your current presentation?

It is easy to reuse a slide from one presentation in another. This technique frees you from creating the same slide from scratch more than once. In addition, some companies store frequently used slides in slide libraries on their file servers, so multiple users can draw from a common pool of premade slides. The following exercise shows you how to locate a slide from a different presentation or from a slide library and insert it into the current presentation.

STEP BY STEP   **Reuse a Slide from a Presentation**

REOPEN the *New Product Preview* presentation that you created earlier in this lesson. Change your file to Normal view if needed.

1. On the Home tab of the Ribbon, click the New Slide button drop-down arrow. At the bottom of the gallery that appears, click Reuse Slides. The Reuse Slides task pane opens on the right side of the PowerPoint window (see Figure 2-27).

Figure 2-27

Reuse Slides task pane provides access to existing content

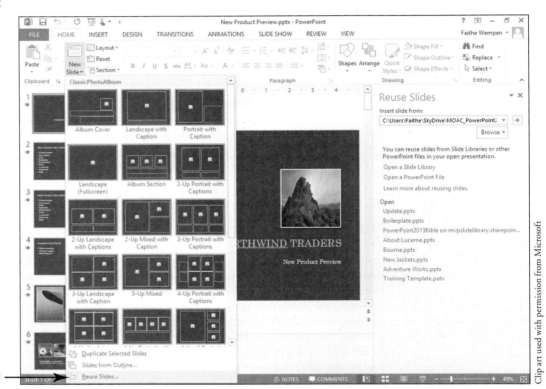

Reuse Slides command

Clip art used with permission from Microsoft

2. In the task pane, click the Browse button. A drop-down list opens. Click Browse File. The Browse dialog box opens.

3. Locate and open *New Jackets*. The presentation's slides appear in the task pane (see Figure 2-28).

Figure 2-28

New Jackets presentation
opens in the Reuse Slides
task pane

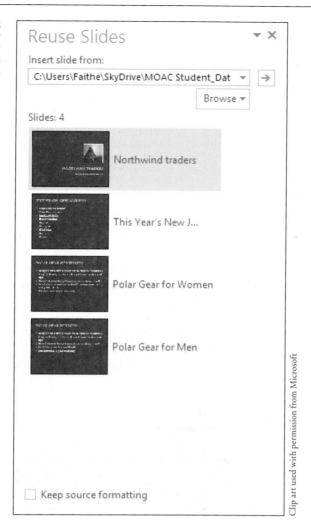

Clip art used with permission from Microsoft

4. In the Slides pane, click slide 2 *(This Year's New Products)* to select it.

5. In the Reuse Slides task pane, click slide 2 *(This Year's New Jackets)* in the *New Jackets* presentation. The slide is inserted into the *New Product Preview* presentation as the new slide 3.

6. Click the Close button in the upper-right corner of the task pane.

7. **SAVE** and **CLOSE** the *New Product Preview* presentation.

PAUSE. LEAVE PowerPoint open to use in the next exercise.

Over time, you will probably create many presentations, and some of them may share common information. The Reuse Slides command lets you copy slides from one presentation to another. By copying finished slides in this manner, you can avoid recreating similar slides over and over again.

You can import slides from other presentations, as you just practiced, or you can import them from slide libraries. A **slide library** is a feature on a SharePoint server that enables people to publish presentations with each slide saved as an individual file, so that others can reuse slides on an individual basis without having to think about which presentation they originally came from. Because using a slide library requires access to a SharePoint server that has special software installed on it for slide libraries, this book does not practice using one. However, the steps for selecting a slide from a slide library are very similar to those for selecting from a presentation. Follow the preceding steps, but in step 2, instead of choosing Browse File, choose Browse Slide Library. The first time you access the slide library, you must type the URL in the Folder Name box; after that, the location defaults to that same library.

CERTIFICATION READY? **1.1.3**

How can you import text files into presentations?

CERTIFICATION READY? **1.1.4**

How can you import a Word outline into a presentation?

Importing Text from Other Sources

PowerPoint readily accepts text from almost any Windows application. One way to import text is to use the Clipboard, because nearly all Windows applications support Clipboard use. You can use the Paste Options icon after pasting text to choose how it will be pasted, or use Paste Special to select special pasting methods. In this exercise, you learn how to paste text from a plain text file and from a Word document into PowerPoint, and you practice using the Paste Special command to maintain the content's original formatting of the text from the Word document. These same techniques also work on graphics.

STEP BY STEP **Import Text into PowerPoint**

START with PowerPoint open.

1. **START** Microsoft Word, and open *Other Resources.docx* in it. The procedure for opening files in Word is the same as in PowerPoint.
2. **SWITCH TO** Microsoft PowerPoint, and open *Cashier Training*. **SAVE** it as *Cashier Training Final*.

3. Switch to Outline view, and scroll down to the bottom of the presentation in the Outline pane. Click after the last bullet point on the last slide and press Enter, creating a new bulleted paragraph.
4. Press Shift+Tab to promote the new paragraph to a new slide (see Figure 2-29).

Figure 2-29

Create a new slide at the end of the presentation to hold the imported content

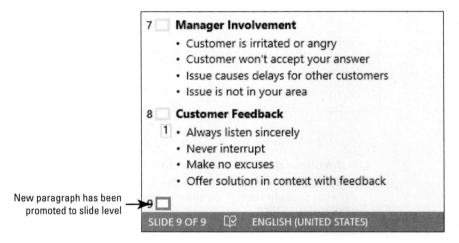

New paragraph has been promoted to slide level

5. Using the Windows taskbar, switch to the *Other Resources* file in Word. Select the heading *(Other Resources)* and press Ctrl+C to copy it to the Clipboard.
6. Switch back to PowerPoint. If the insertion point is not already on the Outline pane next to the slide 9 icon, click to place it there.
7. Press Ctrl+V to paste the text. The text appears as the slide's title, and a Paste Options icon appears beside the text. If you do not see the icon, move the mouse pointer over slide 9's icon to the left of the pasted text.
8. Click the Paste Options icon to open its menu. Its menu contains the Paste Options icons (see Figure 2-30).

Figure 2-30

Use the icons on the Paste Options menu to specify how pasted content should be displayed

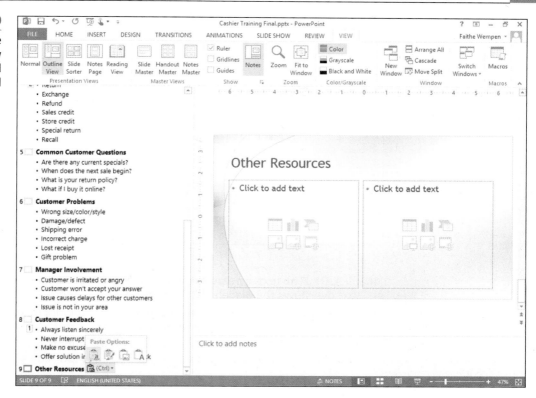

9. Click Keep Source Formatting (the second icon from the left). The pasted text's font changes to the original font it had in the Word document.

10. Switch to the *Other Resources* file in Word, and select the bulleted list. Press Ctrl+C to copy it to the Clipboard.

11. Switch to PowerPoint, and click the Click to add text placeholder on the left side of the slide (in the Slide pane) to move the insertion point into that text box.

12. On the Home tab of the Ribbon, click the Paste button drop-down arrow. A menu opens, containing the same types of icons as found on the Paste Options icon's menu (step 9), and also containing a Paste Special command (see Figure 2-31).

Figure 2-31

Use the Paste button's menu to select special types of pasting

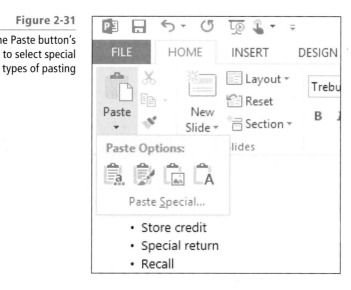

13. Click Paste Special. The Paste Special dialog box opens.

14. Verify that the Paste option button is selected.

15. On the As list, click Formatted Text (RTF) (see Figure 2-32).

Figure 2-32

Paste Special dialog box

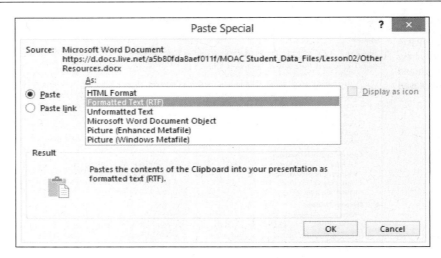

16. Click OK. The text is pasted into the slide keeping the text's original formatting. The text overflows the placeholder's borders. That is normal at this point.

17. Triple-click the last bullet on the slide *(Special training)* to select the entire bullet, and press Ctrl+X to cut the bullet to the Clipboard.

18. Click in the Click to add text placeholder on the right side of the slide, and press Ctrl+V to paste the bullet into that placeholder. The finished slide should resemble Figure 2-33.

Figure 2-33

The completed imported content

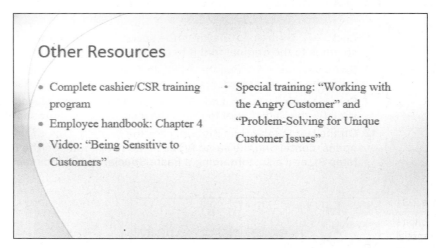

19. In the Slides pane in Normal view, click between slides 8 and 9. A horizontal line appears between them.

20. On the Home tab, click the down arrow below the New Slide button, opening a menu, and then click Slides from Outline.

21. In the Insert Outline dialog box, navigate to the data files for this lesson, select Contacts.txt, and click Insert. A new slide appears containing the content from Contacts.txt.

22. **SAVE** the *Cashier Training Final* presentation.

23. **CLOSE** Word without saving the changes to *Other Resources.docx*.

PAUSE. LEAVE the presentation open to use in the next exercise.

Take Note The text from Contacts.txt imported smoothly because each paragraph after the first one was preceded by a tab stop. PowerPoint understands this to mean that each of those paragraphs should be subordinate to the first paragraph, which forms the slide title. To check this out for yourself, open Contacts.txt in Notepad or some other text editor.

Pasting from one application to another using the Clipboard works for almost all Windows-based applications because they support the Clipboard. You can also drag-and-drop content from the other application's window into PowerPoint, but that works only if the source application supports drag-and-drop (not all applications do).

When you paste content into PowerPoint from other applications via the Clipboard, by default the pasted content takes on the formatting of the PowerPoint slide on which you place it. Using the Paste Options, or Paste Special, you can force the content to keep the formatting it had in its original source file.

There are other uses for Paste Special too. In Figure 2-32, for example, you saw that the Paste Special dialog box lets you choose to either Paste or Paste Link. Pasting a link creates a dynamic connection between the original and the copy, so that if the original changes, the copy in Power-Point changes too.

If you choose a format from the As list that includes the word "Object," as in Microsoft Word Document Object in Figure 2-32, the content is embedded, and you will be able to reopen it in the original application that created it by double-clicking it later. In the preceding exercise, you neither linked nor embedded; you simply pasted using non-default formatting.

You can also import text from any text file (plain text, Word, etc.) using the Slides from Outline command. The result is a new slide that contains the content of the chosen file.

Workplace Ready

PRESENTING WITH A PURPOSE

Many professionals have experienced "death by PowerPoint." They can tell you what it is like to sit through a presentation that is boring or too long and will usually tell you that the presenter did not understand how to use slides effectively. But an ineffective presentation can be worse than dull; it can actually prevent your audience from getting your message.

The following guidelines will help you (and your audience) get the most from a slide show:

- **Be brief:** Make only one major point per slide, using only a few bullets to support that point. A presentation should include only enough slides to support its major points.
- **Write concisely:** Keep your text short; sentence fragments work well on slides.
- **Focus on content:** Formatting is nice, but too much formatting can overwhelm the text and obscure your message.
- **Keep graphics relevant:** A nice picture can enhance a slide's meaning; a chart or table may support your point better than words alone. But use graphics only where they are useful in delivering a clear message.
- **Be consistent:** Use the same fonts, background, and colors throughout the presentation. If you use different design elements on each slide, your audience will become distracted (and maybe irritated).
- **Make sure slides are readable:** Ask someone else to review your slides before you show them to your audience. Make sure the reviewer can read all the text and see the graphics clearly. You may want to check the slides on the screen on which the audience will see them to make sure the text is large enough.
- **Practice, practice, practice:** Never deliver a presentation "cold." Practice running the slide show and delivering your comments along with it. Practice your spoken parts out loud. Be sure to work on your timing, so you know just how long to keep each slide on the screen before going to the next one. Ask someone to watch you practice and offer feedback.

ADDING NOTES TO YOUR SLIDES

The Bottom Line

A **note** is a piece of additional information you associate with a slide. Notes might not fit on a slide, but might contain information which the presenter wants to tell the audience as they view the slide. Suppose, for example, you are using a chart to show financial data to the audience but do not have room on the slide for a lot of details. You can add those details as notes, and they will remind you to share the details with your audience during your presentation. Notes do not appear on the screen when you show your presentation to an audience, but you can view notes in a couple of ways. The following exercises show you how to add notes to your slides.

Adding Notes in the Notes Pane

When you have just a few lines of notes to type, you may find it easier to work in the Notes pane in Normal view than to switch to Notes Page view. Just click in the Notes pane and start typing. Notes you enter here will not be displayed to the audience during the slide show; they are for the presenter's own reference only.

STEP BY STEP | **Add Notes in the Notes Pane**

USE the *Cashier Training Final* presentation that is still open from the previous exercise.

1. Display slide 2 in Normal view.
2. Click in the Notes pane *(below the Slide pane)* to place the insertion point there. If the Notes pane does not appear, display the View tab and click Notes.
3. In the Notes pane, type Emphasize the importance of building customer goodwill as a cashier. Your screen should look like the one shown in Figure 2-34.

Figure 2-34

Type notes in the Notes pane below the slide in Normal view

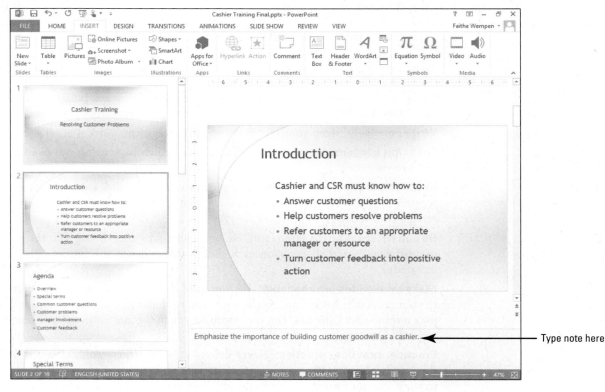

4. **SAVE** the presentation.

PAUSE. LEAVE the presentation open to use in the next exercise.

Take Note   You can edit and delete text in the Notes pane just as you can in the Slide pane or on the Outline pane. Select text with the mouse pointer; use the Delete and Backspace keys to delete text.

Notes do not appear on the screen in Slide Show view, so the audience does not see them. You can see your notes by printing them or by using PowerPoint's **Presenter view**. Presenter view lets you use two monitors when delivering your presentation to an audience. One monitor displays your slides in Slide Show view. You can use the second monitor to view your notes, among other things.

Cross Ref   You will learn more about Presenter view in Lesson 11.

Adding Notes in Notes Page View

Notes Page view is a special view that displays each slide along with its associated notes. Each slide and its notes appear on a white background; the content is sized as it would be when printed on a standard sheet of paper. You can view and edit notes directly in the note placeholder, which is located below the slide. In this exercise, you learn how to add notes in Notes Page view.

STEP BY STEP   **Add Notes in Notes Page View**

USE the *Cashier Training Final* presentation that is still open from the previous exercise.

1. Display slide 2 *(Introduction)* if it is not already displayed.

2. On the View tab, click the Notes Page button to switch to Notes Page view. If a warning appears that edits made in this view will be lost when saved to the server, click Check Out. (This happens if you are accessing the data files from a SharePoint server or your SkyDrive.)

3. On the vertical scroll bar, click below the scroll box once to move to slide 3 *(Agenda)*.

4. Click in the Click to add text box below the slide in the Notes pane, and type Welcome employees to the training session and introduce yourself. Briefly go through the agenda points. The completed slide should resemble Figure 2-35.

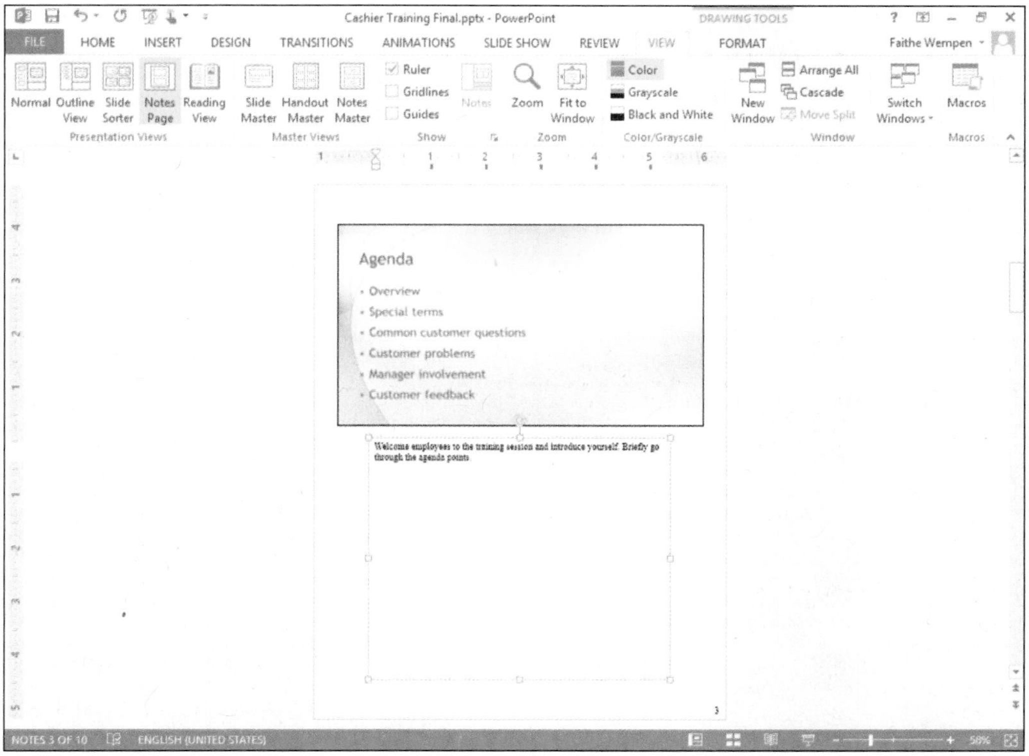

Figure 2-35

Type notes below the slide in Notes Page view

5. **SAVE** the presentation.

PAUSE. LEAVE the presentation open to use in the next exercise.

Take Note   If you have difficulty seeing what you are typing, use the Zoom control to zoom in.

PRINTING A PRESENTATION

The Bottom Line

PowerPoint gives you many options for printing your slides. In the following exercises, you learn how to preview a presentation before printing it, how to choose a printer, how to set print options, and how to print a presentation in both color and grayscale mode.

Using Print Preview and Changing the Print Layout

PowerPoint's Print Preview feature shows you how your slides will look on paper before you print them. When you change to a different print layout, Print Preview reflects the change, so you can try out different potential layouts for your presentation printouts before committing one to paper. This exercise shows you how to use Print Preview, and how to print different layouts, including speaker notes.

STEP BY STEP   **Use Print Preview and Change the Print Layout**

USE the *Cashier Training Final* presentation that is still open from the previous exercise.

1. Switch to **Normal view**, and display **slide 1** *(Cashier Training)*.
2. Click the **File tab**, and click **Print**. A preview of the print job appears in the right pane. The default print layout is Full Page Slides (see Figure 2-36).

Figure 2-36

Print Preview appears to the right of the print options in Backstage view

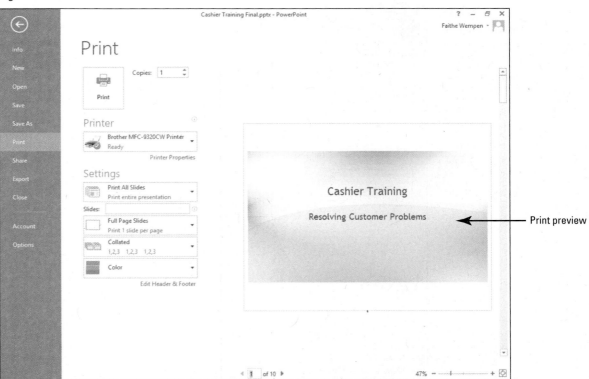

Print preview

Take Note If the printer selected under the Printer heading prints only in black and white, Print Preview will display your slides in grayscale. The default printer is set within Windows, not within PowerPoint; open the Devices and Printers folder in the Control Panel in Windows to change the default printer.

3. Click the Next Page arrow at the bottom of the window. A preview of slide 2 appears.

4. In the left pane, under the Settings heading, click Full Page Slides to open a menu of layouts.

5. Click 6 Slides Vertical under the Handouts section on the menu of layouts. Print Preview changes to show a page containing six small slides (see Figure 2-37).

Figure 2-37

Print Preview shows how the page will print with the chosen layout

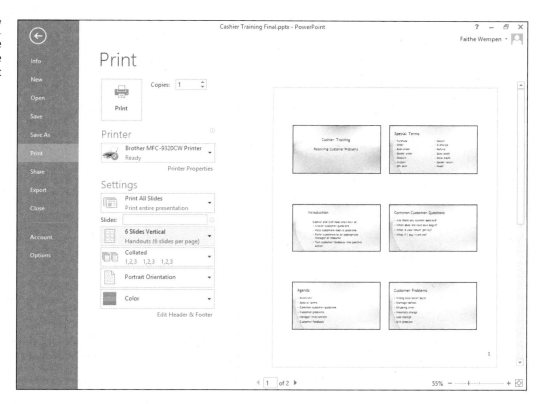

6. Click the 6 Slides Vertical button and click Outline. Print Preview shows the presentation as a text-only outline.

7. Click Outline, and then click Notes Pages. Print Preview shows slide 2 with the notes you typed in an earlier exercise in the notes area below it (see Figure 2-38).

Figure 2-38

Notes Pages printouts
contain the slide images and
any speaker notes you
have created

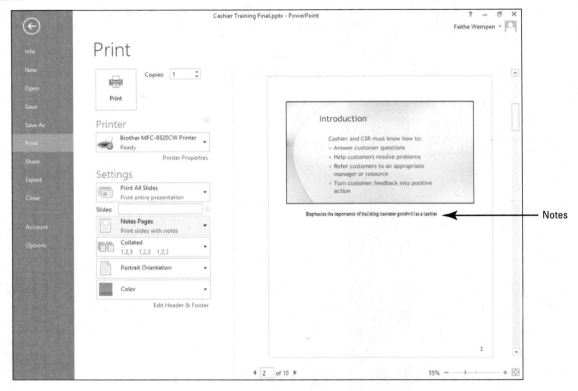

8. Click the **Back button** (the left pointing arrow in the far upper left corner in the Categories pane) or press **Esc** to leave Backstage view without printing anything.

PAUSE. LEAVE the presentation open to use in the next exercise.

Print Preview allows you to see how your slides will appear before you print them. Print Preview is integrated into the Print section of Backstage view, so you can see how the changes you make to the print settings will change the printout.

You can preview and print a presentation in several different formats:

- **Full Page Slides:** One slide prints per page as large as possible.
- **Notes Pages:** One slide prints per page with any notes below it.
- **Outline:** The text of the presentation prints in outline form; graphics do not print.
- **Handouts:** Multiple slides print per page, designed for distribution to an audience. The exact number depends on the setting you choose (between two and nine slides per page).

Setting Print Options

In addition to choosing a layout, PowerPoint lets you set a number of other attributes before printing a presentation. The following exercise shows you how to set some of these printing options. One of these options is grayscale mode, in which there are no colors; each color appears as a shade of gray. Grayscale mode is often used for draft copies because it minimizes the use of expensive colored ink or toner. You can also choose to print only certain slides, and to print multiple copies.

STEP BY STEP   **Set Print Options**

USE the *Cashier Training Final* presentation that is still open from the previous exercise.

1. Click the File tab, and click Print. The printing options and Print Preview appear in Backstage view. The Notes Pages layout is still selected from the previous exercise.

2. In the Copies box at the top of the window, type 2 to print two copies.

Another Way
You can also press Ctrl+P to open the Print section of Backstage view.

3. Under the Printer heading, click the down arrow. A menu appears of other available printers (if any) (see Figure 2-39).

Figure 2-39

Other available printers appear on the Printer list

4. Click away from the open menu to close it without making a change.

5. In the Slides: text box (under Print All Slides), type 1-3. Specifying 1-3 sets only the first three slides to be printed, and Print All Slides changes to Custom Range.

6. Click the Custom Range drop down arrow, and note the command at the bottom of its menu: Print Hidden Slides. That option is not currently available because there are no hidden slides in this presentation.

7. Click away from the menu to close it without making a change.

8. Click the Collated drop down arrow to open a menu of collation options. When you are printing multiple copies, you can choose to have the copies collated or not.

9. Click away from the Collated button's menu to close it without making a change.

10. Click the Color drop down arrow to open a menu of color options.

Take Note   If a black and white printer is selected, the Color button will appear as a Grayscale button instead.

11. Click Pure Black and White from the Color button's menu. Print Preview changes to show how the setting will affect the printouts.

Take Note   In some presentations there is a difference between Grayscale and Pure Black and White modes. In this particular presentation there is not because there are no non-background graphics to convert to grayscale images. Figure 2-40 shows the preview of slide 1 in Pure Black and White mode.

12. If you want to print now, click the **Print button**. Be sure to follow your instructor's instructions before printing. Otherwise, click the **Home tab**, click the **Back button**, or press **Esc** to leave Backstage view without printing.

PAUSE. LEAVE the presentation open to use in the next exercise.

The Print section of Backstage view provides an array of options that help you print your presentations exactly the way you want. You can select a printer and enter a number of copies, a page range, and a color mode as you saw in the preceding exercise. You can also choose a print layout and specify whether a multi-copy print job should be collated or not.

When you click the button that defines the print layout (Full Page Slides, or Notes Pages, or whatever layout is selected), you find some extra commands. These were not used in the preceding exercise, but you may find them helpful in some cases

- **Frame Slides:** This option prints a fine black border around each slide.
- **Scale to Fit Paper:** If your printer uses unusual-size sheets, this option tells PowerPoint to scale the slides to fit on the paper.
- **High Quality:** If your slides are formatted with shadows under text or graphics, choose this option to print the shadows.
- **Print Comments and Ink Markup:** This option lets you print any comments and handwritten notes that have been added to the presentation. The option is not available if the presentation does not include comments or markups.

Cross Ref   Comments are covered in Lesson 10.

Previewing a Presentation on the Screen

Before you show your presentation to an audience, you should preview it in Slide Show view. In Slide Show view, PowerPoint displays every slide in the presentation in order from beginning to end. To advance to the next slide, you can click the left mouse button. To move to other slides besides the next one, you can right-click and select other options from the menu that appears in the bottom left corner of the slide. This exercise shows you how to use PowerPoint's tools for running a slide show on your own computer's screen.

STEP BY STEP	**Preview a Presentation**

USE the *Cashier Training Final* presentation that is still open from the previous exercise.

1. On the Slide Show tab, click **From Beginning**. PowerPoint changes to Slide Show view and the first slide appears in full-screen mode.

Take Note   You can also switch to Slide Show view by pressing F5 or by clicking the Slide Show view icon in the lower-right corner of the status bar.

2. Click the **left mouse button** to move to the next slide. Keep clicking the mouse until all of the slides have been viewed. When you click the mouse on the last slide, PowerPoint displays a black screen.

Take Note   You can exit from Slide Show view at any time by pressing Esc. You do not have to go through every slide.

3. When you are at the end of the slide show, click the **left mouse button** once more to return to Normal view.
4. **SAVE** and **CLOSE** the *Cashier Training Final* presentation.

EXIT PowerPoint.

 Cross Ref   You will learn more about using Slide Show view in Lesson 11.

SKILL SUMMARY

In This Lesson, You Learned How To:	Exam Objective	Objective Number
Create a New Blank Presentation	Create a blank presentation.	1.1.1
Save a Presentation	Embed fonts.	5.3.5
Create a Presentation from a Template	Create presentations using templates.	1.1.2
Add, Delete, and Organize Slides	Duplicate existing slides. Modify slide order. Delete slides.	2.1.2 2.3.2 2.1.4
Create a Presentation from Existing Content	Apply styles to create slides. Reuse slides from other presentations. Import text files into presentations. Import Word document outlines into presentations.	2.1.6. 5.1.2 1.1.3 1.1.4
Add Notes to Your Slides		
Print a Presentation	Print speaker notes. Print selections from presentations. Print presentations in grayscale.	1.4.6 1.4.2 1.4.5

Knowledge Assessment

Matching

Match the term in Column 1 to its description in Column 2.

Column 1	Column 2
1. Note	a. Shows how a presentation will appear on paper
2. Template	b. A black-and-white printing mode that saves colored ink or toner
3. Handout	c. Additional information associated with a slide that the audience will not see
4. Print Preview	d. A predefined arrangement of placeholders
5. Presenter view	e. To decrease the outline level of a paragraph on a slide
6. Demote	f. A small picture of a slide
7. Layout	g. The distance from a placeholder's left border
8. Thumbnail	h. A predesigned presentation
9. Grayscale	i. A printed copy of a presentation for audience use
10. Indent level	j. Lets you see notes on one screen while the audience sees slides on another

True/False

Circle T if the statement is true or F if the statement is false.

T F 1. A new, blank presentation appears on your screen when you launch PowerPoint.

T F 2. Once a layout has been applied to a slide, it cannot be changed.

T F 3. When you save a presentation for the first time, the Save As dialog box appears.

T F 4. If you want to be able to use a presentation with an older version of PowerPoint, you can save it by using the PowerPoint 97-2003 Presentation file format.

T F 5. Many PowerPoint templates feature a set of complementing colors, fonts, and effects called a layout.

T F 6. You can copy and paste content from most Windows applications into PowerPoint.

T F 7. One way to copy a slide is to right-click its thumbnail and then click Copy.

T F 8. Notes appear on the screen with the slides in Slide Show view.

T F 9. PowerPoint can print just the text of your slide without printing any graphics via an Outline layout.

T F 10. If you use a printer that does not print in color, your slides will appear in grayscale when viewed in Print Preview.

Competency Assessment

Project 2-1: Tonight's Guest Speaker

As director of the Citywide Business Alliance, one of your jobs is to introduce the guest speaker at the organization's monthly meeting. To do this, you will create a new presentation from a theme template, and then reuse a slide with information about the speaker from a different presentation.

GET READY. LAUNCH PowerPoint if it is not already running.

1. Click the File tab, and then click New to open the New Presentation window.
2. Click the Ion template. In the dialog box that appears, click the purple sample and then click Create.
3. In the Click to add title placeholder, type Citywide Business Alliance.
4. In the Click to add subtitle placeholder, type Guest Speaker: Stephanie Bourne.
5. On the Home tab, click the arrow below the New Slide button to open its menu, and then click Reuse Slides.

6. In the Reuse Slides task pane, click the Browse drop down arrow, and then click Browse File.
7. Navigate to the location where the sample files for this lesson are stored and open the *Bourne.pptx* presentation file.
8. In the Reuse Slides task pane, click slide 1. The slide is added to your new presentation. Close the task pane.
9. Click the File tab, and then click Print. Only print if instructed by your instructor. The Print controls appear in Backstage view.
10. Click the Color drop down arrow, and on the menu that appears, click Grayscale.
11. Click the Full Page Slides drop down arrow, and on the menu that appears, click 2 Slides under the Handouts section.
12. Click Print to print the handout in grayscale mode. Only print if instructed by your instructor.
13. Click the File tab and click Save As, or click the Save icon on the Quick Access Toolbar. Click Browse and navigate to the folder where you are storing your work for this lesson.
14. Open the Save as type drop-down list and click PowerPoint 97-2003 Presentation.
15. Select the text in the File name box, press Delete, and then type Speaker.
16. Click Save.
17. **CLOSE** the file.

LEAVE PowerPoint open for use in the next project.

Project 2-2: Advertise with Us

As an account manager for The Phone Company, you are always trying to convince potential customers of the benefits of advertising in the local phone directory. A PowerPoint presentation can help you make your case. You need to create a presentation from a Word document that lists some reasons why businesses should purchase advertising space in your directory.

GET READY. LAUNCH PowerPoint if it is not already running.

1. If you just started PowerPoint, press Esc and a new blank presentation appears automatically. If PowerPoint was already running and there is not a new blank presentation open, press Ctrl+N to start a new blank presentation.
2. Click in the slide's title placeholder, and then type Why Advertise with Us?.
3. Click in the subtitle placeholder, and then type The Phone Company.
4. Click outside the text placeholder to deselect it.

5. On the Ribbon's Home tab, click the New Slide drop-down arrow. At the bottom of the gallery of slide layouts, click Slides from Outline.

6. In the Insert Outline dialog box, locate and select the Microsoft Word document named *Ad Benefits*. Click Insert. PowerPoint inserts five new slides using content from the outline.

7. Switch to Slide Sorter view. Drag slide 5 to a new position between slides 1 and 2.

8. Click slide 6, and then press Delete to remove the slide from the presentation.

9. Switch to Notes Page view, and then go to slide 1.

10. Click in the Notes pane below the slide, and then type Give the client a copy of the directory.

11. Switch to Normal view.

12. On the Quick Access Toolbar, click the Save icon.

13. Click Browse and navigate to the folder where you want to save the presentation.

14. Replace the default name in the File name box with Benefits.

15. Click Save. **CLOSE** the file.

LEAVE PowerPoint open for use in the next project.

Proficiency Assessment

Project 2-3: Send People to Their Rooms

You are an assistant marketing manager at Shelbourne, Ltd., which develops process control software for use in manufacturing. You are coordinating a set of panel discussions at the company's annual sales and marketing meeting. At the start of the afternoon session, you must tell the groups which conference rooms to use for their discussions. To help deliver your message, you need to create a single-slide presentation that lists the panels' room assignments. You can display the slide on a projection screen for reference while you announce the room assignments.

1. **CREATE** a new, blank presentation. It contains one slide by default.

2. Change the slide's layout to Title and Content. In the slide's title placeholder, type Panel Discussions.

3. In the second placeholder, type the following items, placing each item on its own line:
   Aligning with Partners, Room 104
   Building Incentives, Room 101
   Creating New Value, Room 102
   Managing Expenses, Room 108
   Opening New Markets, Room 112
   Recapturing Lost Accounts, Room 107
   Strengthening Client Relationships, Room 110

4. In the Notes pane, type Refreshments will be delivered to each room during the 3:00 pm break.

5. Print one copy of the presentation.

6. **SAVE** the presentation as *Room Assignments*, then **CLOSE** the file.

LEAVE PowerPoint open for use in the next project.

Project 2-4: **Editorial Services**

You are the editorial director for Lucerne Publishing, a small publishing house that provides editorial services to other businesses. Your sales manager has asked you to prepare a simple presentation that lists the services offered by your editorial staff. You can create this presentation from an outline that was created earlier.

1. **CREATE** a new, blank presentation.
2. Type Lucerne Publishing in the title placeholder.
3. Type Editorial Services in the subtitle placeholder, and then click outside the placeholder.
4. Use the Slides from Outline command to locate the Microsoft Word document named *Editorial Services*, and then click Insert.
5. In the Outline pane, click slide 6.
6. Use the Reuse Slides command to locate and open the *About Lucerne* presentation, and then add slide 3 from that presentation to the end of your new presentation as the final slide.
7. Print one copy of the presentation in a layout that shows nine slides per page.
8. **SAVE** the presentation as *Lucerne Editorial Services*, and then **CLOSE** the file.

LEAVE PowerPoint open for use in the next project.

Mastery Assessment

Project 2-5: **The Final Gallery Crawl**

As director of the Graphic Design Institute, you have volunteered to coordinate your city's last-ever gallery crawl—an annual charity event that enables the public to visit several art galleries for one price. Fortunately, this year's crawl is almost identical to last year's event; so when you create a presentation for the local arts council, you can use last year's presentation as the basis for a new one.

1. **OPEN** the file *Gallery Crawl*, and save it as *Final Gallery Crawl*.
2. In Slide Sorter view, switch the positions of slides 6 and 7.
3. In Normal view, reword the subtitle of slide 1 to read Our last ever!
4. Print the presentation in grayscale using a 9-slides-per-page layout.
5. View the presentation from beginning to end in Slide Show view.
6. **SAVE** the presentation as *Final Gallery Crawl*, and then **CLOSE** the file.

LEAVE PowerPoint open for use in the next project.

Project 2-6: **The Final, Final Gallery Crawl**

Having just finished your presentation for the last-ever gallery crawl, you realize that one of the museum curators uses an older version of PowerPoint. You need to save a copy of the presentation so he can use it on his computer.

1. **OPEN** *Final Gallery Crawl* from the data files for this lesson, or open the version you created in Project 2-5.
2. **SAVE** the presentation with the file name *Compatible Gallery Crawl* in PowerPoint 97-2003 Presentation format. **CLOSE** the file without making any other changes.

EXIT PowerPoint.

3 Working with Text

LESSON SKILL MATRIX

Skill	Exam Objective	Objective Number
Formatting Characters	Apply formatting and styles to text.	3.1.4
Formatting Paragraphs and Lists	Create bulleted and numbered lists.	3.1.5
Inserting and Formatting WordArt	Change text to WordArt.	3.1.1
Creating and Formatting Text Boxes	Modify shape backgrounds. Create multiple columns in a single shape.	2.2.1 3.1.2
Using Proofing Tools	Proof presentations.	5.3.2

KEY TERMS

- bulleted list
- fonts
- Format Painter
- formatting
- line spacing
- Live Preview
- numbered list
- Quick Style
- text boxes
- texture
- WordArt

©marcomayer/iStockphoto

©marcomayer/iStockphoto

Fourth Coffee is a "boutique" company devoted to producing and distributing fine coffees and teas. As the sales manager for Fourth Coffee, you often produce and deliver presentations to your staff and managers on topics such as realizing the full profit potential of your delivery systems. Whenever you create a presentation, consider how the information appears to your viewers. If the text in your slides is difficult to read, is haphazardly formatted, if you cram too much text into your slides, or you have too much white space, your presentations will not be professional looking. In this lesson, you learn some basics of text formatting, including formatting characters and paragraphs, creating and formatting lists, using WordArt to "jazz up" your text, and creating and modifying text boxes.

SOFTWARE ORIENTATION

Microsoft PowerPoint Basic Text Formatting Tools

Most of the PowerPoint basic text formatting tools are found on the Home tab of the Ribbon (see Figure 3-1). These are the tools you will use most often when working with text.

There are two groups of text formatting tools on the Ribbon: the Font group and the Paragraph group. They allow you to fine-tune the text on your slides, right down to an individual character. These groups also provide access to the Font and Paragraph dialog boxes, which give you even more control over your text's appearance.

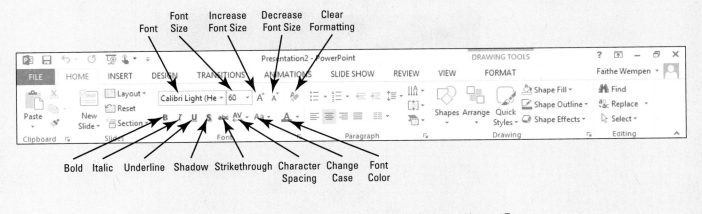

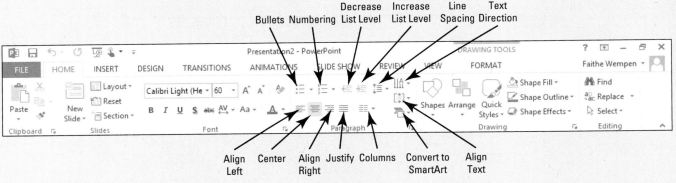

Figure 3-1

Basic text formatting tools (Font group and Paragraph group)

FORMATTING CHARACTERS

The Bottom Line

The term, **formatting**, refers to the appearance of text or objects on a slide. Most of PowerPoint's tools are devoted to formatting the various parts of your slides. All PowerPoint presentations are formatted with specific fonts, font sizes, and font attributes such as style and color. You can change the way characters look on a slide by using commands in the Font group on the Home tab or the Mini toolbar. The Format Painter can save you time by allowing you to copy formats from selected text to other text items.

CERTIFICATION READY? **3.1.4**

How do you apply formatting and styles to text?

Choosing Fonts and Font Sizes

Fonts (sometimes called typefaces) are sets of characters, numbers, and symbols in a specific style or design. You can change the font and font size at any time on your slides. The following exercise shows you how to do this both with the Mini toolbar and with the Ribbon.

STEP BY STEP **Choose Fonts and Font Sizes**

GET READY. Before you begin these steps, make sure that your computer is on. Log on, if necessary.

1. Start PowerPoint, if the program is not already running.
2. Locate and open *Sales Pipeline* and save it as *Sales Pipeline Formats*.
3. Go to slide 2. In the first row of the table, double-click **Timing**. The Mini toolbar appears above the selected text (see Figure 3-2).

Figure 3-2

The Mini toolbar

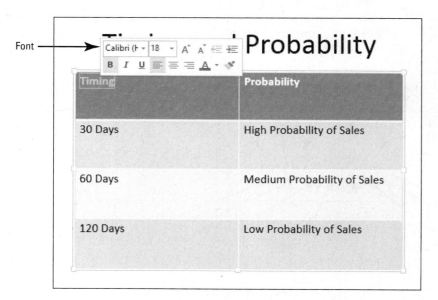

4. Click the **Font drop-down arrow** on the Mini toolbar. A list of fonts appears.
5. Click **Berlin Sans FB Demi**. PowerPoint applies the chosen font to the selected text.
6. Click the **Font Size drop-down arrow** on the Mini toolbar. A list of font sizes appears (see Figure 3-3).

Figure 3-3

Choosing a new font size
from the Mini toolbar

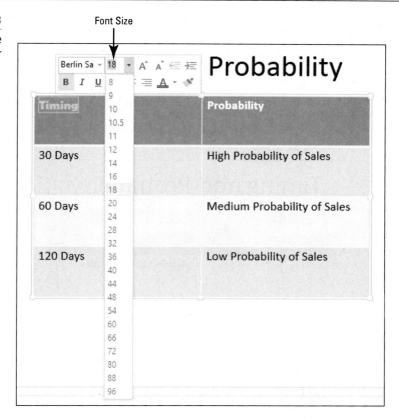

7. Click 32. PowerPoint applies the chosen font size to the selected text.

8. Double-click Probability in the top right cell of the table.

9. On the Home tab of the Ribbon, click the Font drop-down arrow. A list of fonts appears (see Figure 3-4).

Figure 3-4

Choosing a new font
from the Ribbon

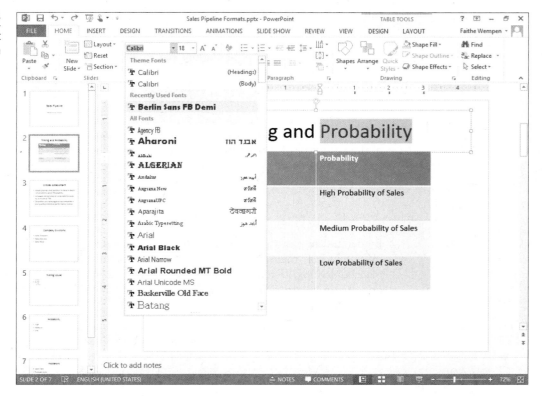

10. Select the Berlin Sans FB Demi font. It is in the Recently Used Fonts section near the top of the list.

11. On the Home tab of the Ribbon, click the Font Size drop-down arrow. A list of font sizes appears.

12. Click 32.

13. Click away from the selected text to deselect it. Your slide should look like the one shown in Figure 3-5.

Figure 3-5

The new font and font size applied to the table headings

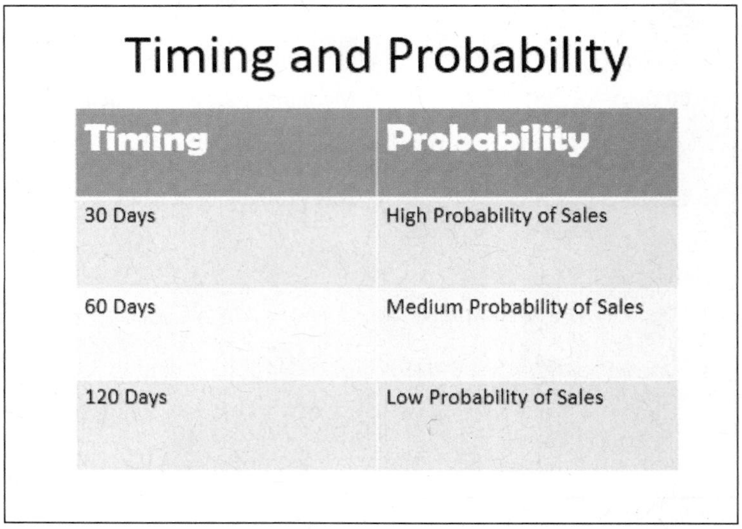

Timing and Probability

Timing	Probability
30 Days	High Probability of Sales
60 Days	Medium Probability of Sales
120 Days	Low Probability of Sales

14. **SAVE** the presentation.

PAUSE. LEAVE the presentation open to use in the next exercise.

Take Note   To maintain formatting consistency between slides in a presentation, you might prefer to change the font and font size on the Slide Master, which flows down the change to all slides automatically. Lesson 4 covers Slide Masters.

By default, PowerPoint presentations have two fonts: one font for the headings and one for the body text. (The same font can be used for both.) These font choices are a result of the theme. A theme is a set of formatting specifications, including the colors, fonts, graphic effects, and slide layouts available. All presentations have a theme, even blank ones.

To return to the default fonts provided by the theme, select a font from the Theme Fonts section of the Font drop-down list (see Figure 3-4). If you choose anything other than a theme font, as in the preceding exercise, applying a different theme will have no effect on that text, because manually applied fonts take precedence over theme fonts.

Using AutoFit to Change Text Size

By default, text in the placeholder boxes on a slide layout are set to AutoFit, so that if you type more text into them than will fit, the text automatically gets smaller so that it will fit into the placeholder box. If you then delete some of the text so that there is more room available, the text once again enlarges, up to its default size. You can change the AutoFit setting for a text box or placeholder as needed.

STEP BY STEP   **Change AutoFit Behavior**

USE the *Sales Pipeline Formats* presentation that is still open from the preceding exercise.

1. On slide 3, type the following additional bullet points at the bottom of the slide:

   • Helps Engineering staff do long-range planning for future product enhancements

   • Provides Marketing staff with critical data about customer needs and preferences

   As you begin to type the second bullet point, AutoFit engages, and makes the text in the text box smaller so that it will all continue to fit.

2. Click the AutoFit icon in the lower-left corner of the text box. A menu appears (see Figure 3-6).

Figure 3-6

Set AutoFit behavior

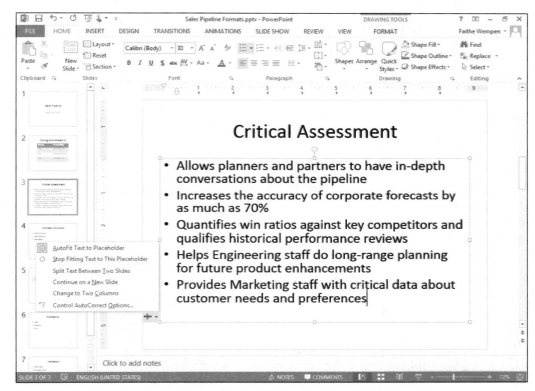

3. Click Stop Fitting Text to This Placeholder. The text returns to its default size and overflows the bottom of the text box.

Take Note   Notice the other choices in Figure 3-6. You can choose to split text between two slides, continue on a new slide, or change to a two-column layout.

4. Click the AutoFit icon again, and click AutoFit Text to Placeholder.
5. **SAVE** the presentation.

PAUSE. LEAVE the presentation open to use in the next exercise.

AutoFit is enabled by default because it is a useful feature that most users appreciate in most situations. Rather than finding the maximum font size by trial and error that will allow the text to fit in the allotted space, you can rely on AutoFit to figure that out for you. There are some situations, though, where AutoFit may not be appropriate. For example, you might want the slide titles to always appear in the same size font.

Take Note   In manually created text boxes (covered later in this lesson), AutoFit is not enabled by default; instead, the text box itself resizes as needed to hold the text.

Applying Font Styles and Effects

Text on a PowerPoint slide can be boldfaced or italicized (called *font styles*), underlined, or formatted with other attributes such as strikethrough or shadow (called *effects*). In the following exercise, you will apply a font style and an effect to text on a slide, as well as adjust character spacing.

STEP BY STEP   **Apply Font Styles and Effects**

USE the *Sales Pipeline Formats* presentation that is still open from the previous exercise.

1. On slide 2, double-click Timing in the top left cell of the table. The Mini toolbar appears above the selected text.

2. Click the Italic button on the Mini toolbar (see Figure 3-7). PowerPoint formats the selected text in italic.

Figure 3-7

Italicize selected text from the
Mini toolbar

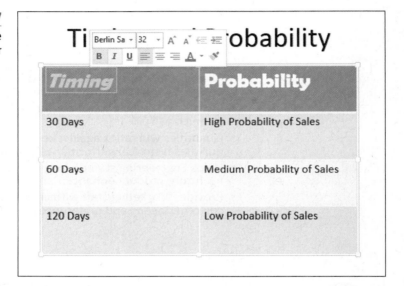

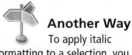

Another Way
To apply italic formatting to a selection, you can also press Ctrl+I or click the Italic button in the Font group of the Ribbon. You can also right-click the selection and choose Font.

3. Double-click Probability in the top right cell of the table, and then italicize it using any method.

4. Double-click Timing in the top left cell of the table, and then click the dialog box launcher in the Font group on the Ribbon (see Figure 3-8) to produce the Font dialog box.

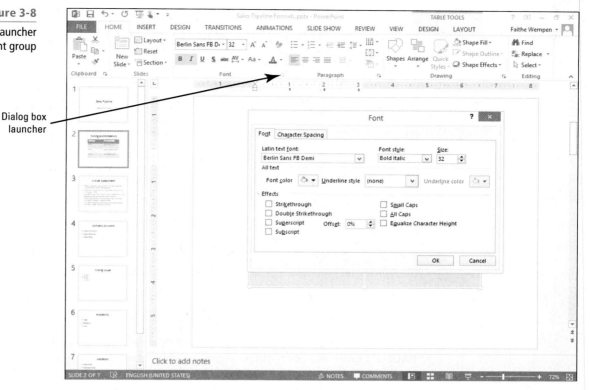

Figure 3-8

Click the dialog box launcher
in the Font group

Dialog box
launcher

5. In the Font dialog box, on the Font tab, click to mark the Small Caps check box.
6. Click the Character Spacing tab.
7. Click the Spacing drop-down arrow, then click Expanded in the list (see Figure 3-9).

Figure 3-9

Character Spacing tab of the
Font dialog box

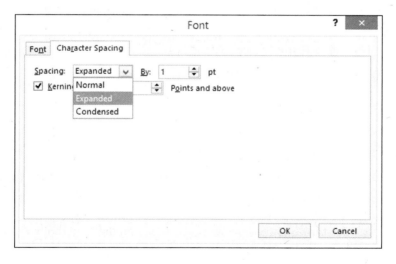

8. Click OK. PowerPoint places 1 point of spacing between the letters and applies the Small Caps effect.
9. Double-click Probability in the top right cell of the table.
10. On the Quick Access Toolbar, click the Repeat button. PowerPoint repeats the last command you issued, applying the new character spacing to the selected text. Click away from the text to deselect it. Your slide should look like the one shown in Figure 3-10.

Figure 3-10

Completed text formatting

Timing and Probability

TIMING	*PROBABILITY*
30 Days	High Probability of Sales
60 Days	Medium Probability of Sales
120 Days	Low Probability of Sales

11. **SAVE** the presentation.

PAUSE. LEAVE the presentation open to use in the next exercise.

Cross Ref   WordArt styles can also be used to format text and apply effects. They are covered later in this lesson.

Use font styles and effects to emphasize text on a slide. Besides the standard font styles—bold, italic, and underline—PowerPoint provides a variety of special effects such as strikethrough and small caps. You can also adjust character spacing and case to give your text a special look. To access more font effects, click the Font group's dialog box launcher to open the Font dialog box.

Changing Font Color

An easy way to change text appearance is to modify its color. Use the Font Color button in the Font group on the Ribbon to access a palette of colors you can apply to selected text.

STEP BY STEP   **Change Font Color**

USE the *Sales Pipeline Formats* presentation that is still open from the previous exercise.

1. On slide 2, double-click Timing in the top left cell of the table. The Mini toolbar appears above the selected text.

2. Click the Font Color drop-down arrow on the Mini toolbar. A palette of colors appears (see Figure 3-11).

Figure 3-11

Choosing a different font color
from the Mini toolbar

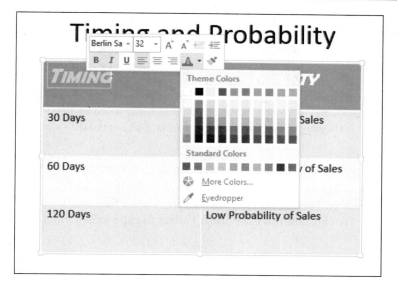

Figure 3-11

Choosing a different font color from the Mini toolbar

3. In the first row of theme colors, click Orange, Accent 6. PowerPoint applies the color to the selected text.

Take Note When you hover the mouse pointer over a color box, the color's name appears in a ScreenTip.

4. Double-click Probability in the top right cell of the table.

5. On the Home tab on the Ribbon, click the Font Color drop-down arrow and apply the color Orange, Accent 6 to the selected text. Your slide should resemble Figure 3-12 when you are finished.

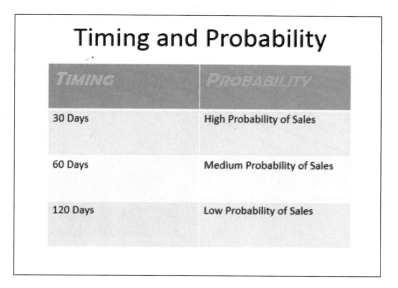

Figure 3-12

Color has been applied to the table headings

6. **SAVE** the presentation.

PAUSE. LEAVE the presentation open to use in the next exercise.

PowerPoint provides an almost limitless selection of colors that can be applied to fonts. You can select any color for your text, but it is usually best to use one of the colors provided by the presentation's theme, as you did in the preceding exercise. Each PowerPoint theme includes a set of coordinating colors, which appear in the color palette when you click the Font Color button. By selecting one of the theme's colors, you can be sure that all the font colors in your slides will look well together on the screen making them easier to read.

If you want to use a color that is not included in the theme, select one of the Standard Colors at the bottom of the color palette (see Figure 3-11), or click More Colors to open the Colors dialog box. In the Colors dialog box, you can choose from dozens of standard colors or create a custom color.

The difference between a theme color and a standard color is apparent when you switch to a different theme or color scheme as you will learn to do in Lesson 4. A theme color will change to match the new colors for the presentation, but a standard color will remain fixed.

Copying Character Formats with the Format Painter

As you format text in your presentations, you will want to keep similar types of text formatted the same way. **Format Painter** is a tool that copies formatting from one block of text to another. In this exercise, you will use Format Painter to copy some formatting.

STEP BY STEP   **Copy Character Formats with the Format Painter**

USE the *Sales Pipeline Formats* presentation that is still open from the previous exercise.

1. On slide 2, select the text in the title placeholder.
2. Change the font color to Blue, Accent 1, Darker 25%.

Take Note   To locate the color requested in step 2, point to the Blue Accent 1 color in the palette (fifth from the left) and then slide the mouse down over the various tints and shades of that color until you find the one for which the ScreenTip shows *Darker 25%*.

3. Click the Bold button in the Ribbon's Font group to apply the bold font style.
4. Click the Text Shadow button in the Font group to apply the shadow font style (see Figure 3-13).

Figure 3-13

Format the title text

Format Painter

Bold

Text Shadow

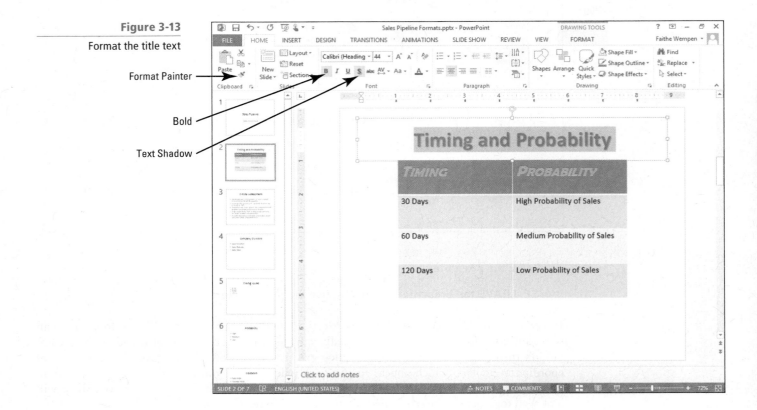

5. With the text still selected, click the Format Painter button in the Clipboard group.

6. Go to slide 3, and then click the word Assessment. The formatting is painted onto that word.

7. Click the Format Painter button again to copy the formatting that is now applied to Assessment.

8. Drag across the word Critical, releasing the mouse button when the word is selected. The formatting is painted onto that word.

9. Double-click the Format Painter button. Double-clicking it makes the feature stay on until you turn it off.

10. Go to each of the remaining slides in the presentation, and drag across all the text in the title of each slide. The Format Painter applies the new formatting to the text.

Take Note If you accidentally click anywhere that does not contain editable text, the Format Painter feature turns off. If that happens, select some of the already formatted text, and then click the Format Painter button to turn the feature back on.

11. When you are finished painting each slide title, press Esc or click the Format Painter button again to turn the feature off.

12. **SAVE** the presentation.

PAUSE. LEAVE the presentation open to use in the next exercise.

Format Painter makes it easy to apply the same formatting to multiple blocks of text no matter where they are in the presentation. If you want to copy a format only once, simply click the button. To copy a format multiple times, double-click the button, and the feature will stay on until you turn it off. Not only does this tool reduce your workload, but it also ensures consistency throughout a presentation. (Another way to achieve consistency is to make changes to the Slide Master rather than to individual slides; you will learn about that in Lesson 4.)

The Format Painter feature can copy not only character formats but paragraph formats such as alignments and line spacing. You will learn about paragraph formats in the next section.

FORMATTING PARAGRAPHS AND LISTS

The Bottom Line

You can change the look of paragraph text by modifying alignment or line spacing. When you apply formatting to a paragraph, all the text within that paragraph receives the same formatting. Lists make the information on slides easy to read and remember. PowerPoint provides for several levels of bulleted lists that you can modify for special effects. You can also create numbered lists when your slide text implies a specific order.

Aligning Paragraphs

By default, PowerPoint aligns text along the left margin. In this exercise, you will change the alignment of items in a bulleted list to customize a slide's appearance.

STEP BY STEP **Align Paragraphs**

USE the *Sales Pipeline Formats* presentation that is still open from the previous exercise.

1. On slide 4, click in the second bulleted item (*Sales Districts*).

2. On the Home tab, click the Center button in the Ribbon's Paragraph group. PowerPoint aligns the paragraph in the center of the text placeholder.

3. Click in the third bulleted item (*Sales Reps*).

4. Click the Align Right button in the Paragraph group. PowerPoint aligns the paragraph to the right side of the text placeholder. Your slide should look like the one shown in Figure 3-14.

Figure 3-14

Aligning paragraphs to the left, center, and right

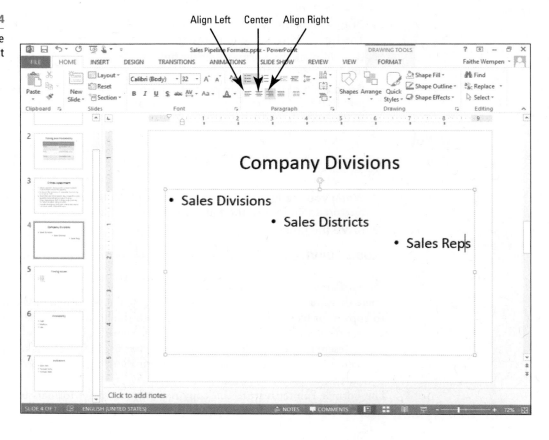

5. SAVE the presentation.

PAUSE. LEAVE the presentation open to use in the next exercise.

When you apply paragraph formats such as alignment, you do not have to select the entire paragraph of text. Just click anywhere in the paragraph and apply the format. The formatting applies to the entire paragraph, even if the paragraph is several lines or sentences long.

When you begin a new paragraph by pressing Enter after an existing paragraph, the new paragraph keeps the same alignment and formatting as the paragraph above it. For example, if you start a new paragraph after a paragraph aligned to the right, the new paragraph aligns to the right as well.

PowerPoint provides four paragraph alignment options:

- **Align Text Left:** Aligns the paragraph at the left edge of the object in which the text resides whether the object containing the text is a placeholder, a table cell, or a text box.
- **Center:** Aligns the paragraph in the center of the object.
- **Align Text Right:** Aligns the paragraph at the right edge of the object.
- **Justify:** Aligns text to both the left and right margins to distribute the paragraph of text evenly across the width of the object, if possible. PowerPoint justifies text by adding spaces between words and characters. The final line of a justified paragraph is left-aligned, so if the paragraph occupies only one line, it will appear left-aligned.

Another Way
The paragraph alignment tools also appear on the Mini toolbar when you right-click within a paragraph.

Another Way
To left-align text, press Ctrl+L. To center text, press Ctrl+E. To right-align text, press Ctrl+R. You can also right-click and choose Paragraph and set alignment in the Paragraph dialog box.

Setting Line Spacing

In this exercise, you learn how to adjust **line spacing** to allow more or less room between lines of a paragraph and also between paragraphs. Line spacing changes can help you display text more attractively or fit more text on a slide. By default, PowerPoint formats your paragraphs so that one line of blank space lies between each paragraph and between the lines within a paragraph. Use the Line Spacing button to adjust the spacing to 1.0, 1.5, 2.0, 2.5, or 3.0. You also can use the Line Spacing Options command to display the Paragraph dialog box. With this dialog box, you can fine-tune the spacing between each paragraph.

STEP BY STEP | **Set Paragraph Line Spacing**

USE the *Sales Pipeline Formats* presentation that is still open from the previous exercise.

1. On slide 3, select the last two bulleted paragraphs, and then press Delete. You are doing this so that AutoFit no longer resizes the text to make it all fit, and so there is enough room in the text box to clearly see the results of the line spacing change you are going to be making.

2. Select all the remaining bulleted paragraphs on the slide. One way to do this is to click inside the text placeholder that contains the bullets and press Ctrl+A. You can also drag across the bullets to select them.

3. Click the Line Spacing button in the Paragraph group. A list of line spacing options appears (see Figure 3-15).

Figure 3-15

Set an amount of spacing between lines

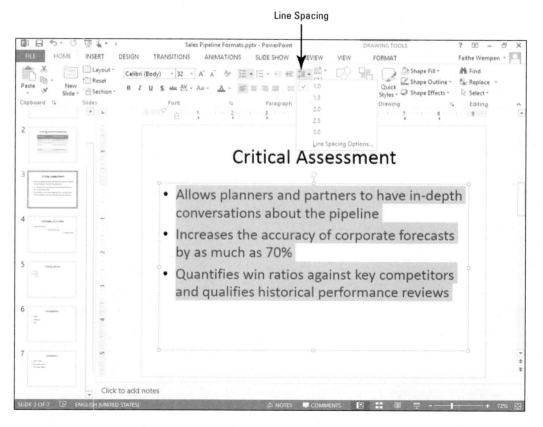

4. Select 1.5. PowerPoint formats the paragraphs so each line is separated by 1.5 lines of blank space.

5. Click the Line Spacing button again, and then click Line Spacing Options at the bottom of the menu. The Paragraph dialog box opens.

Another Way
You can also open the Paragraph dialog box by clicking the dialog box launcher in the Paragraph group.

6. In the Spacing section of the dialog box, set the following values:

Before: 0 pt

After: 9 pt

7. Open the Line Spacing drop-down list, and then click Exactly. Then in the text box to its right, type 38. The dialog box settings should look like Figure 3-16.

Figure 3-16

In the Paragraph dialog box, you can set spacing both between lines within a paragraph and before/after each paragraph

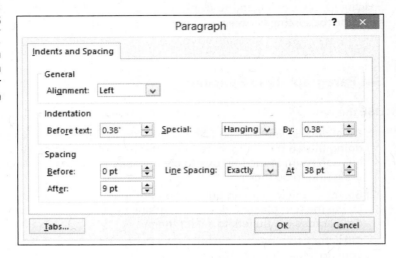

8. Click OK. The settings are applied to all the bullets on the slide.

9. Click away from the bullets to deselect them. The slide should resemble Figure 3-17.

Figure 3-17

The slide with line spacing applied

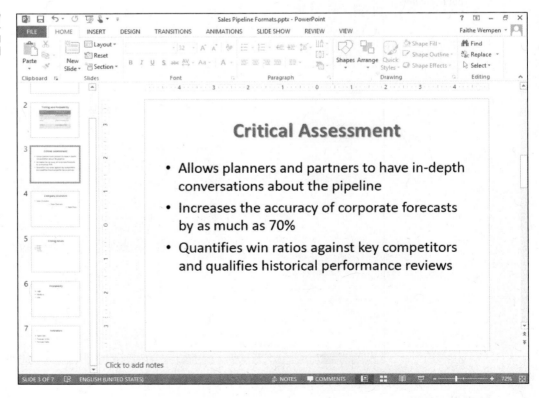

10. **SAVE** the presentation.

PAUSE. LEAVE the presentation open to use in the next exercise.

The Line Spacing drop-down list in the Paragraph dialog box enables you to select from these settings:

- **Single:** Sets the spacing to what single spacing would be for the font size in use. The actual amount changes depending on the largest font size used in that paragraph.
- **1.5 lines:** Sets the spacing halfway between single spacing and double spacing.
- **Double:** Sets the spacing to what double spacing would be for the font size in use.
- **Exactly:** Sets the spacing to a precise number of points. If you change the font size(s) in use, this value does not change automatically.
- **Multiple:** Enables you to specify a multiplier for spacing. For example, you might enter 1.25 for spacing halfway between single-spacing and 1.5 lines spacing.

Setting Indentation

Indentation controls the horizontal spacing of a paragraph, much as line spacing controls its vertical spacing. Indentation determines how far from the text box's left and right margins the text appears. In this exercise you will set the indentation for some paragraphs.

STEP BY STEP　　　**Set Indentation**

USE the *Sales Pipeline Formats* presentation that is still open from the previous exercise.

Another Way
Instead of clicking the dialog box launcher, you can right-click and choose Paragraph.

1. On slide 3, click in the **first bulleted paragraph**.
2. Click the **dialog box launcher** for the Paragraph group. The Paragraph dialog box opens.
3. In the Indentation section of the dialog box, set the **Before text** value to **0.7"** (see Figure 3-18).

Figure 3-18

Change the indentation in the Paragraph dialog box

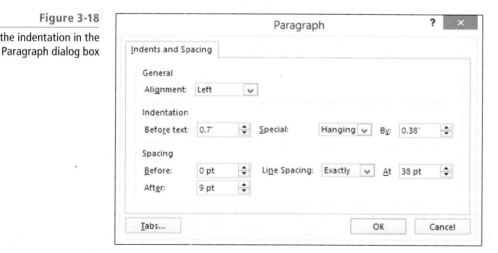

Take Note　　The Before Text setting refers to the paragraph as a whole. A hanging indent is a reverse indent and applies only to the first line.

4. Click **OK**. The new setting is applied. Both lines of the first bullet are indented more than the other bullets (see Figure 3-19). The placement of the bullet in relation to the rest of the text has not changed.

Figure 3-19

The result of a change to the
Before Text indentation setting
for the first paragraph

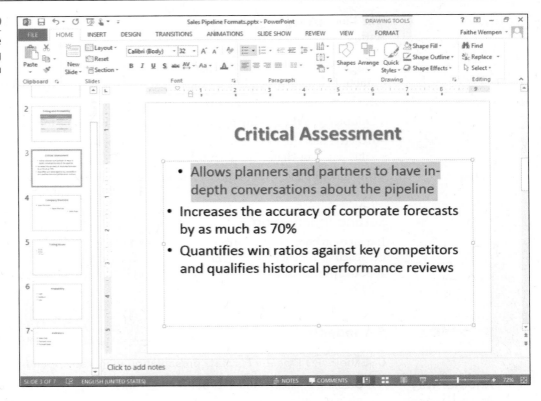

5. Select the other two bulleted paragraphs and repeat steps 3-4.

6. Select all three bulleted paragraphs.

7. Click the dialog box launcher for the Paragraph group. The Paragraph dialog box opens.

8. Set the Hanging indent to 0.6", and then click OK to apply the new setting.

Take Note   The bullet character has moved to the left in relation to the paragraph; the paragraph text has not moved.

9. **SAVE** the *Sales Pipeline Formats* presentation, and then close it.

PAUSE. LEAVE PowerPoint open to use in the next exercise.

By promoting and demoting bulleted paragraphs in the outline level, as you learned to do in Lesson 2, you can indirectly control their indentation. However, you can also directly change paragraphs' indentations via the Paragraph dialog box without altering their outline levels. This is useful when you want to change how a paragraph is formatted without changing its meaning or importance in the presentation's message.

There are two indentation settings. The first one, Before Text, applies to all lines in the paragraph. The second one, Special, is a specialty setting that varies according to the paragraph type:

- **Hanging:** A reverse indent. The first line (which usually contains a bullet character when Hanging is used) is reverse-indented by the specified amount. In other words, the first line has a lesser indent than the other lines, so it hangs off into the left margin. In the preceding steps, the hanging indent was 0.6".

- **First line:** A standard first-line indent. The first line is indented an extra amount on top of what is specified for the Before Text indentation setting.

- **(none):** This setting removes any special indents for the first line.

Indents can be set for any paragraph, but are often the most useful for bulleted and numbered lists. You will learn more about creating and formatting lists in the next section.

CERTIFICATION READY?   **3.1.5**

How can you create numbered lists in PowerPoint?

Creating Numbered Lists

PowerPoint enables you to create **numbered lists** to place a list of itemized information in numeric order. Numbered lists are used for procedural steps, action items, and other information where the order in which the items appear is significant. In the following exercise, you will create a numbered list from a list of items on a slide.

STEP BY STEP   **Create Numbered Lists**

GET READY. To create a numbered list, perform the following steps:

1. **OPEN** the *Leveraging Corporate Cash* presentation, and then save it as *Leveraging Corporate Cash Lists*.
2. On slide 2, click in the first line of the text in the text placeholder (*Determine inventory turnover*).
3. Click the Numbering button in the Paragraph group. PowerPoint formats the sentence with a number 1.
4. Select the last three lines in the text placeholder.
5. Click the Numbering button. PowerPoint applies numbers 2 through 4.
6. Click outside the text placeholder to clear any text selection. Your slide should look like the one shown in Figure 3-20.

Another Way
To number a paragraph, right-click the paragraph, and then click Numbering on the shortcut menu.

Figure 3-20

A numbered list

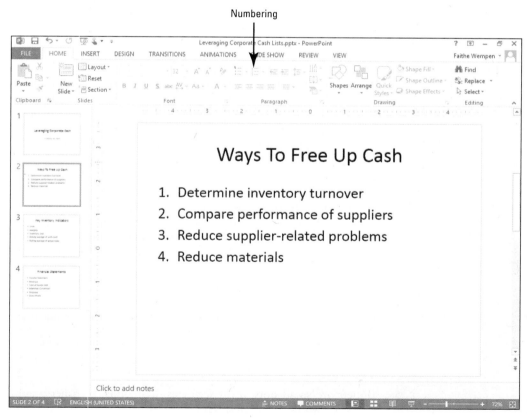

Another Way
You can also drag across the list to select it.

7. Click in the text placeholder containing the numbered list, and then press Ctrl+A to select the entire list.
8. Click the down arrow to the right of the Numbering button, opening a gallery of numbering styles.
9. Click the uppercase Roman numeral style as in Figure 3-21.

Figure 3-21

Changing the numbered list's numbering style

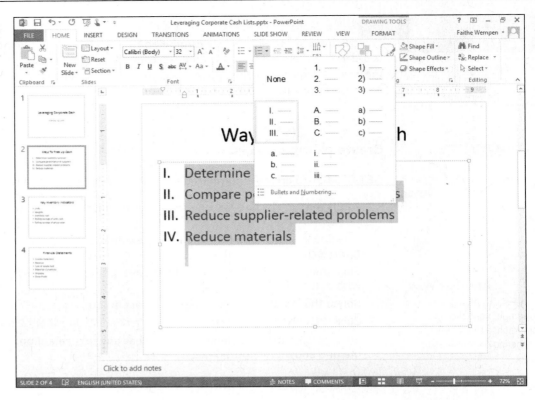

10. **SAVE** the presentation.

PAUSE. LEAVE the presentation open to use in the next exercise.

When you finish typing text in a numbered paragraph, you can press Enter to start a new numbered paragraph that continues the same numbering sequence. PowerPoint automatically numbers the new paragraph with the next number in the sequence of numbers so you can continue the list uninterrupted. To turn off numbering, press Enter twice or click the Numbering button on the Home tab.

By default, PowerPoint numbers items using numerals followed by periods. You can, however, change the numbering format to numerals followed by parentheses, upper or lowercase Roman numerals, or upper or lowercase letters. To change the numbering format, click the Numbering button's drop-down arrow and select a new format from the gallery.

For even more control over the numbering format, click Bullets and Numbering on the gallery to display the Bullets and Numbering dialog box. You can use this dialog box to choose what number to start the list with, change the size of the numbers, or change their color. You will work with that dialog box in the next exercise.

Working with Bulleted Lists

Bullets are small dots, arrows, circles, diamonds, or other graphics that appear before a short phrase or word. A **bulleted list** is a set of paragraphs (two or more) that each start with a bullet symbol. Bulleted lists are the most popular way to present items on PowerPoint presentations. In fact, most of PowerPoint's text placeholders automatically format text as a bulleted list. In the following exercise you will change the formats of a bulleted list.

STEP BY STEP   **Work with Bulleted Lists**

CERTIFICATION
READY?   **3.1.5**

How can you create bulleted
lists in PowerPoint?

USE the *Leveraging Corporate Cash Lists* presentation that is still open from the previous exercise.

1. On slide 3, select all of the bulleted list items in the text box. To do this, you can either drag across them or press Ctrl+A.
2. Click the drop-down arrow to the right of the Bullets button in the Paragraph group. PowerPoint displays a gallery of bullet styles.

Take Note   If a series of paragraphs does not have bullets, you can add them by selecting the paragraphs and then clicking the Bullets button in the Paragraph group.

3. Click Check mark Bullets (see Figure 3-22). PowerPoint applies the bullet style to the selected paragraphs.

Figure 3-22

Select a different bullet character

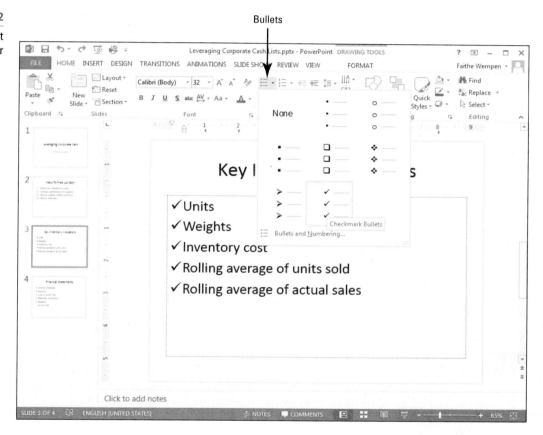

Take Note   If you hover the mouse over a certain bullet style on the list, the selected text on the slide is previewed using that bullet character. This is an example of the **Live Preview** feature, which also works with various other types of formatting too, including borders and fills.

4. With the text still selected, click the Bullets drop-down arrow again, and then click Bullets and Numbering. The Bullets and Numbering dialog box appears (see Figure 3-23).

Figure 3-23

The Bullets and Numbering
dialog box

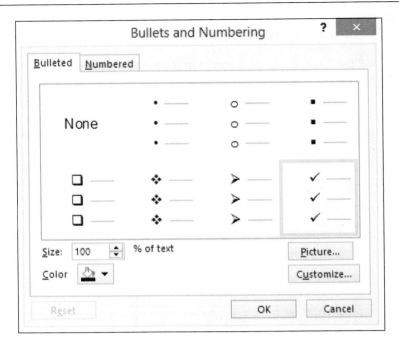

5. In the Size: box, type 80. This reduces the bullets' size to 80% of the text's size.

6. Click the Color drop-down arrow, and then click Blue, Accent 1. (It is the fifth color from the left on the first line.) This changes the color of the bullets.

7. Click OK. PowerPoint applies the changes.

8. SAVE the *Leveraging Corporate Cash Lists* presentation, and then close it.

PAUSE. LEAVE PowerPoint open to use in the next exercise.

Each PowerPoint theme supplies bullet characters for up to nine levels of bullets, and these characters differ according to theme. When you create a bulleted list on your slide, you can continue it automatically after the last item by pressing Enter. PowerPoint automatically adds the new paragraph with a bullet.

INSERTING AND FORMATTING WORDART

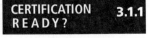

The **WordArt** feature allows you to use text to create a graphic object. PowerPoint's WordArt feature can change standard text into flashy, eye-catching graphics. Use WordArt's formatting options to change the WordArt fill or outline color or apply special effects. You can also apply WordArt styles to any slide text to give it special emphasis.

CERTIFICATION READY? 3.1.1

How can you change regular text to WordArt?

Inserting a WordArt Graphic

In this exercise, you will enhance the appearance of slide titles by converting them to WordArt.

STEP BY STEP **Insert a WordArt Graphic**

GET READY. To insert a WordArt graphic, perform the following steps:

1. **OPEN** the *Full Profit Potential* presentation, and save it as *Full Profit*. Notice that the first slide has a subtitle but no title placeholder.

2. Click the Insert tab on the Ribbon, and click the WordArt button to display a gallery of WordArt styles (see Figure 3-24).

Figure 3-24

Gallery of WordArt styles

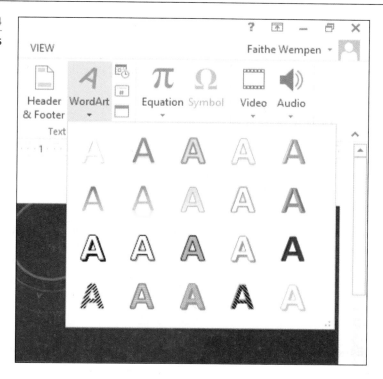

3. Click the Gradient Fill – Gold, Accent 1, Reflection WordArt style. PowerPoint displays the WordArt graphic with the sample text *Your text here*.

4. Type Full Profit to replace the sample text. Your slide should resemble Figure 3-25.

Figure 3-25

A new WordArt graphic on a slide

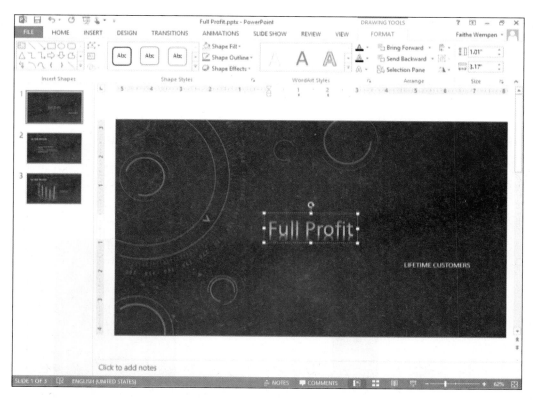

5. **SAVE** the presentation.

PAUSE. LEAVE the presentation open to use in the next exercise.

After you have inserted the WordArt graphic, you can format it in a number of ways. You can change the style from the WordArt gallery, you can modify the fill or the outline, or you can apply a number of interesting special effects. You can also modify the text of the graphic at any time. Click the graphic to open the placeholder just as when editing a slide's title or body text, and then edit the text as desired.

Formatting a WordArt Graphic

To format a WordArt graphic, you use the tools on one of PowerPoint's contextual tabs, the Drawing Tools Format tab. In the next several exercises, you will use these tools to modify the WordArt's fill and outline and apply an effect.

Changing the WordArt Fill Color

The WordArt fill color is the color you see inside the WordArt characters. You can change the fill color by using the color palette for the current theme or any other available color. You can also apply a special effect fill to WordArt such as a texture, gradient, or pattern.

STEP BY STEP   **Apply a Solid Fill Color to WordArt**

USE the *Full Profit* presentation that is still open from the previous exercise.

1. Select the WordArt graphic's text on slide 1. Make sure you select the text itself and not just the outer frame of the WordArt object. Note that the Drawing Tools Format tab becomes active on the Ribbon.
2. Click the Drawing Tools Format tab, and then locate the WordArt Styles group.
3. Click the Text Fill drop-down arrow. PowerPoint displays the Theme Colors palette.
4. Click the Gray-25%, Text 2 theme color as the fill color (see Figure 3-26). It's the fourth color in the top row. PowerPoint changes the fill of the text.

Figure 3-26

Filling a WordArt object with a solid color

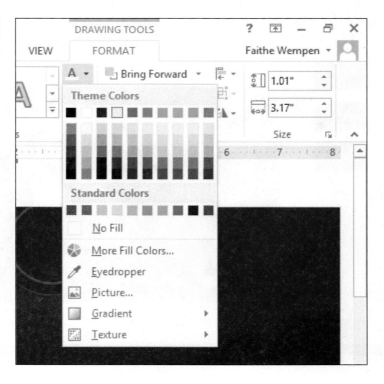

5. SAVE the presentation.

PAUSE. LEAVE the presentation open to use in the next exercise.

One way to fine-tune the graphic you have inserted is to change the fill color of the WordArt object. You can use any of the colors on the Theme Colors palette to make sure the object coordinates with other items in the presentation.

You can also choose from the Standard Colors palette or select another color from the Colors dialog box. To access these colors, click More Fill Colors on the palette (see Figure 3-26) to open the Colors dialog box. You can "mix" your own colors on the Custom tab or click the Standard tab to choose from a palette of premixed colors.

Applying a Texture Fill to WordArt

Textures are graphics that repeat to fill an object with a surface that resembles a familiar material such as straw, marble, paper, or wood. The texture graphics are specially designed so that the left edge blends in with the right edge (and the top edge with the bottom edge), so that when you place copies side by side, it looks like one seamless surface. In this exercise, you will practice applying a texture fill to WordArt.

STEP BY STEP   **Apply a Texture Fill to WordArt**

USE the *Full Profit* presentation that is still open from the previous exercise.

1. Select the WordArt graphic's text on slide 1 if it is not already selected.
2. On the Drawing Tools Format tab, click the Text Fill drop-down arrow. PowerPoint displays the Theme Colors palette.
3. Point to Texture, and then click the Granite texture (see Figure 3-27). PowerPoint changes the fill of the graphic.

Figure 3-27

Filling a WordArt object with a texture

Granite

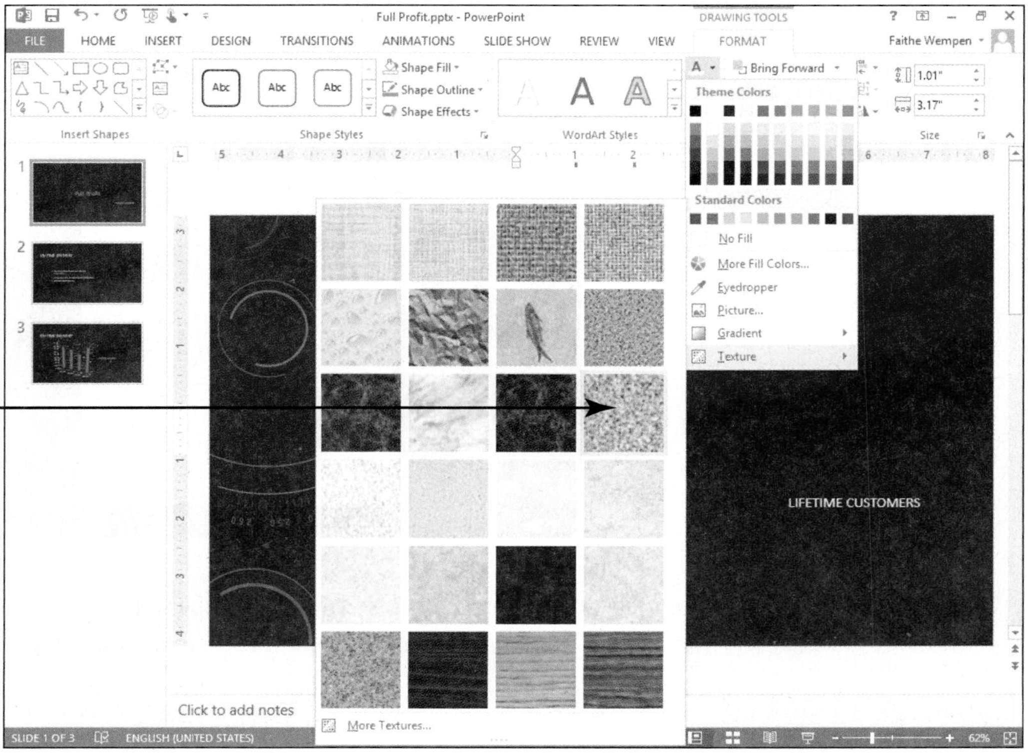

4. Press **Ctrl+B** to make the WordArt bold so you can see the texture applied to it more clearly.

5. **SAVE** the presentation.

PAUSE. LEAVE the presentation open to use in the next exercise.

Changing the WordArt Outline Color

Most WordArt styles include a colored outline around the edges of the WordArt characters. Just as with a WordArt object's fill color, you can fine-tune the outline color of the object. You have the same color options as for changing a fill color. The Text Outline Theme Colors palette also allows you to remove the outline, change its weight, or apply a dash style to the outline. In this exercise you will learn how to change the outline color to fine-tune a WordArt graphic.

STEP BY STEP   **Change the WordArt Outline Color**

USE the *Full Profit* presentation that is still open from the previous exercise.

1. Select the WordArt graphic's text on slide 1 if it is not already selected.

2. On the Drawing Tools Format tab, click the Text Outline drop-down arrow. PowerPoint displays the Theme Colors palette (see Figure 3-28).

Figure 3-28

Changing the border color of a WordArt object

Text Outline

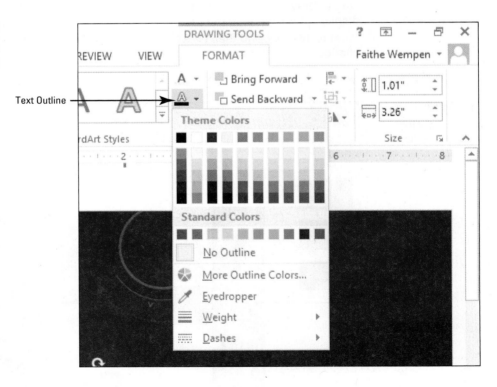

3. Click More Outline Colors. The Colors dialog box opens.

4. On the Standard tab, click a dark blue hexagon (see Figure 3-29).

Figure 3-29

Choose a color from the Colors
dialog box

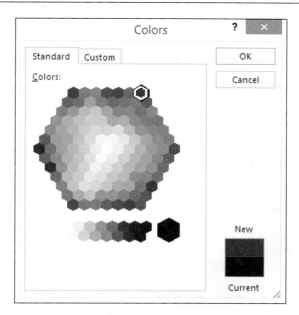

5. Click OK. The dark blue background blends in with the background of the slide, so it is not obvious to see.

6. Zoom in on the object to 200% to see it more clearly. Zoom out to 100% when you are finished looking at the border.

7. Select the WordArt again if necessary, click the Text Outline drop-down arrow again, point to Weight, and click 3 pt. The outline becomes more dramatic and easier to see.

8. Click the Text Outline drop-down arrow again, and click No Outline. The outline disappears.

9. Click the Fit Slide to Current Window icon in the lower right corner of the PowerPoint window to view the entire slide again.

PAUSE. LEAVE the presentation open to use in the next exercise.

Applying Special Effects to WordArt

You can apply special effects to your WordArt objects such as shadows, reflections, glows, transformations, and more. These effects can also be applied to the other object types that you will learn about in later lessons such as drawn lines and shapes.

STEP BY STEP   **Apply Special Effects to WordArt**

USE the *Full Profit* presentation that is still open from the previous exercise.

1. Select the WordArt graphic on slide 1 if it is not already selected.

2. On the Drawing Tools Format tab, click the Text Effects drop-down arrow. PowerPoint displays the Text Effects menu.

3. Hover your mouse over Reflection. PowerPoint displays the Reflection special effects (see Figure 3-30). This WordArt already has one type of reflection applied but not the type we want.

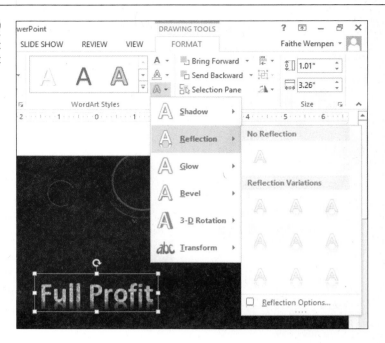

4. Click **Tight Reflection, touching** (the first reflection under the Reflection Variations heading). PowerPoint changes the reflection effect to the chosen one.

5. Click the WordArt graphic and drag it close to the subtitle (see Figure 3-31).

6. **SAVE** the presentation.

PAUSE. LEAVE the presentation open to use in the next exercise.

WordArt special effects provide a way to spice up an ordinary slide. Although you should not use WordArt special effects on all your slides, you may want to look for spots in your presentations where a little artistic punch will liven up your slide show. Always consider your audience and your topic when adding special effects. For example, a presentation discussing plant closings and layoffs would not be an appropriate place for a cheerful-looking WordArt graphic.

Formatting Text with WordArt Styles

You do not have to insert a WordArt graphic to use the WordArt styles. You can apply WordArt styles to any text in a slide. Applying WordArt styles to regular text in a presentation is an additional way to format the text to customize the presentation. You can use the same features you used to format the WordArt graphic to format a title or bulleted text: Text Fill, Text Outline, and Text Effects. In this exercise, you will practice applying WordArt styles to text.

STEP BY STEP | **Format Text with WordArt Styles**

USE the *Full Profit* presentation that is still open from the previous exercise.

1. Go to slide 2.
2. Select the slide title, On-Time Delivery.
3. Zoom in to 100% on the selected text, so you can see the effects more clearly that you will apply.
4. On the Drawing Tools Format tab, click the More button in the WordArt Styles group (see Figure 3-32) to display the WordArt Styles gallery.

Figure 3-32

The More button opens the WordArt Styles gallery

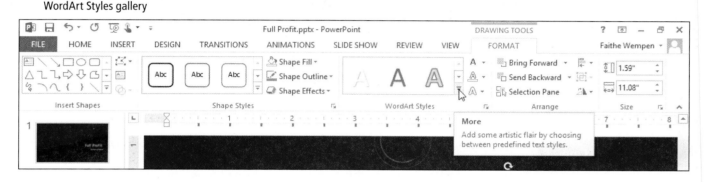

5. Click the Pattern Fill - Purple, Accent 1, 50%, Hard Shadow - Accent 1 WordArt style (see Figure 3-33). The style is applied to the selected text.

Figure 3-33

Select a WordArt style

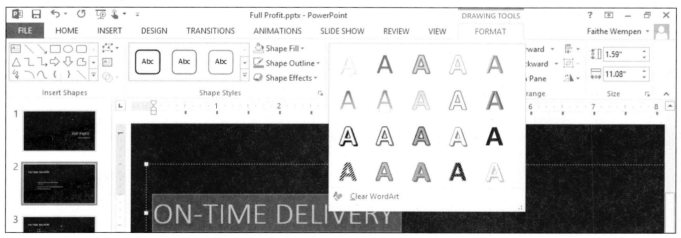

6. On the Home tab, in the Font group, open the Font Size drop-down list and choose 60.
7. Click outside the text placeholder to clear its border. The title should look like the one shown in Figure 3-34.

Figure 3-34

The title with WordArt applied

Figure 3-34

The title with WordArt applied

8. **SAVE** and close the *Full Profit* presentation.

PAUSE. LEAVE PowerPoint open to use in the next exercise.

CREATING AND FORMATTING TEXT BOXES

The Bottom Line

Although PowerPoint layouts are very flexible and provide a number of ways to insert text, you may occasionally need to insert text in a location for which there is no default placeholder. **Text boxes** are the answer in this circumstance. A text box is a free-floating box into which you can type text. You can use text boxes as containers for extra text that is not part of a placeholder. A text box can hold a few words, an entire paragraph of text, or even several paragraphs of text. Text boxes make it easy to position content anywhere on a slide.

Adding a Text Box to a Slide

Text boxes can be used to place text on a slide any place you want it. In this exercise, you will add a text box to a slide and then insert text into the text box.

STEP BY STEP   **Add a Text Box to a Slide**

1. **OPEN** the *Profit Analysis* presentation and save it as *Profit Analysis Boxes*.
2. If the rulers do not appear, on the View tab click to mark the Ruler check box so that rulers appear around the slide.
3. Go to slide 1.
4. On the Insert tab, click Text Box in the Text group. The cursor changes to a text insertion pointer.
5. Move the pointer to the right side of the slide, below the red dot and at the 3" mark on the horizontal ruler.
6. Click and hold down the mouse button. Drag the mouse down and to the right to create a rectangle that is 3" wide. Use the horizontal ruler to gauge the size.

Take Note   The height you draw the text box does not matter because the height automatically fits the content. When blank, the text box is one line high. It expands as you type more lines.

7. Release the mouse button. The rectangle changes to a text box.

Take Note   When you release the mouse button after creating a text box, the Ribbon automatically displays the Home tab.

8. Type Fourth Coffee in the text box.

9. Select the text Fourth Coffee, and then change the Font Size to 28 using the Font drop-down list on the Home tab.

10. Click outside the text box to clear its border. Your slide should look like the one shown in Figure 3-35.

Figure 3-35

Inserting a text box

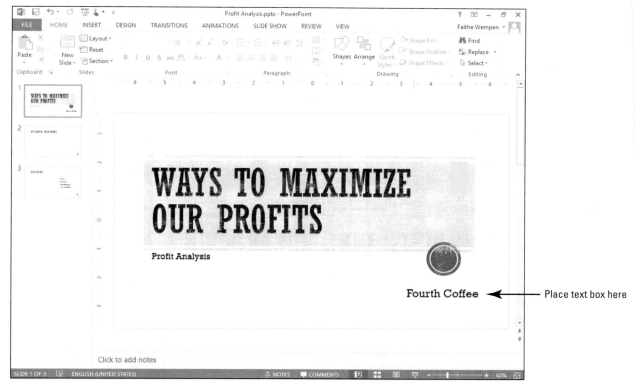

11. **SAVE** the presentation.

PAUSE. LEAVE the presentation open to use in the next exercise.

You have two options when creating a text box. If you simply click the slide with the text box pointer, you create a text box in which text will not wrap. As you enter text, the text box expands horizontally to accommodate the text. If you want to create a text box that will contain the text in a specific area, with text wrapping from line to line, you draw a desired width with the text box pointer as you did in the preceding steps. When text reaches that border, it wraps to the next line.

Take Note You can change a text box's wrap setting. Right-click its border, and then click Format Shape. From the Format Shape task pane, select Shape Options, choose the Size & Properties icon, and under the Text Box settings, mark or clear the Wrap Text in Shape check box.

Resizing a Text Box

Text boxes can be resized to make room for the addition of other text boxes or objects or to rearrange a text box's contents. In this exercise, you will practice resizing text boxes on a PowerPoint slide.

STEP BY STEP **Resize a Text Box**

USE the *Profit Analysis Boxes* presentation that is still open from the previous exercise.

1. Display slide 2.

2. On the Insert tab, click Text Box in the Text group.

3. Drag to **draw a text box** under the Divisional Breakdown title. Make the text box approximately **4"** wide.

4. Type the following items into the text box, pressing **Enter** after each item to start a new paragraph (see Figure 3-36).

   Sales

   Marketing

   Purchasing

   Production

   Distribution

   Customer Service

   Human Resources

   Product Development

   Information Technology

   Administration

Figure 3-36

Type text into the text box

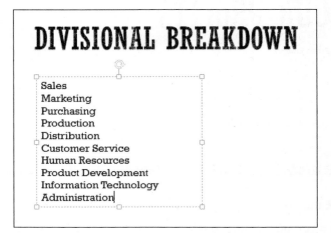

5. Move the **mouse pointer** to the white square in the middle of the text box's right border. This is a resizing handle or selection handle. The pointer changes to a double-headed arrow (see Figure 3-37).

Figure 3-37

Position the mouse pointer over the right-side handle on the text box frame

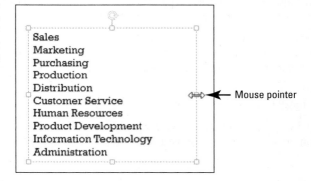

Mouse pointer

6. Click and hold down the mouse button.

Take Note   A text box has eight resizing handles: one in each corner and one in the middle of each side.

7. Hold and Drag the sizing handle to the left until the text box's right border is close to the text (all entries should still be on a single line).

8. Release the mouse button. The text box resizes to a smaller size. Your slide should look like the one in Figure 3-38.

Figure 3-38

The resized text box

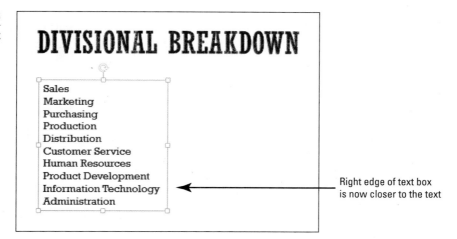

Right edge of text box is now closer to the text

9. Click outside the text box to clear its border.
10. **SAVE** the presentation.

PAUSE. LEAVE the presentation open to use in the next exercise.

Formatting a Text Box

You can apply many different types of formatting to text boxes to make them more eye-catching and graphical. You can apply a Quick Style, add a border, or apply a solid, gradient, texture, or pattern fill to its background.

Applying a Quick Style to a Text Box

PowerPoint's **Quick Styles** allow you to quickly format any text box or placeholder with a combination of fill, border, and effect formats to make the object stand out on the slide. In this exercise, you apply a Quick Style to a text box, but PowerPoint also provides Quick Styles for other features such as tables, SmartArt graphics, charts, and pictures.

STEP BY STEP | **Apply a Quick Style to a Text Box**

USE the *Profit Analysis Boxes* presentation that is still open from the previous exercise.

1. Go to slide 1.
2. Click the Fourth Coffee text box to select it.
3. On the Home tab, click the Quick Styles button to display a gallery of Quick Styles.
4. Select the Intense Effect – Gray-50%, Accent 5 Quick Style, the next-to-last thumbnail in the last row (see Figure 3-39). The Quick Style formatting is applied to the text box.

Figure 3-39

A Quick Style applied to a text box

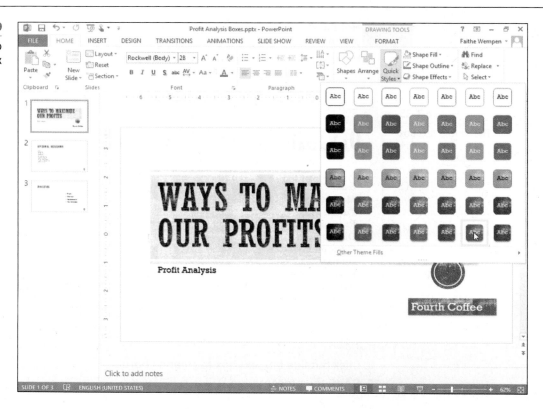

5. **SAVE** the presentation.

PAUSE. LEAVE the presentation open to use in the next exercise.

There are several advantages to using Quick Styles to format an object. Each Quick Style provides a number of formatting options that would take more time to apply separately. Quick Styles give a professional appearance to slides. Using Quick Styles can also make it easy to format consistently throughout a presentation.

CERTIFICATION READY?   **2.2.1**

How can you modify a text box's background?

Applying Fill and Border Formatting to a Text Box

If you want more control over formatting applied to a text box, you can use the Shape Fill and Shape Outline tools to set the formatting for a text box on your own. In this exercise, you apply fill and border formatting to a text box.

STEP BY STEP   **Apply Fill and Border Formatting to a Text Box**

USE the *Profit Analysis Boxes* presentation that is still open from the previous exercise.

1. Go to slide 2.
2. Click inside the text box list. PowerPoint displays the text box border and sizing handles.
3. On the Drawing Tools Format tab, click the Shape Fill drop-down arrow in the Shape Styles group. The Theme Colors palette for the text box fill color appears.
4. Click the Tan, Background 2, Darker 25% theme color. PowerPoint formats the text box fill with this color (see Figure 3-40).

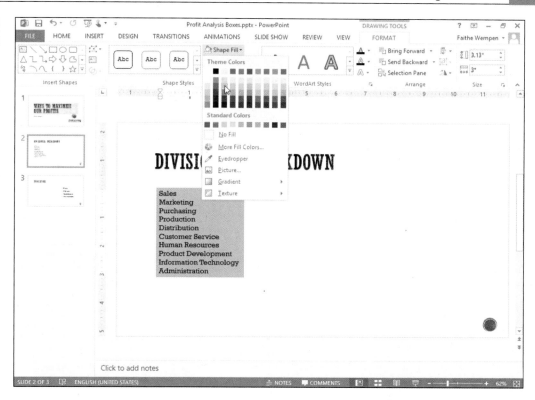

Figure 3-40

Select a shape fill

5. Click the Shape Outline drop-down arrow. The Theme Colors palette for the text box border color appears.

6. Click the Orange, Accent 1, Darker 25% theme color. PowerPoint formats the text box border with this color.

7. Click the Shape Outline drop-down arrow again.

8. Click or hover the mouse pointer over Weight. A menu with line weights appears.

9. Click 3 pt. PowerPoint resizes the text box border to a 3-point border size (see Figure 3-41).

Figure 3-41

A 3-pt shape outline
has been applied

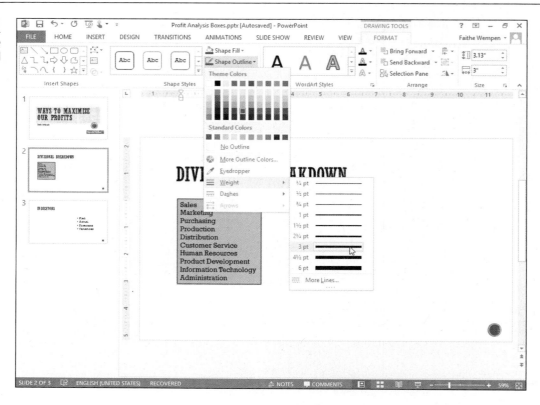

Take Note   You can change the style of a text box's outline from solid to dashed or dotted by selecting the Dashes option from the Shape Outline drop-down menu.

10. **SAVE** the presentation.

PAUSE. LEAVE the presentation open to use in the next exercise.

Applying Special Fills to a Text Box

You are not limited to plain solid colors for text box fills. You can fill using gradients, patterns, textures, and pictures to create interesting special effects. In this exercise, you will insert a picture and apply a gradient color to a text box.

STEP BY STEP   **Apply Picture and Gradient Fills to a Text Box**

USE the *Profit Analysis Boxes* presentation that is still open from the previous exercise.

1. On slide 2, select the text box containing the list of divisions.
2. On the Drawing Tools Format tab, click the Shape Fill button. A menu opens.
3. In the menu, click Picture. The Insert Picture dialog box opens.
4. Click the Browse button that is next to "From a file." Then navigate to the location of the data files for this lesson and click golden.jpg.
5. Click Insert. The Insert Picture dialog box closes and the picture is inserted as a background in the text box (see Figure 3-42).

Figure 3-42

A picture applied as a text box background

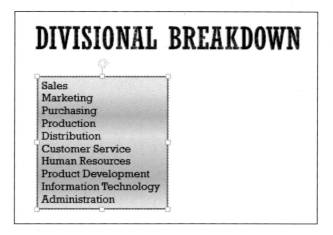

6. With the same text box still selected, on the Drawing Tools Format tab, click the Shape Fill button. A menu appears.

7. Click or hover the mouse over Gradient. A menu of gradient presets appears.

8. Click the Linear Right sample in the Light Variations section (see Figure 3-43). To determine the name of a sample, hover the mouse pointer over each sample, so a ScreenTip appears with its name.

Figure 3-43

Select a gradient preset

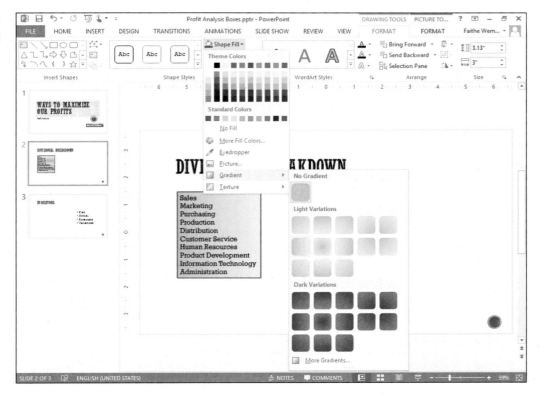

9. On the Drawing Tools Format tab, click Shape Fill, point to Gradient, and click More Gradients. The Format Shape task pane opens.

10. Click the Color button in the task pane, and click Dark Red, Accent 2.

11. Drag the center stop on the Gradient Stops bar until the value in the Position box reads 25 (see Figure 3-44).

Figure 3-44

Select a different color for the gradient

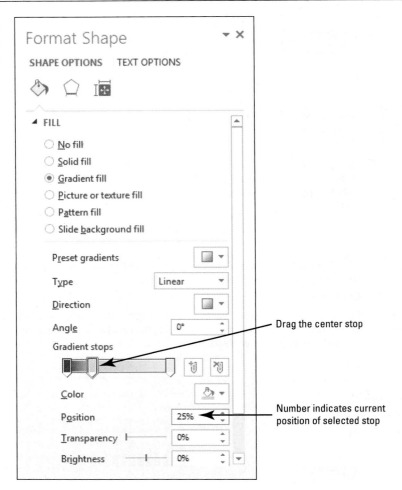

12. Click **Close** in the upper right corner of the task pane to close it.
13. **SAVE** the presentation.

PAUSE. LEAVE the presentation open to use in the next exercise.

Gradient fills can be much more complex than the simple ones you applied in the preceding exercise. You can choose from several preset color combinations in the Format Shape task pane (see Figure 3-44), or create your own color combinations. The slider in the task pane can be adjusted to create multipoint gradient effects in which you choose exactly which colors appear and in what proportions. You can also adjust the brightness and transparency of the gradient at various points in the fill.

Applying Texture and Pattern Fills

Texture and pattern fills are alternatives to plain colored fills. As you learned earlier in the lesson, a texture fill repeats a small graphic to fill the area; texture graphics are specially designed so that the edges blend together and it looks like a single graphic. Texture graphics usually simulate some type of textured material like wood, marble, or fabric. A pattern fill is a repeating pattern that consists of a background color and a foreground color like the pattern on a checked table cloth or a pinstripe suit. In the following exercise you will apply texture and pattern fills to a text box.

STEP BY STEP **Apply Texture and Pattern Fills to a Text Box**

USE the *Profit Analysis Boxes* presentation that is still open from the previous exercise.

1. On slide 2, click the Text Box button on the Insert tab, and drag to draw a new text box to the right of the existing one, approximately 4.5" in width.

2. In the new text box, type the following: Each division makes a unique and valuable contribution to the organization.

3. Select the new text box, and on the Drawing Tools Format tab, click Shape Fill, and hover the mouse pointer over Texture in the menu that appears.

4. Click the Papyrus texture. To locate the correct texture, hover the mouse pointer over each texture to display the ScreenTip (see Figure 3-45). The texture is applied to the text box.

Figure 3-45

Apply a texture fill to a text box

Papyrus texture ⟶

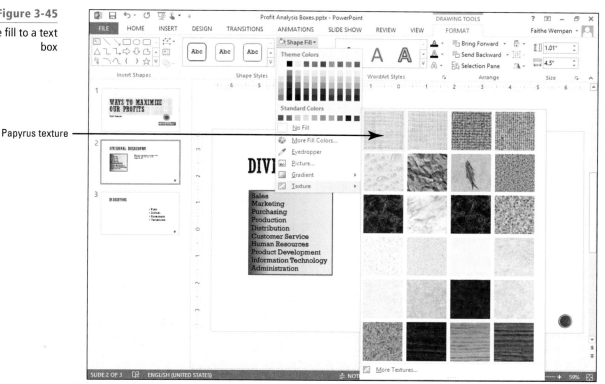

5. On slide 3, select the text box containing the bulleted list.

6. Right-click the text box's border to activate the shortcut menu and click Format Shape. The Format Shape task pane opens.

7. Click Pattern Fill. A selection of patterns appears.

8. Click the Light downward diagonal pattern (first pattern in third row).

9. Click the Foreground button to browse for a color.

10. Click Brown, Accent 6 (see Figure 3-46). The new fill appears in the text box.

Figure 3-46

Apply a pattern fill to
a text box

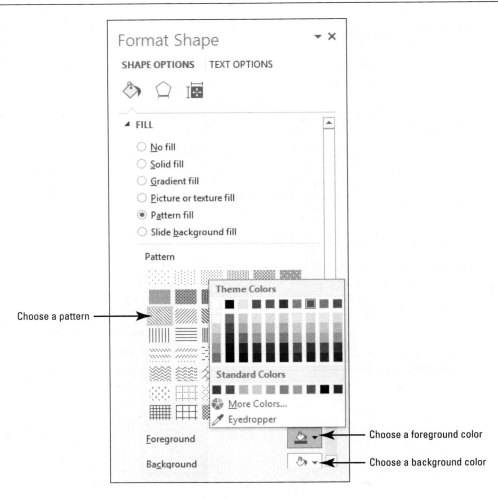

Choose a pattern

Choose a foreground color

Choose a background color

11. Click **Close (X)** to close the task pane.
12. **SAVE** the presentation.

PAUSE. LEAVE the presentation open to use in the next exercise.

Changing Text Box Shape and Applying Effects

You can apply the same special effects to text boxes as you can to WordArt, drawn shapes, and other objects. These special effects include reflection, glow, 3-D effects, shadows, soft edges, and beveling. You can also modify the shape of a text box, using any of the dozens of preset shapes that PowerPoint offers. In this exercise, you learn how to change the shape of a text box and apply shape effects.

STEP BY STEP | **Change Text Box Shape and Apply Effects**

USE the *Profit Analysis Boxes* presentation that is still open from the previous exercise.

1. On slide 1, select the **Fourth Coffee text box**.
2. On the Drawing Tools Format tab, in the Insert Shapes group, click the **Edit Shape button**. A menu opens.
3. Hover the mouse pointer over **Change Shape**. A fly-out menu of shapes appears (see Figure 3-47).

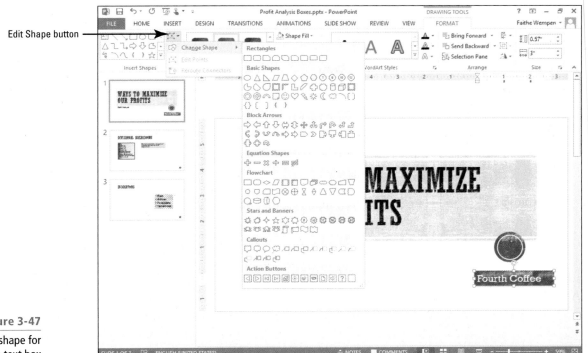

Figure 3-47

Choose a different shape for the text box

4. In the first row, click the Rounded Rectangle; the new shape is applied to the text box.

5. Click away from the shape so that you can see it better. The corners of the text box are now rounded.

6. On slide 2, select the Each division... text box on the right.

7. On the Drawing Tools Format tab, click the Shape Effects button in the Shape Styles group. A menu of effects appears.

8. Hover the mouse pointer over Bevel to produce the Bevel options menu.

9. Click the Circle bevel effect (first effect in the first row of the Bevel section) (see Figure 3-48). The bevel effect is applied to the text box.

Figure 3-48

Select a bevel effect

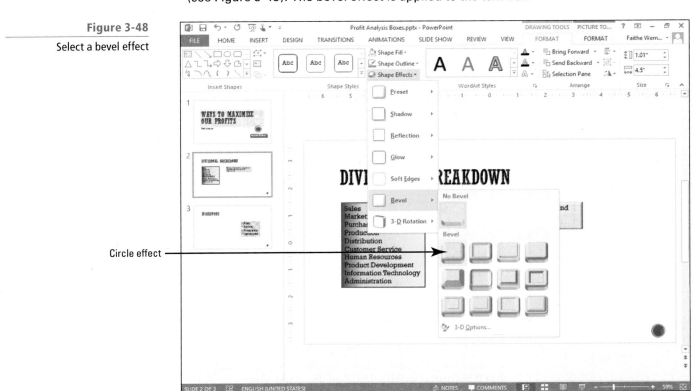

10. Click the Shape Effects button again, and point to Shadow to produce the Shadow options menu.

11. Click the Offset Diagonal Bottom Right shadow (the first shadow in the Outer section).

12. Click away from the text box to see the changes better. It should resemble Figure 3-49.

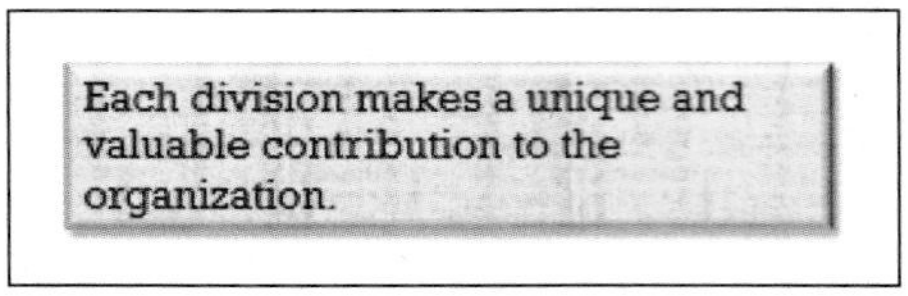

Figure 3-49

The text box with bevel and shadow effects applied

Each division makes a unique and valuable contribution to the organization.

13. SAVE the presentation.

PAUSE. LEAVE the presentation open to use in the next exercise.

Changing the Default Formatting for New Text Boxes

If you are going to create lots of text boxes in a presentation, there are ways you can save time in formatting them. One way is to redefine the default for new text boxes to match your desired settings as you will learn to do in this exercise.

STEP BY STEP

Change the Default Formatting for New Text Boxes

USE the *Profit Analysis Boxes* presentation that is still open from the previous exercise.

1. On slide 2, select the text box on the right.

Take Note   Make sure you select its outer border rather than clicking inside it. (For this activity, it makes a difference.) The outer border should appear solid, not dashed, when selected.

2. Right-click the text box's outer border. A menu appears (see Figure 3-50).

Figure 3-50

Make the current text box's formatting the default for new text boxes

3. Click Set as Default Text Box.

4. On the Insert tab, click Text Box, and drag to draw another text box on slide 2. Notice that it is formatted the same as the other one.

5. Return the text box to the previous default formatting (no outline, no fill). To do so, follow these steps:

   a. Right-click the text box's outer border, and click Format Picture. The Format Picture task pane opens.

Take Note   Ordinarily when you right-click a text box, you would have the Format Shape command available instead of Format Picture, but Format Picture appears in this case because of the text box's fill being an image (the texture).

   b. Click the Fill & Line icon, expand the Fill category, and then choose No fill.

   c. Expand the Line category, and then choose No line.

   d. Close the task pane.

6. Set the text box's current appearance to the new default by repeating steps 2-3.

7. Delete the new text box without typing anything in it. To delete a text box, click its border to select it, and then press Delete on the keyboard.

8. **SAVE** the presentation.

PAUSE. LEAVE the presentation open to use in the next exercise.

Working with Text in a Text Box

You can format the text within a text box in a number of ways: adjust alignment, change text orientation, set text margins, modify the text wrap settings, and even set the text in multiple columns.

Aligning Text in a Text Box.   You use the same alignment options in a text box that are available for a text placeholder: left, center, right, and justify. By default, PowerPoint aligns text in new text boxes to the left. If you align text to a different position, such as right, and then add a new paragraph by pressing Enter from that text, the new paragraph keeps the right-aligned formatting. In the following exercise, you will align text to the center of the text box.

STEP BY STEP   **Align Text in a Text Box**

USE the *Profit Analysis Boxes* presentation that is still open from the previous exercise.

1. On slide 1, click in the Fourth Coffee text box to move the insertion point into it.

2. Click the Center button. PowerPoint aligns the text so that it is centered between the left and right border of the text box.

3. Repeat this process for the Ways to Maximize Our Profits text box.

4. Click outside the text box to clear its border. Your slide should look like the one in Figure 3-51.

Figure 3-51

Center the text in the title and subtitle boxes on the first slide

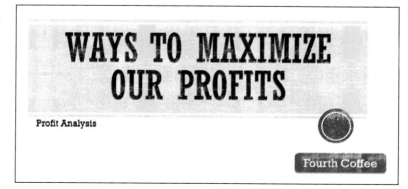

5. **SAVE** the presentation.

PAUSE. LEAVE the presentation open to use in the next exercise.

Take Note   If you resize a text box that has centered text, the text re-centers automatically based on the final size of the text box.

The Justify alignment option keeps long passages of text even on the left and right margins of a text box, similar to the way newspapers and many books align text. PowerPoint adds extra space between words if necessary to stretch a line to meet the right margin. This can result in a very "gappy" look that you can improve by adjusting font size and/or the width of the text box. The last line of each paragraph is not affected, since Justify does not work on single-line paragraphs.

Orienting Text in a Text Box

You can change the text direction in a text box so that text runs from bottom to top or stacks one letter atop the other. This can make text in the text box more visually interesting. You can also change orientation by rotating the text box itself. The following exercise shows how to rotate the text in a text box in two different ways.

STEP BY STEP   **Orient Text in a Text Box**

USE the *Profit Analysis Boxes* presentation that is still open from the previous exercise.

1. Go to slide 3.
2. Select the Indicators text box.
3. On the Home tab, click the Align Text drop-down arrow in the Paragraph group, and then click Top.
4. On the Home tab, click the Text Direction drop-down arrow in the Paragraph group. A menu of text direction choices displays.
5. Click Rotate all text 270° (see Figure 3-52). PowerPoint changes the orientation of the text in the text box to run from the bottom of the text box to the top.

Figure 3-52

Rotate the text 270 degrees

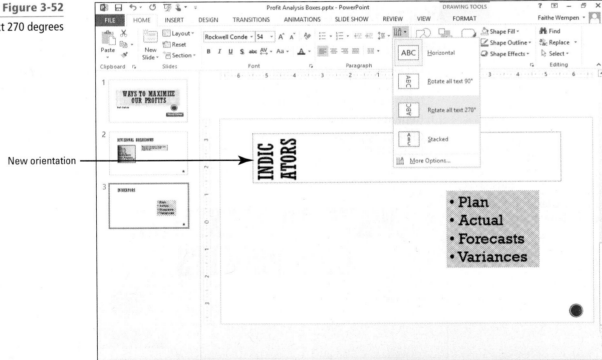

6. Drag the bottom right corner selection handle downward on the text box, increasing the height and decreasing the width of the text box so the text appears in a single vertical column along the left side of the slide. Your slide should look like the one in Figure 3-53.

Figure 3-53

The rotated and resized text box

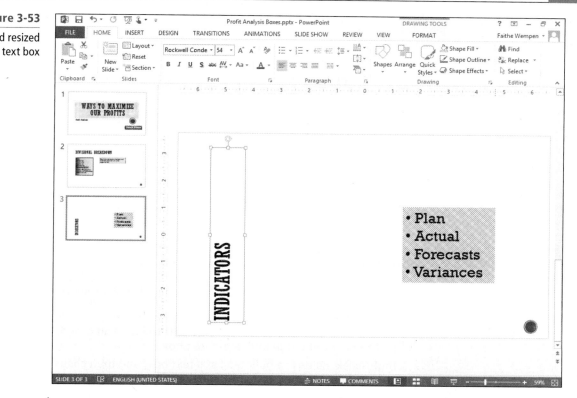

7. Switch to slide 1, and draw another text box on slide 1 in the top left corner. Type Sales Department in the text box.

8. Move the mouse to the round rotation handle at the top center of the text box. The mouse pointer changes to an open-ended circle with an arrow point.

9. Click and hold down the mouse button.

10. Move the mouse to the left so that the outline of the text box starts to rotate around its center (see Figure 3-54).

Figure 3-54

Manually rotating a text box

11. Rotate the text box to about a 30-degree angle, and then release the mouse button.

12. Move the rotated text box so that it overlaps the corner of the title box.

13. Click outside the text box to clear its sizing handles. Your slide should look like the one in Figure 3-55.

Figure 3-55

The completed slide with rotated objects

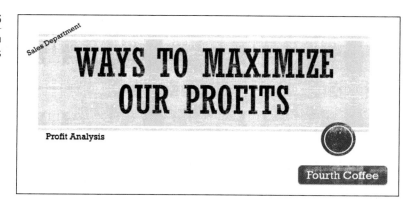

14. SAVE the presentation.

PAUSE. LEAVE the presentation open to use in the next exercise.

Orienting text boxes can be a design enhancement for your slides. For example, you might create a text box that includes your company name in it. Instead of drawing the text box horizontally on the slide, draw it so it is taller than wide and then choose one of the Text Direction button options to change text orientation. You can also rotate a text box or any placeholder for a special effect.

Setting the Margins in a Text Box

PowerPoint enables you to set the margins in a text box. Margins control the distance between the text and the outer border of the text box. In this exercise you will change the right and left margins on a text box.

STEP BY STEP	**Set the Margins in a Text Box**

USE the *Profit Analysis Boxes* presentation that is still open from the previous exercise.

1. Go to slide 3.
2. Select the text box on the right side of the slide, and drag it to the left side of the slide, just to the right of the Indicators text box.
3. Right-click inside the bulleted list's text box, and then click Format Shape on the shortcut menu. The Format Shape task pane opens.
4. Click the Size & Properties icon, and then click the Text Box heading to expand its options. Text box layout options appear (see Figure 3-56).

Figure 3-56

Set the margins in the Format Shape task pane

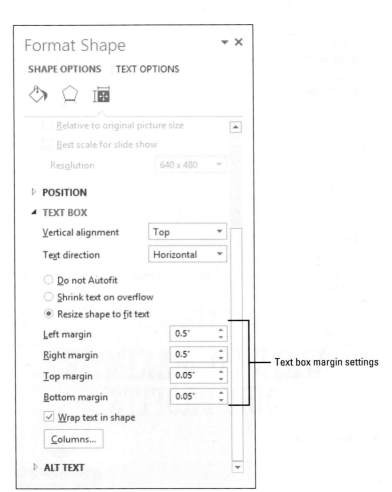

Text box margin settings

5. Click the Left margin spin button (up arrow) to set the left margin at 0.5". PowerPoint applies the margin changes immediately.

6. Click the Right margin spin button to set the right margin at 0.5". Figure 3-56 shows the correct settings.

7. Click Close to close the task pane.

8. Widen the text box to 4.5" so that each bullet point appears on a single line. Your slide should look like the one shown in Figure 3-57.

Figure 3-57

Text box with new margins

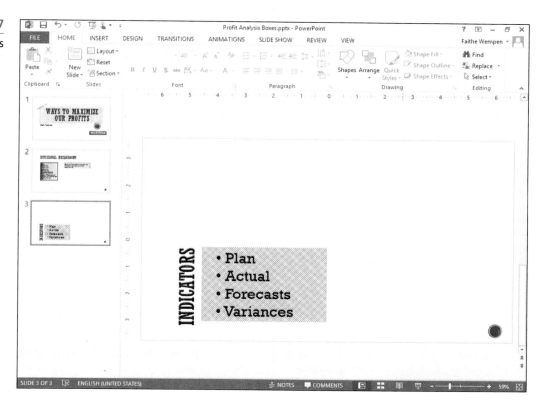

9. **SAVE** the presentation.

PAUSE. LEAVE the presentation open to use in the next exercise.

Resizing text box margins enables you to fine-tune text placement within a text box. For example, if you want text to appear 1 inch away from the left side of the text box, change the Left margin box to 1.0. You might want to do this if your slide design needs to have text align with other items placed on the slide. If you have chosen to format a text box or placeholder with a fill, increasing margins can also prevent the text from appearing to crowd the edges of the text box.

Changing the Text Wrap Setting for a Text Box

Depending on the type of text box and the way it was created, it may or may not be set to wrap the text automatically to the next line when the right margin is reached. In the next exercise you will learn how to view and change this setting.

STEP BY STEP **Change the Text Wrap Setting for a Text Box**

USE the *Profit Analysis Boxes* presentation that is still open from the previous exercise.

1. Go to slide 2.

2. Right-click the Each division... text box, and then click Format Picture. The Format Picture task pane appears.

3. Click **Text Options**, and then click the **Textbox icon**.

4. Click to clear the **Wrap text in shape check box** (see Figure 3-58).

Figure 3-58

The Wrap Text in Shape check box controls text wrap

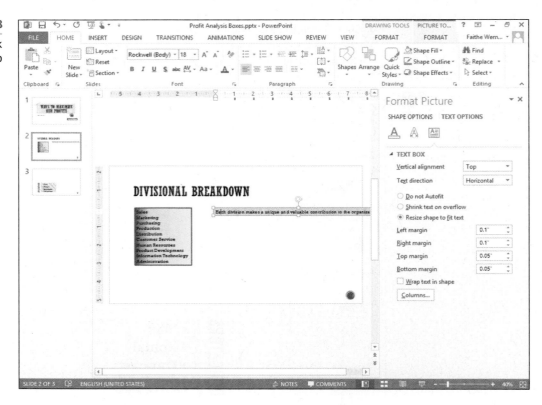

5. Click **Close** to close the task pane. The text now overruns the slide because it is on a single line.

6. Click in the text box, and click after the word *and* to place the insertion point there.

7. Press **Shift+Enter** to manually insert a line break.

8. **SAVE** the *Profit Analysis Boxes* presentation.

PAUSE. LEAVE the presentation open to use in the next exercise.

CERTIFICATION READY?   3.1.2

How can you create multiple columns in a single shape?

Setting Up Columns in a Text Box

PowerPoint enables you to create columns in text boxes to present information you want to set up in lists across the slide but do not want to place in PowerPoint tables. As you enter text or other items into a column, PowerPoint fills up the first column and then wraps text to the next column. Viewers of your presentation may have an easier time reading and remembering lists formatted into multiple columns. You can create columns in any text box, placeholder, or shape. In the following exercise you will change a text box so that it uses two columns.

STEP BY STEP   **Set Up Columns in a Text Box**

USE the *Profit Analysis Boxes* presentation that is still open from the previous exercise.

1. On slide 2, drag the Each division... text box to the bottom of the slide, under the other text box.

2. Click in the text box that contains the list of divisions beginning with Sales.

3. On the Home tab, click the Columns button. A menu appears (see Figure 3-59).

Figure 3-59

Set the text box in two columns

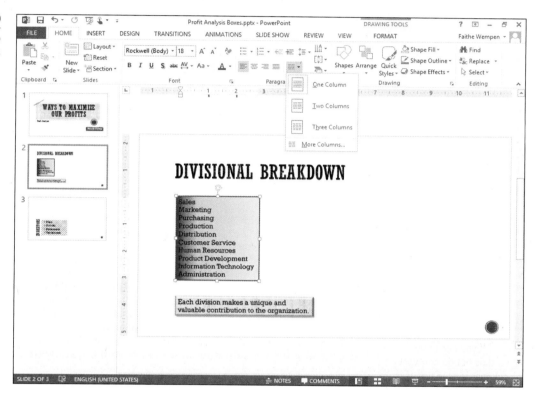

4. Click Two Columns. PowerPoint formats the list of items into two columns. The columns are truncated at this point because the text box is not wide enough.

5. Drag the right border of the text box to the right to widen it enough that two columns can appear side by side with neither one truncated.

6. On the Drawing Tools Format tab, click the Shape Height text box's down-pointing spin arrow, decreasing the shape height until each column contains seven lines of text (see Figure 3-60).

Figure 3-60

Decrease the shape height and increase its width to accommodate the multicolumn list

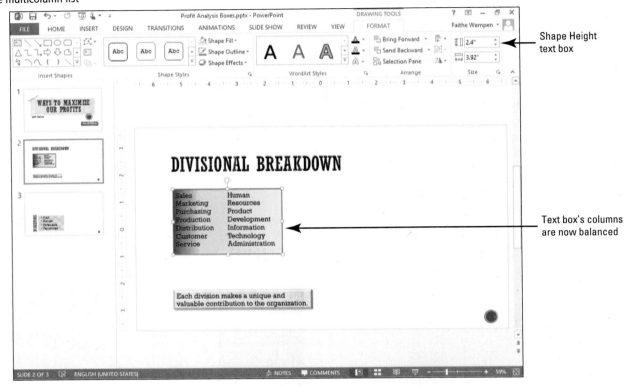

Shape Height text box

Text box's columns are now balanced

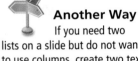

Another Way

If you need two lists on a slide but do not want to use columns, create two text boxes and position them side by side, or switch to a slide layout that contains two side-by-side placeholder boxes.

7. **SAVE** the *Profit Analysis Boxes* presentation.

PAUSE. LEAVE the presentation open to use in the next exercise.

Take Note   If the column choices in the Columns drop-down menu do not meet your needs, click the More Columns option to display the Columns dialog box. Here you can set any number of columns and adjust the spacing between columns.

Aligning Text Boxes on a Slide

In addition to aligning the text within a text box, you can align the text box itself with other objects on the slide, including other text boxes. Doing so ensures that the items on a slide align precisely and neatly with one another when it is appropriate for them to do so. For example, you might have two text boxes side by side, and top-aligning them with one another ensures that the slide's overall appearance is balanced.

STEP BY STEP   **Align Text Boxes**

USE the *Profit Analysis Boxes* presentation that is still open from the previous exercise.

1. On slide 2, click the text box that contains the two column list.
2. Hold down the Shift key and click the text box at the bottom of the slide. It is also selected.
3. On the Drawing Tools Format tab, click the Align Button in the Arrange group. A menu appears (see Figure 3-61).

Figure 3-61

Choose how text boxes should align

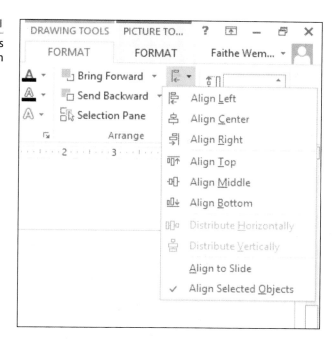

4. Click Align Center. The two text boxes are centered in relation to one another.
5. On the Drawing Tools Format tab, click the Align button again, and click Align to Slide. Nothing changes in the text box placement yet.
6. On the Drawing Tools Format tab, click the Align button again, and click Align Center. Both text boxes become center-aligned in relation to the slide itself.
7. **SAVE** and close the *Profit Analysis Boxes* presentation.

LEAVE PowerPoint open to use in the next exercise.

Take note   The Left, Right, and Center commands on the Align menu refer to horizontal alignment, either in relation to the slide or to other selected content. The Top, Middle, and Bottom commands refer to vertical alignment.

 Workplace Ready _____

PROOFING TOOLS

Even if you are a good typist, errors and inconsistencies can creep into your presentations. The Proofing tools in PowerPoint provide an extra measure of reassurance that an embarrassing typo will not be discovered in the middle of an important meeting.

Can you identify all the proofing errors on the following slide? There are 10 of them, and each of these would be found by the Spelling checker in PowerPoint. If you found all 10, congratulations! If you did not, type this text into PowerPoint exactly as shown here and let PowerPoint identify the errors.

Citiing Sources

When a presntation contains information that is not orignal, it is important to cight the source from which it was derivered. If you do do not, you may be commiting plagarism, which can put youu at risk for legal action.

USING PROOFING TOOLS

The Spelling and Thesaurus features in PowerPoint help you ensure your presentation's text is professionally written and edited, free from spelling errors.

Checking Spelling

The Spelling feature in PowerPoint compares each word in the presentation to its built-in and custom dictionaries, and it flags any words that it does not find plus any instances of repeated words, such as *the the*. You can then evaluate the found words and decide how to proceed with each one. Misspelled words appear with a wavy red underline in the presentation, and you can deal with each one individually by right-clicking it. Alternately, you can open the Spelling dialog box and work through all the possible misspellings at once. In this exercise, you will practice using PowerPoint's Spelling feature using both of those methods.

STEP BY STEP **Check Spelling**

GET READY. To check spelling, perform the following tasks:

1. **OPEN** the *TV Options* presentation and save it as *TV Options Corrected*.
2. On slide 1, notice that the word *Satelite* is misspelled, and that it has a wavy red underline.
3. Right-click the word Satelite. A list of possible spelling corrections appears.
4. In the list, click Satellite (see Figure 3-62). The correction is made.

Figure 3-62

Correct a single misspelled word from the shortcut menu

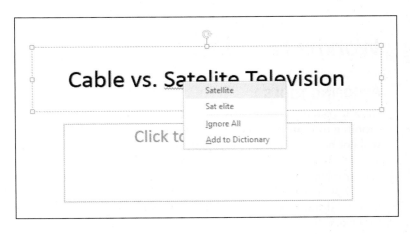

5. On the Review tab, click Spelling in the Proofing group. The Spelling task pane opens, and the Spelling feature finds and flags the next misspelled word (see Figure 3-63). The suggestions list contains only one possible correction.

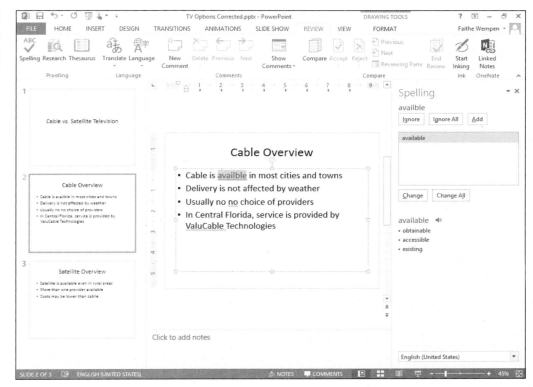

6. Click the Change button to change to the correct spelling of *available*. The next problem identified is a repeated word, *no*.

7. Click the Delete button to delete one of the words *no*. The next problem that appears is a proper name, *ValuCable*, which is actually a correct spelling.

8. Click the Ignore button to ignore the potential misspelling. You could have also clicked Add to add it to the dictionary; but because it is a made-up word for this exercise, Ignore is more appropriate.

9. Click Change to change to the correct spelling of *cable*. A message appears that the spelling check is complete.

10. Click OK to close the dialog box.

11. **SAVE** the presentation.

PAUSE. LEAVE the presentation open for the next exercise.

Use caution with the Change All button because it may make changes you do not intend. For example, if you correct all instances at once where you have typed *pian* instead of *pain*, it will also change all instances of *piano* to *paino*.

Using the Thesaurus

A thesaurus is a reference book or utility that offers suggestions for words that are similar in meaning to the word you are looking up (synonyms) or that are opposite in meaning (antonyms). PowerPoint includes a built-in thesaurus. In the following exercise you will use it to find an alternate word.

STEP BY STEP   **Change a Word with the Thesaurus**

USE the *TV Options Corrected* presentation that is still open from the previous exercise.

1. On slide 3, select the word **Costs**.

2. On the Review tab, click **Thesaurus**. The Thesaurus task pane opens displaying a list of terms related to the word you have selected.

3. In the Thesaurus task pane, hover the mouse pointer over the word Charges. Click the **down arrow** that appears to the right of Charges, then click **Insert** from the menu that appears (see Figure 3-64). The word *Costs* changes to *Charges* on the slide.

Figure 3-64

Find word alternatives with Thesaurus

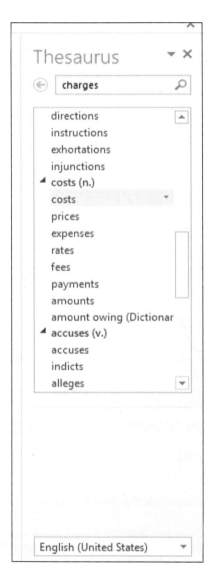

4. In the Thesaurus task pane, click the word **Prices**. The display changes to show synonyms of that word.

5. Click the **Back arrow** in the task pane to return to the list of synonyms for Costs.

SAVE the presentation and **EXIT** PowerPoint.

SKILL SUMMARY

In This Lesson, You Learned How To:	Exam Objective	Objective Number
Format Characters	Apply formatting and styles to text.	3.1.4
Format Paragraphs and Lists	Create bulleted and numbered lists.	3.1.5
Insert and Format WordArt	Change text to WordArt.	3.1.1
Create and Format Text Boxes	Modify shape backgrounds. Create multiple columns in a single shape.	2.2.1 3.1.2
Use Proofing Tools	Proof presentations.	5.3.2

Knowledge Assessment

Fill in the Blank

Fill in each blank with the term or phrase that best completes the statement.

1. A(n) _____ is a container for text on a slide.
2. A(n) _____ is a set of letters, numbers, and symbols in a specific style or design.
3. The _____ feature, when needed, shrinks the size of the text in a text box in order to fit it in the box.
4. A(n) _____ is a symbol that appears to the left of each paragraph in a list.
5. The _____ feature enables you to copy formatting from one block of text to another.
6. _____ text is aligned to both the left and right margins of a text box.
7. A(n) _____ indent is a reverse indent for the first line of a paragraph where the first line is indented less than the other lines.
8. A(n) _____ object is text in the form of a graphic.
9. The _____ in PowerPoint can be used to look up synonyms.
10. To _____ a text box, drag one of its selection handles.

Multiple Choice

Circle the correct answer.

1. You can select a different font from the _____ tab on the Ribbon.
   a. Home
   b. Font
   c. Layout
   d. Review

2. You can select fonts and font sizes either from the Ribbon or the _____.
   a. Status bar
   b. Scroll bar
   c. Mini toolbar
   d. File menu

3. Which of the following is not a paragraph alignment type?
   a. All
   b. Center
   c. Justify
   d. Right

4. When selecting a color, such as from the Font Color button's palette, the colors on the top row are:
   a. standard colors
   b. tints
   c. shades
   d. theme colors

5. Most of PowerPoint's text placeholders automatically format text as a(n) _____ list.
   a. numbered
   b. bulleted
   c. sorted
   d. itemized

6. Reflection is one type of _____ you can apply to WordArt.
   a. effect
   b. font
   c. alignment
   d. spacing

7. A text box's _____ determine(s) how close the text comes to the sides, top, and bottom border of the box.
   a. orientation
   b. margins
   c. padding
   d. alignment

8. To apply a WordArt style to existing text on a slide, you must first:
   a. format the text with a Quick Style
   b. insert a text box
   c. select the text
   d. change the text's alignment

9. What does it mean when a word has a wavy red underline?
   a. The word is inconsistently formatted compared to the surrounding text.
   b. There is a grammar error.
   c. The word is not in the dictionary.
   d. The capitalization does not match that of the surrounding text.

10. A thesaurus enables you to look up synonyms and _____.
    a. alternate spellings
    b. antonyms
    c. translations
    d. pronunciations

Competency Assessment

Project 3-1: Blended Coffees

As director of marketing for Fourth Coffee, you have prepared a product brochure for new company employees. This year's brochure includes a page of new products that you need to format. You will use Quick Styles to format the title and text placeholders. You will also correct a spelling error.

GET READY. LAUNCH PowerPoint if it is not already running.

1. **OPEN** the *Coffee Products* presentation and save it as *Coffee Products Brochure*.
2. Go to slide 2 and click anywhere in the slide title.
3. On the Home tab, click the Quick Styles button to display the Quick Styles gallery.
4. Click the Moderate Effect – Orange, Accent 1 style.
5. Click in any of the product items on slide 2.

6. Click the Quick Styles button.

7. Click the Subtle Effect – Orange, Accent 1 style.

8. Right-click the red-underlined word and select Caffeine as the correct spelling.

9. **SAVE** the presentation and **CLOSE** the file.

LEAVE PowerPoint open for the next project.

Project 3-2: **Typecasting with Typefaces**

As an account representative for Graphic Design Institute, you are responsible for preparing a presentation for potential sponsors. Another employee started a PowerPoint presentation containing a title slide, but when you open the file, you realize that the font choices are not appropriate. You need to modify both the font and size of the slide's text, as well as change the horizontal alignment of the text.

GET READY. LAUNCH PowerPoint if it is not already running.

1. **OPEN** the *Graphic Designs* presentation.

2. On slide 1, select the text Graphic Design Institute.

3. Click the Font drop-down arrow.

4. Click Bodoni MT.

5. Click the Font Size drop-down arrow.

6. Click 60.

7. Click the Center button in the Paragraph group.

8. Click the Format Painter in the Clipboard group.

9. Drag across the subtitle text to change its font and size to the same as the title.

10. With the subtitle text still selected, Click the Font Size drop-down arrow and click 28.

11. Click the Center button in the Paragraph group. Notice that the subtitle is not centered exactly beneath the title; that is because the text boxes for the title and subtitle are different widths.

12. Click in the title text box, and then note the position of its right edge on the slide.

13. Click in the subtitle text box, and then drag its right edge to widen it so it is the same width as the title box.

14. **SAVE** the presentation as *Graphic Designs Final* and **CLOSE** the file.

LEAVE PowerPoint open for the next project.

Proficiency Assessment

Project 3-3: **Destinations**

As the owner and operator of Margie's Travel, you are involved with many aspects of sales, marketing, customer service, and new products and services. Today you want to format the text in a slide presentation that includes new European destinations.

GET READY. LAUNCH PowerPoint if it is not already running.

1. **OPEN** the *New Destinations* presentation.

2. Go to slide 2 and select the slide's title text. Click the Bold button on the Home tab to make the title boldface.

3. Select all the text in the bulleted list. Click the Align Left button to align the list along the left side of the text placeholder.

4. With the list still selected, open the Bullets and Numbering dialog box. Change the bullets' color to Lime, Accent 2, and then resize the bullets so they are 125% of the text's size. Click OK.

5. Click the Font Color drop-down arrow, and then change the list's font color to Lime Accent 2, Lighter 80%.

6. Click Text Box on the Insert tab, and then click in the center of the slide.

7. In the text box, type Companion Flies Free until January 1!.

8. Select the text box you just created, and then on the Home tab, click the Quick Styles button, and then apply the Colored Outline – Lime, Accent 3 Quick Style to the text box.

9. **SAVE** the presentation as *New Destinations Final* and **CLOSE** the file.

LEAVE PowerPoint open for the next project.

Project 3-4: **Business To Business Imports**

You are the lone marketing research person in your company, World Wide Importers. You often find exciting and potentially highly profitable new products that go overlooked by some of the senior staff. You need to draw attention to these products, and PowerPoint can help. Create a short presentation that uses WordArt to jazz up your presentation. This presentation will focus on precision equipment your company can start importing.

GET READY. LAUNCH PowerPoint if it is not already running.

1. **OPEN** the *World Wide Importers* presentation.

2. With slide 1 on the screen (but nothing selected on it), open the WordArt gallery and select Fill – White, Outline – Accent 1, Shadow.

3. In the WordArt text box that appears, type World Wide Importers. Reposition the text box so it is just above the subtitle and centered between the left and right edges of the slide.

4. On the Drawing Tools Format tab, in the WordArt Styles group, open the Text Fill color palette and click Aqua, Accent 1, Darker 25%.

5. Open the Text Effects menu and select the Cool Slant bevel effect. (It is the rightmost style in the first row of the Bevel section.)

6. Go to slide 2 and select all the text in the bulleted list.

7. Change the font size to 24, and then change the line spacing to 1.5.

8. Click the Numbering button to convert the list into a numbered list.

9. Go to slide 3. Insert a text box under the slide's title. Type the following items into the text box, putting each item on its own line:
   Digital controls
   Heat sensors
   Laser guides
   Light sensors
   Motion detectors
   Pressure monitors
   Regulators
   Timing systems

10. Select all the text in the text box and change the font size to 24.

11. On the Home tab, open the Quick Styles gallery and click Colored Fill – Gray 50%, Accent 4.

12. **SAVE** the presentation as *World Wide Importers Final*, and then **CLOSE** the file.

LEAVE PowerPoint open for the next project.

Mastery Assessment

Project 3-5: Pop Quiz

As an instructor at the School of Fine Art, you decide to use a slide show to give beginning students the first pop quiz on art history. You need to finish the presentation by formatting the text and removing some unneeded text boxes.

GET READY. LAUNCH PowerPoint if it is not already running.

1. **OPEN** the *Art History* presentation.
2. On slides 2, 3, and 4, do each of the following:
   a. Format the slide's title with the Intense Effect – Dark Blue, Dark 1 Quick Style.
   b. Convert the bulleted list of answers into a numbered list.
   c. Delete the text box (containing the correct answer) at the bottom of each slide.
3. **SAVE** the presentation as *Art History Final*, and then **CLOSE** the file.

LEAVE PowerPoint open for the next project.

Project 3-6: Graphic Design Drafts

As the account representative that prepared the Graphic Design Institute slide, you want to make sure that nobody uses this presentation before it is approved. To protect against someone inadvertently printing the slide, you need to add a text box across the entire slide that labels the slide as a "Draft."

GET READY. LAUNCH PowerPoint if it is not already running.

1. **OPEN** the *Graphic Designs Final* presentation you completed in Project 3-2.
2. **SAVE** the presentation as *Graphic Designs Draft*.
3. Add a text box at the top of slide 1, and type DRAFT into the text box.
4. Rotate the text box at a 45-degree angle, and then place it in the center of the slide, on top of the existing text.
5. Enlarge the text to 88 points. Resize the text box if needed by dragging its sizing handles so the text fits properly inside the box.
6. Using Text Effects on the Drawing Tools Format tab, apply the Orange, 18 point glow, Accent Color 3 glow effect to the text.
7. **SAVE** and **CLOSE** the presentation.

EXIT PowerPoint.

4 Designing a Presentation

LESSON SKILL MATRIX

Skill	Exam Objective	Objective Number
Formatting Presentations with Themes and Layouts	Modify presentation themes.	1.2.7
Changing Slide Backgrounds	Modify slide backgrounds.	2.1.5
Inserting a Date, Footer, and Slide Numbers	Control slide numbers.	1.2.5
	Insert headers and footers.	1.2.6
Linking to Web Pages and Other Programs	Insert hyperlinks.	3.1.3
Working with Sections	Insert section headers.	2.3.1
Customizing Slide Masters	Apply a slide master.	1.2.1
	Modify existing layouts.	1.2.3
	Add background images.	1.2.4
	Add new layouts.	1.2.2
	Add slide layouts.	2.1.1

KEY TERMS

- action
- action button
- font theme
- footer
- header
- hyperlink
- layout
- layout master
- live preview
- section
- slide master
- target
- theme

©bjones27/iStockphoto

140

©bjones27/iStockphoto

Southridge Video is a small company that offers video services to the community, such as videography for special events, video editing services, and duplication and conversion services. As a sales representative for Southridge Video, you often present information on the company to those who are considering the use of professional-level video services. In this lesson, you will add design elements to a simple presentation to polish and improve its appearance. You will also learn how to break down a presentation into sections and to customize slide masters to make global changes to a presentation.

SOFTWARE ORIENTATION

Microsoft PowerPoint's Themes and Variants

PowerPoint offers dozens of unique themes and variants you can apply to presentations to format the slides with colors, fonts, effects, and backgrounds. Figure 4-1 shows the Design tab with the Variants gallery open showing access to the Colors, Fonts, Effects, and Background Styles commands.

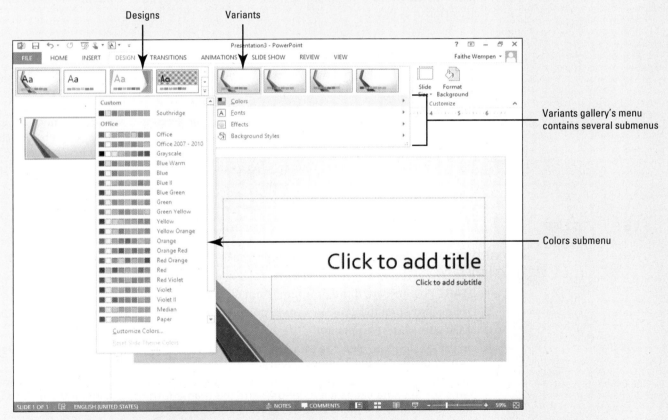

Figure 4-1
The Design tab

Use PowerPoint's built-in themes to give your presentation a polished, professional look without a lot of trial and error. You can preview a theme by pointing at it in the Themes gallery, and then apply it to the presentation by clicking it. After you have chosen a theme, you can select one of its variants from the Variants gallery.

FORMATTING PRESENTATIONS WITH THEMES
AND LAYOUTS

The Bottom Line

A PowerPoint **theme** includes a set of colors designed to work well together, a set of fonts (one for headings and one for body text), special effects that can be applied to objects such as pictures or shapes, and often a graphic background. The theme also controls the layout of placeholders on each slide. Use a theme to quickly apply a unified look to one or more slides in a presentation (or to the entire presentation). You can also modify a theme and save your changes as a new custom theme.

Slide **layouts** control the position of text and objects on an individual slide. For each slide, you can select a layout according to the content you need to add to it.

PowerPoint makes it easy to see how a theme will look on your slides by offering a **live preview**: As you move the mouse pointer over each theme in the gallery, that theme's formats display on the current slide. This formatting feature takes a great deal of guesswork out of the design process—if you don't like a theme's appearance, just move the pointer to a different theme or click outside the gallery to restore the previous appearance.

Clicking a theme applies it to all slides in a presentation. You can also apply a theme to a single slide or a selection of slides by making the selection, right-clicking the theme, and choosing Apply to Selected Slides.

A theme differs from a template in that it contains no sample content—only formatting specifications.

Applying a Theme and Variant to a Presentation

In this exercise, you will learn how to select a theme from the Themes gallery to replace the default blank design and create a more visually appealing design for your PowerPoint presentations.

New in PowerPoint 2013 — you can apply a variant after selecting a theme. Variants are available only in the new themes and templates that come with PowerPoint 2013. The most obvious change that a variant makes is to apply different colors, but some variants also make other changes too, such as a different background graphic. You can select a variant from the Variants group on the Design tab.

STEP BY STEP   **Apply a Theme and Variant to a Presentation**

GET READY. Before you begin these steps, make sure that your computer is on. Log on, if necessary.

1. **START** PowerPoint, if the program is not already running.
2. Locate and open the *Special Events* presentation and save it as *Special Events Final*.
3. Make sure slide 1 is selected.
4. On the Design tab, click the More button in the Themes group. PowerPoint's available themes display in the Themes gallery.
5. Point to any of the themes in the gallery. Notice that a ScreenTip displays the theme's name (or in some cases file location), and the theme formats are instantly applied to the slide behind the gallery. (See Figure 4-2.)

Figure 4-2

The Themes gallery

6. **Right-click** the **Slice theme**; a pop-up menu appears. In the menu, click **Apply to Selected Slides**. The Slice theme is applied only to slide 1.

7. Click the **More button** again in the Themes group to reopen the Themes gallery.

8. **Right-click** the **Ion theme**, and click **Apply to All Slides** to apply it to all slides.

9. Scroll through the **slides** to see how the theme has supplied new colors, fonts, bullet symbols, and layouts.

10. On the Design tab, click the **purple thumbnail image** in the Variants group. The colors change on all slides to reflect the chosen variant. Slide 1 should resemble Figure 4-3.

Figure 4-3

Ion theme applied to all slides
in the presentation

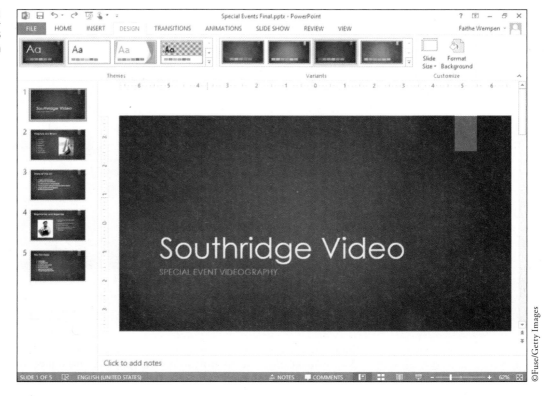

11. **SAVE** the presentation.

PAUSE. LEAVE the presentation open to use in the next exercise.

Take Note   You can display the name of the current theme on the status bar if you'd like. To do so, right-click the status bar and click Theme.

CERTIFICATION READY?   **1.2.7**

How do you modify a presentation's theme?

Changing Theme Colors

If you do not like the colors used in the theme you have chosen, you can change them. One way to do so is to choose a different variant, as you saw in the previous exercise. You can also select a different color theme, or you can create your own color theme. When you apply a different color theme, your current theme fonts, background graphics, and effects remain the same—only the colors change. In this exercise, you will choose a different color theme for a presentation.

STEP BY STEP   **Change Theme Colors**

USE the *Special Events Final* presentation that is still open from the previous exercise.

1. Click the More button in the Variants group, and then point to Colors. A menu appears containing the available color themes.
2. Move the pointer over some of the color themes to see the live preview of those colors on the current slide (see Figure 4-4).
3. Click the Blue Warm color theme. The new colors are applied to the presentation.

Figure 4-4

Apply a different color theme to the presentation

Select a color theme

©Fuse/Getty Images

4. Click the More button again in the Variants group, point to Colors, and then click Customize Colors at the bottom of the gallery. The dialog box opens to allow you to replace colors in the current color palette.

5. Click the **drop-down arrow** next to the color designated for Hyperlink.

6. Click **White, Text 1** on the Theme Colors palette to change the color for Hyperlinks to white (see Figure 4-5).

Figure 4-5

The Create New Theme Colors dialog box

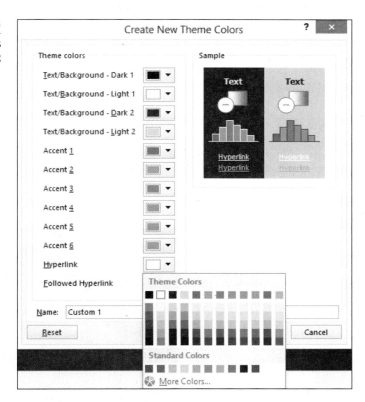

7. Select the **text** in the Name box and type **Southridge** in its place.

8. Click **Save** to save the new theme colors.

9. **SAVE** the presentation.

PAUSE. LEAVE the presentation open to use in the next exercise.

To create a unique appearance you can choose new colors for theme elements in the Create New Theme Colors dialog box. This dialog box displays the theme's color palette and shows you to which element each color applies. A preview area shows the colors in use; as you change colors, the preview changes to show how the new colors work together. If you do not like the choices you have made, use the Reset button on the Create New Theme Colors dialog box to restore the default colors.

You can save a new color theme to make it available for use with any theme. Saved color themes display at the top of the Theme Colors gallery in the Custom section.

Changing Theme Fonts

Each theme supplies a combination of two fonts to be applied to headings and body. Collectively these two fonts are called a **font theme**. A font theme may have two different fonts—one for headings and one for body text—or the same font for both. In the following exercise, you will choose a different font theme for a presentation.

Change Theme Fonts

USE the *Special Events Final* presentation that is still open from the previous exercise.

1. Click the **More button** in the Variants group, and then point to **Fonts**. A gallery displays showing font combinations for all available themes.

2. Move the **pointer** over some of the font combinations to see the live preview of those fonts on the current slide.

3. Click the **Candara font theme** (see Figure 4-6). The new fonts are applied to the presentation.

Figure 4-6

Choose a new font theme

Select a font theme

©Fuse/Getty Images

4. **SAVE** the presentation.

PAUSE. LEAVE the presentation open to use in the next exercise.

PowerPoint supplies a wide variety of font combinations to allow you to choose among traditional *serif fonts* and contemporary *sans serif* fonts. A serif is a tail or flourish on the edges of each letter, such as the tiny vertical lines hanging off the top edges of a capital T. *Sans* in sans serif is Latin for "without." It means the font does not have a "tail" or flourish on the edge of each letter. The body text in this book uses a serif font; the headings use a sans serif font. The choice you make depends a great deal on the subject of your presentation and the impression you are trying to convey with your slides.

As with theme colors, you can select your own theme fonts and save them to be available to apply to any theme. Click Customize Fonts at the bottom of the Theme Fonts gallery, select a heading font and body font, and then save the combination with a new name.

Applying a Different Slide Layout

The slide layout gallery shows the available layouts in the theme you have applied. If more than one theme is in use in the presentation (e.g., if you applied a different theme to only selected slides), the slide layout gallery shows available layouts from all themes in use so you can pick and choose among a greater variety of layout options. In this exercise, you will choose a different layout for a slide.

STEP BY STEP   **Applying a Different Slide Layout**

USE the *Special Events Final* presentation that is still open from the previous exercise.

1. Click the Home tab on the Ribbon.
2. Go to slide 5 and click New Slide in the Slides group. (Click the graphical part of the button, not the button's text.) PowerPoint adds a new slide with the same layout as slide 5, Title and Content.
3. Type the title Contact Information.
4. Type the following information as the first bullet point in the text placeholder:

   457 Gray Road

   North Hills, OH 45678

Take Note   Use Shift+Enter after typing *Road* to start a new line without starting a new paragraph.

5. Type these additional bullet points:

   Phone: (513) 555-6543

   Fax: (513) 555-5432

6. Select the entire bulleted list, and then click the Bullets button on the Home tab to turn off the bullets. Then click away from the text box to deselect the selection. Your slide should look like Figure 4-7.

Figure 4-7

Add contact information to the slide

Bullets button

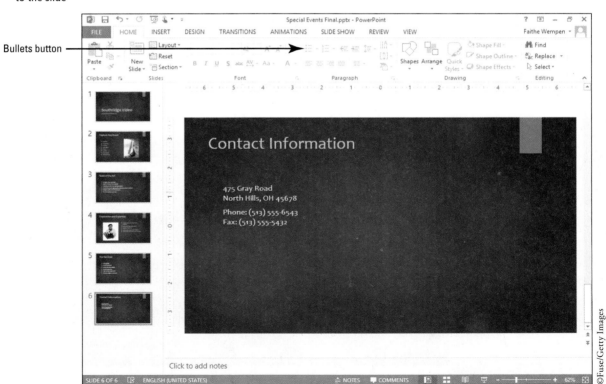

7. On the Home tab, click the Layout button in the Slides group to display the slide layout gallery shown in Figure 4-8.

Figure 4-8

Slide layout gallery

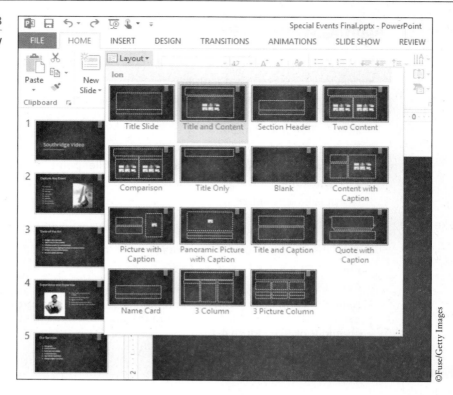

8. Click Two Content to change the layout to two side-by-side content placeholders.

9. In the second placeholder, type the following:

Directions: From I-261 East, take exit 205 South (Crawfordsville Road) to Gray Road. Turn left on Gray Road, and look for us on your left after 2 miles.

10. Click anywhere in the text you just typed, and then click the Bullets button on the Home tab to turn off the bullet. Click away from the text box to deselect it. Your slide should look similar to Figure 4-9.

Figure 4-9

The completed slide

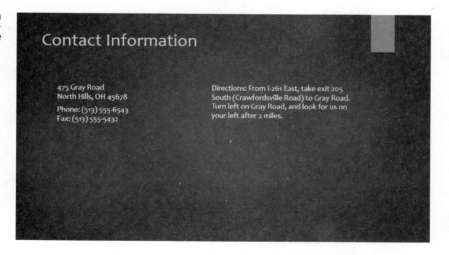

11. SAVE the presentation.

PAUSE. LEAVE the presentation open to use in the next exercise.

The layouts that appear in the slide layout gallery depend on the layouts stored in the Slide Master, which you will learn about later in this lesson.

CHANGING SLIDE BACKGROUNDS

The Bottom Line

Themes provide a default background for all slides formatted with that theme. To customize a theme or draw attention to one or more slides you can apply a different background.

Selecting a Theme Background

CERTIFICATION READY? 2.1.5

How do you modify the slide background?

The Background Styles gallery allows you to choose from plain, light, or dark backgrounds and gradient backgrounds that gradually change from light to dark. Background colors are determined by the theme. Some background styles include graphic effects such as fine lines or textures that cover the entire background. Use the Background Styles gallery to quickly apply a different solid-color or gradient background based on theme colors. You can apply a background to one or more selected slides or to all slides in the presentation. In this exercise, you will select a background style from the preset backgrounds provided by the theme, and then customize it with the Format Background task pane.

STEP BY STEP | **Select a Theme Background**

USE the *Special Events Final* presentation that is still open from the previous exercise.

1. Go to slide 6 if it is not already selected.
2. On the Design tab, click the More button in the Variants group and then point to Background Styles. A gallery (see Figure 4-10) displays some background styles created using the theme's designated background colors.

Take Note Hover the mouse on a background style to see its name and preview it on the current slide.

Figure 4-10

Background Styles gallery

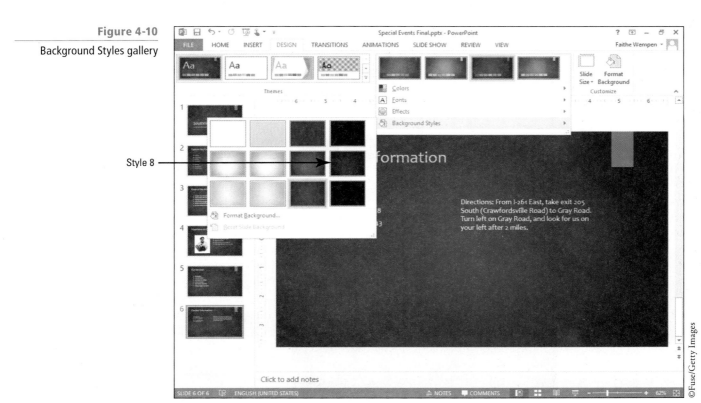

©Fuse/Getty Images

3. Right-click Style 8, then click Apply to Selected Slides. The background style is applied to slide 6 only.

4. SAVE the presentation.

PAUSE. LEAVE the presentation open to use in the next exercise.

The area of the slide that is considered to be "background" can change depending on the theme. For example, some themes have graphics overlaid on a colored background, so that your choice of background color peeks through in only a few spots.

Another Way
Display the Format Background task pane by right-clicking any blank area of the slide background and then clicking Format Background from the shortcut menu. Or, from the Background Styles gallery (used in the previous exercise), click Format Background.

Customize the Background

The same background options that you learned about in Lesson 3 for text boxes also apply to slide backgrounds. Use the Format Background task pane to create and modify any background, even a default theme background. You can apply a solid color or gradient fill, or select a picture or texture for the background. Options for each of these fill types allow you to modify the fill to suit your needs.

STEP BY STEP   **Customize the Background**

USE the *Special Events Final* presentation that is still open from the previous exercise.

1. With slide 6 still active, click the Format Background button on the Design tab. The Format Background task pane opens. A gradient fill is selected because the style you selected in the previous exercise was a gradient.

2. Click the Type drop-down arrow, and then in the drop-down list, click the Linear preset (see Figure 4-11). The slide background changes to a different gradient type.

Figure 4-11

Format Background task pane with gradient controls

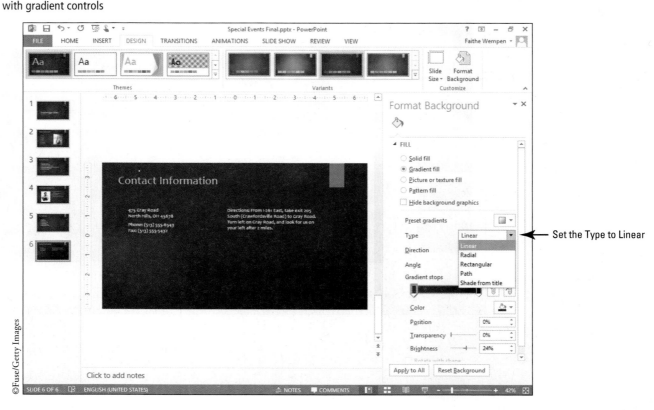

©Fuse/Getty Images

3. Click the Solid Fill option button. The controls change to those for solid colors.

4. Click the Color drop-down arrow and in the gallery that appears, click Dark Purple, Background 2, Darker 50% (the third color in the bottom row of the Theme Colors section).

5. Drag the Transparency slider to 20% or type 20 in the Transparency text box. The fill lightens because it is now partly transparent (see Figure 4-12).

Figure 4-12

Options for solid-color background fills

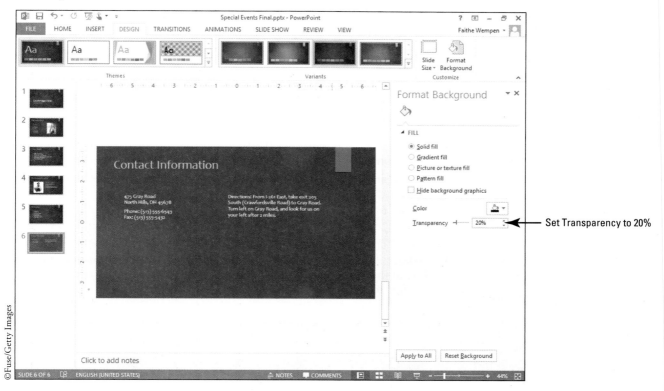

Set Transparency to 20%

©Fuse/Getty Images

Another Way

If you had wanted to apply the new background to all the slides, you could have clicked Apply to All before closing the task pane in step 12.

6. Click Picture or texture fill. The controls change to those for pictures and textures.

7. Click the Texture drop-down arrow, and then click the Green Marble texture.

8. Click Pattern Fill. The controls change to those for patterns.

9. Open the Foreground Color drop-down list and click Dark Purple, Background 2 (the third color in the top row of the Theme Colors section).

10. Open the Background Color drop-down list and click Teal, Accent 5 (next-to-last color in the top row of the Theme Colors section).

11. Click the 90% pattern (the last pattern in the second row).

12. In the Format Background task pane, click Reset Background. The background returns to its original state specified by the theme and variant in use.

13. **CLOSE** the Format Background task pane.

14. **SAVE** the presentation.

PAUSE. LEAVE the presentation open to use in the next exercise.

For any background choice, you can increase transparency to "wash out" the background so it does not overwhelm your text. For a solid color, you might increase its transparency. For a gradient fill background, you can adjust the gradient by adding or removing colors. By default, a new slide background created in the Format Background task pane applies only to the current slide. Click the Apply to All button to apply the background to the entire presentation.

INSERTING A DATE, FOOTER, AND SLIDE NUMBERS

The Bottom Line

Adding a date, footer, and slide numbers to a presentation can help you identify and organize slides. In this exercise, you will learn how to apply these useful elements to one or more slides.

CERTIFICATION READY? **1.2.5**

How do you control slide numbers?

CERTIFICATION READY? **1.2.6**

How do you insert headers and footers?

Inserting a Date, Footer, and Slide Numbers

A **footer** is text that repeats at the bottom of each slide in a presentation (or in whatever location on the slide where the footer placeholder is located). Use a footer to record the slide title, company name, or other important information that you want the audience to keep in mind as they view the slides. In this exercise, you will apply a footer, a date, and slide numbers to a PowerPoint presentation.

STEP BY STEP **Insert a Date, Footer, and Slide Numbers**

USE the *Special Events Final* presentation that is still open from the previous exercise.

1. Click the Insert tab, and then click the Header & Footer button. The Header and Footer dialog box opens.
2. Click the Date and time check box, and then click Update automatically if it is not already selected.
3. Click to select the Slide number check box.
4. Click the Footer check box, and then type Special Events in the text box below the check box.
5. Click the Don't show on title slide check box. The dialog box should resemble Figure 4-13 at this point. The date will be today's date rather than the date shown in Figure 4-13.

Figure 4-13

Header and Footer dialog box

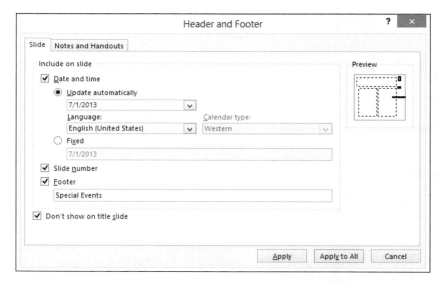

6. Click the Apply to All button to apply the date, footer, and slide number to all slides except the title slide. Slide 6 should look similar to Figure 4-14. In this particular theme, the footer and date appear vertically along the right side of the slide, and the slide number appears in the colored box in the upper right corner.

Take Note   The footer placeholder box is not always at the bottom of the slide; it can be anywhere on the slide, depending on the layout. For example, in Figure 4-14 it is along the right side.

Figure 4-14

A slide number, footer, and date on a slide

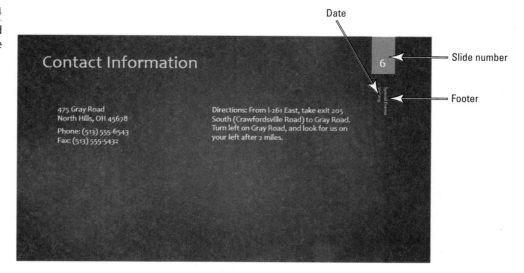

7. Click the Design tab, and move the mouse over several different themes in the Themes group. Notice that the placement of the slide number, footer, and date change with different themes. In many of the themes, these elements appear at the bottom of the slide.

8. **SAVE** the presentation.

PAUSE. LEAVE the presentation open to use in the next exercise.

Another Way
You can also open the Header and Footer dialog box by clicking the Date & Time button or the Slide Number button on the Insert tab, in the Text group.

You have two choices when inserting a date: a date that automatically updates by changing to the current date each time the presentation is opened or a fixed date, which stays the same until you decide to change it. If it is important to indicate when slides were created or presented, use a fixed date.

You may have noticed that the Header and Footer dialog box has another tab, the Notes and Handouts tab. When you create notes, pages, and handouts, you can specify a **header** to appear at the top of every page. A header is repeated text, much like a footer, except it appears at the top of each printed page. Headers do not appear onscreen in Slide Show view—only on printouts. You can also create footers for notes pages and handouts.

Cross Ref

You will work with handouts in Lesson 11.

LINKING TO WEB PAGES AND OTHER PROGRAMS

The Bottom Line

You can set up **hyperlinks** (clickable shortcuts) on slides that allow you to jump to a specific slide in the presentation or to external content. Hyperlinks can be displayed as either text or a graphic.

CERTIFICATION READY? **3.1.3**

How do you insert a hyperlink?

Adding a Text Hyperlink

Use the Insert Hyperlink dialog box to set up links between slides or from slides to other targets. (The **target** is the page, file, or slide that opens when you click a link.) If you select text before inserting the hyperlink, that text will become the link that can be clicked. If you select a graphic before inserting the hyperlink, the hyperlink will be attached to the graphic, so that clicking it activates the hyperlink. In this exercise, you will create a text hyperlink.

STEP BY STEP   **Add a Text Hyperlink**

USE the *Special Events Final* presentation that is still open from the previous exercise.

1. Go to slide 6, position the insertion point at the end of the fax number, and press Enter to start a new paragraph. Then type Visit our website.

2. Select the text you just typed, and then click the Hyperlink button on the Insert tab. The Insert Hyperlink dialog box opens.

3. Click in the Address box and type http://www.southridgevideo.com as the target of the link text (see Figure 4-15).

Figure 4-15

The Insert Hyperlink dialog box

The text you selected on the slide appears here

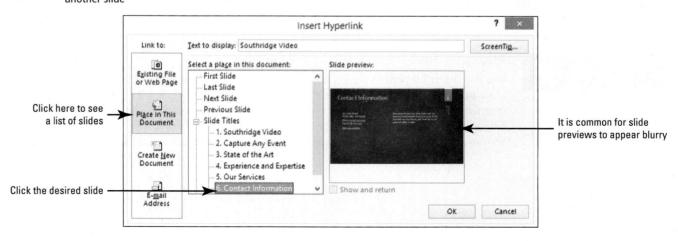

Type the address the hyperlink refers to here

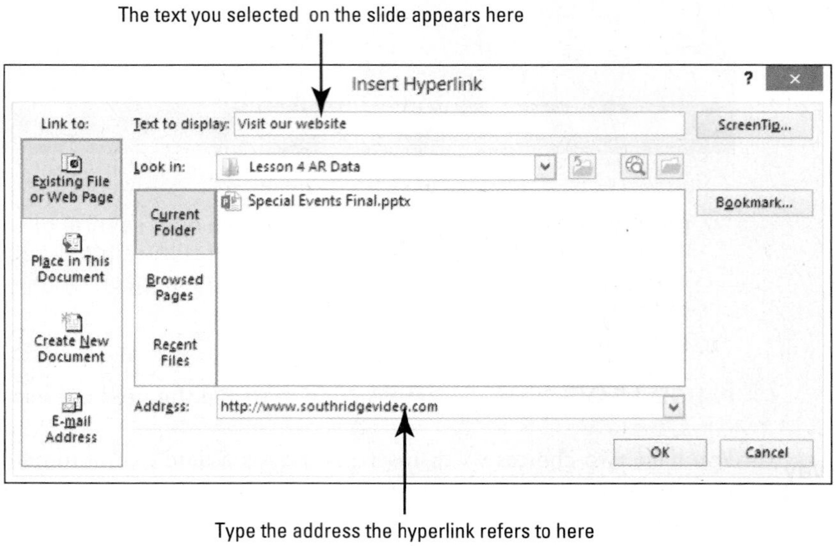

4. Click OK. The website address is formatted with the theme's hyperlink color and an underline.

5. Go to slide 1, and select Southridge Video.

6. Click the Hyperlink button on the Insert tab. The Insert Hyperlink dialog box opens.

7. In the Link To list on the left side of the dialog box, click Place in This Document. A list of slides from the current presentation appears.

8. Click 6. Contact Information (see Figure 4-16).

Figure 4-16

Creating a hyperlink to another slide

Click here to see a list of slides

Click the desired slide

It is common for slide previews to appear blurry

9. Click OK; PowerPoint identifies slide 6 as the target for this hyperlink.
10. **SAVE** the presentation.

PAUSE. LEAVE the presentation open to use in the next exercise.

You can create links to a number of different types of targets using the Insert Hyperlink dialog box.

- Choose **Existing File or Web Page** to link to any web page or any file on your system or network. Use the Look in box, the Browse the Web button, the Browse for File button to locate the desired page or file, or type the URL or path in the Address box.
- Choose **Place in This Document** to display a list of the current presentation's slides and custom shows. Click the slide or custom show that you want to display when the link is clicked.
- Choose **Create New Document** to create a link to a new document. You supply the path and the name for the new document and then choose whether to add content to the document now or later.
- Choose **E-mail Address** to type an e-mail address to which you want to link.

You can add hyperlinks to a slide in Normal view, but the links will work only in Slide Show view.

Adding a Graphical Hyperlink

Hyperlinks can be attached to graphics so that when you click the graphic, the hyperlink executes. In this exercise, you will make an existing graphic into a hyperlink.

STEP BY STEP | **Add a Graphical Hyperlink**

USE the *Special Events Final* presentation that is still open from the previous exercise.

1. Go to slide 4, and click the photo to select it.
2. Press Ctrl+K to open the Insert Hyperlink dialog box. (Ctrl+K is a keyboard shortcut for the Insert Hyperlink command you used previously.)
3. Click Place in This Document. A list of slides from the current presentation appears.
4. Click 6. Contact Information.
5. Click OK.
6. **SAVE** the presentation.

PAUSE. LEAVE the presentation open to use in the next exercise.

Another Way
You can also right-click a graphic and choose Hyperlink to open the Insert Hyperlink dialog box.

If you need to change a link's target, click anywhere in the link, and then click the Hyperlink button, or right-click it and click Edit Hyperlink. The Edit Hyperlink dialog box opens, offering the same functionality as the Insert Hyperlink dialog box. You can remove a link by right-clicking the link and selecting Remove Hyperlink from the shortcut menu.

Adding an Action to a Slide

Use **actions** to perform tasks such as jumping to a new slide or starting a different program. Actions can be applied to text or shapes such as **action buttons**. An action button is a shape from the Shapes gallery to which you can assign a hyperlink or some other action. (You can assign actions to any object, not just an action button. However, action buttons are specifically designed for that purpose.)

Besides allowing you to set up links to specific slides or files, you can use action settings to run a particular program, run a macro, or perform an action with an object such as an embedded Excel worksheet. You can also play a sound from a list of default sounds or any sound file on your system.

STEP BY STEP   Add an Action to a Slide

USE the *Special Events Final* presentation that is still open from the previous exercise.

Another Way
The Shapes button is also available on the Home tab, in the Drawing group.

1. Go to slide 5.
2. Click the Shapes button on the Insert tab to display a gallery of drawing shapes.
3. Click the Action Button: Information shape (in the middle of the last row of shapes in the Action Buttons section, see Figure 4-17).

Figure 4-17

Create an information action button

Action Button: Information shape

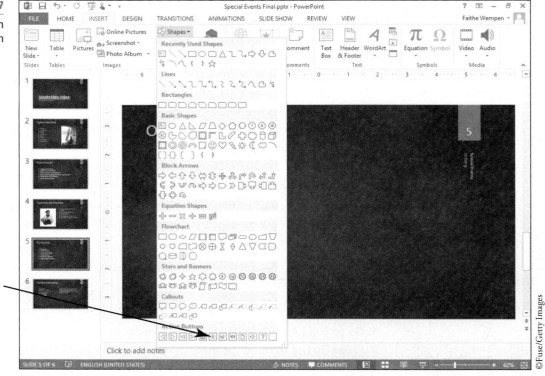

4. The pointer changes to a crosshair. Click near the bottom right corner of the slide to draw the button there at its default size. As soon as you release the mouse button, the Action Settings dialog box opens.
5. Click Hyperlink to, and then click the drop-down arrow of the text box below it.
6. Scroll to the bottom of the list of possible link targets and click Other File (see Figure 4-18). The Hyperlink to Other File dialog box opens.

Another Way
If you drag to draw the button instead of clicking, you can make it any size you like.

Figure 4-18

Choose to hyperlink to another file

Click Hyperlink to...

...and choose Other File

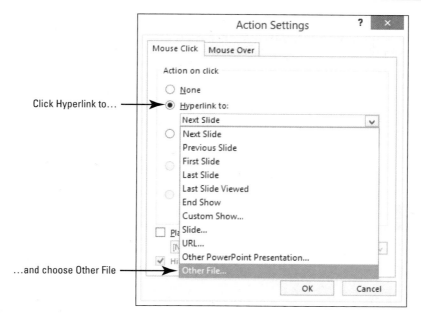

7. Navigate to the data files for this lesson, click the *Service Fees* file, and then click OK to apply your selection and return to the Action Settings dialog box.
8. Click OK again to close the Action Settings dialog box.
9. **SAVE** the presentation.

PAUSE. LEAVE the presentation open to use in the next exercise.

The Action Settings dialog box has two tabs that contain identical options. The default tab, Mouse Click, offers actions that will occur when you click the mouse pointer on the action item, such as the action button you drew in this exercise. The Mouse Over tab offers actions that will occur when you move the mouse pointer over the action item. It is therefore possible to attach two different actions to the same item. For example, you can specify that an action button will play a sound if you rest the mouse pointer on it and display a new slide if you click it.

Testing Links in a Slide Show

Hyperlinks and action buttons work only in Slide Show view, so you must enter Slide Show view in order to test them. In this exercise, you will enter Slide Show view and test hyperlinks.

STEP BY STEP   **Test Links in a Slide Show**

USE the *Special Events Final* presentation that is still open from the previous exercise.

1. **SAVE** the presentation and then press F5 to start the slide show from slide 1.
2. On slide 1, click the underlined Southridge Video text. The show jumps to slide 6.
3. Right-click, and on the menu that appears, choose Last Viewed to return to slide 1.
4. Click the mouse button three times to advance to slide 4, and then click the photo. The show jumps to slide 6.
5. Right-click, and on the menu that appears, choose Last Viewed to return to slide 4.
6. Click the mouse button to advance to slide 5, and then click the Information button. If a security warning appears, click Yes to continue. A spreadsheet opens in Excel.
7. **CLOSE** Excel without making or saving any changes.
8. If the slide show is not active (full screen), switch back to it using the Windows taskbar.

Another Way
You can also enter Slide Show view by clicking the Slide Show tab, and clicking the Start Slide Show group and clicking From Beginning.

9. Press **Esc** to end the slide show or click one more time.

10. **CLOSE** the presentation, saving your changes to it.

PAUSE. LEAVE PowerPoint open to use in the next exercise.

When you activate links or actions during a slide show, the target of the link or action is displayed in the full screen, like the slides in the slide show. After working with the external content, if the slide show does not automatically reappear as the active application, you can return to the slide show by selecting it from the taskbar in Windows.

WORKING WITH SECTIONS

The Bottom Line

To organize a long presentation, you can create **sections**, which are dividers that group slides into logical clusters, as folders organize groups of related papers. You can then work with the sections rather than with individual slides, moving or deleting an entire section as a group.

Creating Sections

You can create sections that organize the slides for easier management. This organization is especially useful in a lengthy presentation that covers multiple topics; each topic can be a section. In this exercise, you create some sections and then use them to manipulate content.

STEP BY STEP   **Create Sections**

USE the *Blue Yonder Introduction* presentation.

1. Locate and open the *Blue Yonder Introduction* presentation and save it as *Blue Yonder Sections*.

2. Go to **slide 2**. In the navigation pane on the left, **right-click** slide 2 and click **Add Section** from the menu that appears (see Figure 4-19). A new section bar labeled Untitled Section appears in the Navigation pane above slide 2, indicating that the new section begins with that slide.

Figure 4-19

Add a section

Right-click the slide the section should begin with →

Click Add Section →

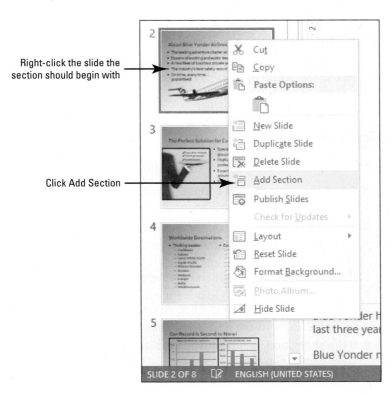

3. Go to slide 5. In the Navigation pane, right-click slide 5 and click Add Section. Another new section (also labeled Untitled Section) appears above slide 5 in the Navigation pane. Repeat these actions to create another new section above slide 7.

4. Click the Untitled Section bar above slide 2. Slides 2, 3, and 4 become selected.

5. Right-click the Untitled Section bar you just clicked and choose Rename Section from the menu that appears. The Rename Section dialog box opens.

6. Type Introduction in the Section name box (see Figure 4-20), and click Rename.

Figure 4-20

Rename a section

7. Rename the other two sections, Detail and Conclusion, using the same actions you used in steps 4-6.

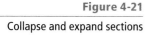

8. Right-click the Detail section heading in the Navigation pane and click Move Section Up to move that section to appear before the Introduction section.

9. Right-click the Detail section heading again and click Move Section Down. The Detail section moves back to its original location.

10. Right-click the Introduction section heading in the Navigation pane and click Collapse All. All the sections collapse in the Navigation pane.

11. Double-click the Conclusion section heading. That section is expanded so you can see the individual slides in it (see Figure 4-21).

Figure 4-21

Collapse and expand sections

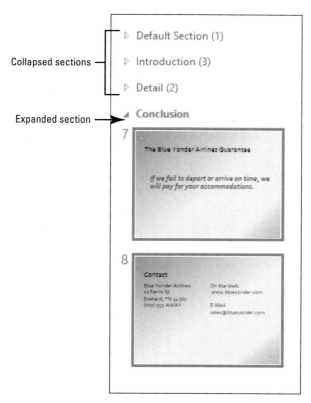

12. Right-click the Conclusion section and click Remove Section. The section heading is removed, but the slides remain; they are added to the Detail section.

13. Right-click either of the remaining section headings and choose Expand All.

14. Click the Introduction section heading to select it, and then on the Design tab, click the More button in the Variants group and point to Background Styles. On the Background Styles palette that appears, right-click Style 1 (the white background) and click Apply to Selected Slides. Only the slides in the selected section change their background color.

15. **SAVE** the presentation and **CLOSE** it.

PAUSE. LEAVE PowerPoint open to use in the next exercise.

Sections offer an easy way of selecting groups of slides, so you can move them, format them, or even delete them. To delete an entire section, right-click the section header and click Remove Section & Slides. In the preceding exercise, you removed a section but kept the slides. Sections also enable you to rearrange groups of slides easily, by moving a section up or down in order.

Sections are invisible to the audience when you present a slide show. If you want to make it more obvious that you have organized the presentation into sections, you may wish to insert summary slides at the beginning or end of each section.

SOFTWARE ORIENTATION

PowerPoint's Slide Master View

Slide Master view (see Figure 4-22) provides tools for modifying the master slides, on which all of the current presentation's layouts and formats are based. You can modify the slide master itself, or any of the individual layout masters subordinate to it.

Figure 4-22
Slide Master view

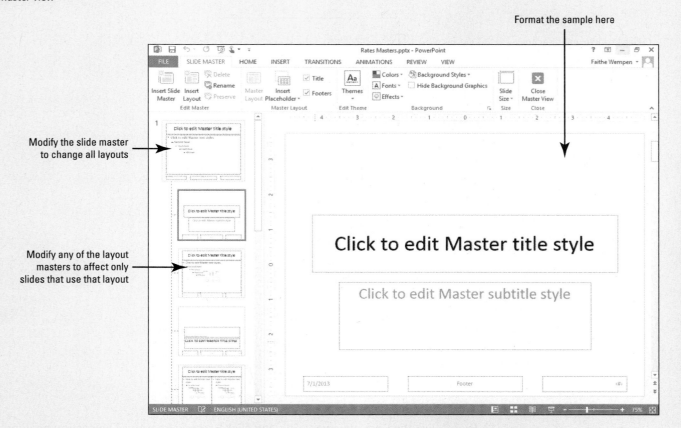

Use the tools on the Slide Master tab and the slide in the Navigation pane to customize formats that will apply to all slides in a presentation. If you make changes to the topmost slide in the left pane, the changes apply to all layouts. If you click a specific layout below it to change, the changes apply to all slides that use that layout.

Workplace Ready

ENSURING CONSISTENCY WITH SLIDE MASTERS

When multiple people in the same company or department create business materials with Power-Point, it can be a challenge to keep them consistent in their font, color, and layout choices. A slide master can help by providing a common template from which everyone can start.

For example, some companies require all employees to use very specific fonts and shades of colors in all company-related materials. Rather than having to set up the specific fonts and colors each time in each new presentation you create, you can set up the colors once in a slide master, and then save the presentation as a template file. You can then start new presentations based on that template.

A template file can contain multiple slide masters, so a company can provide a single template file to employees that contains all the slide masters they will need to create PowerPoint presentations that conform to the company's official standards.

CUSTOMIZING SLIDE MASTERS

The Bottom Line

The **slide master** for a presentation stores information on the current theme, layout of placehold-ers, bullet characters, and other formats that affect all slides in a presentation. If you want to make design changes that will apply to many or all slides in a presentation, you can save a great deal of time by modifying the slide master rather than applying changes on each slide. Slide Master view makes it easy to change formats globally for a presentation by displaying the slide master and all layouts available in the current presentation. Customizing a slide master makes it easy to apply changes consistently throughout a presentation.

CERTIFICATION READY?   1.2.1

How do you apply a slide master?

Applying a Theme to a Slide Master

To customize a slide master, you use Slide Master view. Slide Master view has its own tab on the Ribbon to provide tools you can use to change the masters. In this exercise, you will apply a theme to a slide master to change its look.

STEP BY STEP   **Apply a Theme to a Slide Master**

GET READY. To apply a theme to a slide master, perform the following steps:

1. Locate and open the *Rates* presentation and save it as *Rates Masters*.
2. With slide 1 active, click the View tab.
3. Click the Slide Master button. Slide Master view opens with the Title Slide Layout selected in the left pane (see Figure 4-23).

Figure 4-23

Slide Master view with the Title Slide layout selected

Title Slide layout selected ——→

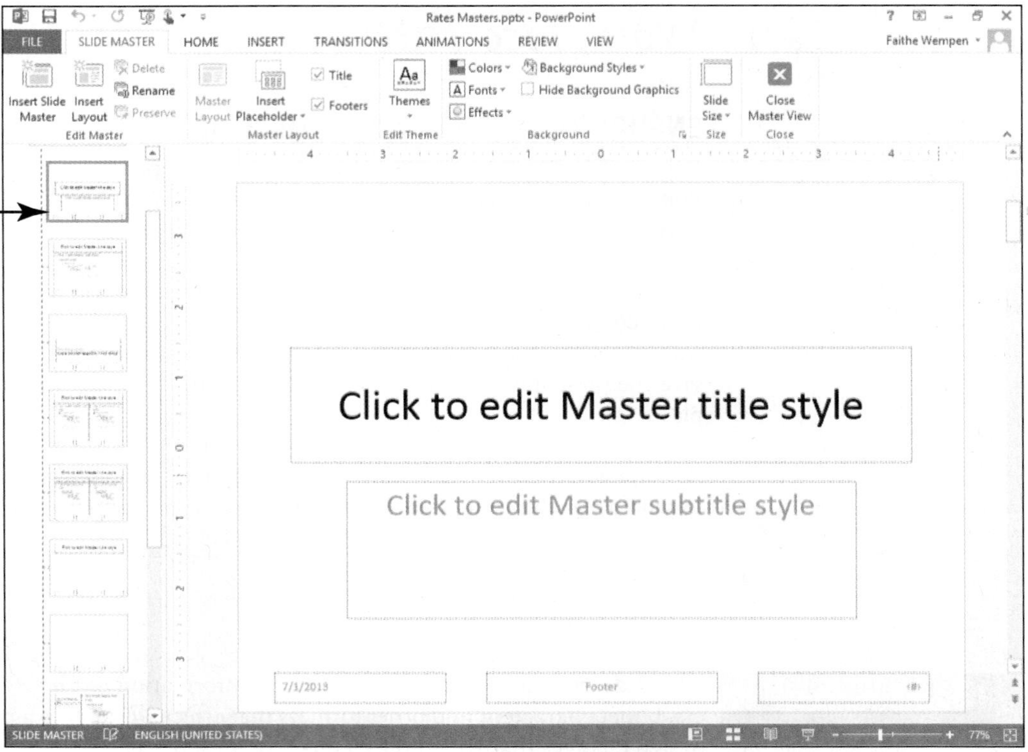

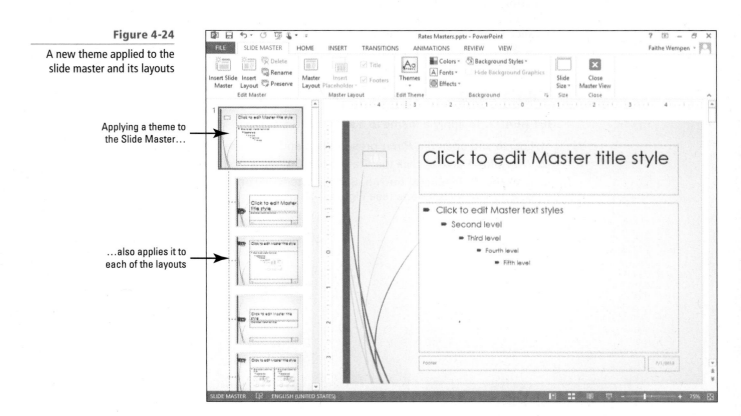

4. Click the **first slide** in the left pane, which is the slide master for the current theme. (It is the top slide in the left pane—the one that is slightly larger than the others.)

5. Click the **Themes button** in the Slide Master tab to open the Themes gallery; click the **Wisp theme** in the gallery. The theme is applied to the slide master as well as all slide layouts in the left pane (see Figure 4-24).

Figure 4-24

A new theme applied to the slide master and its layouts

Applying a theme to the Slide Master...

...also applies it to each of the layouts

Take Note   Remember, you can find a layout or theme's name by hovering the mouse over it.

6. **SAVE** the presentation.

PAUSE. LEAVE the presentation open in Slide Master view to use in the next exercise.

The slide master, displayed at the top of the left pane, looks like a blank Title and Content slide. To make a change to the master, edit it just the way you would edit any slide using tools on any of the Ribbon's tabs. For example, to change the font of the slide title, click the title, display the Home tab, and use the Font list to select a new font. Change bullet characters by clicking in any of the nine levels of bullets and then selecting a new bullet character from the Bullets and Numbering dialog box.

Some changes you make to the slide master display on the masters for other slide layouts. You can also click any of these layouts to display it in the Navigation pane so you can make changes to that layout. Any changes you make to these layouts will display on slides that use those layouts. Your changed masters display in the slide layout gallery to be available when you create new slides.

Moving and Resizing Placeholders

You may have noticed that some designs place slide content in different locations from others. This is because the placeholders on the slide master are positioned differently. You can move and resize the placeholders on the slide master to create different effects yourself. Each slide master has a set of **layout masters** that determine the number, type, and position of the placeholders on a particular type of slide. In Slide Master view, the layout masters are beneath the Slide Master and slightly indented in the left pane to show that they are subordinate to it. Any changes you make to the placeholders on the Slide Master itself flow down to the layout masters. In this exercise, you will change the layout for a particular layout master.

STEP BY STEP   **Move and Resize Placeholders on a Layout Master**

USE the *Rates Masters* presentation that is still open from the previous exercise.

1. In Slide Master view, click to select the layout master for the Title Slide Layout in the left pane (hover the mouse pointer over the slide to see a ScreenTip indicating the layout master's name). The Title Slide Layout master appears in the right pane.

2. In the right pane, click the outer border of the subtitle placeholder (click to edit Master subtitle style) to select that text box.

3. On the Drawing Tools Format tab, in the Size group, set the Height value to 1" (see Figure 4-25).

Another Way
You can also resize a placeholder by dragging one of its selection handles on its border, as with any other object.

Figure 4-25

Resizing a placeholder

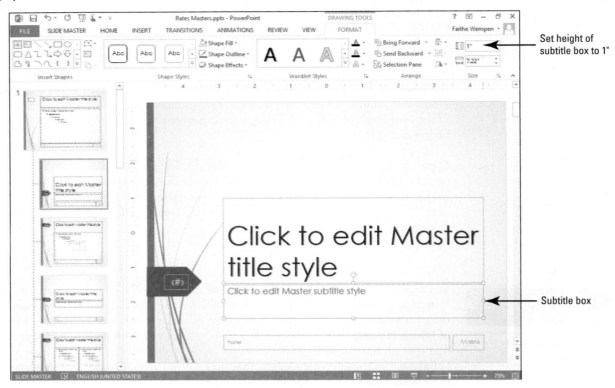

Set height of
subtitle box to 1"

Subtitle box

4. Position the mouse pointer over the border of the subtitle placeholder, but not over a selection handle. The mouse pointer becomes a four-headed arrow. Click and drag the box to the top of the slide (see Figure 4-26).

Figure 4-26

Moving a placeholder

Drag subtitle
placeholder box here

5. Using the same process as in step 4, move the title placeholder immediately below the subtitle placeholder (see Figure 4-27).

Figure 4-27

The completed slide
layout master

6. **SAVE** the presentation.

PAUSE. LEAVE the presentation open in Slide Master view to use in the next exercise.

Adding New Elements to a Master

Adding a new element to a layout, such as a text box or a graphic, places it on all slides that use that layout. Adding such elements to the Slide Master itself places them on every slide that uses that theme, regardless of the layout. You might place the company's logo on each slide, for example, or a copyright notice. In this exercise, you will add a copyright notice to the Slide Master, affecting every layout master that is subordinate to it.

STEP BY STEP | **Add a New Element to a Master**

USE the *Rates Masters* presentation that is still open in Slide Master view from the previous exercise.

1. Click the Slide Master at the top of the left pane.
2. On the Insert tab, click the Text Box button in the Text group.
3. In the bottom left corner of the slide master, below the footer, click to place a new text box, and type Copyright 2015 Southridge Video.

4. Select the text you just typed, and then click the Decrease Font Size button on the Home tab twice to change the font size to 14 point. Resize the text box as necessary so that the text fits on one line (see Figure 4-28).

Figure 4-28

A copyright notice added to the Slide Master will appear on all slides

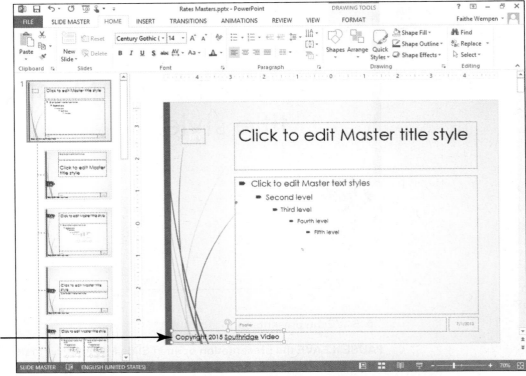

Insert the new text box here

5. With the text still selected, change the text fill color to Light Green, Background 2, Darker 75%.

6. Click the Slide Master tab, and then click the Close Master View button to return to Normal view.

7. View each slide to confirm that the copyright text appears on each one.

PAUSE. LEAVE the presentation open to use in the next exercise.

CERTIFICATION READY? 1.2.4

How do you add a background image?

Working with Background Images

Many of PowerPoint's themes include background images that enhance the look of the slides. You can hide these images if you like for a particular layout master, or delete them entirely from the Slide Master. You can also add your own background images.

STEP BY STEP   **Work with Background Images**

USE the *Rates Masters* presentation that is still open from the previous exercise.

1. Go to slide 1.

2. On the Design tab, click Format Background to display the Format Background task pane.

3. Mark the Hide background graphics check box in the task pane (see Figure 4-29). The background image disappears from slide 1. It remains on the other two slides.

Figure 4-29

Use the Hide Background Graphics check box to hide the background images for an individual slide

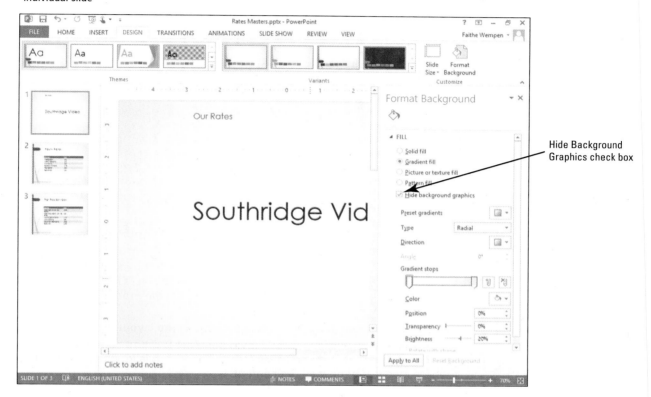

Hide Background Graphics check box

4. Clear the Hide background graphics check box. The background image reappears on slide 1.

5. Close the Format Background task pane.

6. On the View tab, click Slide Master to enter Slide Master view, and select the Title and Content Layout in the left pane.

7. On the Slide Master tab, mark the Hide Background Graphics check box. The background graphic is removed from the chosen layout. This method of removal hides the background for all slides that use the chosen layout, whereas the method in step 3 hid the background just for the selected slide.

8. Clear the Hide Background Graphics check box to restore the background graphic to the Title and Content Layout.

9. Select the Title Slide Layout in the left pane, and then in the right pane, select the brown polygon on the left side of the slide. Hold down the Shift key and click the page number code inside it, so that both objects are selected.

10. Drag the selected objects up so that the point of the polygon points at the word "Click" in the title placeholder (see Figure 4-30).

Figure 4-30

Reposition background
graphics by dragging them

Drag the polygon and the
slide number placeholder here

11. Click the Slide Master thumbnail at the top of the left pane, and then in the right pane, click the leaf graphic on the left side of the slide to select it. Then press Delete to remove it. The leaf graphic is in two parts; repeat the process for the remaining part to remove the entire graphic.

    Notice that the leaf graphic is removed from all the layouts.

12. On the Insert tab, click Pictures. Navigate to the location containing the files for this lesson, select Store.jpg, and click Insert. The image is inserted on the Slide Master where it covers almost all the content.

13. Drag the upper and lower selection handles on the image so that it covers the entire slide. The image will distort slightly; that is okay.

14. On the Picture Tools Format tab, click the Color button located in the Adjust group, and then click Washout (fourth thumbnail in the first row in the Recolor section) (see Figure 4-31).

Figure 4-31

Select Washout as the image
color setting

Color

Washout

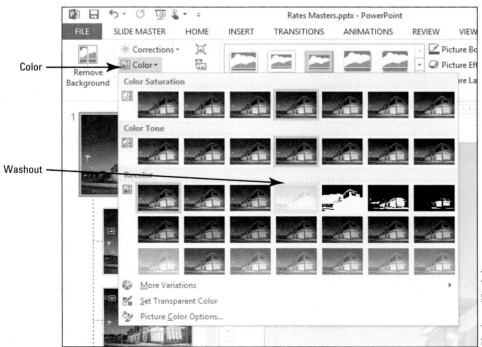

©buzbuzzer/iStockphoto

15. In the Arrange group, click the Send Backward drop-down arrow and click Send to Back. Now the background image is behind all other objects on the Slide Master as well as on each layout master (see Figure 4-32).

Figure 4-32

The new background image is behind all other content

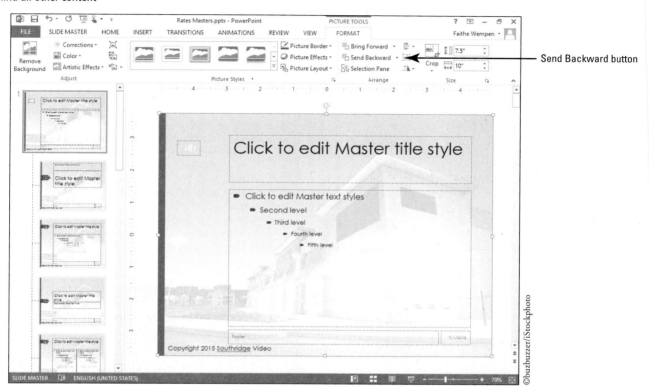

Send Backward button

©buzbuzzer/iStockphoto

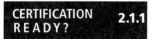
How do you create a new layout?

How do you add a slide layout?

Creating a New Layout

If you need to create a number of slides with a layout different from any of the default layouts, you can create a new custom layout to your own specifications. Or, if you want some slides to use a modified version of one of the default layouts, but you also want to retain that original layout, you may want to create your own custom slide layout. In this exercise you will create a custom layout.

STEP BY STEP   **Create a New Layout**

USE the *Rates Masters* presentation that is still open in Slide Master view from the previous exercise.

1. Click the Slide Master at the top of the left pane.

2. On the Slide Master tab, click Insert Layout. A new blank layout appears at the bottom of the left pane. It is blank except for a title placeholder and the copyright information (see Figure 4-33).

Figure 4-33

A new layout has been created

Insert Layout button →

New layout →

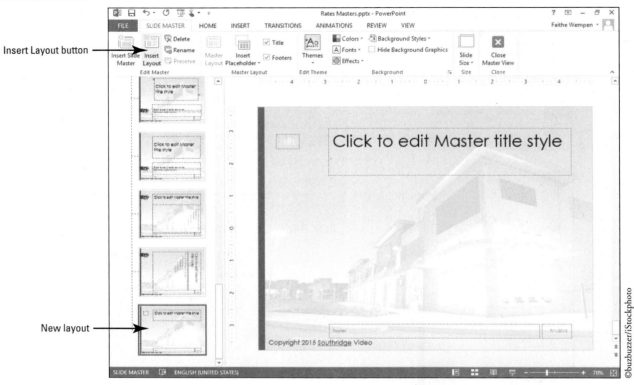

©buzbuzzer/iStockphoto

3. On the Slide Master tab, click the **Insert Placeholder button's drop-down arrow**. A menu opens (see Figure 4-34).

Figure 4-34

Select a type of placeholder

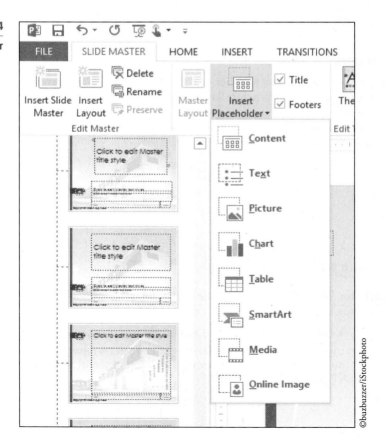

©buzbuzzer/iStockphoto

4. In the menu, click Text. The mouse pointer turns into a crosshair.

5. Draw a new text placeholder on the slide below the title placeholder that will cover most of the empty space on the slide vertically and about ¾ of the empty space on the slide horizontally (see Figure 4-35).

Figure 4-35

Draw a text placeholder as shown here

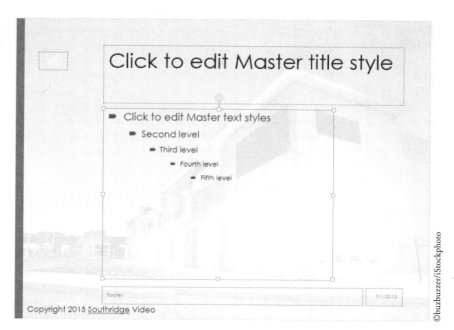

6. Click the Insert Placeholder drop-down arrow again, and click Picture in the menu that appears. Draw a placeholder box to the right of the text placeholder (see Figure 4-36).

Figure 4-36

Draw a picture placeholder as shown here

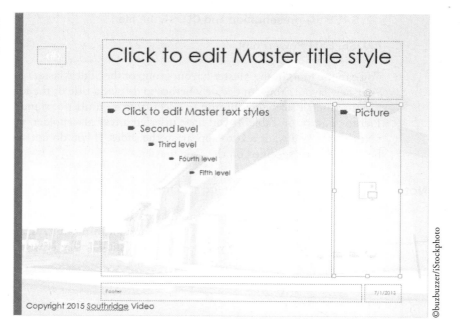

7. Right-click the new layout master in the left pane and click Rename Layout in the menu that appears.

8. In the Rename Layout dialog box, replace the current name with Text and Side Picture and click Rename.

9. On the Slide Master tab, click Close Master View.

10. Go to slide 1.

11. On the Home tab > Slides group, click the New Slide button's drop-down arrow. On the gallery of layouts that appears, click your new layout, Text and Side Picture, to create a new slide using it (see Figure 4-37).

Figure 4-37

Use the new layout when creating a new slide

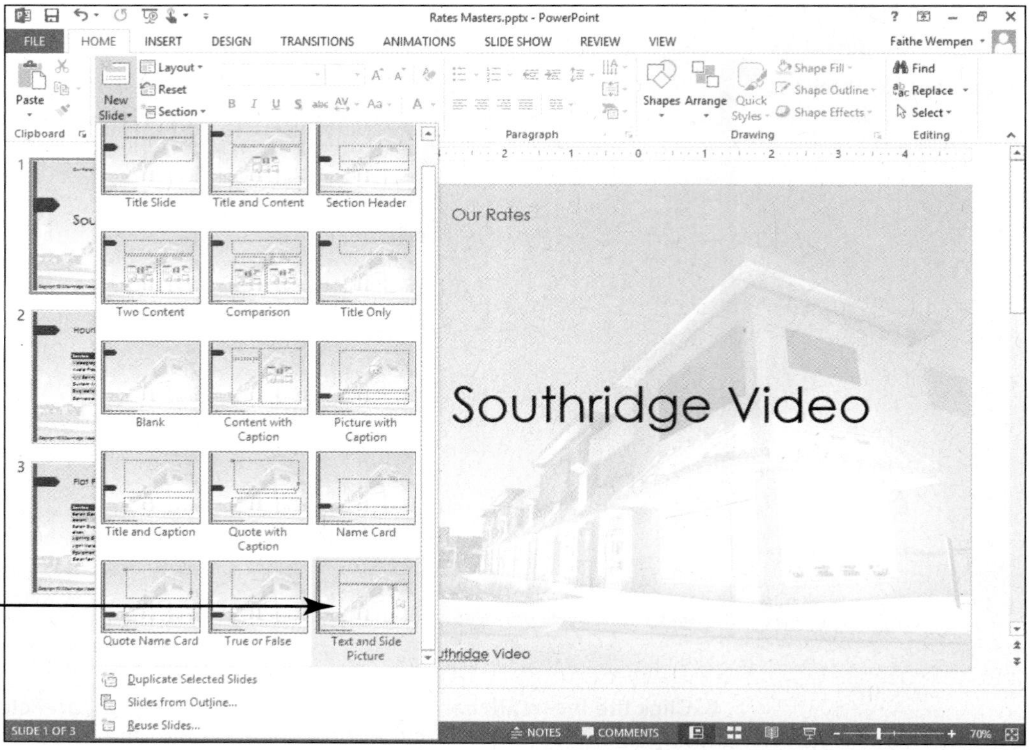

New layout

12. **SAVE** the presentation and **CLOSE** the file.

PAUSE. EXIT PowerPoint.

You can use tools in the Master Layout group of the Slide Master tab to customize placeholders for your new layout. You can decide whether to display a title or the footer placeholders, and you can use the Insert Placeholder button to select from a number of standard placeholders, such as Text, Picture, Chart, or Table. If you have inserted a text placeholder, you can format the placeholder text the way you want text to appear on the slides. If you do not specify formatting, the text will be formatted as specified on the slide master.

Take Note   Custom layouts are stored in the presentation in which they are created.

When you have completed the custom layout, use the Rename button on the Slide Master tab > Edit Master group to give the custom layout a meaningful name. It will then be available in the slide layout gallery any time you want to add a slide in that presentation.

SKILL SUMMARY

In This Lesson, You Learned How To:	Exam Objective	Objective Number
Format Presentations with Themes and Layouts	Modify presentation themes.	1.2.7
Change Slide Backgrounds	Modify slide backgrounds.	2.1.5
Insert a Date, Footer, and Slide Numbers	Control slide numbers. Insert headers and footers.	1.2.5 1.2.6
Link to Web Pages and Other Programs	Insert hyperlinks.	3.1.3
Work with Sections	Insert section headers.	2.3.1
Customize Slide Masters	Apply a slide master. Modify existing layouts. Add background images. Add new layouts. Add slide layouts.	1.2.1 1.2.3 1.2.4 1.2.2 2.1.1

Knowledge Assessment

Fill in the Blank

Fill in each blank with the term or phrase that best completes the statement.

1. A(n) _____ contains color, font, layout, and effect settings that you can apply to a presentation to change its appearance.
2. A slide's _____ determines the positioning and types of placeholders on it.
3. Text that repeats at the bottom of each slide is a(n) _____.
4. Underlined text on a slide usually means that the text is a(n) _____ and opens a web page or another slide when clicked.
5. A(n) _____ button can be placed on a slide to perform a certain activity or jump to a certain slide when clicked.
6. You can organize slides into _____, which group slides together for easier handling.
7. To ensure consistency, make formatting changes to the _____ rather than individual slides.
8. The individual layouts associated with a particular slide master are called _____ masters.
9. To create your own layout, start a new layout and then add one or more _____.
10. Hyperlinks must be tested in _____ view.

Multiple Choice

Circle the correct answer.

1. Which of these does a theme *not* include?
   a. A color palette
   b. Fonts
   c. Graphic effects
   d. Sample content

2. Themes are applied from which tab?
   a. Home
   b. Insert
   c. Design
   d. Transitions

3. How many fonts are in a font theme?
   a. 1
   b. 2
   c. 4
   d. It varies

4. From which tab do you apply a different layout to a slide?
   a. Home
   b. Insert
   c. Design
   d. Transitions

5. Which of these is *not* a type of fill you can use for a slide background?
   a. Solid color
   b. SmartArt
   c. Texture
   d. Gradient

6. To link to a slide in the current presentation, choose —————— in the Insert Hyperlink dialog box.
   a. Existing File or Web Page
   b. Place in This Document
   c. Create New Document
   d. Show Current Slides

7. Where do slide headers appear, if used?
   a. Onscreen during Slide Show view
   b. On printouts of handouts and notes pages
   c. Neither place
   d. Both places

8. After assigning a hyperlink to a graphic, you can test it in —————— view.
   a. Normal
   b. Slide Show
   c. Slide Sorter
   d. Notes Pages

9. Action buttons are selected and inserted from the —————— button's menu on the Insert tab.
   a. Clip Art
   b. SmartArt
   c. Shapes
   d. WordArt

10. What happens when you move a section header?
    a. All the slides in the section move along with it.
    b. The header moves but not the slides in its section.
    c. a new slide master is created
    d. none of the above

Competency Assessment

Project 4-1: **Service with a Smile**

You are the sales manager for a large chain of auto dealerships that prides itself on service and warranty packages that give customers a sense of security. The company, Car King, is rolling out a new line of extended warranties to offer its customers. You have created a presentation that details three levels of warranties. Now you need to improve the look of the slides to make customers take notice.

GET READY. LAUNCH PowerPoint if it is not already running.

1. **OPEN** the *Warranty Plans* presentation and save it as *Warranty Plans Final.*
2. With slide 1 active, insert a new Title and Content slide.
3. Change the slide layout to Title slide.
4. Type the title Car King and the subtitle Extended Warranty Plans.
5. Drag the title slide above slide 1 so the title slide becomes the first slide.
6. Click the Design tab, and then click the More button in the Themes group to display the Themes gallery.
7. Click the Wood Type theme to apply this theme to all slides.
8. Click the More button in the Variants group. On the menu that appears, point to Fonts, and then scroll down to locate and click the Times New Roman-Arial theme font combination.
9. Click the More button in the Variants group, and on the menu that appears, point to Colors, and then click Customize Colors.
10. Click the Accent 1 drop-down arrow, then click the 25% darker version of the current color. For example, if the current color is Orange, Accent 1, then choose Orange, Accent 1, Darker 25%.
11. Click the Accent 2 drop-down arrow, then click the 50% darker version of the current color.
12. Type CarKing as the color scheme name, and then click Save.
13. Go to slide 1, if necessary.
14. Change the Themes Background Style to Style 9.
15. **SAVE** the presentation and **CLOSE** the file.

LEAVE PowerPoint open for use in the next project.

Project 4-2: **Special Delivery**

As a marketing manager for Consolidated Delivery, you have been asked to prepare and present information on the company's services to a prospective corporate client. You need to add some interactive features to a standard presentation to make your delivery especially interesting.

1. **OPEN** the *Messenger Service* presentation and save it as *Messenger Service Links.*
2. Go to slide 2. Change slide's layout to Title and Content.
3. Select the text Contact Consolidated in the text box at the bottom of the slide.
4. Insert a hyperlink to slide 6. Our Numbers, in the same document.
5. Go to slide 5, Our Rates, and insert an Information action button.

6. Draw a button near the bottom of the slide and set the action to Hyperlink to: Other File. Select the file *Contract Plans.*
7. Go to slide 6, select the website address, and then create a hyperlink to http://www.consolidatedmessenger.com.
8. Insert an automatically updating date, slide numbers, and the footer Consolidated Messenger on all slides except the title slide. (You may need to adjust the location of your action button on slide 5 after you add slide numbers and the footer.)
9. Using a Function key, run the slide show from slide 1, Consolidated Messenger.
10. Use the Navigation tool on slide 2, Our Services, to go to slide 6, Our Numbers.
11. Advance to slide 4 and then to slide 5.
12. On slide 5, click the action button to open the *Contract Plans* file. Close Microsoft Word to return to the slide show.
13. Advance to slide 6 and click the website link. Close the browser and end the slide show.
14. **SAVE** the presentation and **CLOSE** the file.

LEAVE PowerPoint open for use in the next project.

Proficiency Assessment

Project 4-3: Travel Tips

You are an assistant at Sunny Day Travel, and your boss has created the beginnings of a presentation containing travel tips for various destination types. Because there will eventually be many slides per destination, you will organize the slides into sections for the destination types and make some changes to the slide master that will improve the slides' look.

1. **OPEN** the *Travel Tips* presentation and save it as *Travel Tips Sections*.
2. Go to slide 2. Notice that the title is obscured by the graphic.
3. Switch to Slide Master view, and select the slide master.
4. Drag the bottom border of the title placeholder upward so its height is 0.75". Use the Height box on the Drawing Tools Format tab to gauge the height, or use the vertical ruler.
5. Close Slide Master view, and confirm on slide 2 that the title no longer overlaps the graphic.
6. Create a section that starts with slide 3. Name it Sand and Sun.
7. Create a section that starts with slide 6. Name it Adventure.
8. Create a section that starts with slide 9. Name it Cruise.
9. Create a section that starts with slide 12. Name it City.
10. Create a section that starts with slide 15. Name it Summary.
11. Move the City section before the Cruise section.
12. On slide 2, select the graphic for Sand and Sun, and then create a hyperlink that jumps to slide 3.
13. Create additional hyperlinks for the other three graphics, jumping to the first slide in their respective sections.
14. **SAVE** the presentation and **CLOSE** the file.

LEAVE PowerPoint open for use in the next project.

Project 4-4: Senior Meals

As the activities director for Senior Meal Services, you are responsible for educating your staff about the dietary recommendations for senior citizens. You have created a presentation, and now you will modify its slide master, theme, and colors to make it more appealing.

1. **OPEN** the *Meals* presentation and save it as *Senior Meals*.
2. Apply the Slice theme to the entire presentation.
3. Change the font theme to Century Gothic.
4. Change to the variant with the red background.
5. Display the Slide Master, and then change the background on the Slide Master to Style 2 from the Background Styles list.
6. Close Slide Master view, and then go to slide 1.
7. Select the website address on slide 1, and make it into a live hyperlink.
8. Set the current date to appear at the bottom of each slide, and set the date to *not* automatically update.
9. **SAVE** the presentation and **CLOSE** the file.

LEAVE PowerPoint open for use in the next project.

Mastery Assessment

Project 4-5: The Art of the Biography

You work for the editorial director of Lucerne Publishing. She has asked you to fine-tune a presentation on new biographies she plans to deliver to the sales force. You want to make some global changes to the presentation by customizing the presentation's slide masters, and you need to create a new layout that you will use to introduce sections of biographies.

1. **OPEN** the *Biographies* presentation and save it as *Biographies Masters*.
2. Switch to Slide Master view and apply the Parallax theme to the slide master.
3. On the Title and Content layout, create a new layout.
4. Deselect Title in the Master Layout group to remove the title placeholder from the new layout.
5. Insert a text placeholder in the center of the slide. Delete the sample bulleted text, remove bullet formatting, and change font size to 40 point. Center the text in the placeholder.
6. Apply a different background style to this new layout.
7. Rename the new layout Introduction.
8. Close Slide Master view.
9. Insert a new slide after slide 1 using the Introduction layout. Type American History in the placeholder.
10. **SAVE** the presentation and **CLOSE** the file.

LEAVE PowerPoint open for use in the next project.

Project 4-6: Adventure Works

You are a coordinator for Adventure Works, a company that manages outdoor adventures for children and teenagers. To introduce your programs you have created a presentation to show at local schools and recreation centers. Finalize the presentation with design elements and effects that will catch the eye.

1. **OPEN** the *Adventures* presentation.
2. Apply the Celestial theme to the presentation, and apply the green-and-blue variant (which may be the second variant from the left in the Variants gallery).
3. Customize theme fonts by applying the Corbel font theme.
4. Make the e-mail address and website address on slide 5 active hyperlinks.
5. Change the layout on slide 1 to Title Slide.
6. Add a footer that contains the text Adventure Works to all slides, including the title slide.
7. **SAVE** the presentation as *Adventures Final* and **CLOSE** the file.

EXIT PowerPoint.

Circling Back 1

You are a sales representative for Contoso Food Services. You are preparing a brief presentation to introduce your company to the Food Services Committee at Trey College, in hopes of receiving a contract to provide food services for the campus dining hall.

Project 1: Create a Presentation

Begin by creating slides from a blank presentation. Then add slides from another presentation, rearrange the slides, and print the presentation.

GET READY. LAUNCH PowerPoint if it is not already running.

1. Create a new blank presentation and save it as *Trey Proposal*.
2. On the title slide, type Contoso Food Services in the title placeholder.
3. Type Trey College Proposal in the subtitle placeholder.
4. Reuse slides 2-4 from the *Boilerplate* presentation.
5. Rearrange slides so that slide 2 becomes slide 3.
6. Print the presentation as slides in Grayscale mode.
7. **SAVE** the presentation.

PAUSE. LEAVE PowerPoint and your presentation open for the next project.

> **Online**
>
> The *Boilerplate* file is available on the book companion website or in WileyPLUS.

Project 2: Format Your Presentation

Now that you have the bare bones of your presentation written, you can concentrate on formatting to improve the presentation's appearance. You will use WordArt, a theme, font styles, and other formatting options to give your slides punch.

USE the presentation that is open from the previous project.

1. Apply the Wisp theme, and then apply the third variant (blue tint).
2. On slide 1, delete the title text and the title placeholder box.
3. Create a WordArt graphic using the Fill - Black, Text 1, Shadow preset (the first one in the WordArt Styles gallery). Type the text CONTOSO FOOD SERVICES.
4. Make these changes to the WordArt graphic:
   a. Set the font size to 56 pt. (Hint: Click in the Font Size box on the Ribbon and type 56 directly into it.)
   b. Change the WordArt text fill to Purple, Accent 6, Darker 50%. (Hint: Use the Text Fill button in the WordArt Styles group on the Drawing Tools Format tab.)
   c. Change the WordArt text fill to a gradient, using the Linear Down option in the Dark Variations section of the Gradient gallery.
   d. Change the WordArt outline color to Purple, Accent 6.
   e. Apply the Tight Reflection, touching effect to the WordArt graphic.
   f. Reposition the WordArt graphic 0.5" above the slide's subtitle box.
5. Apply italics to the slide 1 subtitle.
6. Center the subtitle horizontally under the title. Figure 1 shows the completed slide 1.

Figure 1

Slide 1 completed

CONTOSO FOOD SERVICES

Trey College Proposal

7. Go to slide 2. Make these changes to the text in the right-hand placeholder:

   a. Select all text in the right-hand placeholder and change the font size to 24 pt.

   b. Right-align the last three paragraphs (the attribution), and adjust line spacing so there is no extra space above these lines. (Hint: Choose Line Spacing Options at the bottom of the Line Spacing menu.)

   c. Use the Format Painter to copy formats from the quote paragraph and the quote attribution on slide 2 to the quote text and attribution on slide 3.

8. Go to slide 4. Insert a text box below the picture that is as wide as the picture and type the following text:

   Contoso Food Services is proud to serve institutions in fifteen states in this country and three Canadian provinces. Our reputation for quality is second to none.

9. Format the text box as follows:

   a. Center the text in the text box.

   b. Apply a Shape Style of your choice to the text box.

10. **SAVE** the presentation.

PAUSE. LEAVE PowerPoint and your presentation open for the next project.

Project 3: Add Design Touches to Your Presentation

You are ready to do the final formatting and add the finishing touches to the presentation. You will adjust the slide master, add a slide, and change the background.

USE the presentation that is open from the previous project.

1. Insert an automatically updating date and slide numbers that appear on all slides except the title slide.

2. In Slide Master view, move the Date placeholder to the left of the Footer placeholder. Close Slide Master view.

3. Insert a new slide at the end of the presentation using the Two Content layout.

4. Type the slide title Contact Us.

5. Insert the following contact information in the left-hand text placeholder. Format the information as desired.

   Mailing address:

   17507 Atlantic Blvd

   Boca Raton, FL 33456

   Phone:

   561 555 3663

   561 555 3664

6. Insert the following information in the right-hand text placeholder:

E-mail:

sales@contoso.com

Website:

www.contoso.com

7. Create a hyperlink from the website text to the website at http://www.contoso.com if PowerPoint did not make it a hyperlink when you typed it.

8. Apply a different background style to slide 5 only to make it stand out. (Hint: Right-click the desired background style and click Apply to Selected Slides.)

9. Go to slide 3. Insert an Information action button above the date in the lower-left corner of the slide that links to the *Pricing* Excel file.

10. Go to slide 2, and apply the Blue Tissue Paper texture fill to the text box that contains the quotation. Repeat for the text box on slide 3.

11. Run the presentation in Slide Show view. Test the action button on slide 3 to make sure it works in Slide Show view.

12. **SAVE** your changes to the presentation.

13. **SAVE** the presentation again as *Trey 2003* in the 97-2003 format, and then **CLOSE** the file.

EXIT PowerPoint.

Online

The *Pricing* file is available on the book companion website or in WileyPLUS.

LESSON SKILL MATRIX

Skills	Exam Objective	Objective Number
Creating Tables	Create new tables.	3.2.1
Importing Tables from External Sources	Import tables from external sources.	3.2.4
Modifying Table Layout	Modify the number of rows and columns.	3.2.2
Formatting Tables	Apply table styles.	3.2.3

KEY TERMS

- cells
- embedded
- linked
- table
- worksheet
- workbook
- rows
- columns

©rramirez125/iStockphoto

©rramirez125/iStockphoto

You are an assistant director of ATM operations at Woodgrove Bank. Your job is to help oversee the placement and use of ATMs in your bank's branches and other locations. You often deliver presentations to bank officers to keep them up to date on ATM activities. The best way to organize information that has several related components is to use a table. Distributing information in rows and columns makes the data easy to read and understand. Use the table features of Microsoft Office PowerPoint 2013 to modify the structure and appearance of a table to improve readability and visual interest.

SOFTWARE ORIENTATION

A PowerPoint Table

Tables are designed to organize data in columns and rows (see Figure 5-1).

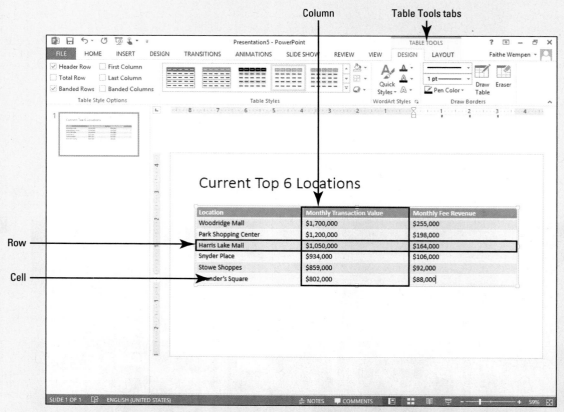

Figure 5-1

A PowerPoint table and the table tools on the Ribbon

The Table Tools Design tab, shown above, and the Table Tools Layout tab provide tools for modifying and formatting a table. These tabs become active only when a table is selected.

CREATING TABLES

When you want to organize complex data on a slide, use a **table**. A table is a grid into which you can type text in the individual **cells** at the intersection of each **column** and **row**. A table's column and row structure makes data easy to understand. If you need to organize numerical data that may be used in calculations, you can insert an Excel worksheet right on a slide and use Excel's tools to work with the data.

Inserting a Table

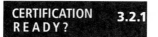

CERTIFICATION READY?   3.2.1

How do you create a new table?

PowerPoint has automated the process of creating a table so that you can simply specify the number of columns and rows and then type data to achieve a professionally formatted result. Power-Point offers several ways to insert a table. The simplest is to click the Insert Table icon in any content placeholder. You can also insert a table with the Table button on the Insert tab. In this exercise, you will create tables using both methods.

STEP BY STEP   **Insert a Table**

GET READY. Before you begin these steps, make sure that your computer is on. Log on, if necessary.

1. **START** PowerPoint, if the program is not already running.
2. Locate and open the *ATMs* presentation and save it as *ATMs Final*.
3. Click below slide 4 in the left pane and press Enter to insert a new slide with the Title and Content layout after slide 4.
4. On the new slide, click in the title placeholder and type the slide title, Proposed ATM Locations.
5. Click the Insert Table icon [ ] in the content placeholder. The Insert Table dialog box opens (see Figure 5-2).

Figure 5-2

The Insert Table dialog box

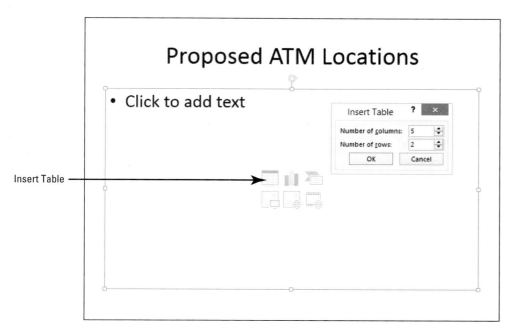

Another Way

You can open the Insert Table dialog box by clicking the Table drop-down arrow on the Insert tab >Tables group and then clicking Insert Table.

6. In the Number of Columns text box, type 3 to specify three columns, press Tab to move to the Number of Rows text box, and then type 6 to specify six rows. Click OK. PowerPoint creates the table in the content area (see Figure 5-3). Notice that formats specified by the current theme have already been applied to the table.

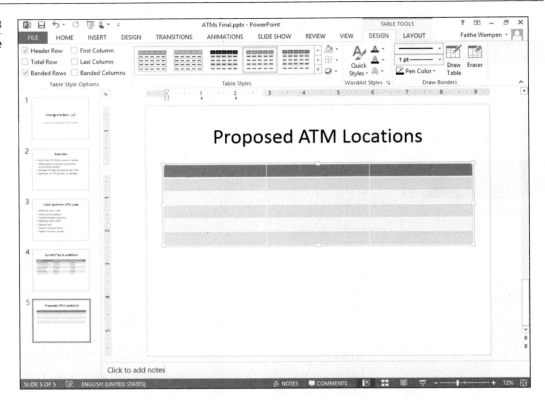

7. Click in the **first table cell** in the top row and type **Location**. Press **Tab** to move to the next cell and type **Site Study Complete**. Press **Tab** to move to the third cell in the row and type **Nearest Competing ATM**.

8. Type the **following information** in the table cells, pressing **Tab** to move from cell to cell. Your table should look like Figure 5-4 when you complete it.

Springdale Cineplex	Yes	More than 2 miles
Glen Avenue BIG Foods	No	Three blocks
Findlay Market Square	Yes	One block
Center City Arena	Yes	One block
Williams State College	No	Half a mile

Figure 5-4

The table with data typed in it

Location	Site Study Complete	Nearest Competing ATM
Springdale Cineplex	Yes	More than 2 miles
Glen Avenue BIG Foods	No	Three blocks
Findlay Market Square	Yes	One block
Center City Arena	Yes	One block
Williams State College	No	Half a mile

9. Insert a **new slide** with the Title and Content layout at the end of the presentation, and click to **display** the new slide.

10. On the Insert tab, click **Table** to produce the Table menu and grid.

11. Drag **across the grid** to select a 5×5 block (see Figure 5-5), and then release the **mouse button** to create the table.

Figure 5-5

Use the Table button to
select a 5×5 block

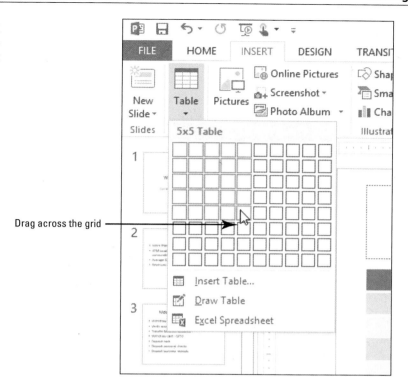

Drag across the grid

12. Delete the new slide on which you just created the table.
13. **SAVE** the presentation.

PAUSE. LEAVE the presentation open to use in the next exercise.

By default, PowerPoint sizes a new table to fill the width of the content placeholder. If you have only a few columns, you may find the table a little too spacious. You will learn later in this lesson how to adjust column widths and row heights to more closely fit the data you have entered.

If you need to reposition a table on a slide, you can do so by simply dragging its outer frame, as with any other object on a slide. You can resize a table overall by positioning the mouse pointer over one of the corners of its frame, so the mouse pointer becomes a double-headed arrow, and then dragging in or out. Dragging the corners of a table's frame changes the sizes of all rows and columns proportionally.

Drawing a Table

Drawing a table enables you to create a table with different row and column sizes, and with different numbers of rows per column (or columns per row). In this exercise, you will draw a table.

STEP BY STEP   **Draw a Table**

USE the *ATMs Final* presentation that is still open from the previous exercise.

1. Insert a new slide at the end of the presentation with the Title Only layout.
2. On the Insert tab, click Table to open the Table menu, and then click Draw Table. The mouse pointer changes to a pencil.
3. Click and drag the mouse pointer to draw a frame approximately 3" high and the same width as the slide's title placeholder box.

   When you release the mouse button, the new table appears (which has only one big cell), and the Table Tools Design tab is displayed (see Figure 5-6).

Figure 5-6

Draw the outer frame for a
new table

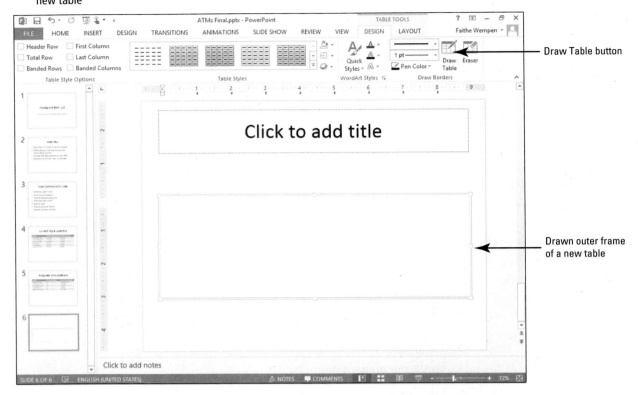

Draw Table button

Drawn outer frame
of a new table

4. On the Table Tools Design tab, click Draw Table in the Draw Borders command group. The mouse pointer becomes a pencil again.

5. Click and drag to draw a horizontal line that divides the table horizontally. A dotted horizontal line appears. Release the mouse button to accept it.

Take Note Drag to draw the lines starting slightly inside the border rather than on the border's edge. If you start dragging too close to the border, PowerPoint creates a new table frame rather than adding to the existing table.

The drawing pencil mouse pointer should stay on; if it turns itself off, click the Draw Table button again to re-enable it.

6. Drag a vertical line through the middle of the table to divide it vertically.

7. Drag another vertical line that divides only the lower-right cell of the table vertically.

8. Drag another horizontal line that divides only the lower-right cells of the table horizontally. Figure 5-7 shows the completed table.

Figure 5-7

A drawn table

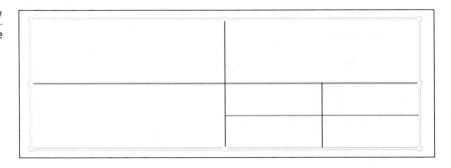

9. Press **Esc** to turn off the pencil cursor on the mouse pointer.

10. Type the text shown in Figure 5-8 into the slide's title placeholder and into the table. You will format this table later in the lesson.

11. **SAVE** the presentation.

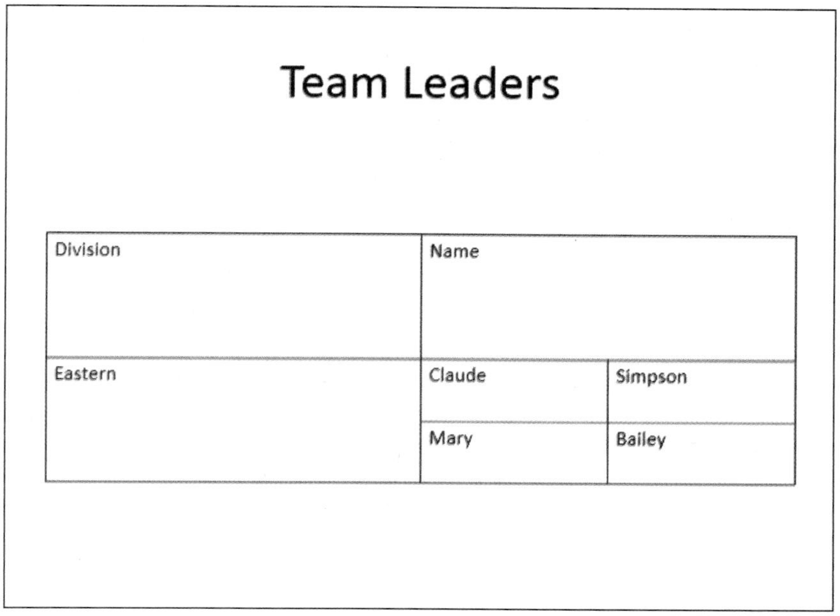

Figure 5-8

The table with text added

Team Leaders

Division	Name	
Eastern	Claude	Simpson
	Mary	Bailey

PAUSE. LEAVE the presentation open to use in the next exercise.

Drawing a table is useful when you need a table that has different numbers of rows or columns in different spots as you saw in the preceding exercise. You can also draw a table to create rows and columns of different heights and widths. Later in this lesson you will learn how to resize, merge, and split table rows and columns to create the same kinds of effects after the initial table creation.

IMPORTING TABLES FROM EXTERNAL SOURCES

The Bottom Line

Microsoft Office 2013 allows a great deal of integration among its programs. If you need to show numerical data on a slide, for example, you can insert an Excel worksheet directly on the slide and use it to manipulate data just as you would in Excel.

 Workplace Ready

APPLICATION-INDEPENDENCE

Because the core Office applications (Word, Excel, and PowerPoint) are designed to work closely together, the application you choose to create a certain type of content is a matter of personal preference. Some applications work better for certain types of content than others, so you can create content in the application that is easiest for you, and then import it into any of the other applications as needed.

For example, Excel is the best application for numeric data that you need to perform calculations on. Word and PowerPoint both enable you to create tables, but the calculation capabilities are much less. Therefore, if you need a calculation-heavy table in PowerPoint, it is easier to input that data into an Excel file and then import that data into your PowerPoint presentation afterwards.

CERTIFICATION READY?   3.2.4

How do you import tables from external sources?

Using an Excel Worksheet in PowerPoint

If you need to show numeric data on a PowerPoint slide, you can insert an Excel worksheet directly on the slide and use it to manipulate data just as you would in Excel. Inserting an Excel **worksheet** (a spreadsheet from an Excel **workbook**) gives you access to all of Excel's data manipulation and formatting tools. If you want to show Excel data on a slide and have not yet created the worksheet, it makes sense to create the worksheet directly on the PowerPoint slide. A worksheet you insert in this way is **embedded** on the slide—it is stored within the PowerPoint presentation but can be edited using the tools of its source application, Excel.

When you insert a worksheet using the Excel Spreadsheet command, the worksheet consists of only four visible cells. Drag the bottom or side sizing handle (or the lower-right corner handle) to reveal more cells. When you have finished inserting data, use these handles to adjust the border to hide empty cells that would otherwise show on the PowerPoint slide.

You can also resize a worksheet object by clicking it once to display the heavy, light-blue container border, then dragging a bottom, side, or corner of the placeholder. This action enlarges or reduces the object itself; however, it does not change the font size of the embedded data even though the text may look larger. You can edit an embedded worksheet at any time by double-clicking the worksheet object to open it in Excel. You can remove the object by clicking it once to display the heavy, light-blue container border and then pressing Delete.

In this exercise, you will insert an Excel worksheet in a PowerPoint presentation. In some ways the worksheet is like a table; in other ways it differs. You will see the differences as you work through the exercise.

STEP BY STEP   **Insert an Excel Worksheet**

USE the *ATMs Final* presentation that is still open from the previous exercise.

1. Insert a new slide at the end of the presentation with the Title Only layout.
2. Type the slide title ATM Cost Analysis.
3. Click away from the title text box, and then click the Insert tab, click the Table drop-down arrow, and then click Excel Spreadsheet. PowerPoint creates a small Excel worksheet on the slide. Note that the PowerPoint Ribbon has been replaced by the Excel Ribbon but the title bar still shows ATMs Final.
4. Resize the worksheet object by dragging the lower-right corner handle diagonally to the right to display columns A through F and rows 1 through 10 (see Figure 5-9).

Figure 5-9

A new Excel worksheet on a slide

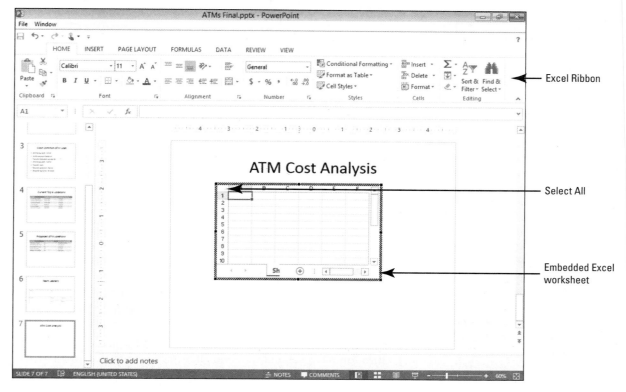

Take Note   When an Excel worksheet is open on the slide, you are actually working in Excel. To return to PowerPoint, click outside the worksheet object.

5. Click the **Select All** area in the upper-left corner of the worksheet where the column headers and row headers intersect. The entire worksheet is selected.

6. Click the **Font Size drop-down arrow** on the Home tab and click **18**.

7. Type **data in the worksheet cells** (see Figure 5-10). To move between cells use the **arrow keys** on the keyboard or press **Tab**. To adjust column widths, position the **pointer** on the border between column headings so the pointer turns into a two-headed arrow and drag to the right until all data appears. The overall size of the embedded Excel spreadsheet expands as needed as you widen the columns.

Figure 5-10

Type the data as shown

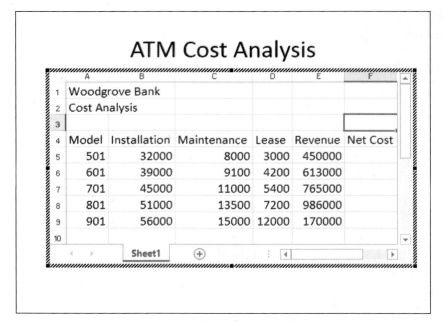

8. Click cell **F5** and type the following formula: **=E5–(B5+C5+D5)**. This formula sums the values in B5, C5, and D5, and then subtracts that total from the value in E5.

9. Press **Enter** to complete the formula.

10. Click cell **F5**, and then click the **Copy** button on the Home tab. Then click and drag over cells **F6** through **F9** to select them and click the **Paste** button to paste the formula in each of the selected cells.

11. Click and drag over the range **B5:F9** to select those cells. Then click the **Accounting Number Format** button in the Number group on the Home tab to apply a currency format to the selected cells. (Do not worry if some of the cells fill up with # signs.)

12. With B5:F9 still selected, click the **Decrease Decimal** button in the Number group twice to remove the decimal points and trailing zeros for the numbers.

13. Widen the **columns** as needed so that there are no #### entries in any of the cells.

14. Click cell **A1** and change the font size to **24**.

15. Click **outside the worksheet** to return to PowerPoint. Your slide should look similar to Figure 5-11. You may need to resize and/or reposition the object to center it on the slide.

Figure 5-11

The completed Excel worksheet embedded in a slide

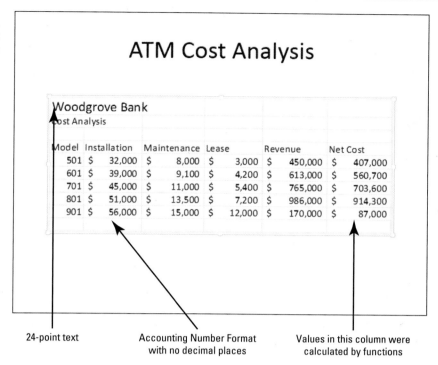

24-point text

Accounting Number Format with no decimal places

Values in this column were calculated by functions

16. **SAVE** the presentation.

PAUSE. LEAVE PowerPoint open to use in the next exercise.

Take Note   You know a worksheet is open and ready to edit in Excel when it displays the heavy hatched border.

If you have already created an Excel worksheet and want to use the data on a slide, you have several additional options for moving it from Excel to PowerPoint:

* Select the data in Excel, copy it to the Clipboard, and paste it on a PowerPoint slide. This action pastes the Excel data as a PowerPoint table that cannot be edited in Excel but can be modified like any other PowerPoint table. This action also works for Word tables as well as data from other applications.

* Select the data in Excel, copy it to the Clipboard, click the Paste button drop-down arrow in PowerPoint, and select Paste Special. In the Paste Special dialog box, choose to Paste the data as a Microsoft Excel Worksheet Object. The data is then embedded on the slide just as when you used the Excel Spreadsheet command.

* Select the data in Excel, copy it to the Clipboard, and open the Paste Special dialog box in PowerPoint. Choose to Paste link the data as an Excel worksheet object. The data is then **linked** to the Excel worksheet, so that if you make a change to the worksheet in Excel, the data on the slide will show that same change.

* Click the Object button on the Insert tab to open the Insert Object dialog box. Here you can choose to create a new worksheet file or navigate to an existing file and paste it on the slide, with or without linking.

Take Note   The Insert Object dialog box allows you to create a number of objects other than worksheets. You can create Excel charts, graphics, and even Word documents of various versions.

You can use the same procedures to copy Excel charts to slides. When simply pasted on a slide, an Excel chart can be formatted using the same tools you use to work with a PowerPoint chart.

 Cross Ref   You will work with PowerPoint charts in Lesson 6.

MODIFYING TABLE LAYOUT

The Bottom Line

It is often necessary to modify the layout as you work with a table. For example, you may need to add or delete rows or columns, move data in the table, adjust column widths, or merge or split table cells.

CERTIFICATION READY?   **3.2.2**

How do you modify the number of rows and columns?

Adding Rows and Columns

One of the most common reasons to change a table's structure is to add data to or remove data from the table. You will learn in this exercise that you can easily insert rows and columns in PowerPoint tables to keep data accurate and up to date. In the following exercise, you will add a row and a column to a table.

STEP BY STEP   **Add a Row and a Column**

USE the *ATMs Final* presentation that is still open from the previous exercise.

1. Go to **slide 6** (the Team Leaders slide).
2. Click at the end of the word **Bailey** in the last cell, and press **Tab**. A new row appears.
3. In the new row, type the data as shown in Figure 5-12.

Figure 5-12

Adding a row at the bottom of a table

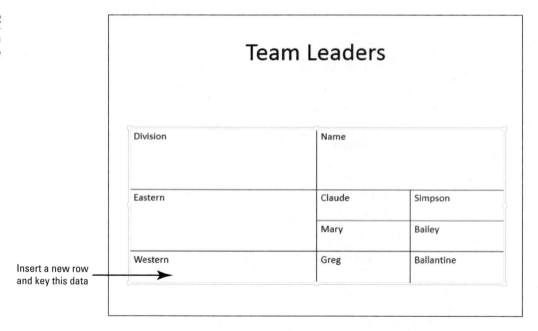

Insert a new row and key this data

   **Another Way**
You can also right-click in a cell, and click the Insert button on the Mini toolbar to see the options for inserting cells above, below, left, or right.

4. Click in the cell containing **Eastern** and on the Table Tools Layout tab, click **Insert Above** in the Rows & Columns group. A new blank row appears above that cell's row.
5. Drag the **lower border** of the first row upward, decreasing that row's height as much as possible. (The text within that row prevents the height from being smaller than will accommodate that text.)
6. In the new row, type the **data** shown in Figure 5-13.

Figure 5-13

Adding a row between two
existing rows

Insert Above button

New row inserted

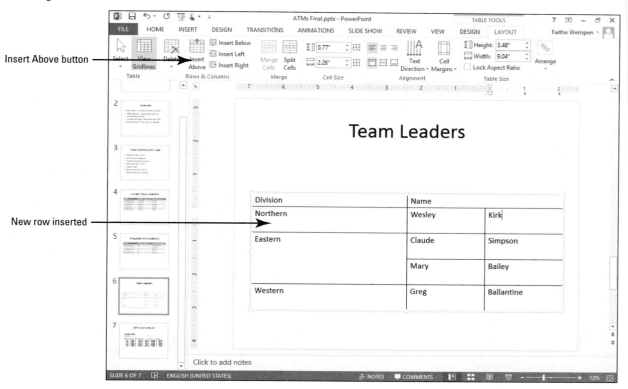

7. Click and drag across all the cells in the Division column to select that column.

8. On the Table Tools Layout tab, click Insert Right. A new blank column appears.

9. In the new column, type the data shown in Figure 5-14. If the table becomes so tall that it overruns the bottom of the slide, move the table upward on the slide as needed by dragging its outer border.

Figure 5-14

Adding a new column

New column added

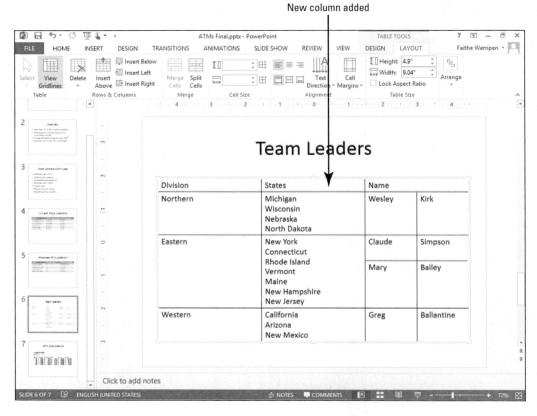

10. **SAVE** the presentation.

PAUSE. LEAVE the presentation open to use in the next exercise.

To add a new row at the bottom of a table, simply move into the last cell of the table (bottom right) and press Tab. Alternatively, the Tools in the Rows & Columns group on the Table Tools Layout tab make it easy to insert new rows and columns exactly where you want them in the table. Click in a cell near where you want to add the row or column, and then click the appropriate button on the tab.

Deleting Rows or Columns

When you delete rows and columns, the table automatically resizes to account for the removal of the data. Note, however, that columns do not automatically resize to fill the area previously occupied by a column. After removing columns, you may need to resize the remaining columns in the table to adjust space. You will learn about resizing later in this lesson. In this exercise, you will delete a column and a row.

STEP BY STEP   **Delete Rows or Columns**

USE the *ATMs Final* presentation that is still open from the previous exercise.

1. On slide 6, click in the upper left cell (**Division**).
2. On the Table Tools Layout tab, click the **Delete** button in the Rows & Columns group, and on the menu that appears, click **Delete Columns** (see Figure 5-15). The first column is deleted.

Figure 5-15

Deleting a column

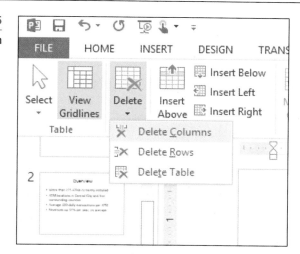

Figure 5-15

Deleting a column

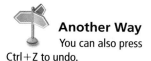

Another Way
You can also press
Ctrl+Z to undo.

3. Click the Undo button on the Quick Access Toolbar to undo the delete operation.

4. Click in the lower-left cell (Western).

5. On the Table Tools Layout tab, click the Delete button, and on the menu that appears, click Delete Rows. The bottom row is deleted.

6. Click the Undo button on the Quick Access Toolbar to undo the delete operation.

7. **SAVE** the presentation.

PAUSE. LEAVE the presentation open to use in the next exercise.

Moving Rows and Columns

Move rows and columns when you need to reorder data. You can use drag and drop or the Cut and Paste commands to move row or column data into a new, blank row or column. In this exercise, you will insert a new column and then move content into it.

STEP BY STEP **Move a Column**

Another Way
You can also click
in the rightmost column and
then on the Table Tools Layout
tab, click Select and click Select
Column.

USE the *ATMs Final* presentation that is still open from the previous exercise.

1. Go to slide 4, click in the second column, and on the Table Tools Layout tab, click Insert Left. A new column is inserted between the first and second columns.

2. Drag across all the cells in the rightmost column to select them.

3. Drag the selected column and drop it on top of the first cell in the blank column you inserted in step 1. The data from the selected column is moved to the new column, and a blank column remains in the data's previous location (see Figure 5-16).

Figure 5-16

Moving a column

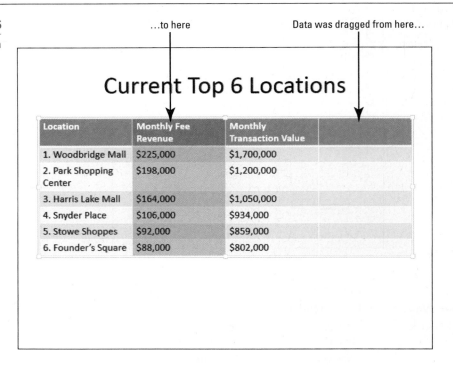

...to here   Data was dragged from here...

Current Top 6 Locations

Location	Monthly Fee Revenue	Monthly Transaction Value	
1. Woodbridge Mall	$225,000	$1,700,000	
2. Park Shopping Center	$198,000	$1,200,000	
3. Harris Lake Mall	$164,000	$1,050,000	
4. Snyder Place	$106,000	$934,000	
5. Stowe Shoppes	$92,000	$859,000	
6. Founder's Square	$88,000	$802,000	

Another Way
You can use the Cut and Paste commands on the Home tab to cut and paste if you prefer, or right-click and choose the Cut or Paste Options commands from the shortcut menu.

4. With the second column still selected, press **Ctrl+X** to cut the column's data to the Clipboard. The column disappears entirely. When you use the Ctrl+X command to cut all data from a column, a blank column is not left behind as with drag and drop.

5. Click in the first row of the empty column on the right side of the table and press **Ctrl+V** to paste the data into that column. The data is placed in the empty column, and the table returns to having only three columns.

6. Drag the table's frame to re-center it on the slide if needed. (It may be slightly skewed to the left.)

7. **SAVE** the presentation.

PAUSE. LEAVE the presentation open to use in the next exercise.

Moving rows and columns in PowerPoint is similar to moving rows and columns in a worksheet program such as Excel: you must make sure you have a blank row or column in which to insert the new data. If you simply drag a row or column to a new location, you will overwrite the existing data at that location.

Resizing and Distributing Rows and Columns
Row heights and column widths can be easily resized by dragging or double-clicking cell borders.

Adjust column widths or row heights to eliminate unused space or add space to make table text more readable. Dragging allows you to "eyeball" column widths or row heights so that they look attractive on the slide. Double-clicking on the divider bar between columns allows you to immediately set column width to the width of its widest line. Double-clicking does not adjust row height, however. To resize a row that has been enlarged, drag its bottom border. To make all the rows or columns the same width, you can use the Distribute Rows or Distribute Columns buttons.

In this exercise, you will resize rows and columns in two different ways and distribute the column widths evenly.

STEP BY STEP   **Resize and Distribute Rows and Columns**

USE the *ATMs Final* presentation that is still open from the previous exercise.

1. Go to slide 6, and double-click the vertical border between the first and second columns.

Take Note   Double-clicking a column border adjusts column width to fit the column's widest entry.

2. Drag the horizontal border between the Claude Simpson and Mary Bailey lines in the table upward, so that the Claude Simpson cells are as short as possible (see Figure 5-17).

Figure 5-17

Resize a row by dragging its bottom border

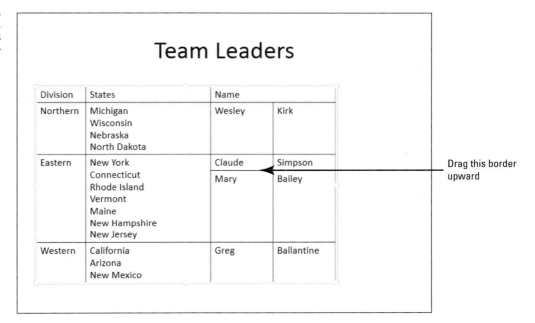

If you need to be more precise in resizing, you can use the tools in the Cell Size group on the Table Tools Layout tab to specify exact widths and heights for table cells.

3. Click in the cell that contains States.

4. On the Table Tools Layout tab, in the Table Size group's Width box, set the value to exactly 7" by clicking the increment arrows or typing over the existing value.

5. In the Cell Size group's Width box, set the value to exactly 3.1" by clicking the up increment arrow or by typing over the existing value (see Figure 5-18).

Take Note   The Width setting in the Table Size group controls the width of the entire table; the Width setting in the Cell Size group controls the width of only the column in which the active cell is located. The active cell is the one containing the insertion point.

Figure 5-18

Specify an exact width from the Table Tools Layout tab

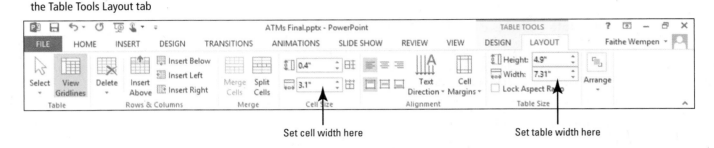

Set cell width here   Set table width here

6. Drag the **outer border** of the table to the right as needed to re-center the table beneath the Team Leaders title.

7. Select the **entire table** by dragging across it.

8. On the Table Tools Layout tab, click the **Distribute Columns** button ⊞. Each column becomes the same width.

9. **SAVE** the presentation.

PAUSE. LEAVE the presentation open to use in the next exercise.

You do not have to select an entire column or row to resize all cells in that column. When you click in any cell and resize a row or column, all cells in that row or column are adjusted at the same time.

If space in a table is extremely tight, you may be able to fit more text in columns and rows by adjusting cell margins. The Cell Margins button in the Alignment group on the Table Tools Layout tab allows you to select from four different cell margin options ranging from None to Wide, or create custom margins.

Merging and Splitting Table Cells

The merge and split features allow you to adjust how content fits in table cells and to modify the internal structure of a table without increasing or reducing its overall width. By merging cells, you can position content so it spans more than one column or row. When two cells merge, all the content is retained; a paragraph break is inserted between their content. Use the split feature when you want to divide a single row or column to accommodate additional entries without modifying the remainder of the table. When you split a cell that contains content, the content goes with the leftmost or upper cell; you may choose to move some or all of the content into the new blank cell(s) after the split. Merging and splitting can modify the internal structure of a table without increasing or reducing its overall width. In this exercise, you will practice merging and splitting table cells.

STEP BY STEP   **Merge and Split Table Cells**

USE the *ATMs Final* presentation that is still open from the previous exercise.

1. Go to **slide 6** and select the cells containing **Wesley** and **Kirk**.

2. On the Table Tools Layout tab, click **Merge Cells**. The two cells become one, and the text from both cells appears in the merged cell separated by a paragraph break (see Figure 5-19).

Figure 5-19

Merging cells

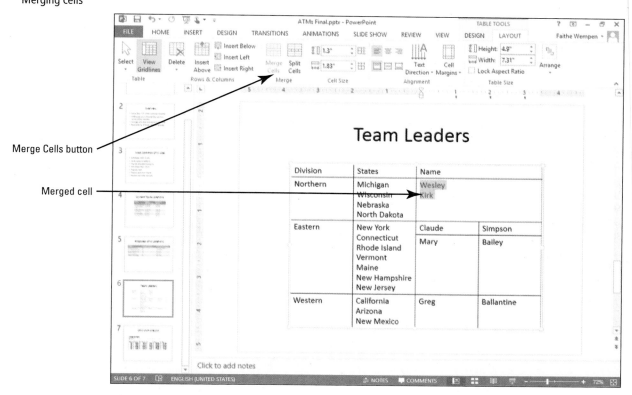

Merge Cells button

Merged cell

3. Click at the beginning of the second name and press Backspace to delete the paragraph break between the two names, so they appear on the same line. Press the space bar once if needed to add a space between the two names.

4. Use the procedures in steps 1-3 to merge each of the other three names (Claude Simpson, Mary Bailey, and Greg Ballantine) in the table in the same way.

5. Use the procedures in steps 1-3 to merge the cells containing the two names of the representatives for the Eastern region, and leave each name on a separate line as in Figure 5-20.

Figure 5-20

The table after all first and last names have been merged

Team Leaders

Division	States	Name
Northern	Michigan Wisconsin Nebraska North Dakota	Wesley Kirk
Eastern	New York Connecticut Rhode Island Vermont Maine New Hampshire New Jersey	Claude Simpson Mary Bailey
Western	California Arizona New Mexico	Greg Ballantine

6. Select **all three cells** that contain state names, and on the Table Tools Layout tab, click **Split Cells**. The Split Cells dialog box opens (see Figure 5-21).

Figure 5-21

Splitting a cell into
multiple cells

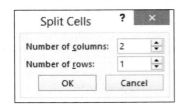

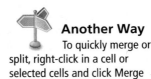
To quickly merge or split, right-click in a cell or selected cells and click Merge Cells or Split Cells on the shortcut menu.

7. In the Number of Columns text box, type **2** to set the number of columns to 2 if it is not already at that value. In the Number of Rows box, type **1** to set the number of rows to 1 if it is not already at that value. Then click **OK**.

8. Select the **entire table**, and then click the **Distribute Columns** button on the Table Tools Layout tab to equalize the column widths.

9. For each division, move **approximately half** of the names from the existing cell to the empty cell to its right (see Figure 5-22). You can move the text either with drag and drop or cut and paste.

Figure 5-22

Move some of the state names
into the new cells

Move some of the state
names into the new column

Team Leaders

Division	States		Name
Northern	Michigan Wisconsin	Nebraska North Dakota	Wesley Kirk
Eastern	New York Connecticut Rhode Island Vermont	Maine New Hampshire New Jersey	Claude Simpson Mary Bailey
Western	California Arizona	New Mexico	Greg Ballantine

10. **SAVE** the presentation file and **CLOSE** it.

PAUSE. LEAVE PowerPoint open to use in the next exercise.

You can also split columns or rows by drawing additional lines with the Draw Table feature, as you did earlier in the lesson. You can use the Eraser tool on the Table Tools Design tab to merge cells by erasing the divider between them.

FORMATTING TABLES

The Bottom Line

PowerPoint provides default formats to all new tables so that they have an appealing look. You may want to modify formatting, however, because you do not like the default colors or you want a different look. Use the tools on the Table Tools Design and Table Tools Layout tabs to apply new formatting options.

Changing Table Text Alignment and Orientation

Text can be aligned both vertically and horizontally within a cell. You can also change the text's orientation (rotation) to create visual interest. Use the same tools to align content horizontally in a table cell that you use to align text in a text placeholder. Changing alignment in table cells can improve readability as well as make a table more attractive.

Vertical alignment options control how content appears from the top to the bottom of a cell. The default option is top alignment, but column headings often look better centered vertically in table cells. When column headings have differing numbers of lines, standard procedure is to align all headings at the bottom.

Use options on the Text Direction menu in the Alignment group of the Table Tools Layout tab to change the orientation of text for a special effect. Vertical text or text that reads from bottom to top makes a unique row header, for example. In this exercise, you will change the text direction and alignment in table cells.

STEP BY STEP	Align and Orient Text in a Table

GET READY. To align and orient text in a table, do the following:

1. **OPEN** the *Bids* presentation and save it as *Final Bids*.
2. Go to slide 2, and click in the merged cell at the far left of the table.
3. Click the Table Tools Layout tab, and then click the Text Direction button to display a menu of orientation options.
4. Click Stacked. This option will stack text with each letter below the previous one.
5. Type Vendor in the merged cell. The text stacks in the merged cell (see Figure 5-23).

Figure 5-23

Stacked text orientation

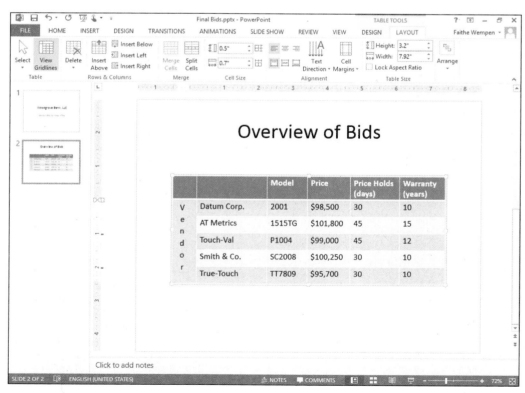

6. Select the text you just typed. Click the Home tab, and then click the Character Spacing button in the Font group. Click Very Tight (see Figure 5-24).

Figure 5-24

Set the character spacing

Character Spacing button

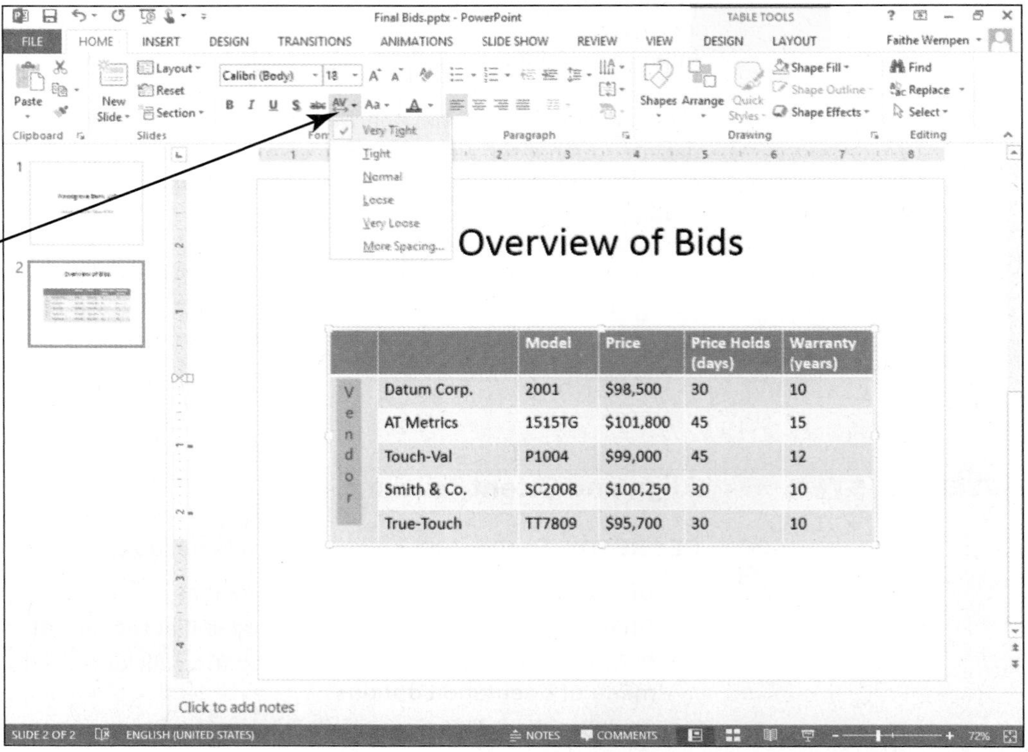

Take Note When you move the I-beam pointer over rotated or stacked text, its orientation changes to match the text orientation.

7. With text still selected, click the Bold button in the Font group on the Home tab.
8. Select the cells with numbers in the Price column. Click the Align Right button ☰ in the Paragraph group to align all text in that column along the right side of the cells.
9. Select the cells with numbers in the last two columns. Click the Center button ☰ to center the contents of those cells.
10. Select the cells in the column header row. Because they are already blue, it will not be obvious that they are selected.
11. Click the Center button on the Home tab to center the contents of those cells.
12. Click the Table Tools Layout tab, and click the Align Bottom button ⊟ in the Alignment group. All column headings now align at the bottom of the cells (see Figure 5-25).

Figure 5-25

Set vertical alignment

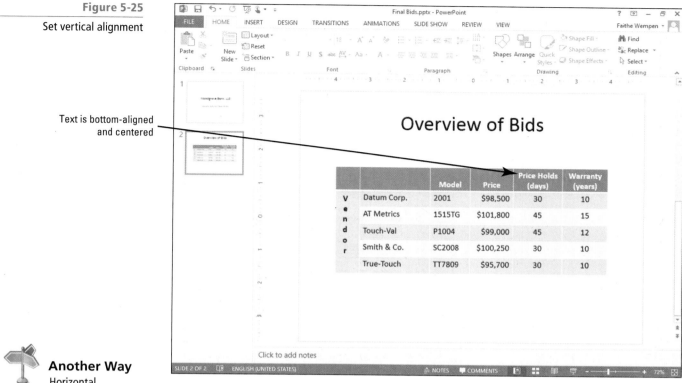

Text is bottom-aligned
and centered

Figure 5-25

Set vertical alignment

Another Way
Horizontal
alignment buttons also appear
on the Table Tools Layout tab.

13. **SAVE** the presentation.

PAUSE. LEAVE the presentation open to use in the next exercise.

Applying a Table Style

PowerPoint tables are formatted by default with a Quick Style based on the current theme colors. You can choose another table style to change color and shading formats. In this exercise, you will apply a table style.

STEP BY STEP   **Apply a Table Style**

USE the *Final Bids* presentation that is still open from the previous exercise.

1. Click anywhere in the table on slide 2, and then click the Table Tools Design tab.
2. Click the More button in the Table Styles group to display the Table Styles gallery (see Figure 5-26). Note that the table styles are organized into several groups—Best Match for Document, Light, Medium, and Dark.

Figure 5-26

Table Styles gallery

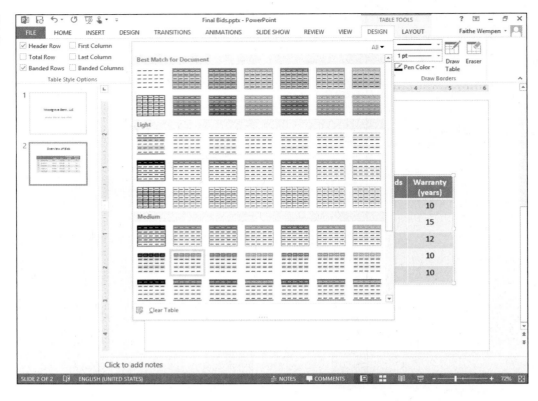

3. Click the Themed Style 2 – Accent 6 table style. This style is a colorful alternative, but not exactly what you want.

4. Click the More button again, and then click the Medium Style 3 style, a black and gray combination in the first column of the gallery. Your table should look similar to Figure 5-27.

Figure 5-27

New style applied to entire table

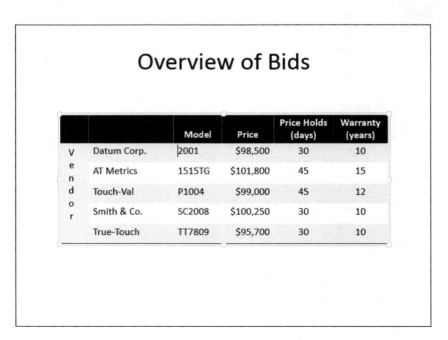

PAUSE. LEAVE the presentation open to use in the next exercise.

Colors available for Table Style formats are controlled by theme. If you apply a Quick Style and then change the theme, the Table Style colors will adjust to those of the new theme.

You may on occasion want to remove all table formatting to present data in a simple grid without shading or border colors. You can remove formatting by clicking Clear Table at the bottom of the Table Styles gallery. Once you have cleared formats, you can reapply them by selecting any table style.

Turning Table Style Options On or Off

The options in the Table Style Options group on the Table Tools Design tab allow you to adjust what part of a table receives special emphasis. If your table has a row that shows totals of calculations, for example, the Total Row option applies color to that row so it stands out. You can use any number of these options in a single table, or you can deselect all of them for a plainer effect. Keep in mind that there is sometimes a fine line between effective emphasis and the visual confusion that can result from too much emphasis. In this exercise, you will modify the formatting applied by a table style by turning certain options on and off.

STEP BY STEP	Turn Table Style Options On and Off

USE the *Final Bids* presentation that is still open from the previous exercise.

1. Click anywhere in the table to select it if necessary.
2. Click the Table Tools Design tab if it is not already displayed.
3. Click the Banded Rows option in the Table Style Options group to deselect the option.
4. Click the First Column option. The first column receives special emphasis.
5. Click the Banded Columns option. Color bands are applied to the columns. Your table should look similar to Figure 5-28.

Figure 5-28

New table style options have been applied

Overview of Bids

Vendor		Model	Price	Price Holds (days)	Warranty (years)
V e n d o r	Datum Corp.	2001	$98,500	30	10
	AT Metrics	1515TG	$101,800	45	15
	Touch-Val	P1004	$99,000	45	12
	Smith & Co.	SC2008	$100,250	30	10
	True-Touch	TT7809	$95,700	30	10

6. **SAVE** and close the presentation.

PAUSE. LEAVE PowerPoint open to use in the next exercise.

Adding Shading to Cells

If you do not like the Table Style options or want more control over formatting, use the Table Tools Design tab's options for creating shading fills, border styles, and effects. Use the Shading button to display a color palette with the current theme colors. You can also select a color from the

Standard Colors palette or from the Colors dialog box, or choose a picture, gradient, or texture fill. In this exercise, you will learn to use the Shading button on the Table Tools Design tab to select your own fill options for table cells. In this exercise, you will add shading to cells.

STEP BY STEP   Add Shading to Cells

GET READY. To add shading to cells, perform the following steps:

1. **OPEN** the *Warranties* presentation and save it as *Warranties Final*.
2. Go to slide 2, and select the cells in the top row of the table (*the* column header row).
3. Click the Table Tools Design tab, and then click the Shading button drop-down arrow in the Table Styles group. The Shading color palette displays.
4. Click the Gold, Accent 1 color to fill the column header cells with gold.
5. With the column header cells still selected, click the Shading drop-down arrow again, point to Gradient, and select the From Top Right Corner gradient style in the Dark Variations section of the gallery (see Figure 5-29).
6. **SAVE** the presentation.

PAUSE. LEAVE the presentation open to use in the next exercise.

Figure 5-29

Select a gradient fill

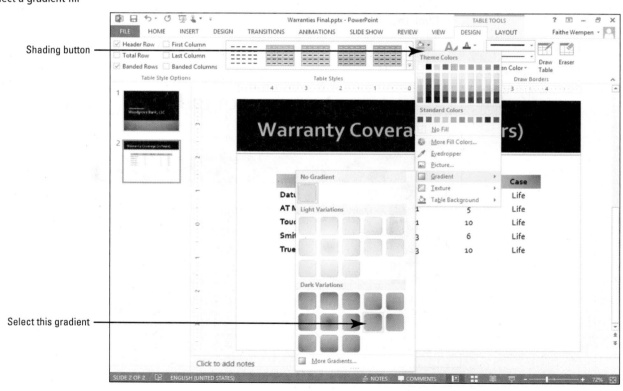

The Shading menu also offers the Table Background option. You can use this command to insert a color or a picture to fill all cells of a table. You will learn more about inserting pictures as backgrounds later in this lesson.

Be careful when applying picture or texture fills to an entire table. Your text must remain readable, so choose a light background, adjust transparency if necessary, or be prepared to boldface text.

Adding Borders to Table Cells

The Borders menu allows you to quickly apply borders to all sides of selected cells or to any specific side of a cell, giving you considerable flexibility in formatting table cells. You can also remove all borders from a cell or selected cells by selecting No Border. After you have selected a border option, it displays on the button. You can easily reapply that border option by simply clicking the button. In this exercise, you will add borders to table cells.

STEP BY STEP   **Add Borders to Table Cells**

USE the *Warranties Final* presentation that is still open from the previous exercise.

1. In the table on slide 2, select all cells *except those in the first column and the column header cells*. (You are selecting the numbers and the Life entries.)
2. On the Table Tools Design tab, click the Borders drop-down arrow in the Table Styles group. A menu of border options appears.
3. Click Inside Horizontal Border (see Figure 5-30).

Figure 5-30

Apply an inside horizontal border to the selected cells

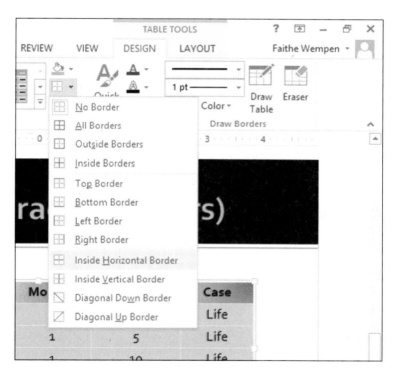

4. Click outside the table to deselect the cells, and then select only the bottom row of the table.
5. Click the Borders drop-down arrow, and then click Bottom Border. A border is applied to the entire bottom row of the table.
6. Click outside the table to deselect the cells. Your table should look like Figure 5-31.

Figure 5-31

Borders applied to the
selected cells

Vendor	Keypad	Monitor	Electronics	Case
Datum Corp.	5	2	5	Life
AT Metrics	3	1	5	Life
Touch-Val	7	1	10	Life
Smith & Co.	5	3	6	Life
True-Touch	7	3	10	Life

7. **SAVE** the presentation.

PAUSE. LEAVE the presentation open to use in the next exercise.

Take Note   The Shading button also shows the latest shading color you chose making it easy to apply the same color again.

Note that you can also choose diagonal borders from the Borders menu. Use a diagonal border to split a cell so you can insert two values in it, one to the left side of the cell and the other to the right on the other side of the diagonal border.

Take Note   To insert two values in a cell, set left alignment and type the first value, then press **Ctrl+Tab** or use the spacebar to move to the other half of the cell to type the second value.

Adding Special Effects to a Table

The Table Styles group offers an Effects button to let you apply selected special effects. Using the Effects menu, you can apply cell bevel, shadow, and reflection effects to a table. Bevels can apply to individual cells or selections of cells, but shadows and reflections are applied to the entire table.

STEP BY STEP   **Add Special Effects to a Table**

USE the *Warranties Final* presentation that is still open from the previous exercise.

1. Click anywhere in the table on slide 2.
2. Click the **Effects** button in the Table Styles group (Table Tools Design tab), point to Shadow, and click **Offset Diagonal Bottom Right in the Outer section** (see Figure 5-32).

Figure 5-32

Apply a shadow effect
to the table

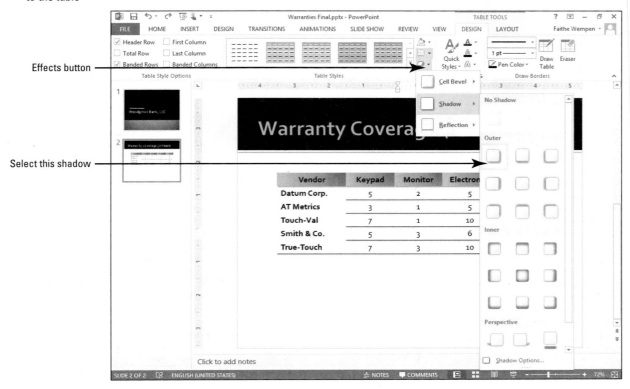

3. Click **outside the table** to see the effect.
4. **SAVE** the presentation.

PAUSE. LEAVE the presentation open to use in the next exercise.

Adding an Image to a Table

An image can serve as the background in one or more table cells. The image is not the cell content, but rather a background fill, just as a color fill would be. The text in the cell appears on top of the background fill. In this exercise, you will learn how to add an image behind the text in some cells in a table.

STEP BY STEP	**Add an Image to a Table**

USE the *Warranties Final* presentation that is still open from the previous exercise.

1. In the table on slide 2, select the **vendor names** in the first column of the table. (Do not select the Vendor column heading.)
2. Right-click in one of the **selected cells**, then click **Format Shape** on the menu that appears. The Format Shape task pane displays.
3. In the task pane, click **Fill** to expand that category if it is not already expanded.
4. Click **Picture or texture fill**.

5. Click the **File** button and in the Insert Picture dialog box, navigate to the **location of your data files**. Select *ATM.jpg* and click **Insert**.
6. In the Format Shape task pane, click to place a checkmark in the **Tile picture as texture** check box.
7. Drag the **Transparency** slider until the box to the right of the slider reads **80%** or **type 80** in the Transparency box (see Figure 5-33).

Figure 5-33

Apply a picture fill

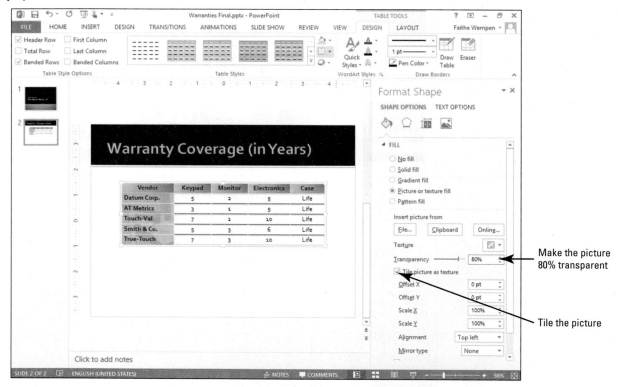

8. **Close the task pane.** Click **outside the table.** The selected cells have a semi-transparent fill using the selected graphic.

9. **SAVE** the presentation.

PAUSE. LEAVE the presentation open to use in the next exercise.

You learned earlier that you can specify a picture as a background using the Table Background command on the Shading menu. Use this option if the picture you want to use is already formatted in such a way that it will not overwhelm the text in the table.

For the most control over an image to be used as a table background, insert it using the Format Shape task pane, as you did in this exercise. You can insert a picture in a single cell or selected cells by right-clicking a selected cell and choosing Format Shape. Or, you can insert the picture in all cells by right-clicking the table's container frame and then choosing Format Shape. Tiling options in the task pane allow you to adjust how the tiles display over the table. If you choose not to tile, a separate copy of the picture will appear in every cell of the table. The Transparency slider lets you wash out the picture to make it appropriate for a background.

Images can be used for more than background effects in tables. You can also insert an image as table content. To do so, click in a cell and use the Picture command on the Shading menu. The picture you select is automatically resized to fit into the selected table cell.

Arranging a Table with Other Objects

PowerPoint enables you to stack one object on top of another and then arrange them to control which one is at the top of the stack. Any transparent areas on the object on top show the underlying object behind them. In this exercise, you will arrange a shape with a table so that the shape serves as a decorative frame.

STEP BY STEP   **Arrange a Shape and a Table**

USE the *Warranties Final* presentation that is still open from the previous exercise.

1. Display slide 2 and on the Insert tab, click the Shapes button to open the Shapes gallery. Then click the rounded rectangle in the first row of shapes.

2. Drag to draw a rounded rectangle that completely covers the table (see Figure 5-34).

Figure 5-34

Cover the table with a rounded rectangle

Shapes button

Select the rounded rectangle

Draw a rectangle that covers the table

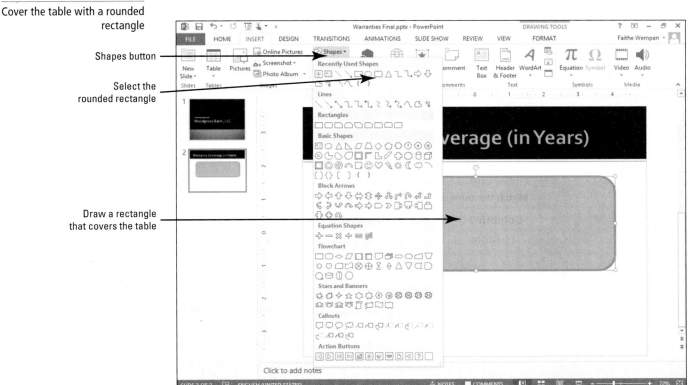

3. On the Drawing Tools Format tab, click Send Backward in the Arrange command group. The shape is sent behind the table.

4. With the shape still selected, click the Shape Fill button in the Shape Styles group and click More Fill Colors from the menu that appears. The Colors dialog box opens.

5. Drag the Transparency slider to 85%, and then click OK. The rectangle appears as a lightly shaded background behind the table (see Figure 5-35).

Figure 5-35

The table and the shape are stacked together, and arranged so that the table is in front

Vendor	Keypad	Monitor	Electronics	Case
Datum Corp.	5	2	5	Life
AT Metrics	3	1	5	Life
Touch-Val	7	1	10	Life
Smith & Co.	5	3	6	Life
True-Touch	7	3	10	Life

6. **SAVE** and **CLOSE** the presentation.

EXIT PowerPoint.

SKILL SUMMARY

In This Lesson, You Learned How To:	Exam Objective	Objective Number
Create tables	Create new tables.	3.2.1
Import tables from external sources	Import tables from external sources.	3.2.4
Modify table layout	Modify the number of rows and columns.	3.2.2
Format tables	Apply table styles.	3.2.3

Knowledge Assessment

Matching

Match the term in Column 1 to its description in Column 2.

Column 1	Column 2
1. Table	a. Insert data so that it maintains a connection to a source document.
2. Draw Table	b. A document used to manipulate numerical data.
3. Table Tools Design	c. A background color for table cells.
4. Merge	d. Insert data so that it can be edited using its original application.
5. Quick Style	e. Tab that allows you to insert a new table row.
6. Link	f. An arrangement of columns and rows used to organize data.
7. Shading	g. Tab that allows you to apply a Quick Style to a table.
8. Embed	h. Option you can use to create a table frame and insert columns and rows where you want them.
9. Table Tools Layout	i. To combine two or more cells to create a larger cell.
10. Worksheet	j. A set of preset formatting that can be applied to a table.

True/False

Circle T if the statement is true or F if the statement is false.

T F 1. To create a new table, click the Insert Object button and then select the type of table to create.

T F 2. By default, a new table is sized to fit the content placeholder in which it was created.

T F 3. To edit a worksheet object on a slide, double-click the object to display Excel's tools.

T F 4. You can copy and paste data from Excel to a PowerPoint slide using the Clipboard.

T F 5. You must select an entire row before you can insert a new row above or below it.

T F 6. When moving a column, you do not have to create an empty column first for the moved data to be placed in; the existing content will move over to accommodate it.

T F 7. Use Distribute Columns to quickly resize all columns to the same width.

T F 8. Use the Blank Table option to quickly remove all formatting from a table.

T F 9. Bevel effects automatically apply to an entire table.

T F 10. If you do not specify that a picture should be tiled over selected cells, it will display in each table cell.

Project 5-1: Job Fair

You work for Lucerne Executive Recruiters, a company that specializes in finding employees for a variety of clients. You are planning to give a brief presentation at a local job fair and need to prepare a slide that lists some currently available jobs for which you are recruiting candidates. You can use a table to display this information.

GET READY. LAUNCH PowerPoint if it is not already running.

1. **OPEN** the *Jobs* presentation and save it as *Jobs Final*.

2. Go to slide 2, and click the Insert Table icon in the content placeholder.

3. Create a table with three columns and seven rows.

4. Type the following information in the table:

Title	Company	Salary Range*
Senior Editor	Litware, Inc.	$30K–$42K
Sales Associate	Contoso Pharmaceuticals	$55K–$70K
District Manager	Tailspin Toys	$65K–$80K
Accountant	Fourth Coffee	$53K–$60K
Production Assistant	Fabrikam, Inc.	$38K–$45K

*Starting salary based on experience

5. Click in the Salary Range column, and then click the Insert Right button on the Table Tools Layout tab to insert a new column.

6. Type the following information in the new column:

Posted
5/01
5/10
4/30
4/27
5/07

7. Click the Production Assistant cell, then click the Insert Below button on the Table Tools Layout tab to insert a new row.

8. Type the following information in the new row:

Loan Officer   Woodgrove Bank $42K –$54K   5/12

9. Select all the cells in the last row of the table (where the starting salary note is), and then click the Merge Cells button on the Table Tools Layout tab.

10. Adjust column widths by dragging or double-clicking cell borders so that all table entries in a given row are on a single line.

11. Format the table as follows:

   a. Select the Salary Range and Posted columns, and then click the Center button on the Home tab.

   b. Click in the last row of the table, and then click the Align Right button.

   c. With the insertion point still in the last row, click the Shading button on the Table Tools Design tab, and then click No Fill.

   d. Click the Borders button, and then click No Border.

   e. Click the First Column table style option to apply emphasis to the first column of the table. Adjust column widths again if necessary to avoid runover lines.

   f. Select all cells in the Loan Officer row of the table, click the Borders button, and then click Bottom Border.

   g. Apply the Circle bevel effect to the column header cells and the first column cells.

12. **SAVE** the presentation and then **CLOSE** the file.

LEAVE PowerPoint open for use in the next project.

Project 5-2: Making the Upgrade

You are a production manager at Tailspin Toys. You have been asked to give a presentation to senior management about anticipated costs of upgrading machinery in the assembly area. Because you want to sum the costs, you will use an Excel worksheet to present the information.

1. **OPEN** the *Upgrades* presentation and save it as *Upgrades Final*.
2. Go to slide 2, click the Insert tab, click the Table drop-down arrow, and then click Excel Spreadsheet.
3. Drag the lower-right corner handle of the worksheet object to reveal columns A through D and rows 1 through 7.
4. Type the following data in the worksheet.

Machine	Upgrade	Cost	Time Frame
Conveyor #2	New belt, drive	$28,000	30 days
Conveyor #3	Update software	$5,800	14 days
Drill Press #1	Replace	$32,000	30 days
Vacuum system	New pump, lines	$12,750	30 days
Docks #2 - #5	Doors, motors	$14,500	10 days

5. Click the Excel Page Layout tab, click the Themes button, and then click Retrospect to apply the same theme to the worksheet that your presentation uses.
6. Adjust column widths by dragging or double-clicking column borders to display all data. Widen the overall worksheet object if needed.
7. Click in cell B7, type Total Costs, and then press Tab.
8. Click the Sum button in the Editing group on the Home tab, and then press Enter to complete the SUM function. The result should be $93,050.
9. Apply Quick Styles to the worksheet as follows:
   a. Select the column headings, and then click the Cell Styles button in the Styles group on the Home tab.
   b. Click the Accent5 style.
   c. Click the Total Costs cell, click the Cell Styles button, and click the Accent1 style.
   d. Click the cell that contains the sum of costs, click the Cell Styles button, and click the Total style.
   e. Apply bold formatting to the column headings and the Total Costs cell.
10. Click the Select All area at the top left corner of the worksheet, then click the Font Size drop-down arrow and click 20. Adjust column widths again if necessary to display all data.
11. Select the entries in the Time Frame column, and click the Center button.
12. Click outside the worksheet twice to review your changes.
13. **SAVE** the presentation and **CLOSE** the file.

LEAVE PowerPoint open for use in the next project.

Proficiency Assessment

Project 5-3: Power Up

You are an operations manager for City Power & Light. You have been asked to give a presentation to department heads about scheduled maintenance of power substations around the city. Use a table to present the maintenance schedule.

1. **OPEN** the *Power* presentation and save it as *Power Final*.
2. Go to slide 3. Insert a table with two columns and seven rows. Move the table below the slide title, centered on the side.
3. Type the following information in the table:

Substation	Week of
Eastland	July 13
Morehead	October 1
Huntington	June 6
Parkland	May 21
Midtown	July 28
Elmwood	December 11

4. Apply a Table Style Medium Style 1 – Accent 2 to the table.
5. Turn on the First Column table style option. Change the font style for the entire presentation to Calibri (from the Design tab's Variant group).
6. Delete the last row of the table.
7. Rearrange the rows so that the dates in the second column are in chronological order. Recenter the table on the slide, if necessary.

   Tip: Create a new blank row, and use it as a temporary holding area when moving rows and then delete the blank row when you are finished.

8. **SAVE** the presentation and **CLOSE** the file.

LEAVE PowerPoint open for use in the next project.

Project 5-4: Is It on the Agenda?

You are an assistant director of finance at Humongous Insurance Company. You have been tasked with establishing the agenda for a management meeting. You have created the agenda as a table on a slide which will appear onscreen throughout the day. You think the table could use some additional formatting to make it easier to read and understand.

1. **OPEN** the *Agenda* presentation and save it as *Agenda Final*.
2. Center all entries in the second column, and then center the column heading only for the third column.
3. Clear all formatting from the table.
4. Remove all borders from the table.
5. Format the table's header row as follows:
   a. Increase the height of the column header row to 0.6", and then center the column header text vertically in the row.
   b. Apply bold, 20-point formatting to the column header text.
   c. Select the header row cells and use the Format Shape task pane to apply the Granite texture. Change the transparency of the texture to 65%.
   d. Apply the Circle cell bevel effect to the header row cells.
6. Change the height of each of the rows except the first one to 0.4".
7. Select the first Break row and apply a shading of Aqua, Accent 3, Lighter 40%.

8. Select the **second Break row** and apply a shading of **Lavender, Accent 5, Lighter 40%**.

9. Apply the **Inside Diagonal Bottom Right** shadow effect to the entire table.

10. Add a **border** around the outside of the table and along the bottom of the header row.

11. **SAVE** the presentation and **CLOSE** the file.

LEAVE PowerPoint open for use in the next project.

Mastery Assessment

Project 5-5: Scaling the Summit

You are a district manager for Adventure Works, a travel agency specializing in adventurous destinations. You are preparing a presentation that contains a list of mountain climbing excursions you can use at a travel fair and need to format the table that contains the excursion information.

1. **OPEN** the *Adventures* presentation.

2. Go to **slide 3** and select **all the cells** in the table.

3. Use the *Mountain.jpg* picture file as a **background fill** for the selected cells. Tile the **picture**, and adjust transparency to **80%**.

4. Change the text in the first row to **White**, and change the background fill of those two cells to **Black**. Make the text in that row **bold** and assign a font size of **20 points**.

5. Apply all borders to the table.

6. Apply an Offset Diagonal Top Right shadow to the entire table.

7. **SAVE** the presentation as *Adventures Final* and **CLOSE** the file.

LEAVE PowerPoint open for use in the next project.

Project 5-6: Complaint Process

Your employer, Trey Research, has been asked by Center City Hospital to help the hospital conduct an extensive study on patient complaints. You have been asked to tally complaints for the past year and categorize them. You have begun the process of creating a presentation to detail your findings. Your first step is a summary table that lays out the major categories of complaints.

1. **OPEN** the *Complaints* presentation.

2. Go to **slide 2** and adjust **column widths** so that all the summary items are on **one line**.

3. Reorder the **rows** so that the categories are in **alphabetical order**.

4. Set the **height** of each of the rows (except the header row) to exactly .4".

5. Split the **Complaints column** (except the column header cell) into two columns, and move **all information** from the original Complaints column, except the column header, into the right-hand split.

6. Merge the table cells in the **left-hand split**. (Do not merge the column header row, only the banded cells.)

7. In the merged cell, rotate the text direction **270 degrees** and type **Over 350 complaints received from patients in past 12 months**.

8. Apply **different shading colors** to each category of complaint, with a border at the bottom of each category section.

9. Adjust **column widths** again, if necessary, and adjust **alignment** as necessary to improve table appearance.

10. **SAVE** the presentation as *Complaints Final* and **CLOSE** the file.

EXIT PowerPoint.

Using Charts in a Presentation 6

LESSON SKILL MATRIX

Skill	Exam Objective	Objective Number
Building Charts	Insert charts.	3.3.2
	Import charts from external sources.	3.3.6
Modifying the Chart Type and Data	Modify chart type.	3.3.3
Modifying Chart Elements	Add legends to charts.	3.3.4
	Modify chart parameters.	3.3.5
Formatting a Chart	Create and modify chart styles.	3.3.1

KEY TERMS

- charts
- chart area
- chart element
- data marker
- data series
- legend
- plot area

©Tongshan/iStockphoto

You are the general manager of the Alpine Ski House, a small ski resort. One of your responsibilities is to provide information to the group of investors who share ownership of the resort. You will use PowerPoint presentations to convey that information. PowerPoint's charting capabilities enable you to communicate financial data in a visual way that makes trends and comparisons easy to understand. In this lesson, you will learn how to insert different types of charts, as well as how to modify and format a chart so it displays your data in the most attractive and useful way.

©Tongshan/iStockphoto

SOFTWARE ORIENTATION

A PowerPoint Chart

Charts can help your audience understand relationships among numerical values. Figure 6-1 shows a sample PowerPoint chart with some standard chart features labeled.

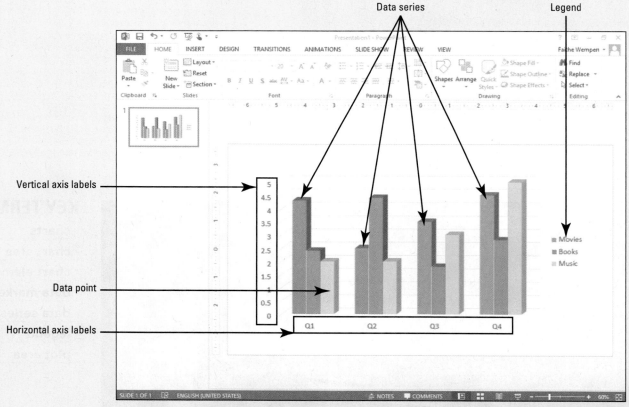

Figure 6-1
Components of a chart

A chart can compare multiple data series (see Figure 6-1) with each series represented by a different color or pattern. A **legend** explains what each color represents. Category axis labels explain what the groupings of bars represent (on the horizontal axis) and vertical axis labels explain the meaning of the numeric values (on the vertical axis). Optional elements such as gridlines behind the chart help make the chart more readable.

BUILDING CHARTS

Charts are visual representations of numerical data. Chart features such as columns, bars, lines, or pie slices make it easy to understand trends or compare values. Once you have created a chart in PowerPoint, you can easily modify the data on which the chart is based, choose a different type of chart to display the data, change the layout of the chart, and modify its formats.

CERTIFICATION READY? 3.3.2

How do you insert charts?

Inserting a Chart from a Content Placeholder

Excel opens when you create a chart in PowerPoint, and you enter the data in Excel that you want to plot on the chart. Then when you return to PowerPoint, the chart appears with the data presented. As with tables and other objects such as diagrams and pictures, the easiest way to insert a chart is to click the Insert Chart icon in any content placeholder. PowerPoint guides you the rest of the way to complete the chart. In the following exercise, you will place a chart on a slide using a content placeholder.

STEP BY STEP   **Insert a Chart**

GET READY. Before you begin these steps, make sure that your computer is on. Log on, if necessary.

1. **START** PowerPoint if the program is not already running.

2. Locate and open the *Revenues* presentation and save it as *Revenues Final*.

3. Go to slide 3. Click the Insert Chart icon in the center of the content placeholder. The Insert Chart dialog box opens (see Figure 6-2), showing chart types and subtypes.

Figure 6-2

Select a chart type and subtype

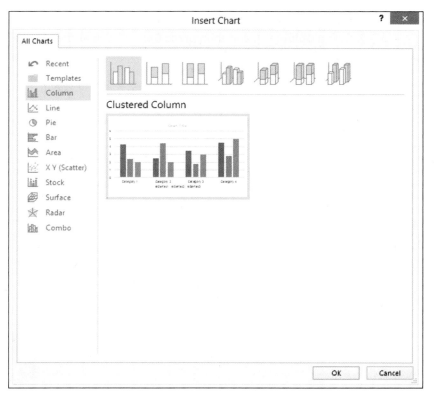

4. Click the **3D Clustered Column** chart subtype (the fourth from the left in the row of icons across the top of the dialog box).

Another Way
To insert a chart on a slide that does not have a content placeholder, click the Chart button on the Insert tab.

5. Click **OK**. A Chart in Microsoft PowerPoint window opens on top of the PowerPoint window containing the sample data on which the chart is based (see Figure 6-3). It is similar to an Excel worksheet. Notice the bright-blue border that surrounds the data range. This range border is used to indicate the data being charted.

Figure 6-3

A worksheet opens for entering the data for the chart

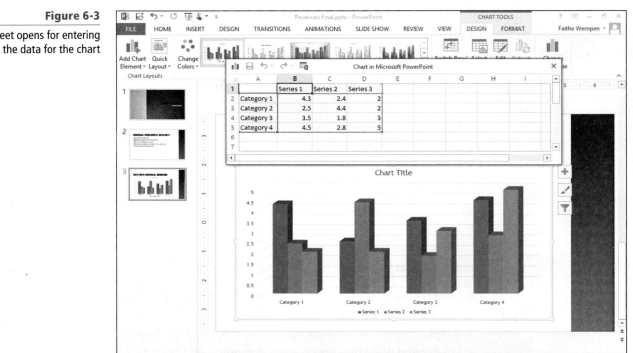

6. Drag the marker in the **bottom right corner of the range border** so that the range includes only cells **A1:C5**.

7. Select **Column D**, and then press **Delete** to clear the selected cells.

8. Click cell **B1** and type **2013**, replacing the current entry. Then press **Tab** to move to cell **C1**. Type **2014**, and press **Enter**.

9. Beginning in cell **A2**, type the following data in Excel to complete the chart:

Spring	**$89,000**	**$102,000**
Summer	**$54,000**	**$62,000**
Fall	**$102,000**	**$118,000**
Winter	**$233,000**	**$267,000**

10. Close the **worksheet window**. The chart appears with the data you entered (see Figure 6-4).

Figure 6-4

The completed chart

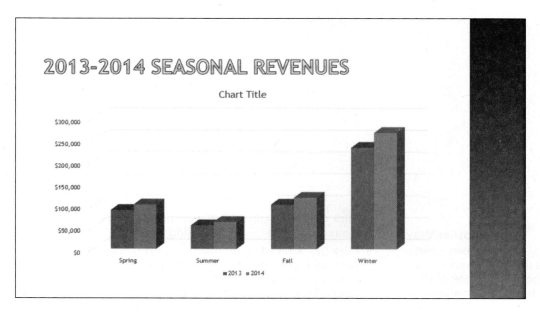

11. **SAVE** the presentation.

PAUSE. LEAVE the presentation open to use in the next exercise.

As you saw in the previous exercise, a worksheet window opens to allow you to insert the data that creates the chart. You can edit the worksheet data any time you want by clicking the Edit Data button on PowerPoint's Chart Tools Design tab (which appears when a chart is selected). When you click Edit Data in the Data group, a menu appears offering for you to edit the data in Power-Point (Edit Data) or in Excel (Edit Data in Excel 2013).

If you want to use data from an existing Excel workbook, open that workbook and Copy and Paste the data into the sheet created for the chart's data. Adjust the range border as needed.

Each PowerPoint chart type is designed to present a specific type of data. When you create a chart, you should select the chart type that will best display your data. Some of the most commonly used chart types are described below:

- **Column charts:** Column charts are generally used for showing data changes over a period of time or for comparing items. Categories (such as Quarter 1 or 2014) display on the horizontal axis (the X axis), and values display on the vertical axis (the Y axis).

- **Bar charts:** Bar charts are often used to compare individual items. They are especially useful when values are durations. Categories display on the vertical axis and values display on the horizontal axis.

- **Line charts:** Line charts are best used to display values over time or trends in data. Categories are usually evenly spaced items, such as months or years, and display on the horizontal axis.

- **Pie charts:** Pie charts are used to show the relationship of an individual category to the sum of all categories. Data for a pie chart consists of only a single column or row of data in the worksheet.

- **Area charts:** Area charts are used to show the amount of change over time as well as total value across a trend. Like a pie chart, an area chart can show the relationship of an individual category to the sum of all values.

You can learn more about chart types and subtypes and how they are designed to be used by consulting PowerPoint's Help files.

CERTIFICATION READY? 3.3.6

How do you import charts from external sources?

Importing a Chart from Excel

You can create the chart in Excel, and then copy the completed chart to PowerPoint using the Clipboard. Excel's charting tools are virtually identical to those in PowerPoint, so there is little reason to create the chart in Excel first, but if the chart already exists in Excel, copying it to PowerPoint can save some time.

STEP BY STEP | **Import an Excel Chart**

USE the *Revenues Final* presentation that is still open from the previous exercise.

1. With slide 3 selected, click **New Slide** on the Home tab. A new slide appears at the end of the presentation.

2. Open Microsoft Excel, and open the *Beverages* file from the data files for this lesson. Select the **chart**, and then press **Ctrl+C** to copy it to the Clipboard.

3. Switch back to PowerPoint and select the **outer frame of the content placeholder** box. Click **twice** on it to make sure the placeholder box itself is selected.

4. Press **Ctrl+V** to paste the chart into the placeholder.

5. Click in the slide's title **placeholder box** and type **Beverage Sales** (see Figure 6-5). Do not worry that the same title also appears above the chart; you will learn later in this lesson how to fix that.

Figure 6-5

The imported chart

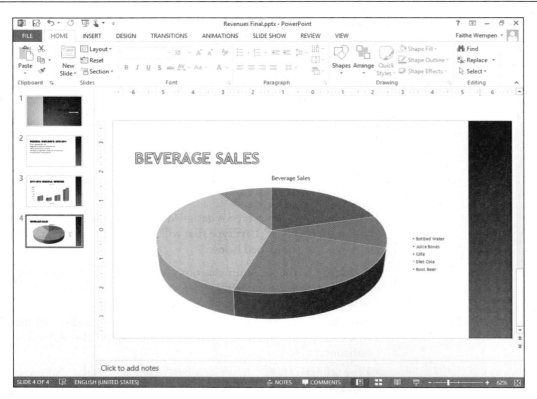

6. Switch back to Excel, and exit Excel.
7. In PowerPoint, **SAVE** the presentation.

PAUSE. LEAVE the presentation open to use in the next exercise.

Resizing and Moving a Chart

In addition to moving the individual elements within a chart, you can move and resize the chart itself. The dotted areas on the chart's border are sizing handles. You can resize any object by dragging a side or corner handle of its container. Note that if you drag a side handle, you may "stretch" the container, distorting its contents. Hold down Shift to maintain the height-width ratio (the aspect ratio). You can move any object, including a chart, by dragging it by its border. When you see the four-headed pointer, just click and drag. In this exercise, you will resize and move a chart.

STEP BY STEP **Resize and Move a Chart**

USE the *Revenues Final* presentation that is still open from the previous exercise.

1. Select the chart on slide 3.
2. Position the pointer on the lower-right corner of the chart's frame, so the mouse pointer becomes a double-headed arrow.
3. Drag inward to decrease the size of the chart by about 2" in width.

Take Note Optionally, you can hold down Shift while resizing to maintain the aspect ratio.

4. Position the pointer anywhere on the chart's frame except on one of the sizing handles. The mouse pointer becomes a four-headed arrow.
5. Drag to reposition the chart so that it is centered attractively on the slide (see Figure 6-6).
6. Click outside of the placeholder, and then **SAVE** the presentation.

Figure 6-6

The chart has been
resized and moved

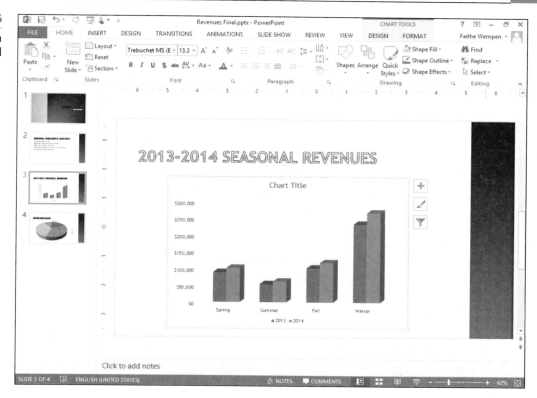

Figure 6-6

The chart has been
resized and moved

PAUSE. **LEAVE** the presentation open to use in the next exercise.

MODIFYING THE CHART TYPE AND DATA

The Bottom Line

It is not uncommon to have to modify a chart after it has been created. You can change the data on which the chart is based at any time or change the way in which the data is plotted. You can also add or remove chart elements as desired to customize your chart.

CERTIFICATION READY? 3.3.3

How do you modify
the chart type?

Choosing a Different Chart Type

After creating a chart, you may choose to change its type and/or its layout. If you decide that the chart type you have chosen does not display the data the way you want, you can choose a different chart type or subtype.

Different chart types display the data series differently. A **data series** consists of all the data points for a particular category, such as all the points for each season's 2014 values. A data point, sometimes called a **data marker**, is one point in a series. The default chart type is a Column chart. In this exercise, you will change a chart's type.

STEP BY STEP **Choose a Different Chart Type**

USE the *Revenues Final* presentation that is still open from the previous exercise.

Another Way

You also can use a shortcut to change the chart's type. Right-click almost anywhere in the chart and then click Change Chart Type on the shortcut menu.

1. In PowerPoint, select the chart on slide 3 and then click the Change Chart Type button on the Chart Tools Design tab. The Change Chart Type dialog box opens showing the same chart types that appeared when you first created the chart.

2. On the list of chart types at the left, click Bar.

3. Click the 3-D Clustered Bar subtype, and then click OK. The columns change to horizontal bars (see Figure 6-7).

4. **SAVE** the presentation and close it.

Figure 6-7

A new chart type applied

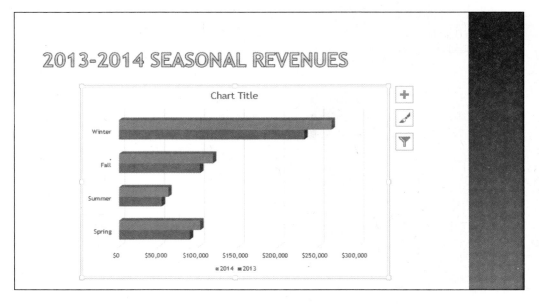

Figure 6-7

A new chart type applied

PAUSE. Leave PowerPoint open for the next exercise.

You can change any chart type to any other type, but the result may not always be what you expect, and you may lose some data. For example, when you change from any multi-series chart (such as a clustered bar or line) to a pie chart, only the first data series appears on the chart since a pie chart can only display one set of data.

If you apply a chart type that does not display your data as you want, use Undo to reverse the change, and then try another chart type.

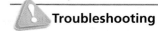

Troubleshooting   Changing from a 2-D chart type to a 3-D type can yield unexpected results. For some chart types, PowerPoint may display the new chart type in a rotated perspective view that you might not like. It is best to decide when you create the original chart whether you want it to use 2- or 3-D and then stick with those dimensions when making any change to the chart type.

Editing a Chart's Data

Chart data remains "live" as long as the chart remains on the slide. You can reopen the chart worksheet at any time to adjust the data. Changes you make to the chart worksheet window are immediately reflected on the PowerPoint chart. Use the Edit Data button to reactivate the worksheet window in Excel, and make your changes there. You can also use the Switch Row/Column button to plot the data on different axes.

Before you can edit chart data, you must select it. To select an individual cell in the data sheet, click that cell. To select ranges of cells, drag across them, or click a column or row header to select the entire row or column. In the following exercise, you will practice editing chart data, including selecting individual cells and entire columns.

STEP BY STEP   **Edit a Chart's Data**

GET READY. To edit a chart's data, do the following:

1. **OPEN** the *Pricing* presentation and save it as *Pricing Final*. Examine the information on the slides, and notice that the dates on the title slide do not agree with the dates on the chart.
2. Go to slide 2 and click the chart to select it.

3. On the Chart Tools Design tab, click the **Edit Data** button in the Data group. The worksheet window opens.

4. Click cell **B1** and type **2011**, replacing the current entry there. Then press **Tab** to move to cell **C1**, and type **2012**, replacing the current entry. Repeat the process for **D1 (2013)** and **E1 (2014)**.

5. Click **column B's column header** to select the entire column, and then **right-click** the column and click **Delete**. The data in the worksheet should now resemble Figure 6-8.

Figure 6-8

The edited data for the chart

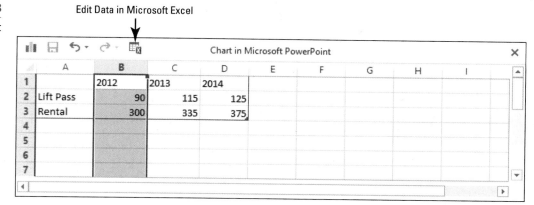

6. Click the **Edit Data in Microsoft Excel** icon on the worksheet window's toolbar. The data opens in Excel.

7. Click cell **A3** and type **Equipment Rental**, replacing the current entry there.

8. Close the **Excel window** and return to **PowerPoint**. Select the chart again if it is not still selected.

9. If the Switch Row/Column button is available on the Chart Tools Design tab, click it to **switch rows and columns**. If it is not, do the following to switch rows and columns:

   a. Click **Select Data**. The Select Data Source dialog box opens.

   b. Click **Switch Row/Column** (see Figure 6-9).

   c. Click **OK**.

Figure 6-9

Switch rows and columns from the Select Data Source dialog box if the Switch Row/Column button is unavailable on the Chart Tools Design tab

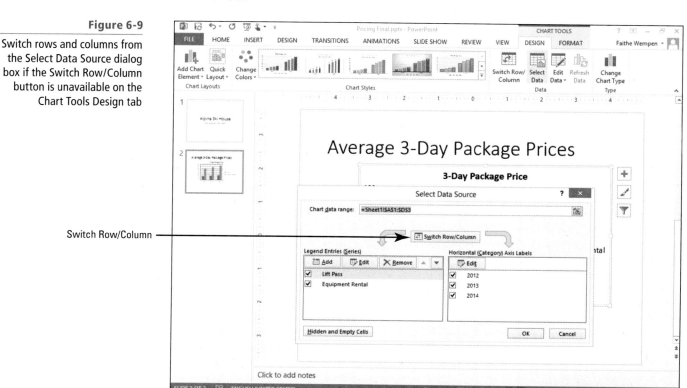

10. Click the **Switch Row/Column** button on the Chart Tools Design tab to switch the rows and columns back to their original settings. (Even if the button was unavailable in step 9, it will be available now.)
11. Close the worksheet window if it is still open.
12. **SAVE** the presentation.

PAUSE. LEAVE the presentation open to use in the next exercise.

The Switch Row/Column feature can be very helpful in adjusting the way data appears in a chart. In essence, the legend entries and the horizontal axis labels switch places. If you find that your chart does not seem to show the data as you wish, try switching rows and columns for a different perspective on the data.

MODIFYING CHART ELEMENTS

The Bottom Line

Chart elements are the optional parts of a chart, such as the legend, title, data labels, data table, axes, axis labels, and so on. You can apply Quick Layouts that apply preset combinations of these elements, and you can turn each element type on or off individually and apply different options to it.

Applying and Modifying a Quick Layout

PowerPoint supplies several preformatted chart layouts that you can apply quickly to modify the default layout. These layouts may adjust the position of features, such as the legend, or add chart components such as titles and data labels. In this exercise, you will choose a different chart layout.

PowerPoint charts can be customized in a variety of ways by adding and removing chart elements such as titles, labels, and gridlines. If you do not want to take the time to add elements, Power-Point's quick layouts can provide you with some standard appearance options to choose from. You will learn how to add elements yourself later in this lesson.

STEP BY STEP   **Apply and Modify a Quick Layout**

USE the *Pricing Final* presentation that is still open from the previous exercise.

1. With the chart on slide 2 selected, click the **Quick Layout** button on the Chart Tools Design tab. The Chart Layout gallery displays (see Figure 6-10).

Take Note   The thumbnails in the Chart Layout gallery show in miniature the new layout and elements of the chart.

Figure 6-10

The Chart Layout gallery

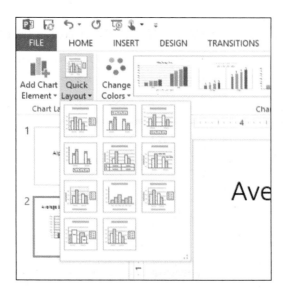

2. Click Layout 2 in the gallery. The layout is modified to place the legend above the chart and add data labels to each of the bars (see Figure 6-11).

Figure 6-11

The chart with Layout 2 applied to it

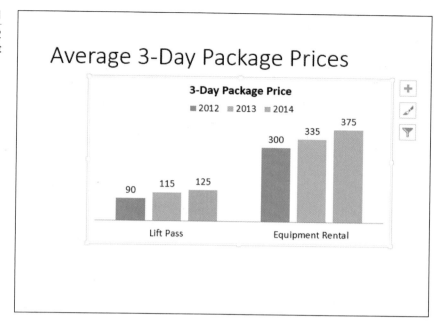

3. Click the Add Chart Element button to open a menu, point to Chart Title, and click None. The chart title is removed. (It is not necessary because the slide itself provides a title.)
4. **SAVE** the presentation.

PAUSE. LEAVE the presentation open to use in the next exercise.

Working with a Legend

As you learned earlier in this lesson, a legend is a key that tells what each color or pattern in a chart represents. There are many options available for adding, positioning, and customizing legends.

A *legend* is a very important chart element, because without it, the audience has no way of knowing what each colored bar, dot, line, or pie slice represents. In this exercise, you will practice adding, modifying, and moving a legend.

STEP BY STEP | **Work with a Legend**

USE the *Pricing Final* presentation that is still open from the previous exercise.

1. With the chart on slide 2 selected, click the Chart Elements button ➕ to the right of the chart. The Chart Elements list appears.
2. Click the Legend check box. The legend disappears.
3. Click the Legend check box again. The legend reappears.
4. An arrow appears to its right. Then click the arrow to display a submenu.
5. Click Bottom. The legend moves below the chart (see Figure 6-12).

Figure 6-12

Set legend options from the
Legend submenu

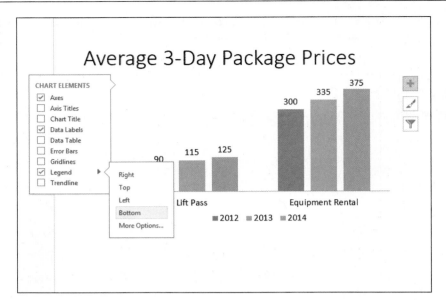

Figure 6-12

Set legend options from the
Legend submenu

6. Click the arrow next to Legend to redisplay the submenu, and click More Options. The Format Legend task pane opens.

7. Under Legend Position, click Left. The legend moves to the left of the chart area.

8. Close the task pane.

9. Position the mouse pointer over the border of the legend and drag it to place it in the empty space above the Lift Pass bars (see Figure 6-13).

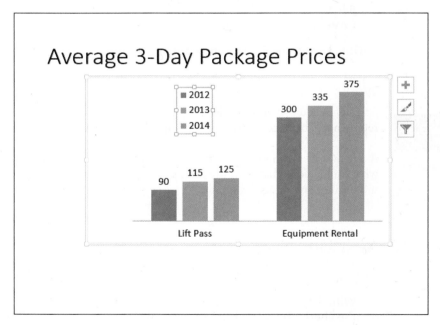

Figure 6-13

Position the legend over the
first set of bars

10. Drag the left side selection handle on the legend's frame to widen the legend so that all its content fits on a single line, and drag the bottom selection handle to decrease the legend height (see Figure 6-14).

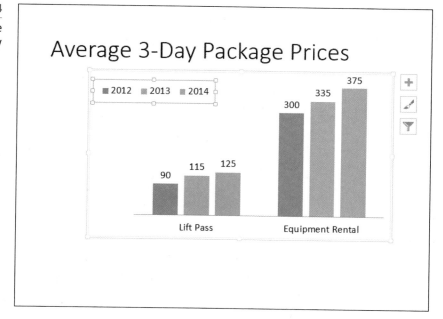

11. On the Chart Tools Design tab, click Add Chart Element, point to Legend, and click Bottom to move the legend below the chart.

12. **SAVE** the presentation.

PAUSE. LEAVE the presentation open to use in the next exercise.

Adding and Deleting Other Chart Elements

Elements such as axis labels, a chart title, and data labels make your chart more informative. Use the tools on the Chart Tools Design tab to turn chart elements on or off or adjust settings for a particular element. The controls for these elements are very similar to the controls for the legend that you learned about in the preceding exercise.

As you saw in the preceding exercise, the Chart Tools Design tab has an Add Chart Element button that opens a menu system for controlling chart elements of many different types. Each type of that menu opens a submenu that includes several basic choices (including None) plus a More command that opens a task pane for controlling that element.

You can remove chart elements by choosing None from their submenu, or in some cases by simply clicking the item to select it and then pressing Delete.

In this exercise, you will practice adding and deleting chart elements.

**CERTIFICATION
READY?**   **3.3.5**

How do you modify chart
parameters?

STEP BY STEP   **Add and Delete Chart Elements**

USE the *Pricing Final* presentation that is still open from the previous exercise.

1. Click the chart on slide 2 to select it, and click the Chart Tools Design tab.

2. Click the Add Chart Element button, point to Gridlines, and click Primary Major Horizontal (see Figure 6-15). Horizontal gridlines are added to the chart.

Figure 6-15

Adding horizontal gridlines
to the chart

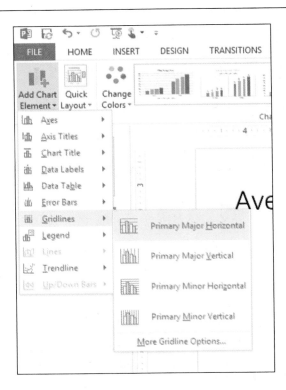

3. Click the **Add Chart Element** button, point to **Data Labels**, and click **None**. The data labels disappear from the chart.

4. Click the **chart's outer frame** to re-select the entire chart if it is not already selected.

5. Click the **Add Chart Element** button, point to **Axes**, and click **Primary Vertical**. Numbers appear along the vertical axis.

6. Click the **Add Chart Element** button, point to **Data Table**, and click **More Data Table Options**. The Format Data Table task pane opens.

7. Clear the **Show legend keys** check box.

8. Clear the **Vertical** and **Outline** check boxes (see Figure 6-16).

Figure 6-16

Customize the data
table options

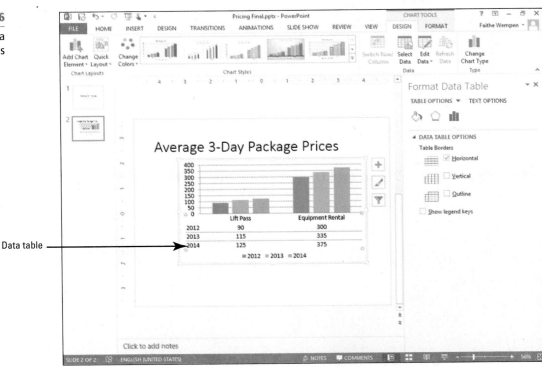

9. Close the task pane.

10. Drag the bottom selection handle on the chart frame downward to increase the chart's height by approximately 1", so that it is less crowded-looking.

11. **SAVE** the presentation and close it.

PAUSE. LEAVE PowerPoint open to use in the next exercise.

Applying elements such as a chart title or axis titles generally reduces the size of the plot area and the data markers. You can offset this adjustment by resizing the chart, as you did in step 10, and/ or by reducing the font size of axis labels and titles, as you will learn later in this lesson.

FORMATTING A CHART

The Bottom Line

Once you have final data and have added the elements you want to include in the chart, you can make final adjustments to the size and position of the chart and its elements and apply final formatting. Use the tools on the Chart Tools Format tab to apply formats to any part of a chart, including the entire chart area, the data series markers, the legend, and the chart's labels and titles.

Applying Chart Styles

CERTIFICATION READY? 3.3.1

How do you create and modify chart styles?

Chart styles provide instant formatting to change the look of a chart. A style can change colors and borders of data markers, apply effects to the data markers, and apply color to the chart or plot area. You can use a style to format a chart if you do not have time to adjust formatting of chart elements such as data series or the individual data points in a series. In this exercise, you apply a style to a chart and then modify it.

STEP BY STEP   **Apply and Modify a Chart Style**

GET READY. To apply a quick style to a chart, perform the following steps:

1. **OPEN** the *Conditions* presentation and save it as *Conditions Final*.

2. Go to slide 2 and click the chart to select it.

3. On the Chart Tools Design tab, click the More button in the Chart Styles group. The Chart Styles gallery appears (see Figure 6-17).

Figure 6-17

The Chart Styles gallery

4. Click Style 8. This style applies a new theme color, bevel effects, and a different chart background color (see Figure 6-18).

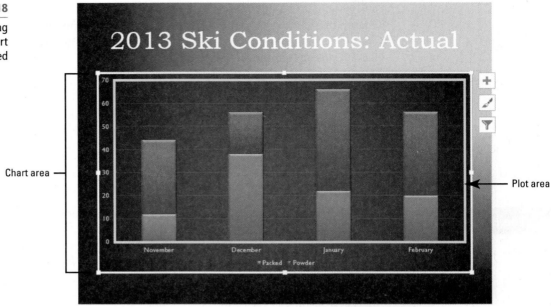

5. **SAVE** the presentation and then **CLOSE** the file.

PAUSE. LEAVE PowerPoint open to use in the next exercise.

Changing the Fill of the Chart Area

To make a chart really "pop" on a slide, you can change its default fill. When you change the **chart area** fill, you format the entire area within the chart's frame. When choosing a fill for the chart area, you have familiar choices: you can select a theme color, picture, gradient, or texture. Take care that colors harmonize with the current theme and that pictures or textures do not overwhelm the other chart elements.

Do not confuse the chart area with the **plot area**. Look back at Figure 6-18 to see the difference. Whereas the chart area includes everything inside the chart's frame the plot area includes only the area within the chart's frame where the data is plotted. The plot area typically excludes the extra elements such as the legend, the chart title, and the data table, but some chart styles place the legend overlapping the plot area.

In this exercise, you will select the chart area and change the chart area's fill.

STEP BY STEP **Change the Chart Area Fill**

GET READY. To apply a chart area fill, follow these steps:

1. **OPEN** the *Admissions* presentation and save it as *Admissions Final*.
2. Select the chart on slide 2, and then click the Chart Tools Format tab.
3. If Chart Area does not already appear in the Chart Elements box, open the drop-down list in the Current Selection group and select it (see Figure 6-19).

Figure 6-19

Make sure the chart area is selected

Another Way

You can also right-click on a blank area of the chart and then click Format Chart Area on the shortcut menu.

4. Click the **Format Selection** button below the Chart Elements box. The Format Chart Area task pane opens.

5. If the Fill options are collapsed in the task pane, click the **Fill** heading to expand it.

6. Click **Picture or texture fill**, and then click the **Texture** button. The texture gallery opens.

7. Click the **Granite** texture, and then drag the **Transparency** slider to **50%**. The chart area has been formatted with a light texture background that makes it stand out from the slide (see Figure 6-20).

8. Close the **Format Chart Area** task pane.

9. **SAVE** the presentation.

Figure 6-20

The chart with background texture applied

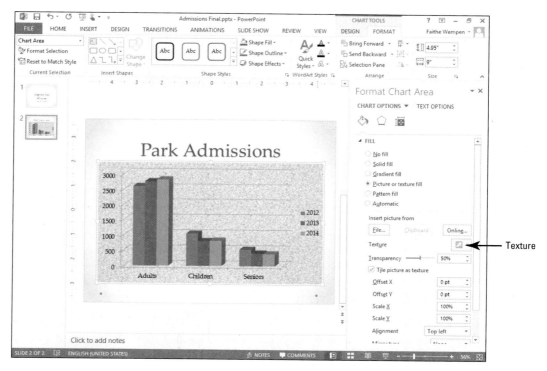

PAUSE. LEAVE the presentation open to use in the next exercise.

When formatting parts of a chart, it is sometimes a challenge to make sure you have selected the element you want to change. Use the Chart Elements list in the Current Selection group on the Chart Tools Format tab to help you select the element you want. This list clearly identifies all elements of the current chart so that you can easily select the one you want to modify.

You can also select any element on the chart to format by right-clicking it. The shortcut menu displays a Format command at the bottom that corresponds to the element you have clicked. If you right-click one of the columns in the chart, for example, the shortcut menu offers the Format Data Series command.

The task pane that opens when you select a chart element to format provides options specifically for that element. The Format Axis task pane, for instance, allows you to change the interval between tick marks on the axis, number style, line color and style, and alignment of axis labels.

Applying a Border to the Chart Area

By default, the chart area does not display a border. The lack of a border enables the chart to blend in seamlessly with the background of the slide on which you place it. If you prefer, you can apply a border that clearly identifies the chart area. In this exercise, you will add a border to a chart.

STEP BY STEP   **Apply a Border to the Chart Area**

USE the *Admissions Final* presentation that is still open from the previous exercise.

1. Click the outer border of the chart to select the chart area.
2. On the Chart Tools Format tab, click Format Selection in the Current Selection group to open the Format Chart Area task pane.
3. Click the Fill heading to collapse the Fill options. Then click the Border heading to expand the border options.
4. Click the Solid line option button.
5. Click the Color button, then click the Black, Text 1, Lighter 35% theme color.
6. Click the Width up increment arrow until the width is 3 pt.
7. Close the task pane.
8. Click outside the chart so you can see the chart area border. Your slide should look similar to Figure 6-21.

Figure 6-21

The chart with a border applied

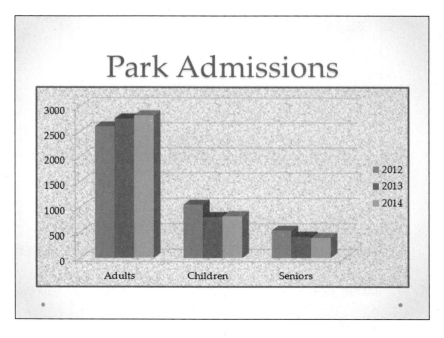

9. **SAVE** the presentation.

PAUSE. LEAVE the presentation open to use in the next exercise.

Applying Formatting Effects

You can apply some of the same types of effects to charts that you apply to other objects in PowerPoint. For example, you can add bevels, 3-D effects, and shadows. Some of these effects apply to individual elements in the chart, while others apply to the chart as a whole. In this exercise, you will apply formatting effects to a chart.

STEP BY STEP   **Apply Formatting Effects**

USE the *Admissions Final* presentation that is still open from the previous exercise.

1. In the chart on slide 2, click one of the blue bars to select it. All three blue bars become selected.

2. On the Chart Tools Format tab, click the Shape Effects button in the Shape Styles group, and on the menu that appears, point to Bevel, and then click the Circle bevel (see Figure 6-22).

Figure 6-22

Applying a bevel effect to a data series

Circle bevel ——————

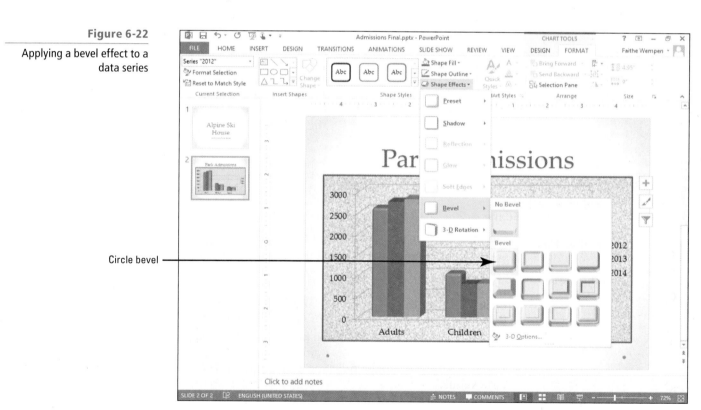

3. Repeat steps 1 and 2 for the red, and then the orange bars, so that all bars are formatted using the same bevel effect.

4. Select Chart Area from the drop-down list in the Current Selection group.

5. Click the Shape Effects button again, point to 3-D Rotation, and click the Perspective Heroic Extreme Right effect (the last one in the Perspective section). The entire chart receives a 3-D effect (see Figure 6-23).

6. **SAVE** the presentation.

Figure 6-23

Apply 3-D rotation to the chart

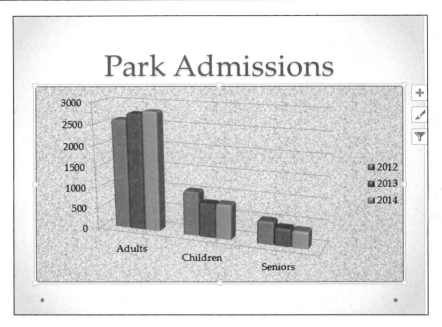

PAUSE. LEAVE the presentation open to use in the next exercise.

Formatting a Chart's Data Series

As you learned earlier, a chart's data series is the visual display of the actual data points. Data series can be columns, bars, lines, or pie slices. You can give a chart considerably more visual appeal by customizing data series fill and border options and by applying effects. In this exercise, you will format a data series.

STEP BY STEP   **Format a Chart's Data Series**

USE the *Admissions Final* presentation that is still open from the previous exercise.

1. Click the chart to select it if it is not already selected.
2. Click one of the red bars to select the entire data series (all the red bars).

Take Note   If you want to format a single data bar, click on it twice.

3. Click the Chart Tools Format tab, and notice that the Chart Elements box in the Current Selection group shows that Series "2013" is selected.
4. Click the Format Selection button in the Current Selection group. The Format Data Series task pane opens.
5. Under the Column Shape heading, click Cylinder. The bars turn to cylinders for the 2013 series.
6. Repeat step 5 for each of the other two data series.
7. Drag the Gap Width slider to the 50% setting. This action decreases the amount of space between the categories on the horizontal axis (see Figure 6-24).

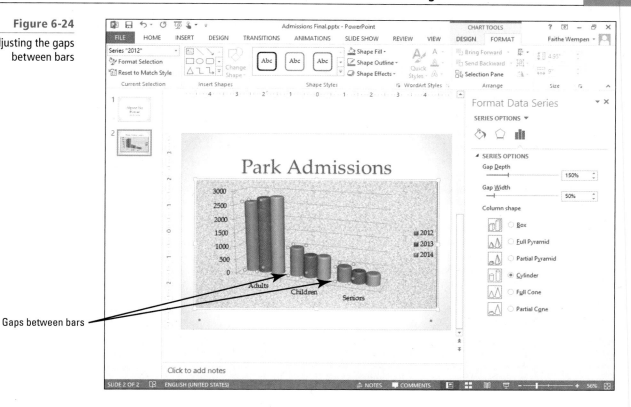

Figure 6-24

Adjusting the gaps between bars

8. Close the task pane.
9. **SAVE** the presentation.

PAUSE. LEAVE the presentation open to use in the next exercise.

You have almost limitless options in formatting the data series for a chart. If you have plenty of time, you can use options in the Format Data Series task pane and the Shape Fill, Shape Outline, and Shape Effects menus to apply colors, pictures, textures, gradients, shadows, bevels, and many other choices. If your time is limited, you can achieve sophisticated effects by simply applying a Chart Style from the Chart Styles gallery.

In some situations, you may want to apply formats to a specific data marker rather than to the entire data series. To select a single data marker, click it once to select the data series, and then click it again to remove selection handles from the other markers.

Adjusting and Formatting Chart Axes

PowerPoint automatically determines the numeric scale to be used for the chart's axes, with the minimum value at zero (usually) and the maximum value slightly higher than the largest value to be plotted. You can adjust the axis scale if you like, however, to create different effects. You can also apply formatting to the axis labels, such as formatting the numbers as currency or changing their font, font size, and font color, or any of the other font-formatting actions you have learned in earlier lessons. In this exercise, you will practice formatting chart axes.

STEP BY STEP   **Adjust a Chart Axis**

USE the *Admissions Final* presentation that is still open from the previous exercise.

1. Click the chart on slide 2 to select it, if necessary.
2. Double-click one of the numbers on the vertical axis. The Format Axis task pane opens.

3. If the Axis Options icon is not selected at the top of the task pane (rightmost icon), click it. Then, if the Axis Options section is collapsed, click the heading to expand that category.

4. Under Bounds, in the Maximum text box, change the value to 4000 to establish that as the maximum value for the chart's vertical axis (see Figure 6-25).

Figure 6-25

Adjust the maximum value for the vertical axis

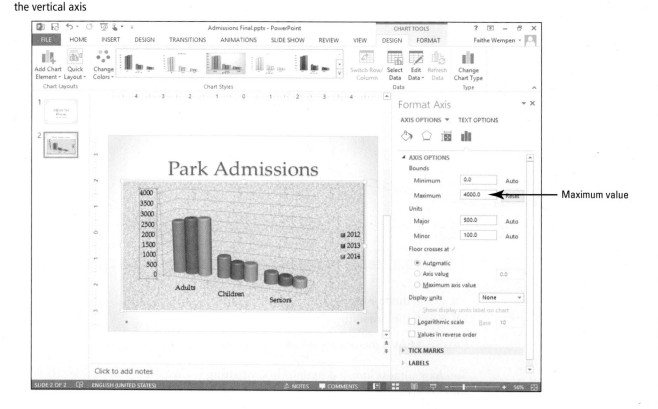

5. Click the Auto button next to Maximum to reset the axis scale.

6. Click the Axis Options heading to collapse that category. Then click the Number heading to expand that category.

7. Open the Category drop-down list and choose Currency.

8. Select the value in the Decimal places box and type 0 to reduce decimal places to zero (see Figure 6-26).

Figure 6-26

Change the number type
to Currency with no
decimal places

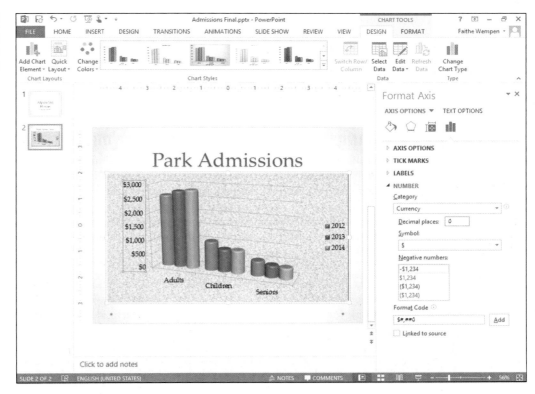

Figure 6-26

Change the number type
to Currency with no
decimal places

9. Close the task pane.

10. On the Home tab, open the Font Size drop-down list and click 16.

11. Click the Font Color button's drop-down arrow to open its palette, and click the dark blue square in the Standard Colors section. The chart should resemble Figure 6-27.

Figure 6-27

The chart's vertical axis has
been formatted

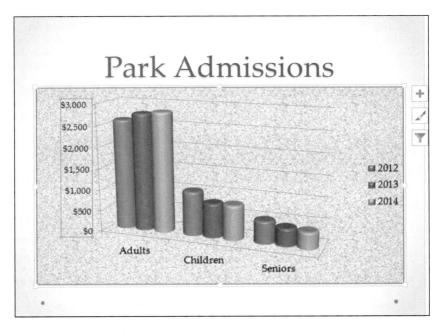

12. **SAVE** the presentation and close it.

PAUSE. Exit PowerPoint, or leave PowerPoint open to complete the end-of-lesson exercises that follow.

By default, a chart's axis and formatting are automatically adjusted as needed when you make changes to the chart. Be aware, however, that if you specify exact values for settings, those settings will remain fixed even if you make changes to the chart.

Workplace *Ready*

MANIPULATING A CHART TO CONVEY A DIFFERENT MESSAGE

Numbers do not lie, but you can present the same numbers in different ways to create a very different impression. For example, adjusting an axis's scale can be useful if you are trying to make the data convey a certain message. If you want to accentuate the differences between values, tighten up the axis scale. For example, if all the data points are between 110 and 120, you might make the minimum value 100 and the maximum value 120 instead of a minimum of 0 and a maximum of 200. Conversely, if you want to minimize the differences between values, make the axis scale a wider range of values.

On a bar or line chart with multiple series, you can also present data in rows rather than columns to convey a different message. For example, suppose you are presenting sales figures for three salespeople for three months. If the chart presents each salesperson's data in a different series, the values for each salesperson are clustered together, inviting a comparison between the salespeople's performances. In contrast, if you present each month in a different series, the values for each month are clustered together, inviting a comparison between the months' data.

SKILL SUMMARY

In This Lesson, You Learned How To:	Exam Objective	Objective Number
Build Charts	Insert charts.	3.3.2
	Import charts from external sources.	3.3.6
Modify the Chart Type and Data	Modify chart type.	3.3.3
Modify Chart Elements	Add legends to charts.	3.3.4
	Modify chart parameters.	3.3.5
Format a Chart	Create and modify chart styles.	3.3.1

Knowledge Assessment

Fill in the Blank

Fill in each blank with the term or phrase that best completes the statement.

1. On a bar chart, the bars that share a common color are a data _____.

2. If you want to change a column chart to a line chart, click the _____ button on the Chart Tools Design tab.

3. A(n) _____ is a visual depiction of numeric data.

4. _____ charts show the relationship of parts to a whole.

5. A chart's _____ provides a key to the information plotted on the chart.

6. On a column chart, the data is charted along the _____ axis.

7. Hold the _____ key as you drag a chart's corner handle to resize it to maintain its aspect ratio.

8. The _____ is the entire area within the chart's border, including not only the plot area but also the chart title and legend.

9. You can quickly tell what part of a chart you have selected by looking at the _____ box on the Chart Tools Format tab.

10. The _____ contains the gridlines and elements such as columns or bars, but excludes elements like the chart title.

Multiple Choice

Circle the correct answer.

1. PowerPoint's charting feature includes a worksheet window that is similar to which other Office application?
   a. Microsoft Word
   b. Microsoft Excel
   c. Microsoft Equation
   d. Microsoft Chart

2. If you want to select a different range of cells for a chart, use the
   a. Edit Data button on the Chart Tools Design tab
   b. Source Data button on the Chart Tools Design tab
   c. Edit Data button on the Chart Tools Format tab
   d. Data Source button on the Chart Tools Format tab

3. The default PowerPoint chart type is a:
   a. column chart
   b. bar chart
   c. line chart
   d. pie chart

4. If you want to show the amount of change over time and the total values across a trend, use a(n):
   a. column chart
   b. line chart
   c. area chart
   d. pie chart

5. You can move a chart on a slide by:
   a. dragging its border
   b. cutting from one location and pasting elsewhere on the slide
   c. dragging a sizing handle
   d. issuing the Move command

6. _____ enables you to quickly format a chart with different colors, effects, and background.
   a. WordArt
   b. A Chart Style
   c. Master Themes
   d. SmartArt

7. Select a single data point by:
   a. clicking once on it
   b. clicking once to select the whole series, and then clicking again to select only that data point
   c. right-clicking on it
   d. Shift+clicking on it

8. To change the numbers along the vertical axis on a column chart, adjust the:
   a. legend
   b. data labels
   c. titles
   d. axis scale

9. The _____ area can be formatted with a different background than the chart area.

   a. Axis
   b. Plot
   c. Artwork
   d. Title

10. Text that identifies information about the values on an axis is called a(n):

    a. legend
    b. chart title
    c. plot title
    d. axis label

Competency Assessment

Project 6-1: **Voter Turnout**

You are a member of the Center City Board of Elections. You have been asked to create a presentation to deliver to the Board showing how turnout has varied in the city over the past four presidential elections. You can create a line chart to display this data clearly.

GET READY. LAUNCH PowerPoint if it is not already running.

1. **OPEN** the *Turnout* presentation.
2. Go to slide 2, click the Insert Chart icon in the content placeholder, and then click Line. Click OK to accept the default subtype.
3. Starting in cell A1, type the following data in the Excel worksheet:

Year	Turnout
2000	0.62
2004	0.74
2008	0.49
2012	0.40

4. Adjust the range border to include only the data you typed, and then delete all extra data on the sheet.
5. Close the worksheet window.
6. Click Layout 9 in the Quick Layout gallery.
7. Click Style 9 in the Chart Styles gallery.
8. Click the legend to select it, and then press Delete.
9. Click the Add Chart Element button, and then point to Data Labels, and click Above.
10. Right-click one of the data labels, then click Format Data Labels. Change the number format to Percentage with 0 decimal places.
11. **SAVE** the presentation as *Turnout Final* and **CLOSE** the file.

LEAVE PowerPoint open for use in the next project.

Project 6-2: **And the Results Are . . .**

You are a project manager for Trey Research. You have been asked to create a slide show to present results of a survey you conducted on opinions about violence in the media. You saved your research results as an Excel file that you can use to create a chart in PowerPoint.

1. **OPEN** the *Survey* presentation.
2. Go to slide 2, click the Insert Chart icon in the content placeholder, click 3-D Clustered Column, and click OK to create the chart.

3. In Excel, open the *Media* workbook. Select the cell range A3:C6 and click the Copy button on the Excel Home tab.

4. In PowerPoint, in the worksheet window, click in cell A1, and press Ctrl+V to paste.

5. Delete any unnecessary sample data in the worksheet, and make sure the range border surrounds the range A1:C4.

6. Switch back to Excel and close it.

7. Switch back to PowerPoint and close the worksheet window and select the chart again if it is not already selected.

8. On the Chart Tools Design tab, click Add Chart Element, point to Legend, and click Bottom to ensure the legend is located at the bottom of the chart.

9. Change the fill colors of both series to two different colors of your choice using the Shape Fill palette.

10. Click a vertical axis label to select the axis, click the Home tab, click the Font Size box, and click 16 to change the font size of all axis labels.

11. Change the horizontal axis labels and the legend labels to 16 points as directed in step 10.

12. **SAVE** the presentation as *Survey Final* and **CLOSE** the file.

LEAVE PowerPoint open for the next project.

Proficiency Assessment

Project 6-3: Visitors Welcome

You work in the Tourist Bureau for the town of Lucerne. As part of your regular duties, you compile a presentation that shows information on visitors. You have created a slide that shows visitors by age. The chart needs some modification and formatting.

1. **OPEN** the *Tourists* presentation.

2. Go to slide 2 and view the chart. The line chart type does not seem appropriate for the data.

3. With the chart selected, click the Change Chart Type button on the Chart Tools Design tab and select the first chart in the Pie category.

4. Apply Layout 2 from the Quick Layout gallery and Style 5 from the Chart Styles gallery.

5. Click the pie and apply a Circle bevel effect.

6. Reduce the width of the chart area by dragging the selection handles on the right and left sides so the chart area is approximately 5" in width.

7. Delete the chart title Percent.

8. Select the legend and increase the font size to 16 point.

9. Apply a light-colored fill to the legend, and a dark-colored border. Change the text color if needed for better text readability.

10. Apply a Circle bevel effect to the legend.

11. Increase the font size for the data labels on the slices to 18 point.

12. **SAVE** the presentation as *Tourists Final* and **CLOSE** the file.

LEAVE PowerPoint open for use in the next project.

Project 6-4: Free for All

You are a marketing consultant hired by Woodgrove Bank. The bank's managers have asked you to determine which freebies customers would find most attractive when opening a new checking account. One of your assistants has created a chart of the survey results. You need to improve the look of the chart by editing the data and applying formats.

1. **OPEN** the *Freebies* presentation.
2. Go to slide 2 and select the chart area.
3. Use the Format Chart Area task pane to apply a gradient fill of your choice to the chart area.
4. Apply a border color and weight of your choice to the chart area.
5. Change the color of at least one of the data series. (You may change more than one or all colors if desired.)
6. Move the legend to the top of the chart. Then apply a new background fill for the legend and add a border to it.
7. Format the vertical axis to show numbers as percentages rather than numeric values.
8. Set the vertical axis scale to have a maximum value of 1 (100%).
9. Show data labels in percentages with no decimal places.
10. **SAVE** the presentation as *Freebies Final* and **CLOSE** the file.

LEAVE PowerPoint open for use in the next project.

Mastery Assessment

Project 6-5: **More Power**

You are a financial analyst for City Power & Light. Senior managers have asked you to determine how much power sales increased from 2012 to 2013, based on customer types. You can compare rates of power sales using a bar chart.

1. **OPEN** a new blank presentation and apply a theme of your choice. Set the slide size to Standard (4:3).
2. Change the layout of the first slide to Title and Content, and type the slide title 2012 – 2013 Sales.
3. Create a Clustered Bar chart, and type the following chart data:

	Industrial	Commercial	Residential
2012	$3,010	$4,273	$5,777
2013	$2,588	$3,876	$4,578

4. Apply Quick Layout 3 to the chart, and change the chart title to Sales by Customer Type.
5. Apply a Chart Style of your choice to the chart.
6. Add a horizontal axis title and type the axis title In Millions.
7. Change the size of the horizontal axis labels to 16-point.
8. Add a border around the legend.
9. **SAVE** the presentation as *Power Sales* and **CLOSE** the file.

LEAVE PowerPoint open for use in the next project.

Project 6-6: **Patient Visits**

You are a veterinarian hoping to attract investors to your clinic. You have created a chart to be used in a presentation for prospective investors. You want to show investors the reasons for patient visits during a given month, by percentage. You are not satisfied with your chart, however, so you want to improve it before the investor meeting.

1. **OPEN** the *Patients* presentation.
2. In the chart worksheet, edit the values to become percentages (e.g., change 38 to 0.38).
3. Format the horizontal axis to show numbers using Percentage format with 0 decimal places.
4. Change the chart type from Bar to a 3-D Pie Chart.
5. Apply Quick Layout 6.
6. Delete the chart title.
7. Use the 3-D Rotation settings in the Format Chart Area task pane (Effects section) to set the Perspective to 5° and the Y Rotation to 40°.
8. Select the data labels and increase their size to 24 point. Apply bold formatting.
9. With data labels still selected, open the Format Data Labels task pane and specify a solid white fill for the labels.
10. Change the fill color of the plot area to Tan, Background 2, and apply the Offset Center shadow effect to the plot area.
11. Apply the same fill and effect to the legend as you applied to the plot area in step 10.
12. **SAVE** the presentation as *Patients Final* and **CLOSE** the file.

EXIT PowerPoint.

7 Creating SmartArt Graphics

LESSON SKILL MATRIX

Skill	Exam Objective	Objective Number
Adding SmartArt to a Slide	Convert lists to SmartArt.	3.4.5
Modifying SmartArt	Change the color of SmartArt.	3.4.2
	Add shapes to SmartArt.	3.4.1
	Reverse direction.	3.4.4
	Move text within SmartArt shapes.	3.4.3

KEY TERMS

- assistant
- demote
- organization chart
- promote
- SmartArt graphic
- SmartArt layout
- subordinates
- Text pane
- top-level shape

©mediaphotos/iStockphoto

You are the director of software development for Litware, Inc., which creates computer games that help children learn to read. One of your responsibilities is orienting new software designers who have just joined the company. You can use SmartArt to explain your company's organization and standard processes to the newcomers. SmartArt provides an easy way to share complex information in the form of sophisticated graphics that clearly show relationships and processes.

©mediaphotos/iStockphoto

SOFTWARE ORIENTATION

Choosing a SmartArt Graphic

PowerPoint offers eight different types of SmartArt with many layouts for each type. Figure 7-1 shows the dialog box that appears when you choose to insert a SmartArt graphic.

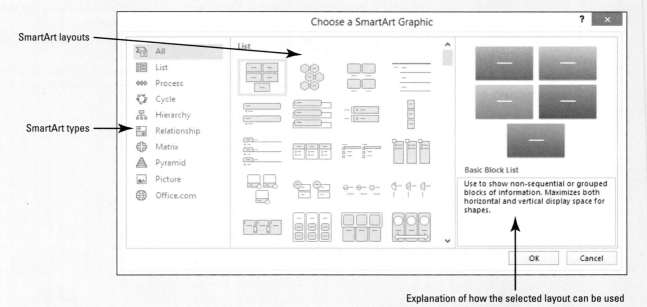

Figure 7-1

Choose a SmartArt Graphic dialog box

When you click a layout, the right pane of the dialog box shows you a close-up view of the selected layout and provides information on how to use the layout. This description can help you decide whether the layout will be appropriate for your information.

ADDING SMARTART TO A SLIDE

The Bottom Line

Use the Insert a SmartArt Graphic icon in any content placeholder to start a new SmartArt graphic. After you have selected a type and a layout, you can add text to the SmartArt graphic. PowerPoint also lets you use existing bullet items to create SmartArt.

Inserting a SmartArt Graphic

SmartArt graphics (also called SmartArt diagrams, or just SmartArt) are visual representations of information you want to communicate. SmartArt shows items of related information in a graphical way that makes their relationships easy to understand. You can use SmartArt to present text information in a more visually interesting way than the usual bulleted or numbered formats. An **organization chart** is a type of SmartArt that shows the relationships among personnel or departments in an organization. Organization charts are included in the Hierarchy layouts. In this exercise, you will insert an organization chart.

STEP BY STEP   **Create SmartArt**

GET READY. Before you begin these steps, make sure that your computer is on. Log on, if necessary.

1. **START** PowerPoint, if the program is not already running.
2. Locate and open the *Litware* presentation and save it as *Litware Final*.
3. Go to slide 3, and click the Insert a SmartArt Graphic icon in the center of the content placeholder. The Choose a SmartArt Graphic dialog box opens.
4. Click Hierarchy in the type list in the left side of the dialog box. The layouts for the Hierarchy type are displayed.
5. Click the first layout in the first row, the Organization Chart. Read the description of the Organization Chart layout in the right pane of the dialog box (see Figure 7-2).

Another Way
To insert SmartArt on a slide that does not have a content placeholder, click the SmartArt button on the Insert tab.

Figure 7-2

The Hierarchy layouts in the Choose a SmartArt Graphic dialog box

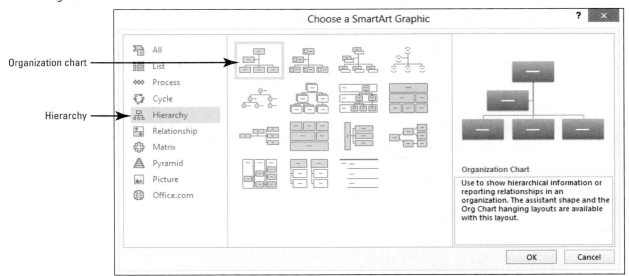

6. Click OK to insert the chart. The chart appears on the slide (see Figure 7-3).

Figure 7-3

A new, blank organization chart

Text Pane button on Ribbon

Text Pane button on SmartArt

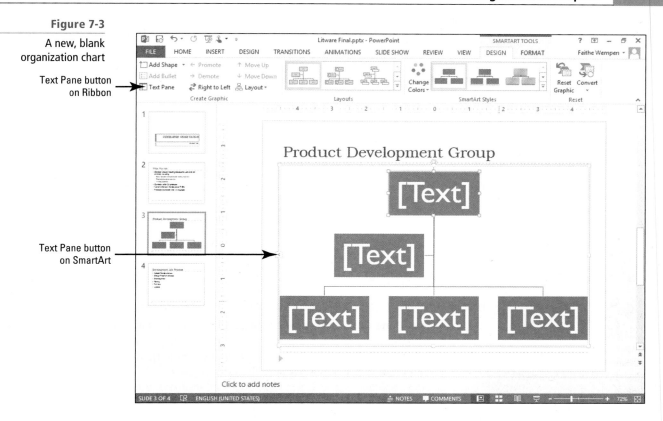

7. **SAVE** the presentation.

PAUSE. LEAVE the presentation open to use in the next exercise.

The Choose a SmartArt Graphic dialog box sorts its many layouts by types such as List, Process, Hierarchy, and so on. A **SmartArt layout** is a particular arrangement of shapes that a SmartArt graphic can have. The following general descriptions of SmartArt types can help you choose a type and a specific layout within that type:

- **List** layouts display information that does not have to be in a particular order, such as a list of items to purchase.
- **Process** layouts show the steps in a process or timeline, such as the steps in a manufacturing process.
- **Cycle** layouts are useful for showing a repeating process, such as a teaching cycle of preparing for a semester, teaching a class, and submitting grades.
- **Hierarchy** layouts show levels of subordination, such as in an organization chart or a tournament bracket.
- **Relationship** layouts show connections among items, such as the relationship between supply and demand.
- **Matrix** layouts show how parts relate to a whole, similar to a pie chart.
- **Pyramid** layouts display relationships in terms of proportion, from largest at the bottom to smallest at the top.
- **Picture** layouts include placeholders for one or more graphics in addition to the text placeholders.

More layouts can also be found at Office.com. Click the Office.com category to see what is available.

Some layouts appear in more than one type's listing. For example, most of the Picture layouts are also categorized as other types.

Adding Text to SmartArt

A new SmartArt graphic appears on the slide with empty shapes to which you add text (and in some cases, pictures) to create the final version. The appearance and position of these shapes are guided by the layout you chose, and shape color is controlled by the current theme. As you enter text, PowerPoint resizes the shapes to accommodate the longest line of text. Font size is also adjusted for the best fit, and PowerPoint keeps the font size the same for all shapes. In this exercise, you will learn how to add text to the organizational chart you created in the previous exercise.

An organization chart, such as the one you create in this section, has some special terminology and layout requirements. In an organization chart, there can be only one **top-level shape**, which is typically occupied by the name of the person or department at the head of the organization. Persons or departments who report to the top-level entity are **subordinates**. An **assistant** is a person who reports directly to a staff member and usually appears on a separate level.

STEP BY STEP	**Add Text to SmartArt**

USE the *Litware Final* presentation that is still open from the previous exercise.

Another Way
You can also display or hide the Text pane by clicking the arrow symbol on the left side of the SmartArt's frame.

1. Click Text Pane on the SmartArt Tools Design tab. This action opens the Text pane.
2. At the top of the Text pane, type Ted Hicks to enter the name in the top-level shape. Notice that as you type the text in the Text pane, it appears in the top shape (see Figure 7-4), and that the text automatically resizes to fit in the shape.

Figure 7-4

Type a name in the top-level shape

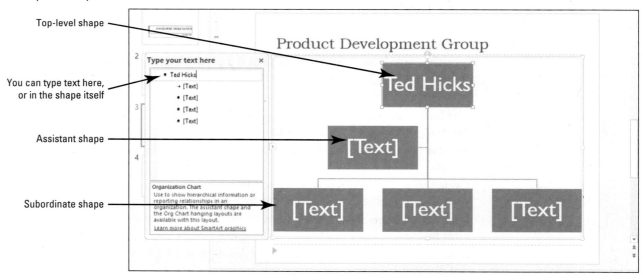

Top-level shape

You can type text here, or in the shape itself

Assistant shape

Subordinate shape

3. Click in the bullet item below Ted Hicks in the Text pane, then type Rose Lang. Rose Lang is an assistant to Ted Hicks, and as such, she has an assistant shape on a level between the top-level shape and the subordinate shapes.
4. Click in the next bullet item in the Text pane and type Marcus Short. Marcus Short is a subordinate to Ted Hicks.

Troubleshooting Do not press Enter after typing the names because that inserts a new shape. If you accidentally do so, click the Undo button on the Quick Access Toolbar to undo the addition.

5. Click in the next bullet item and type Ellen Camp.

Another Way
You can also hide the Text pane by clicking the arrow symbol on the left side of the SmartArt's frame, or by clicking the Text Pane button again on the SmartArt Tools Design tab.

6. Click in the last bullet item and type Pat Cramer.

7. Click the Close button (X) in the Text pane to hide it. You will complete the text entry by typing directly in the shapes.

8. Click just to the right of the name Hicks in the top-level shape, press Enter, and type Director. Notice that the text size adjusts in all the shapes to account for the additional entry in the top-level shape.

9. Click after the name Lang in the assistant shape, press Enter, and type Assistant Director.

10. Use the same process to type the title Reading Products for Marcus Short, Linguistics Products for Ellen Camp, and Writing Products for Pat Cramer.

11. Click away from the SmartArt to deselect it. Your slide should look similar to Figure 7-5.

Figure 7-5

The completed organization chart

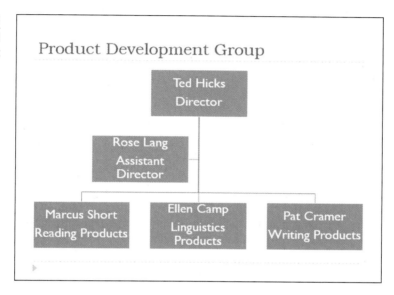

12. **SAVE** the presentation.

PAUSE. LEAVE the presentation open to use in the next exercise.

Text in a SmartArt graphic appears either within a shape or as a bulleted list, depending on the type and layout. In the previous exercise, you inserted text only in shapes because an organization chart does not offer the option of bulleted text. Figure 7-6 shows a list type that contains both shape text and bulleted text.

Figure 7-6

Shape text and bulleted text

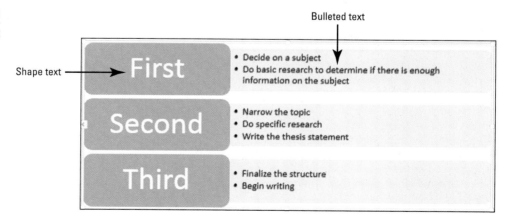

You can display or hide the **Text pane**, which is an optional panel to the left of a SmartArt graphic in which you can type its text. In the Text pane, shape text (that is, text that appears in shapes) appears as the top-level bullet items, and text that appears on the graphic in bulleted text format is indented below the shape text. This format is similar to the way several levels of bulleted text appear in a content placeholder.

You can use the Text pane to enter text, or you can enter text directly in each shape. Click next to a bullet in the Text pane or click any [Text] placeholder and begin typing text. If you need more bullet items than are supplied in the default layout, press Enter at the end of the current bullet item to add a new one, or click the Add Bullet button in the Create Graphic group on the SmartArt Tools Design tab.

If you do not want to use the Text pane, you can close it to get it out of the way. To redisplay it, click the Text Pane button on the left border of the SmartArt container, or click the Text Pane button in the Create Graphic group on the SmartArt Tools Design tab. You can also right-click anywhere in the SmartArt graphic and then click Show Text Pane on the shortcut menu.

Take Note   If you need to edit text you have entered in a shape, you can click the text to activate it and then edit the text as necessary. You can also right-click a shape, click Edit Text on the shortcut menu, and make the necessary changes.

Converting Text or WordArt to SmartArt

As you work with slide text, you may realize that the information would work well as a SmartArt graphic. In this situation, you do not have to retype the text in the SmartArt shapes. Simply convert the bulleted list to a SmartArt graphic. You can create SmartArt from any bulleted list on a slide or any WordArt object. You can choose one of the common layouts in the Convert to SmartArt gallery, or you can access the Choose a SmartArt Graphic dialog box to choose any type or layout. In this exercise, you will learn how to convert a list into a SmartArt Cycle graphic, and you will convert WordArt text into a single SmartArt object.

CERTIFICATION READY?   3.4.5

How do you convert lists to SmartArt?

STEP BY STEP   **Convert Text or WordArt to a SmartArt Graphic**

Another Way
Right-click in a bulleted list, and then click Convert to SmartArt on the shortcut menu.

USE the *Litware Final* presentation that is still open from the previous exercise.

1. Go to slide 4 and select the bulleted list.
2. Click the Home tab, if necessary, and then click the Convert to SmartArt button in the Paragraph group. PowerPoint displays the gallery (see Figure 7-7).

Figure 7-7

The Convert to
SmartArt Gallery

Convert to
SmartArt button

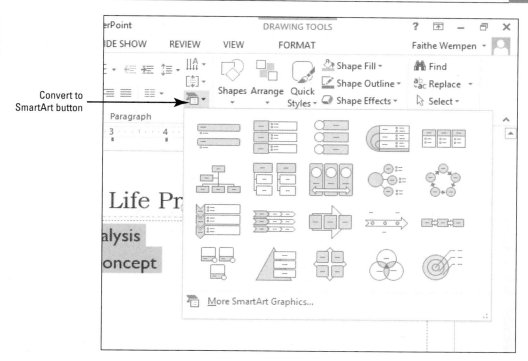

3. Click **More SmartArt Graphics** at the bottom of the gallery. The Choose a SmartArt Graphic dialog box opens.

4. Click **Cycle**, and then click the **Block Cycle** layout (third layout in the first row). Read the **description** of how best to use the Block Cycle layout.

5. Click **OK**. The bulleted list is converted to a cycle graphic (see Figure 7-8).

Figure 7-8

Bulleted list converted to a cycle graphic

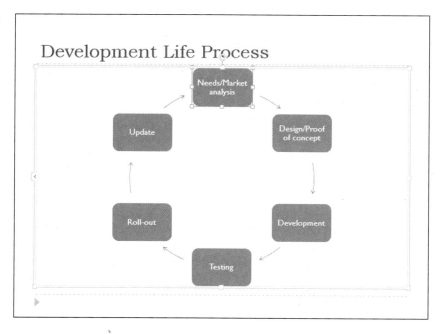

Take Note   You may notice that the text in the shapes is quite small. You will learn how to modify shape and text size later in the lesson.

6. Go to **slide 1**, and triple-click the **Developer Orientation** WordArt object to select it.

7. On the Home tab, click **Convert to SmartArt**, then click **Vertical Bullet List** (the first layout in the first row). The WordArt text is converted to a single-item SmartArt object (see Figure 7-9).

Figure 7-9

WordArt converted
to SmartArt

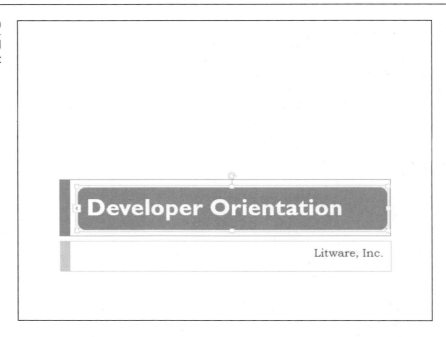

8. **SAVE** the presentation.

PAUSE. LEAVE the presentation open to use in the next exercise.

MODIFYING SMARTART

The Bottom Line

Although a SmartArt graphic makes an interesting visual statement on a slide in its default state, you will probably want to make some changes to the graphic to customize it for your use. You can apply a wide variety of formatting changes to modify appearance, and you can also change layout or orientation and add or remove shapes. You can even change the SmartArt type to another that better fits your data.

Applying a Style to SmartArt

Like other graphic objects, SmartArt can be quickly and easily formatted by applying a SmartArt style. Styles apply fills, borders, and effects to improve the appearance of the graphic's shapes. In this exercise, you will apply a style.

STEP BY STEP   **Apply a Style to SmartArt**

USE the *Litware Final* presentation that is still open from the previous exercise.

1. Go to slide 3 and click once on the SmartArt graphic to select it. Take care to select the SmartArt itself, and not a particular shape within it.
2. Click the SmartArt Tools Design tab to activate it.
3. Click the More button in the SmartArt Styles group. The SmartArt Styles gallery appears (see Figure 7-10).

Figure 7-10

The SmartArt Styles gallery

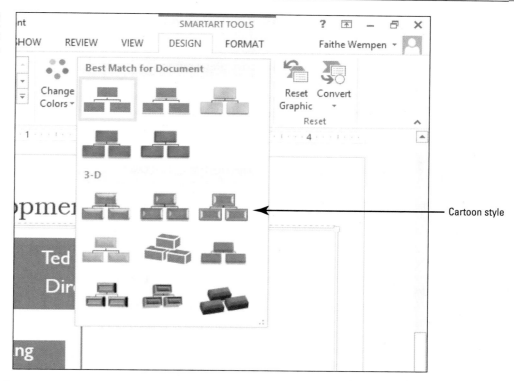

Cartoon style

4. Click the Cartoon style. (It is the third style in the first row of the 3-D section.) PowerPoint applies the style (see Figure 7-11).

Figure 7-11

A style applied to a SmartArt graphic

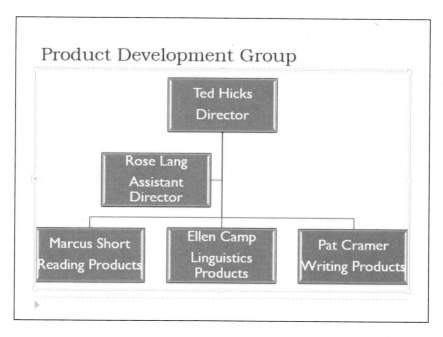

5. Go to slide 1, click the SmartArt object, and repeat steps 2-4 to apply the same style.

6. Go to slide 4, click the SmartArt object, and repeat steps 2-4 to apply the same style.

7. SAVE the presentation.

PAUSE. LEAVE the presentation open to use in the next exercise.

SmartArt styles can instantly improve a new graphic by applying visual effects to the shapes. Review the results carefully, however, after applying a SmartArt style. If your shapes contain several lines of text, some of the 3-D styles may obscure the text or cause it to run over on the edges—not a very attractive presentation.

If you do not like the formatting you have applied, you can easily revert to the original appearance of the SmartArt. Click the Reset Graphic button on the SmartArt Tools Design tab to restore the SmartArt to its default appearance.

CERTIFICATION READY?   **3.4.2**

How do you change the color of SmartArt?

Selecting a Color Theme for SmartArt

By default, SmartArt uses variants of a single theme color. Use the Change Colors gallery to apply a different theme color. In this exercise, you will apply a different color theme to a SmartArt graphic.

STEP BY STEP   **Apply a Color Theme to a SmartArt Graphic**

USE the *Litware Final* presentation that is still open from the previous exercise.

1. Go to **slide 3** and click the **SmartArt graphic** to select it. Click the **SmartArt Tools Design** tab.
2. Click the **Change Colors** button in the SmartArt Styles group. The Change Colors gallery opens.
3. Click the **fourth style** in the Colorful section (**Colorful Range – Accent Colors 4 to 5**). PowerPoint applies theme colors differentiated by level (see Figure 7-12).

Figure 7-12

Apply different colors

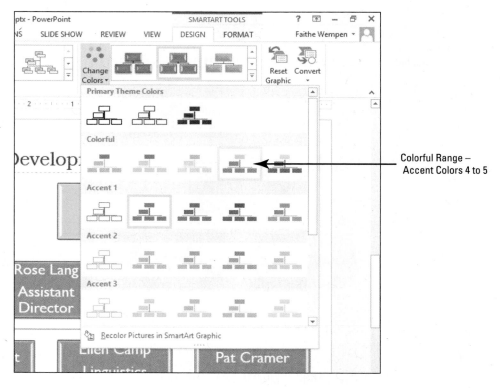

Colorful Range – Accent Colors 4 to 5

Take Note   Differentiating levels or processes by color gives your audience further visual cues that help them understand the SmartArt graphic.

4. Go to **slide 4** and click the **SmartArt graphic** to select it.

5. Click the Change Colors button in the SmartArt Styles group, opening the Change Colors gallery, and then click the first style in the Colorful section (Colorful-Accent Colors). PowerPoint uses theme colors to apply different tints to each shape.

6. **SAVE** the presentation.

PAUSE. LEAVE the presentation open to use in the next exercise.

Another Way
You can also format a shape by right-clicking the shape, selecting Format Shape, and using the options in the Format Shape task pane.

The Change Colors gallery provides a quick way to apply variations of theme colors to an entire SmartArt graphic. If the gallery choices do not provide what you are looking for, you can manually apply theme colors (or any non-theme color) by using tools on the SmartArt Tools Format tab. Click an individual shape or use the Shift or Ctrl keys to select more than one shape, and then choose a shape style from the Shape Styles gallery. You can also use the Shape Fill, Shape Outline, and Shape Effects buttons to choose new colors, outlines, or effects for the selected shapes.

If you do not like the changes you have made to a particular shape, you can reset the shape formats. Right-click the shape, then click Reset Shape on the shortcut menu.

Changing a SmartArt Graphic's Layout

If you decide a particular layout does not present your data as you like, you can easily choose a new layout. A different layout can dramatically change the way the data appears. Different layouts may be more or less suited to your data, so you may want to try several different layouts to find the best match. In this exercise, you will change a SmartArt graphic to a different layout.

STEP BY STEP   **Change a SmartArt Layout**

USE the *Litware Final* presentation that is still open from the previous exercise.

1. Click the SmartArt graphic on slide 4 to select it, if necessary. Make sure you select the outer frame of the graphic—not an individual shape.

2. Click the More button in the Layouts group to display the Layouts gallery.

Take Note   The Layouts gallery displays alternative layouts for the current type.

3. Click Continuous Cycle (see Figure 7-13). PowerPoint applies the new cycle layout to the current chart (see Figure 7-14).

Figure 7-13

The Layouts gallery for the Cycle type

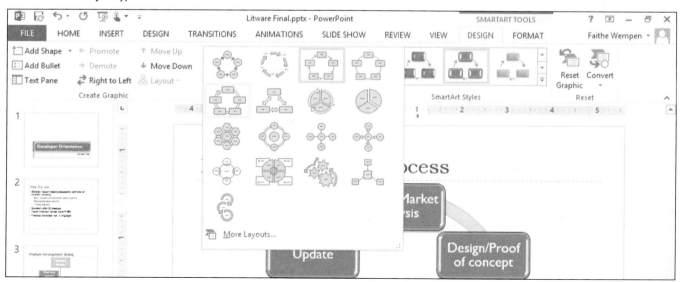

Figure 7-14

A new layout has been applied

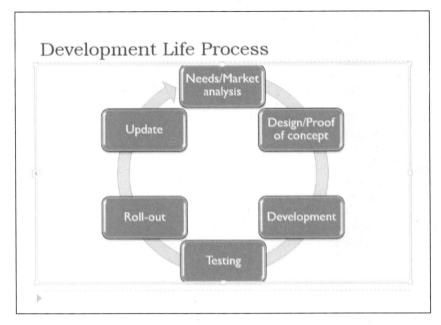

4. **SAVE** the presentation.

PAUSE. LEAVE the presentation open to use in the next exercise.

When changing a layout, you should generally choose from among the layouts of the current SmartArt type. In many cases, changing a layout will not result in any additional work for you; PowerPoint simply adjusts the current text into new shapes or configurations, as happened in this exercise.

Take Note   It is also possible to convert one type of SmartArt to another. You will learn more about making this kind of change later in this lesson.

In some cases, however, your information will not convert seamlessly from one layout to another. Some layouts allow only a limited number of shapes, and if your original layout had more than the number allowed in the new layout, information that cannot be displayed in the new layout may disappear.

CERTIFICATION READY?   **3.4.1**

How do you add shapes to SmartArt?

Adding a New Shape to a SmartArt Graphic

As you work with SmartArt, you may need to add shapes to accommodate your information. Use the Add Shape button to choose what kind of shape to add and where to insert it in the graphic. Adding a new shape to a graphic causes all the existing shapes to resize or reposition to make room for the new shape.

STEP BY STEP   **Add a Shape to a SmartArt Graphic**

USE the *Litware Final* presentation that is still open from the previous exercise.

1. Go to slide 3 and click the SmartArt graphic to select it. Make sure you select the graphic's outer frame, and not a specific shape within it.
2. Click the SmartArt Tools Design tab.
3. Click the last shape in the last row (Pat Cramer) to select it.
4. Click the Add Shape drop-down arrow in the Create Graphic group. PowerPoint displays a menu of options for adding a shape relative to the current shape (see Figure 7-15).

Figure 7-15

The Add Shape menu

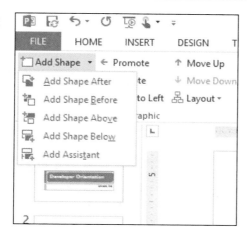

5. Click **Add Shape Below**. PowerPoint adds a subordinate shape to the Pat Cramer shape.

Take Note Notice that the new shape, which is on a new level, has a different theme color to differentiate it from the level above.

6. Type **Hannah Wong** in the new shape, press **Enter**, and type **Product Coordinator**. Then click away from the graphic to **deselect** it. The slide should look similar to Figure 7-16.

Figure 7-16

A new shape has been added

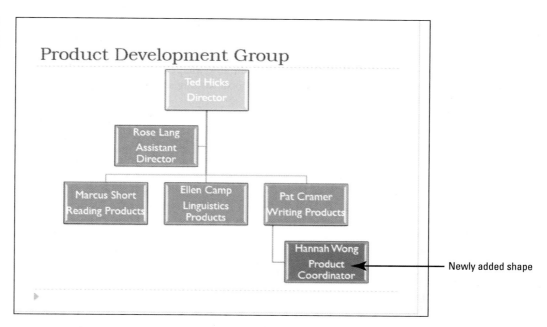

Newly added shape

7. Select **Hannah Wong's shape**. On the SmartArt Tools Design tab, click the **Add Shape drop-down arrow**, and then click **Add Shape Below**. PowerPoint adds a subordinate shape.

8. Type **Allan Morgan** into the new shape, press **Enter**, and type **Software Design**.

9. With Allan Morgan's shape still selected, click the **Add Shape drop-down arrow**, and then click **Add Shape After**. PowerPoint adds a shape on the same level.

Take Note In step 9, had you clicked the face of the Add Shape button rather than its arrow, PowerPoint would have added a new shape subordinate to the selected one.

10. Type **Kyle Porter** in the new shape, press **Enter**, and type **Package Design**.

11. Click away from the graphic to **deselect** it. Your slide should look similar to Figure 7-17.

Figure 7-17

New subordinate shapes have been added

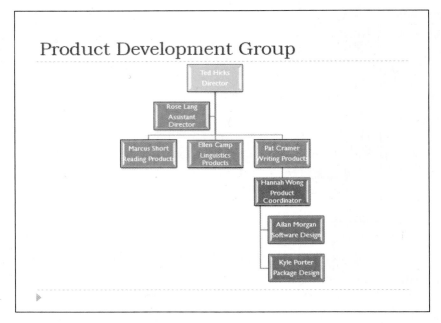

12. **SAVE** the presentation.

PAUSE. LEAVE the presentation open to use in the next exercise.

The choices available on the Add Shape drop-down menu depend on the type of SmartArt you are working with. You can choose among some or all of these options:

- **Add Shape After:** a new shape to the right of the selected shape on the same level. (If the SmartArt graphic displays shapes vertically, the new shape may appear below the selected shape.)
- **Add Shape Before:** a new shape to the left of the selected shape on the same level. (If the SmartArt graphic displays shapes vertically, the new shape may appear above the selected shape.)
- **Add Shape Above:** a new shape on the level above the selected shape. The new shape is superior to the selected shape.
- **Add Shape Below:** a new shape in the level below the selected shape. The new shape is subordinate to the selected shape.
- **Add Assistant:** a new assistant shape subordinate to the selected shape. This option is available only in organization charts.

Take Note   You cannot add a shape above the top-level shape in an organization chart.

Removing a Shape from a SmartArt Graphic

You can easily delete shapes you do not need. When you remove a shape, PowerPoint resizes the other shapes to take advantage of the increased space in the SmartArt container. Font sizes usually increase accordingly too. For this reason, you should not do any manual formatting of text and shape size until you have finalized the number of shapes. You will learn about manually formatting the text and shapes later in this lesson.

STEP BY STEP   **Remove a Shape from a SmartArt Graphic**

USE the *Litware Final* presentation that is still open from the previous exercise.

1. Go to slide 4, and click the SmartArt graphic to select it.

2. Click the Update shape to select it. Make sure you select the shape and not the text within it.

3. Press Delete. PowerPoint removes the shape and reconfigures the SmartArt graphic (see Fitware 7-18).

Figure 7-18

A shape has been deleted, and the remaining shapes spread out to take up its space

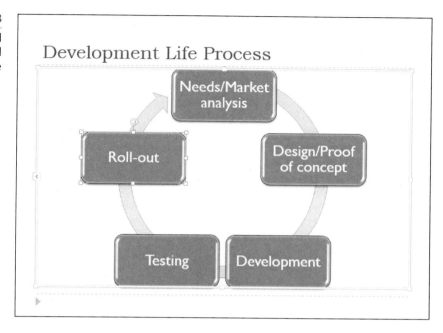

4. **SAVE** the presentation.

PAUSE. LEAVE the presentation open to use in the next exercise.

CERTIFICATION
READY? 3.4.4

How do you reverse direction in a SmartArt graphic?

Reversing Direction

You can change the look of a SmartArt graphic by modifying the way shapes are positioned. You can use the Right to Left and Layout buttons to adjust the orientation. In this exercise, you will reverse a graphic's direction and change the layout of a section of an organization chart.

STEP BY STEP **Reverse Direction**

USE the *Litware Final* presentation that is still open from the previous exercise.

1. Go to slide 3 and click the SmartArt graphic to select it. Make sure you select the entire graphic.

2. Click the SmartArt Tools Design tab if it is not already displayed.

3. Click the Right to Left button in the Create Graphic group. PowerPoint flips the graphic horizontally so that shapes on the right side are now on the left side (see Figure 7-19).

Figure 7-19

Use Right to Left to switch
the orientation

Right to Left button

Product Development Group

4. Click in the top-level shape (**Ted Hicks**). Make sure you select the shape, and not the text within it.

5. Click the **Layout** button in the Create Graphic group. PowerPoint displays options for positioning the shapes relative to the top-level shape.

6. Click **Left Hanging**. The subordinate shapes are arranged vertically below the top-level shape, rather than horizontally (see Figure 7-20).

Figure 7-20

The subordinate shapes
appear vertically

Layout button

Product Development Group

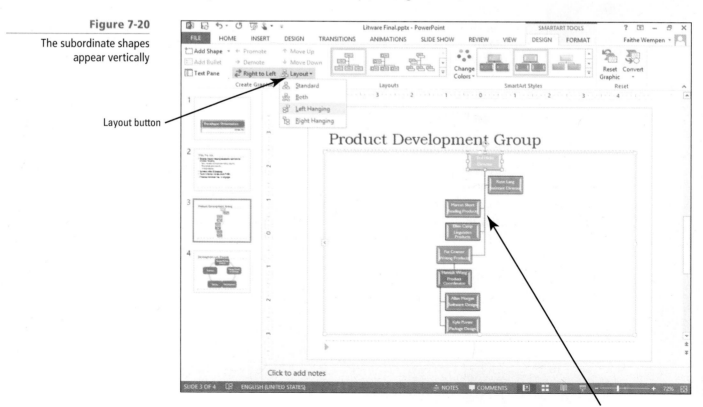

Left hanging layout

7. Click the Layout button, and then click Standard to restore the previous layout.

8. Click the Hannah Wong shape, click the Layout button, and then click Both. The subordinate shapes display horizontally rather than vertically (see Figure 7-21).

Figure 7-21

Layout has been changed for Hannah Wong's subordinates

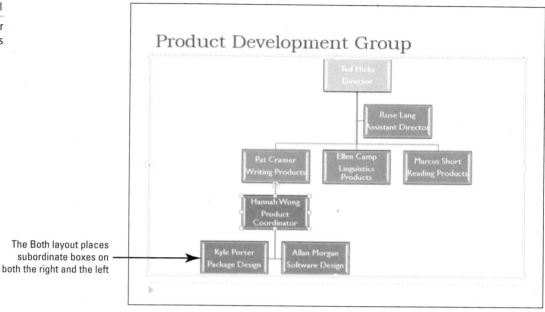

The Both layout places subordinate boxes on both the right and the left

9. **SAVE** the presentation.

PAUSE. LEAVE the presentation open to use in the next exercise.

You can use the Right to Left button with any SmartArt graphic that distributes shapes and information horizontally across the slide. Right to Left has no impact on layouts that center information, such as Pyramid.

The Layout button is available only in organization charts with a shape that is superior to subordinate shapes selected.

You do not have to use the default orientation and positioning of shapes if you would prefer another arrangement. You can click any shape to select it and drag it to a new location. If the shape is connected to other shapes, as in an organization chart, the connector lines shift position or change shape to maintain the connection.

Reordering Shapes

<table>
<tr><td>

CERTIFICATION READY?   3.4.3

How do you move text within SmartArt shapes?

</td><td>

In addition to changing the SmartArt graphic's entire orientation, you can also reorder the individual shapes by using the Move Up and Move Down buttons. Be aware, however, that the directions "up" and "down" are relative and, depending on the position of the shape, may not correspond to the actual direction being moved. In this exercise, you will move a shape to a different location in a SmartArt graphic.

</td></tr>
</table>

STEP BY STEP   **Move a SmartArt Shape**

USE the *Litware Final* presentation that is still open from the previous exercise.

1. Go to slide 4 and click the SmartArt graphic to select it.

2. Click the Testing shape.

3. On the SmartArt Tools Design tab, click Move Down. The shape moves one position in a clockwise direction. Note that in this example, Move Down actually moves the shape upward in the graphic.

4. Click Move Up. The shape moves one position in a counter-clockwise direction.

5. **SAVE** the presentation.

PAUSE. LEAVE the presentation open to use in the next exercise.

Promoting and Demoting Shapes

You can add, remove, or modify shapes by promoting or demoting text. When you **promote** an item, you move it up a level. When you **demote** an item, you make it subordinate to the item above it in the hierarchy. This procedure is similar to changing the indent level of items in a bulleted list. In the following exercise, you will learn how to promote a shape.

STEP BY STEP	Promote a Shape

USE the *Litware Final* presentation that is still open from the previous exercise.

1. Click the SmartArt graphic on slide 3 to select it if necessary.

2. If the Text pane is not already open, click the Text Pane button on the SmartArt Tools Design tab.

3. In the Text pane, click the Hannah Wong bulleted item. Notice in the Text pane that this item is indented below the Pat Cramer bulleted item.

4. Click the Promote button in the Create Graphic group. Hannah Wong's shape jumps up one level, and her two subordinates are also promoted (see Figure 7-22).

Figure 7-22

Promoting a shape

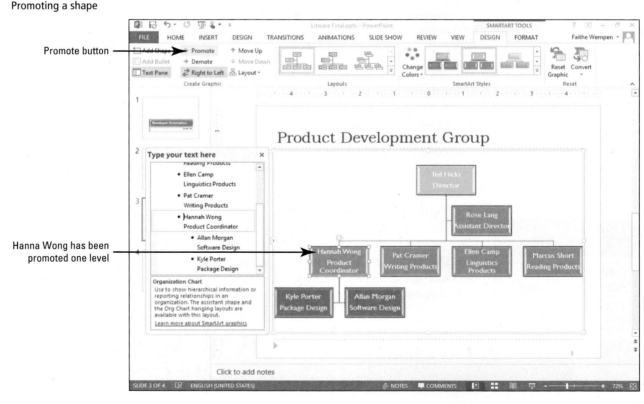

Promote button

Hanna Wong has been promoted one level

5. Click the Text Pane button to hide the Text pane again.

6. **SAVE** the presentation.

PAUSE. LEAVE the presentation open to use in the next exercise.

What happens when you promote or demote an item depends on whether you are promoting shape text or bulleted text:

- In many types of SmartArt graphics, you cannot promote shape text at all because shapes are already first-level items by default. An exception is hierarchical charts such as organization charts. You can promote any shape except the top-level shape; when you promote a shape, it moves up to the level superior to its original position.
- If you promote a bulleted text item, it becomes a shape containing first-level shape text.
- If you demote shape text, it becomes a bullet item.
- If you demote a bulleted text item, it indents further just as when you make a bullet item subordinate on a slide.

When you promote one bulleted item in a placeholder that contains several bulleted items, the other bulleted items may become subordinate to the new shape text. You may need to move bulleted items back to their original shape in this case. You can use Cut and Paste in the Text pane to move bulleted items from one location to another.

Choosing a Different SmartArt Type

Sometimes the hardest part about working with SmartArt is selecting the type and layout that will best display your data. Fortunately, you can easily change the type even after you have created and formatted a SmartArt graphic. Some types of SmartArt will convert very well to a different type, while others will not fit the shape layout of the new type at all. You may need to retype information to display it properly in a different type. The following exercise shows how to select a different type and layout.

STEP BY STEP | **Choose a Different SmartArt Type and Layout**

USE the *Litware Final* presentation that is still open from the previous exercise.

1. Go to slide 4 and click the SmartArt graphic to select it.
2. Click the More button in the Layouts group, and then click More Layouts at the bottom of the gallery to open the Choose a SmartArt Graphic dialog box.
3. Click the Process type in the left pane, then click the Upward Arrow layout in the center pane.
4. Click OK. PowerPoint converts the SmartArt graphic to the Upward Arrow type (see Figure 7-23).

Figure 7-23

The cycle graphic is changed to a process graphic using the Upward Arrow layout.

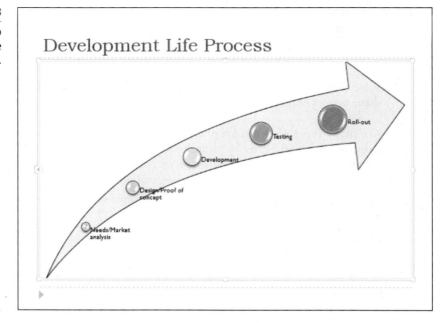

Figure 7-23

The cycle graphic is changed to a process graphic using the Upward Arrow layout.

5. **SAVE** the presentation.

PAUSE. LEAVE the presentation open to use in the next exercise.

Changing Shape Appearance

Final adjustments to a SmartArt graphic include tweaking the size of shapes and modifying text formatting. PowerPoint formats shapes so that all will fit comfortably in the placeholder. If you have only a few shapes, you might find that these adjustments result in a graphic where shapes are much larger than they need to be to hold their text. Conversely, you may want to increase shape size to draw attention to one specific shape. These types of appearance changes can improve the look of a graphic and make it easier to read. In this exercise, you will learn how to change the size of a shape.

STEP BY STEP   **Change Shape Size**

USE the *Litware Final* presentation that is still open from the previous exercise.

1. Close the Text pane if it is open.
2. Select the SmartArt graphic on slide 4 if it is not already selected, and then click the Needs/Market Analysis circle (the circle nearest the thin end of the arrow graphic) to select it. Make sure you select the circle, not the text.
3. Click the SmartArt Tools Format tab.
4. Click the Larger button in the Shapes group twice to increase the size of the smallest circle.
5. Click the Design/Proof of Concept circle shape, and then click the Larger button once to increase the shape's size.
6. Click the Roll-out circle shape, and then click the Smaller button in the Shapes group once to decrease the shape size. Then click away from the graphic to deselect it. Your SmartArt graphic should look like Figure 7-24.

Figure 7-24

Several shapes have been resized

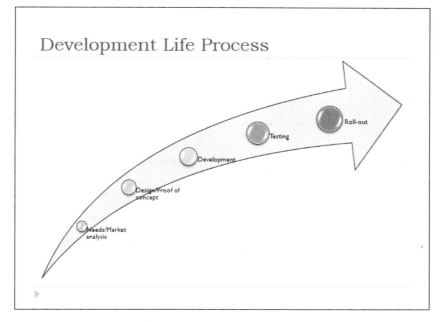

Troubleshooting If you select the text box rather than the shape, click outside the text box to deselect it, and then try again by clicking the left edge of the shape with the four-headed pointer.

　　7. **SAVE** the presentation.

PAUSE. LEAVE the presentation open to use in the next exercise.

Take Note You can also change shape appearance by selecting a completely new shape: right-click a shape, click Change Shape, and select the desired shape from the Shapes gallery.

Take care when enlarging or reducing shapes. You risk ending up with an inconsistent-looking graphic that is much less attractive than one in which shape sizes are identical or graduated according to an obvious pattern.

Changing Text Formatting

PowerPoint automatically adjusts font sizes to fit in or around shapes. If you do not find the size or color of text in a SmartArt graphic attractive or easy to read, you can use the Home tab formatting options to adjust font formats such as size, color, or style. You can also adjust alignment in shapes just as you would in any PowerPoint placeholder.

If you modify text formats with the SmartArt graphic selected, all text within the graphic will display the new format. To apply a new text format to a single shape, select that shape first. Text placeholders are selected the same way as other slide placeholders are. In this exercise, you will format the text in a SmartArt graphic.

STEP BY STEP　　**Change Text Formatting**

USE the *Litware Final* presentation that is still open from the previous exercise.

　　1. On slide 4, select the outer frame of the SmartArt graphic (not a specific shape within it).

　　2. On the Home tab, click the Font Size drop-down arrow, and then click 20. PowerPoint changes the size of all text in the graphic to 20 point (see Figure 7-25).

Figure 7-25

The text size has been enlarged for easier reading

Figure 7-25

The text size has been enlarged for easier reading

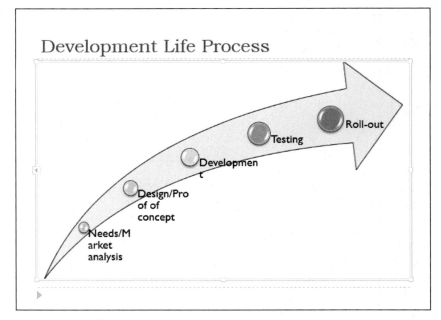

3. Click the Needs/Market analysis text box and drag its border to reduce its width slightly so that the word *Market* moves completely to the second line.

4. Click the Design/Proof of concept text box and expand its width so that the word *Proof* displays completely on the first line.

5. With the Design/Proof of concept text box selected, press the right arrow key on the keyboard three times to move the text box slightly to the right so its text does not overlap the circle shape.

6. Widen the *Development* text box so the word fits on a single line, and move the text box to the right slightly, as you did in step 5. Then click away from the graphic to deselect it. Your completed graphic should look similar to Figure 7-26.

Figure 7-26

The completed process graphic

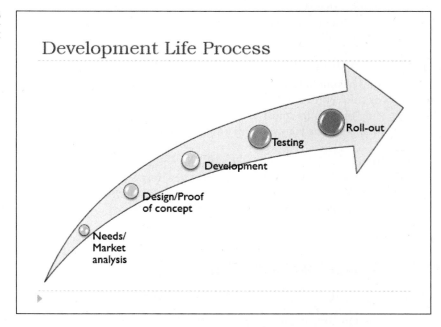

7. Go to slide 3 and click the SmartArt graphic to select it.

8. Click the outside edge of the Ted Hicks shape.

9. Click the Font Color drop-down arrow on the Home tab, and then click Black, Text 1. The text in that shape is now easier to read against the light green fill.

10. Click the Bold button on the Home tab. All text in the shape is bolded. Then click away from the graphic to deselect it. Your graphic should look like Figure 7-27.

Figure 7-27

The completed organization chart

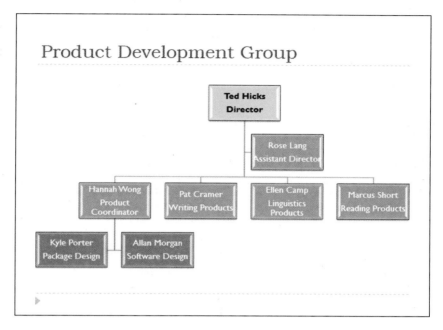

11. **SAVE** the presentation.

PAUSE. LEAVE the presentation open to use in the next exercise.

Converting SmartArt

When you convert SmartArt to text, the text in the SmartArt object changes to a bulleted list. Top-level shape text becomes top-level bullet points, and subordinate shapes become subordinate bullets. When you convert SmartArt to shapes, the diagram changes to a set of drawn shapes and lines, like the ones you might draw yourself using the Shapes button on the Insert tab. In this exercise, you will convert SmartArt diagrams to text and graphics.

STEP BY STEP   **Convert SmartArt**

USE the *Litware Final* presentation that is still open from the previous exercise.

1. Go to slide 4 and select the SmartArt object.

2. On the SmartArt Tools Design tab, click the Convert button, then click Convert to Text from the menu that appears. The SmartArt is converted to a bulleted list.

3. Go to slide 3 and select the SmartArt object.

4. On the SmartArt Tools Design tab, click the Convert button, and then click Convert to Shapes. The diagram changes to a set of shapes.

5. Click inside the diagram to confirm that the SmartArt tabs on the Ribbon do not appear.

6. Click one of the diagram's shapes. Notice that the Drawing Tools Format tab becomes available, indicating it is a drawn shape object.

7. **SAVE** the presentation and **CLOSE** it.

EXIT PowerPoint.

SKILL SUMMARY

In This Lesson, You Learned How To:	Exam Objective	Objective Number
Add SmartArt to a Slide	Convert lists to SmartArt	3.4.5
Modify SmartArt	Change the color of SmartArt	3.4.2
	Add shapes to SmartArt	3.4.1
	Reverse direction	3.4.4
	Move text within SmartArt shapes	3.4.3

Knowledge Assessment

Matching

Match the term in Column 1 to its description in Column 2.

Column 1

1. Promote
2. Assistant
3. SmartArt

4. Organization chart
5. Process
6. Top-level shape
7. Matrix
8. Text pane
9. Demote

10. Subordinates

Column 2

a. SmartArt graphic type that shows relationships among departments or personnel

b. SmartArt graphic type that can show steps in a timeline

c. Holds the name of the person or department at the head of the organization

d. Person who reports directly to a staff member

e. Panel in which you can type SmartArt graphic text

f. Decrease the level of the item in the hierarchy

g. Increase the level of the item in the hierarchy

h. Visual representation of information

i. Departments that report to the head of the organization

j. SmartArt graphic type that shows how parts relate to a whole

True/False

Circle T if the statement is true or F if the statement is false.

T F 1. List type SmartArt shows information that has to be in a particular order.

T F 2. Text in a SmartArt graphic can appear either in a shape or in a bulleted list.

T F 3. Use a Cycle type of SmartArt if you want to show a repeating process.

T F 4. The Standard Colors gallery allows you to apply variations of theme colors to a SmartArt graphic.

T F 5. You can apply a style to a SmartArt graphic from the SmartArt Tools Layout tab.

T F 6. The Add Shape Below option inserts a subordinate shape.

T F 7. The Layout button is available for all SmartArt types.

T F 8. To remove a shape, select it and press the Delete key on the keyboard.

T F 9. You have to retype text if you change from one SmartArt layout to another.

T F 10. SmartArt can be converted to a bulleted list or to shapes.

Project 7-1: Corporate Reorganization

You are the director of operations at Fabrikam, Inc., a company that develops fabric treatments for use in the textile industry. Your company is undergoing reorganization, and you need to prepare a presentation that shows how groups will be aligned in the new structure. You can use a SmartArt graphic to show the new organization.

GET READY. LAUNCH PowerPoint if it is not already running.

1. **OPEN** the *Reorganization* presentation and save it as *Reorganization Final*.
2. Go to slide 2 and click the Insert a SmartArt Graphic icon in the content placeholder.
3. Click the Hierarchy type, click the Hierarchy layout, and then click OK.
4. Click in the top-level shape and type Operations.
5. Click in the first second-level shape and type Production.
6. Click in the second second-level shape and type R & D.
7. Click in the first third-level shape and type Manufacturing.
8. Delete the other third-level shape under Production.
9. Click in the remaining third-level shape (under R & D) and type Quality Assurance.
10. Click the Manufacturing shape to select it. Then click the Add Shape drop-down arrow and select Add Shape Below.
11. Type Fulfillment in the new shape. Then click away from the new shape.
12. Display the SmartArt Styles gallery and click the Polished style (which might be the first style under 3-D, depending upon your screen size).
13. Display the Change Colors gallery and click one of the Colorful gallery choices.
14. Display the Layouts gallery and click the Horizontal Hierarchy layout.
15. **SAVE** the presentation and **CLOSE** the file.

LEAVE PowerPoint open for use in the next project.

Project 7-2: Meeting Agenda

You work for the city manager of Center City. She has asked you to create an agenda to display at an upcoming meeting of the city's department heads. She has supplied the bulleted text on an existing slide. You can use this text to make the agenda look more interesting.

1. **OPEN** the *Meeting Agenda* presentation.
2. Click in the content placeholder, click the Convert to SmartArt button, and then click More SmartArt Graphics.
3. In the List category, click the Vertical Box List layout, and then click OK.
4. Click the first shape to select it, click the Add Shape drop-down arrow, and then click Add Shape After.
5. Type Budget Cuts in the new shape.
6. Display the Layouts gallery and click the Vertical Bullet List layout.
7. Display the Change Colors gallery and under the Accent 5 heading, click the Transparent Gradient Range – Accent 5 option.
8. **SAVE** the presentation as *Meeting Agenda Final* and **CLOSE** the file.

LEAVE PowerPoint open for use in the next project.

Project 7-3: **New Menu**

You are the general manager of the Northwind Traders Restaurant and you are about to present some new entrees to your staff. You can make the information more visually exciting using a SmartArt graphic.

1. **OPEN** the *New Menu* presentation.
2. Convert the bulleted list on slide 2 to the Vertical Block List SmartArt graphic.
3. Click the empty shape at the top of the graphic and remove it.
4. Click at the end of the one Fish bulleted item, press Enter, and type Shrimp Scampi - $19.99.
5. Click the Right to Left button on the SmartArt Tools Design tab to change the orientation of the SmartArt graphic so that the top level text is at the right and the subordinate text at the left.
6. Reduce the size of the shapes (Beef, Pork, Chicken, and Fish) by selecting each and clicking the Smaller button on the SmartArt Tools Format tab one time.
7. Apply the Subtle Effect SmartArt Style of your choice to the graphic.
8. Apply Colorful - Accent Colors to the graphic using the Change Colors button on the SmartArt Tools Design tab.
9. Change the text color to Aqua, Accent 3, and Darker 50% in the shapes at the right side of the graphic.
10. **SAVE** the presentation as *New Menu Final* and **CLOSE** the file.

LEAVE PowerPoint open for use in the next project.

Project 7-4: **On Paper**

You are the plant manager for Northwind Paper Company. You are scheduled to give a presentation to a class of art students to explain how paper is made. You can use a SmartArt graphic to make the process more visually interesting.

1. **OPEN** the *Paper* presentation.
2. Go to slide 4 and insert a new SmartArt graphic. In the Relationship type, choose the Funnel layout.
3. Display the Text pane and replace the placeholder text with the following four items:
   Pulp
   Stock
   Press & Dry
   Paper
4. Apply the Subtle Effect style to the SmartArt graphic.
5. Change the graphic to the Staggered Process layout in the Process type.
6. Change the font size of the text in all shapes in the graphic to 32 pt.
7. **SAVE** the presentation as *Paper Final* and **CLOSE** the file.

LEAVE PowerPoint open for use in the next project.

Mastery Assessment

Project 7-5: Tiger Tales

You are the owner of a karate studio that specializes in teaching youngsters. You are working on a presentation to give at local schools and after-school care centers. You want to add a SmartArt graphic to your presentation to stress the importance of having the proper attitude when learning karate.

1. **OPEN** the *Tigers* presentation.
2. Go to slide 3 and use the bulleted list to create a new SmartArt graphic using the Titled Matrix layout. Note that only the first bulleted item displays in the graphic.
3. Display the Text pane, and click the Respect item, which is currently grayed out with a red X over the bullet.
4. Demote this item. It will then display in the upper-left matrix shape. However, you still cannot see it because its text is the same color as the background.
5. Change the text color for the demoted text to white.
6. Repeat steps 3-5 for each of the other bullet points, so they all become visible.
7. Change the orientation of the SmartArt graphic to Right to Left.
8. Apply a SmartArt style of your choice.
9. Use the Shape Fill menu to apply a fill color to the Core Beliefs shape that is not a theme color but coordinates well with the other shape colors.
10. On the SmartArt Tools Design tab, click Convert, then Convert to Shapes. The SmartArt is converted to a graphic.
11. **SAVE** the presentation as *Tigers Final* and **CLOSE** the file.

LEAVE PowerPoint open for use in the next project.

Project 7-6: Pie Time

You are the franchising manager for Coho Pie Safe, a chain of bakeries specializing in fresh-baked pies and other bakery treats. You are working on a presentation to help potential franchisees understand the company. Use a SmartArt graphic to display information about revenue sources.

1. **OPEN** the *Pies* presentation.
2. Go to slide 2 and in the empty content placeholder, insert a Basic Pie SmartArt graphic from the Relationship graphic type.
3. Use the Text pane to insert the following information in the graphic:

    Birthdays

    Weddings

    Reunions
4. Add two new shapes to the pie with the text Restaurants and Church Socials.
5. Change the graphic type to a Vertical Arrow List layout.
6. Click in the arrow shape to the right of the Birthdays shape and type All ages.
7. Add bulleted text as follows for the remaining arrows:

Weddings	Both formal and informal
Reunions	Per item or bulk sales
Restaurants	Steady income year round
Church Socials	Per item or bulk sales
8. Apply the Cartoon SmartArt style and the Colorful - Accent Colors color scheme of your choice.
9. **SAVE** the presentation as *Pies Final* and **CLOSE** the file.

EXIT PowerPoint.

8 Adding Graphics to a Presentation

LESSON SKILL MATRIX

Skill	Exam Objective	Objective Number
Inserting and Formatting Images	Display gridlines.	2.3.4
	Crop images.	3.5.2
	Resize images.	3.5.1
	Apply styles.	3.5.4
	Apply effects.	3.5.3
	Compress media.	5.3.4
Adding Shapes to Slides	Resize shapes.	2.2.3
	Insert shapes.	2.2.4
	Apply borders to shapes.	2.2.2
	Apply styles to shapes.	2.2.6
	Create custom shapes.	2.2.5
Ordering and Grouping Shapes	Align and group shapes.	2.3.3
Creating a Photo Album Presentation		

KEY TERMS

- aspect ratio
- clip art
- constrain
- crop
- gridlines
- guides
- keyword
- order
- recolor
- reset
- rulers
- saturation
- Smart Guides
- tone

©FrankyDeMeyer/iStockphoto

You are the director of promotions for the Baldwin Museum of Science. The museum is especially interested in attracting teachers and students to their permanent exhibits, so you have scheduled appearances at a number of high schools in your area, where you plan to present PowerPoint slide shows about the museum and various aspects of science. PowerPoint's graphics capabilities allow you to include and customize pictures, shapes, and movies to enliven your presentations. You can also add sounds to provide the finishing touch to a presentation.

©FrankyDeMeyer/iStockphoto

SOFTWARE ORIENTATION

Picture Tools

The Picture Tools Format tab (see Figure 8-1) enables you to apply formatting effects to images. After selecting the picture, apply formatting by clicking a button on this tab.

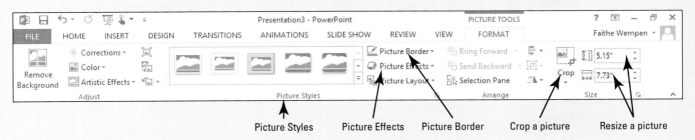

Figure 8-1

Picture Tools Format tab

You can use the tools on the Picture Tools Format tab to apply picture styles, to add or remove its border, and to apply special effects like shadow, reflection, and 3-D rotation. You can also crop and size the picture, correct the colors, and add artistic effects.

INSERTING AND FORMATTING IMAGES

The Bottom Line

Images can be used to illustrate a slide's content or provide visual interest to help hold the audience's attention. You can insert images from the Office.com image collection or a Bing image search, or you can insert a picture that you have created yourself or acquired from some other source. PowerPoint provides many options for improving the appearance of images after you have inserted them. You can reposition and resize them, rotate them, apply special effects such as Quick Styles, adjust brightness and contrast, and even recolor a picture for a special effect. If you do not like formatting changes you have made, you can reset an image to its original appearance.

Inserting Images from Office.com

Microsoft provides a large collection of images that PowerPoint users may use royalty-free in their presentations. To find an appropriate image for your presentation at Office.com, you search by keyword using the Online Pictures feature in PowerPoint. A **keyword** is a descriptor of an image's content, such as dog, tree, or flower. Each image has multiple keywords assigned to it, and so it can be found using a variety of keyword searches.

Some of the images from Office.com are photographs, whereas others are clip art illustrations. **Clip art** illustrations are drawings composed of mathematically generated lines and shapes, similar to the lines and shapes users can create using PowerPoint's own drawing tools. Clip art illustrations increase the size of the presentation file less than photographs do, but they are less realistic-looking. PowerPoint 2013 does not distinguish between clip art and photographs when it searches Office.com, and so your search results will likely contain a mixture of image types.

Take Note Office 2013 uses the terms *image* and *picture* interchangeably. For example, the exam objectives reference *images* but those images are inserted using the *Pictures* and *Online Pictures* commands in the applications. The term *illustration* refers to drawn artwork such as clip art, and the term *photograph* refers to an image that was originally captured with a digital camera or scanned with a scanner.

| STEP BY STEP | **Insert an Image from Office.com** |

GET READY. Before you begin these steps, make sure that your computer is on. Log on, if necessary.

1. **START** PowerPoint, if the program is not already running.
2. Locate and **OPEN** the *Exhibits* presentation and save it as *Exhibits Final*.
3. Go to slide 4 and click the Online Pictures icon in the empty content placeholder. The Insert Pictures dialog box opens.
4. Click in the Office.com Clip Art text box and type gears (see Figure 8-2).

Figure 8-2

Search for images with the keyword *gears*

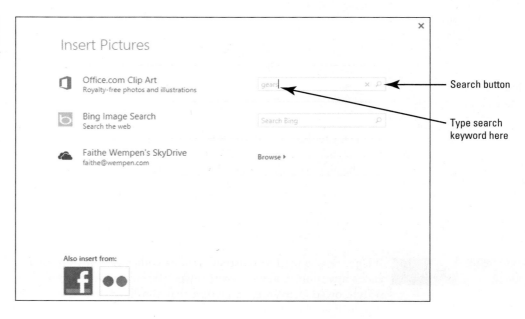

5. Press Enter, or click the Search icon [BTN-SEARCH]. PowerPoint searches for images that match the keyword and displays them in the dialog box.
6. Scroll down through the results and click a picture of gears. Choose a photo, rather than a line drawing.
7. Click Insert. The image is inserted in the content placeholder.
8. **SAVE** the presentation.

PAUSE. LEAVE the presentation open to use in the next exercise.

Another Way
To insert Office.com images on a slide that does not have a content placeholder, click the Online Pictures button on the Insert tab.

This exercise inserted a photograph, rather than a clip art illustration. Photographs provide a more sophisticated and professional look for a presentation. Many clip art illustrations are humorous in appearance and may not be suitable for corporate communications or presentations on serious topics.

When you insert an image into a content placeholder, PowerPoint tries to fit the graphic you select into the content placeholder. The image may not use up the entire placeholder area, depending on its size and shape. If you insert an image on a slide that does not have a placeholder, it will generally appear in the center of the slide. You can adjust the image's size and position by dragging it, as you will learn later in this lesson.

If you decide you do not like an image you have inserted, you can easily delete it. Click the image to select it and then press Delete to remove it from the slide.

Inserting a Picture from a File

You do not have to rely on PowerPoint's clip art files to illustrate your presentation. You can download many pictures for free on the Internet or create your own picture files using a digital camera. In this exercise, you will insert a picture from a file that has already been created.

STEP BY STEP	**Insert a Picture from a File**

USE the *Exhibits Final* presentation that is still open from the previous exercise.

Another Way
Click the Pictures icon in any content placeholder to open the Insert Picture dialog box.

1. Go to slide 3 and on the Insert tab, click the Pictures button. The Insert Picture dialog box opens.
2. Navigate to the location of the data files for this lesson, click *Astronomy.jpg* (see Figure 8-3), and then click Insert. The dialog box may look different from the one shown in Figure 8-3, depending on your Windows version, the view in effect, and the other files in the folder. The picture appears on the slide (see Figure 8-4).

Figure 8-3

Locate a picture file in the Insert Picture dialog box

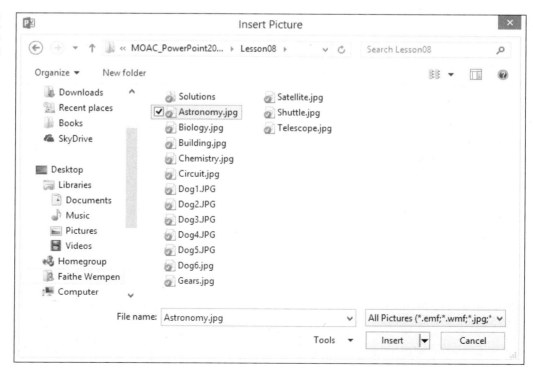

3. **SAVE** the presentation.

PAUSE. LEAVE the presentation open to use in the next exercise.

PowerPoint supports a variety of picture file formats, including GIF, JPEG, PNG, TIFF, BMP, and WMF. Be aware that graphic formats differ in how they store graphic information, so some formats create larger files than others.

If you take your own pictures using a digital camera, you do not have to worry about copyright issues, but you should pay attention to copyright permissions for pictures you locate from other sources. It is extremely easy to save any picture from a web page to your system. If you are going to use the picture commercially, you need to contact the copyright holder, if there is one, and ask for specific permission to reuse the picture.

Take Note   Some U.S. government sites, such as NASA (the source of the picture you inserted in the previous exercise), make images available without requiring copyright permission.

Changing a Picture

After inserting a picture, if it is not what you want you can easily delete it and insert a different one, either from an online source or from another file. However, if you have applied formatting to the picture, as you will learn to do in the remainder of this chapter, you might not want to lose the formatting and start over. In situations such as this, you can use the Change Picture command to swap out the picture without losing any of the formatting you have applied to the previous picture.

STEP BY STEP   **Change a Picture**

USE the *Exhibits Final* presentation that is still open from the previous exercise.

1. Go to slide 4.
2. Right-click the picture and click Change Picture. The Insert Pictures dialog box opens.
3. Click the Browse hyperlink next to From a file. The Insert Picture dialog box opens. (This is a different dialog box from the one in step 2.)
4. Navigate to the folder containing the data files for this lesson and click *Gears.jpg*.
5. Click Insert. The picture is replaced.
6. **SAVE** the presentation.

PAUSE. LEAVE the presentation open to use in the next exercise.

CERTIFICATION READY? 2.3.4

How do you display gridlines?

Using the Ruler, Gridlines, and Guides

In Normal, Outline, and Notes Page views, you can turn on PowerPoint's horizontal and vertical **rulers**, which help you measure the size of an object on the slide, as well as the amount of space between objects. **Smart Guides** appear automatically as you drag objects on a slide to help you line them up with other content on the slide. If you want guide lines that stay visible, turn on the Guides feature. These drawing **guides** are movable vertical and horizontal non-printing lines that you can use when positioning objects on a slide. PowerPoint also provides **gridlines**, a set of dotted horizontal and vertical lines that overlay the entire slide. In this exercise, you learn how to use the ruler, guides, and gridlines to position objects so that they align with other objects on a slide and appear consistently throughout a presentation.

STEP BY STEP   **Use the Ruler, Gridlines, and Guides**

USE the *Exhibits Final* presentation that is still open from the previous exercise.

1. Go to slide 3. On the View tab, click Ruler if this option is not already selected. The vertical and horizontal rulers appear in the Slide pane.

2. Click to mark the Gridlines check box. A grid of regularly spaced dots overlays the slide (see Figure 8-4).

Another Way
Right-click a slide outside of any placeholder, and then click Ruler.

Figure 8-4

Rulers and gridlines

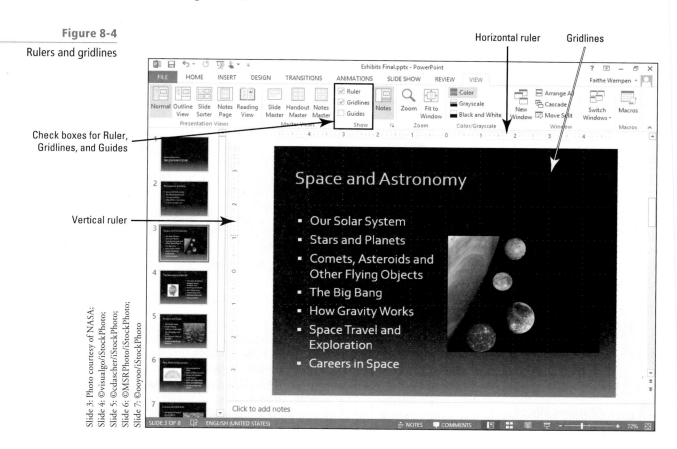

Check boxes for Ruler, Gridlines, and Guides

Vertical ruler

Horizontal ruler   Gridlines

Slide 3: Photo courtesy of NASA;
Slide 4: ©visualgo/iStockPhoto;
Slide 5: ©cdascher/iStockPhoto;
Slide 6: ©MSRPhoto/iStockPhoto;
Slide 7: ©ooyoo/iStockPhoto

3. Click to mark the Guides check box. The default vertical and horizontal drawing guides display, intersecting at the center of the slide, as shown in Figure 8-5.

Figure 8-5

A ScreenTip shows the guide's position on the ruler

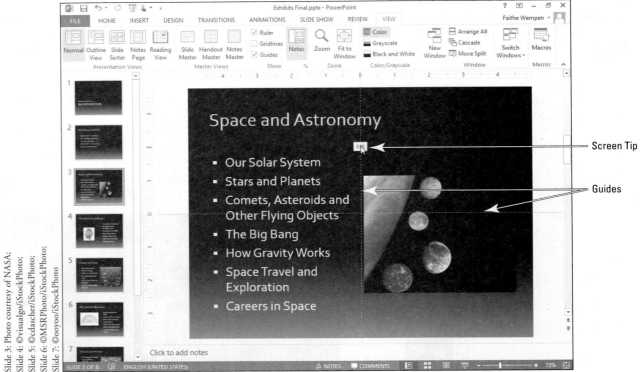

Screen Tip

Guides

Slide 3: Photo courtesy of NASA;
Slide 4: ©visualgo/iStockPhoto;
Slide 5: ©cdascher/iStockPhoto;
Slide 6: ©MSRPhoto/iStockPhoto;
Slide 7: ©ooyoo/iStockPhoto

4. The guides will be more useful for positioning pictures in this presentation, so you can turn off the gridlines: click the View tab, and click Gridlines in the Show group to remove the check mark and hide the gridlines.

5. Click the text box on slide 3 that contains the bulleted list to activate it. You will use the text box's border to help you position guides.

6. Click the vertical guide. As you hold down the mouse button, a ScreenTip appears that shows the current position of the guide—0.0, indicating the guide is at the 0 inch mark on the horizontal ruler.

7. Click and drag the guide to the left until it aligns on the left border of the text placeholder. The ScreenTip should read approximately 4.50 with a left-pointing arrow. Release the mouse button to drop the guide at that location.

8. Click the horizontal guide to the right of the planet picture and drag upward until the ScreenTip reads 1.67 with an upward-pointing arrow. Drop the guide. It should align with the top of the capital letters in the first line of the text placeholder.

9. Click the vertical guide you positioned near the left edge of the slide, hold down Ctrl, and drag a copy of the guide to the right until the ScreenTip reads 4.50 with a right-pointing arrow. Drop the guide by first releasing the mouse button and then releasing the Ctrl key. Your slide should look like Figure 8-6.

Another Way
Right-click an empty area of the slide, point to Grid and Guides, and select Guides from the submenu. Or, click the dialog box launcher in the Show group on the View tab to open the Grid and Guides dialog box and then mark or clear the Guides check box. You can also press Alt+F9 to toggle guides on or off.

Figure 8-6

Drawing guides positioned on the slide

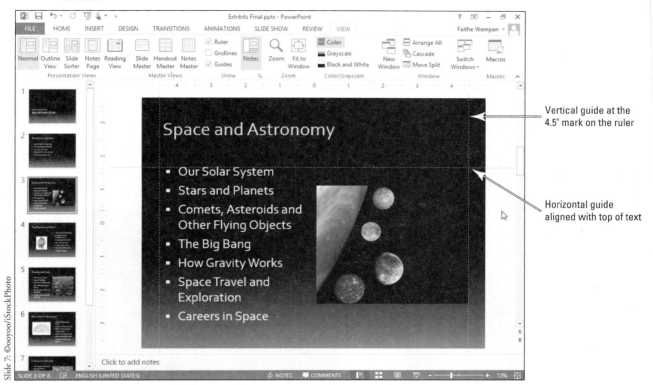

10. Go to slide 4, click the gear picture, and drag it until the upper-left corner of the picture snaps to the intersection of the vertical and horizontal guides. Your slide should look like Figure 8-7.

Figure 8-7

Picture repositioned using the guides

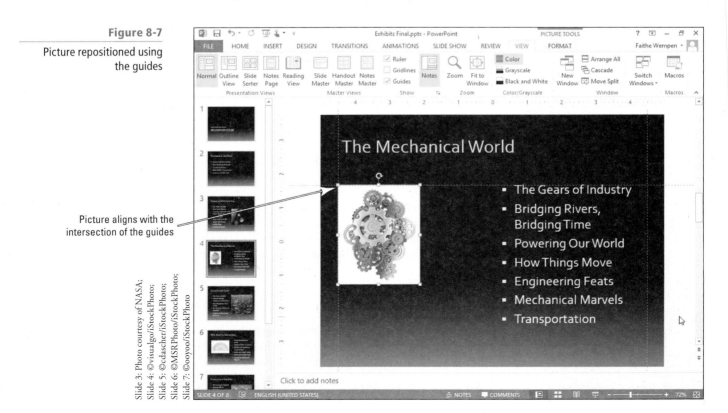

11. Go to slide 5 and drag the picture down and to the left so its upper-right corner snaps to the intersection of the guides.

12. Go to slide 6 and drag the picture up and to the left to snap to the intersection of the two guides.

13. On the View tab, clear the Guides check box to turn off the guides.

14. Go to slide 7 and drag the picture up on the slide until you see a faint red dotted horizontal line at its top. This Smart Guide indicates that the picture is at the same vertical position as the text box to its left (see Figure 8-8). Release the mouse button to drop the picture in the new location.

Figure 8-8

Smart Guides can help you position objects without using traditional guides

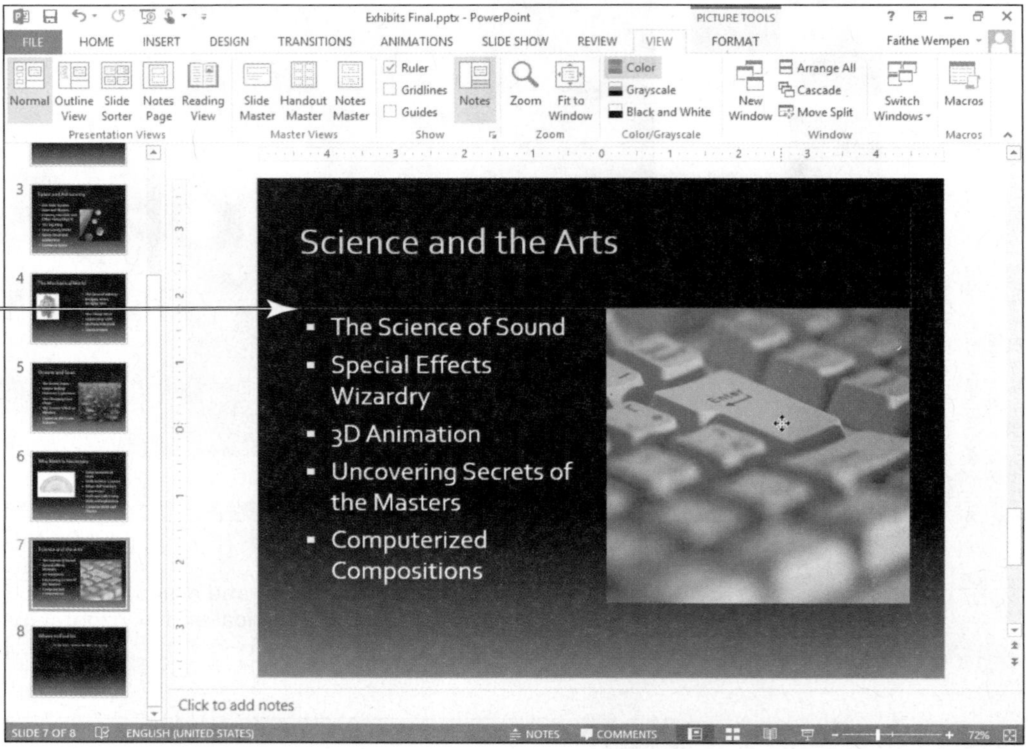

Slide 3: Photo courtesy of NASA;
Slide 4: ©visualgo/iStockPhoto;
Slide 5: ©cdascher/iStockPhoto;
Slide 6: ©MSRPhoto/iStockPhoto;
Slide 7: ©ooyoo/iStockPhoto

Take Note If you do not like the Smart Guides feature, you can turn it off. Right-click an empty area of the slide, point to Grid and Guides, and click Smart Guides. Repeat that same procedure to re-enable the feature.

15. **SAVE** the presentation.

PAUSE. LEAVE the presentation open to use in the next exercise.

By default, objects "snap"—automatically align—to the gridlines even if the gridlines are not currently displayed. This feature can be helpful when you are positioning objects, but you may sometimes find that it hinders precise positioning. You can temporarily override the "snapping" by holding down Alt as you drag an object. Or, you can display the Grid and Guides dialog box (by clicking the dialog box launcher in the Show group on the View tab) and deselect the *Snap objects to grid* check box.

Rotating and Flipping an Image

You can rotate or flip pictures to change their orientation on a slide. Rotating spins the picture around its center; flipping creates a mirror image of it. Rotating and flipping can provide additional visual interest for a graphic or fit it more attractively on a slide.

STEP BY STEP   **Rotate and Flip an Image**

USE the *Exhibits Final* presentation that is still open from the previous exercise. Save the file as *Exhibits Final Version 2*.

1. Go to slide 3, and click the picture to select it.

2. Click the Picture Tools Format tab, click Rotate Objects in the Arrange group, and then click Flip Horizontal in the drop-down menu that appears. The picture reverses its orientation so the planet is on the right and its moons are on the left (see Figure 8-9).

Figure 8-9

The picture has been flipped horizontally

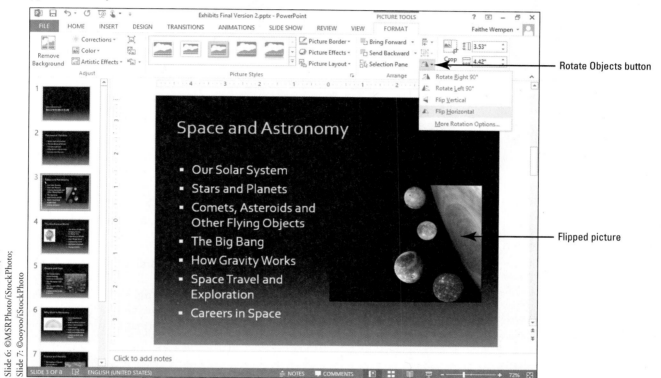

Rotate Objects button

Flipped picture

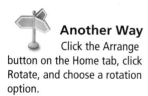

Another Way
Click the Arrange button on the Home tab, click Rotate, and choose a rotation option.

3. Drag the picture up into the upper-right corner of the slide, so that the top and right edges of the picture align with the top and right edges of the slide (see Figure 8-10).

Figure 8-10

Drag the picture to the
upper-right corner of the slide

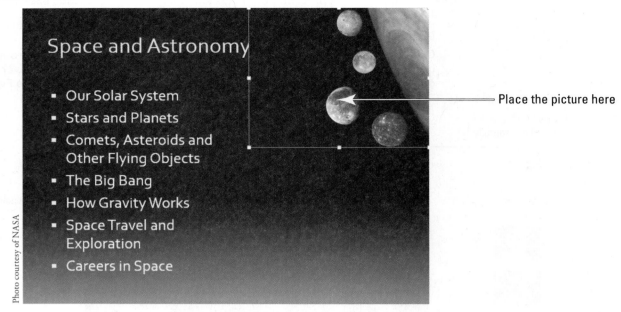

Photo courtesy of NASA

Place the picture here

4. Go to slide 4 and click the picture to select it.
5. Click the Picture Tools Format tab, click Rotate Objects, and then click Rotate Left 90°.
6. **SAVE** the presentation.

PAUSE. LEAVE the presentation open to use in the next exercise.

PowerPoint offers some set rotation options, such as rotating right or left 90 degrees. For more control over the rotation, you can drag the rotation handle above the selected object, or click More Rotation Options on the Rotate button's menu to open the Format Picture task pane, where you can type a specific rotation amount in the Rotation text box.

Cropping an Image

CERTIFICATION READY? 3.5.2

How do you crop an image?

You have several options for adjusting the size of a picture or other graphic object. You can crop an object to remove part of the object, drag a side or corner, specify exact measurements for an object, or scale it to a percentage of its original size. When you **crop** a picture, you remove a portion of the graphic that you think is unnecessary in order to focus attention on the most important part of a picture. The portion of the picture you cropped is not deleted. You can restore the cropped material by using the crop pointer to drag outward to reveal the material that was previously hidden.

STEP BY STEP **Crop an Image**

USE the *Exhibits Final Version 2* presentation that is still open from the previous exercise.

1. Go to slide 6 and click the picture to select it.
2. Click the Picture Tools Format tab.
3. Click the Crop button in the Size group. (Click the upper part of the button, not the arrow below it.) The pointer changes to a crop pointer and crop handles appear around the edges of the picture.

4. Click to position the pointer on the left side crop handle and drag inward to crop the picture so that there is an approximately equal amount of white space to the left of the protractor and to the right of it (see Figure 8-11).

Figure 8-11

Drag the crop handle inward to remove a portion of the picture

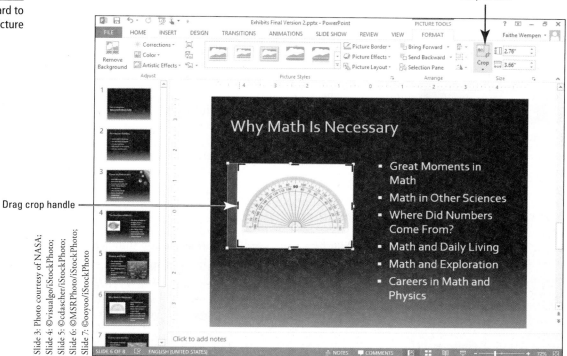

Drag crop handle

5. Release the mouse button, and then click the Crop button again to complete the crop.
6. On the View tab, mark the Guides check box to turn the guides back on.
7. Click and drag the cropped picture back up to the intersection of the two guides. Your slide should look similar to Figure 8-12.

Figure 8-12

The picture has been cropped and repositioned

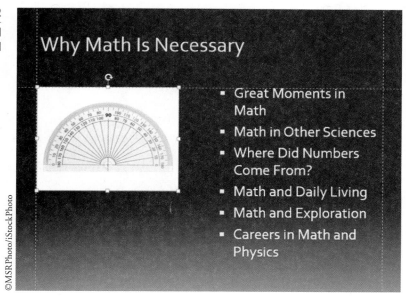

8. On the View tab, clear the Guides check box to turn the guides off.
9. **SAVE** the presentation.

PAUSE. LEAVE the presentation open to use in the next exercise.

Resizing an Image

In this exercise, you will learn three ways to adjust the size of a picture: by simply dragging a corner, by setting measurements in the Size and Position controls in the Format Picture task pane, and by setting a measurement in the Size group on the Picture Tools Format tab. You can use these options to resize any object on a slide.

Generally, you will want to maintain a picture's **aspect ratio** when you resize it. The aspect ratio is the relationship of width to height. By default, a change to the width of a picture is also applied to the height to maintain aspect ratio. In some instances, you may want to distort a picture on purpose by changing one dimension more than the other. To do so, you must deselect the *Lock aspect ratio* check box in the Size section of the Format Picture task pane. You are then free to change width and height independently. Alternatively, you can drag a side selection handle on the object (not a corner); this action allows you to adjust each dimension separately.

In the following exercise, you will resize an object and change its aspect ratio.

CERTIFICATION READY? **3.5.1**

How do you resize an image?

STEP BY STEP   **Resize an Image**

USE the *Exhibits Final Version 2* presentation that is still open from the previous exercise.

1. Go to slide 3 and click the picture to select it.
2. Click and drag the lower-left corner of the picture diagonally until the left edge of the picture aligns with the 0 mark on the horizontal ruler (see Figure 8-13). (Do not worry that the slide title is partially covered; you will fix this problem in a later exercise.)

Figure 8-13

Resize a picture by dragging a corner

Left edge aligns with 0 on horizontal ruler

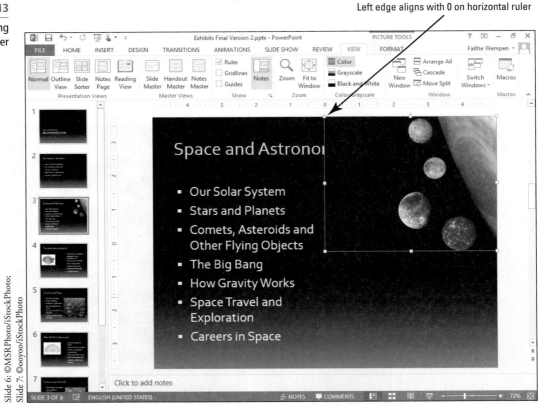

Slide 3: Photo courtesy of NASA;
Slide 4: ©visualgo/iStockPhoto;
Slide 5: ©cdascher/iStockPhoto;
Slide 6: ©MSRPhoto/iStockPhoto;
Slide 7: ©ooyoo/iStockPhoto

Take Note   If you have difficulty getting the size right because Smart Guides pop up to snap the image into alignment with other objects on the slide, turn off Smart Guides temporarily. Right-click an empty area of the slide, point to Grid and Guides, and click Smart Guides. Repeat that same procedure to re-enable the feature.

3. Go to slide 4 and click the picture to select it.

4. Right-click the picture, and then click Size and Position from the shortcut menu. The Format Picture task pane appears.

5. Click the Lock aspect ratio check box to deselect this option. You can now specify the height and width independently.

6. In the Size area of the task pane, click the Reset button to remove previous modifications made to this picture (rotation) from an earlier exercise.

7. Click the Height up arrow until the height is 3.7 inches. Click the Width down arrow until the width is 3 inches.

8. Click to expand the Position heading in the task pane, and set the Vertical position to 2.1 (see Figure 8-14). This action is an alternate way of moving a picture.

Another Way
You can open the Format Picture task pane by clicking the dialog box launcher in the Size group on the Picture Tools Format tab.

Figure 8-14

Format Picture task pane

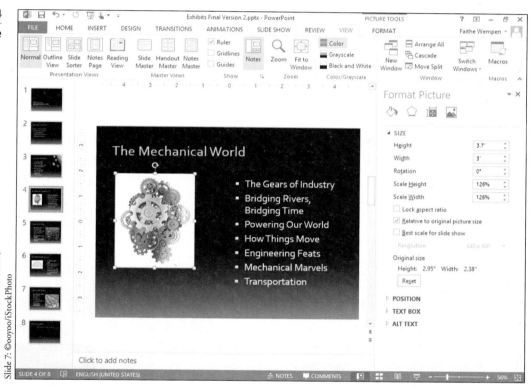

Slide 3: Photo courtesy of NASA;
Slide 4: ©visualgo/iStockPhoto;
Slide 5: ©cdascher/iStockPhoto;
Slide 6: ©MSRPhoto/iStockPhoto;
Slide 7: ©ooyoo/iStockPhoto

Another Way
You can also specify a percentage of the original dimensions, instead of an exact size. This action is called **scaling.**

9. Close the task pane.

10. Go to slide 5 and click the picture to select it.

11. Click the Picture Tools Format tab, and then click the Width down arrow in the Size group until the picture's width is 4.2 inches (see Figure 8-15).

Figure 8-15

Set the width on the Ribbon

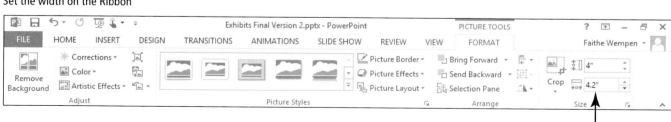

Set Width to 4.2"

12. Turn the guides back on, and then drag the picture to align its upper-right corner with the intersection of the two guides near the right edge of the slide. Then turn the guides off again.

13. **SAVE** the presentation.

PAUSE. LEAVE the presentation open to use in the next exercise.

As you saw in step 6, you can **reset** a picture to its original appearance from the task pane to remove any changes you have made to it. You can also reset a picture on the Picture Tools Format tab. To do so, click the down arrow on the Reset Picture button, and then click Reset Picture & Size. This action resets not only the picture size, but also any formatting you may have applied to it (which you will learn to do later in this lesson).

Applying a Style to an Image

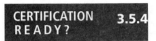

PowerPoint provides a number of styles you can use to apply borders and other effects to images. You can easily apply styles with heavy borders, shadow and reflection effects, and different shapes such as ovals and rounded corners. Use styles to dress up your images or format them consistently throughout a presentation.

CERTIFICATION READY? 3.5.4

How do you apply styles to images?

STEP BY STEP **Apply a Style to a Picture**

USE the *Exhibits Final Version 2* presentation that is still open from the previous exercise.

1. Go to **slide 5** and click the **picture** to select it if necessary.
2. On the Picture Tools Format tab, click the **More** button in the Picture Styles group. The Picture Styles gallery appears.
3. Click the **Soft Edge Oval style**. Your picture should look like the one in Figure 8-16.

Figure 8-16

The Soft Edge Oval style gives the picture a different look

Soft Edge Oval →

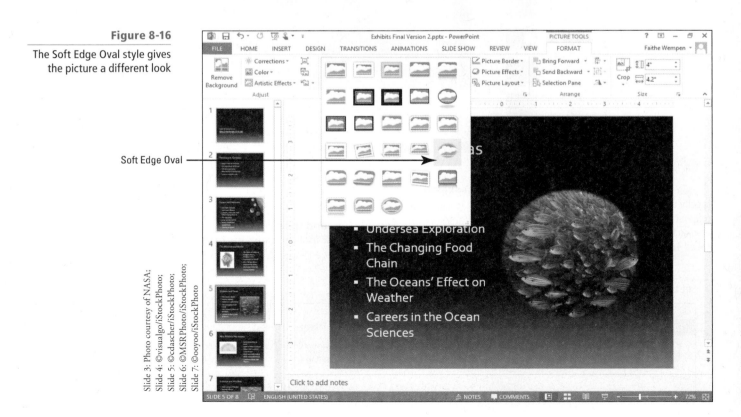

Slide 3: Photo courtesy of NASA;
Slide 4: ©visualgo/iStockPhoto;
Slide 5: ©cdascher/iStockPhoto;
Slide 6: ©MSRPhoto/iStockPhoto;
Slide 7: ©ooyoo/iStockPhoto

4. **SAVE** the presentation.

PAUSE. LEAVE the presentation open to use in the next exercise.

Take Note The style's picture borders are black or white by default, but you can apply any color to the border using the Picture Border button after applying the style.

If you have a number of pictures in a presentation, be careful not to apply too many different styles to the pictures. Using just one or two styles throughout a presentation makes it seem more unified and consistent.

Correcting Brightness and Sharpness

You may need to modify a picture's appearance to make it show up well on a slide. This action can be particularly important with pictures you insert from files, which may not have been photographed using the optimal settings. In PowerPoint 2013 Brightness, Contrast, and Sharpness/Softness are all controlled from the same section of the Format Picture task pane. For presets, you can select from the Corrections button's menu. For precise amounts, you can use the task pane.

STEP BY STEP | **Adjust a Picture's Brightness and Sharpness**

USE the *Exhibits Final Version 2* presentation that is still open from the previous exercise.

1. Go to slide 6 and click the picture to select it. This picture is a bit too bright.
2. Click the Picture Tools Format tab.
3. In the Adjust group, click Corrections. A palette of corrections appears (see Figure 8-17). Notice that there are two sections: Sharpen/Soften and Brightness/Contrast. The center selection in each section is the current setting.

Figure 8-17

Select from the Corrections button's palette

Current setting for sharpness/softness

Current setting for brightness/contrast

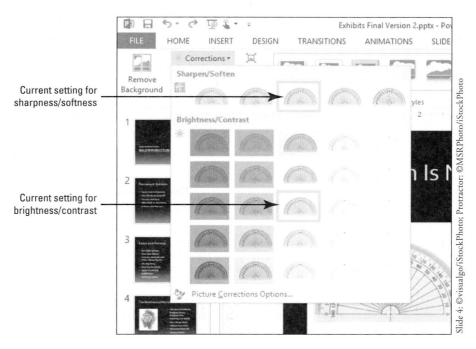

Slide 4: ©visualgo/iStockPhoto; Protractor: ©MSRPhoto/iStockPhoto

4. In the Brightness/Contrast section, click the Brightness −20% Contrast; 0% (Normal) setting.
5. Click the Corrections button again, reopening the menu.
6. In the Sharpen/Soften section, click Sharpen: 25%.
7. Click the Corrections button again, and click Picture Corrections Options. The Format Picture task pane opens.
8. Drag the Sharpness slider to 30% and drag the Contrast slider to 5% (see Figure 8-18).

Another Way
You can use the increment arrow buttons to set the values instead of dragging if you find that easier.

Figure 8-18

Correct a picture from the
Format Picture task pane

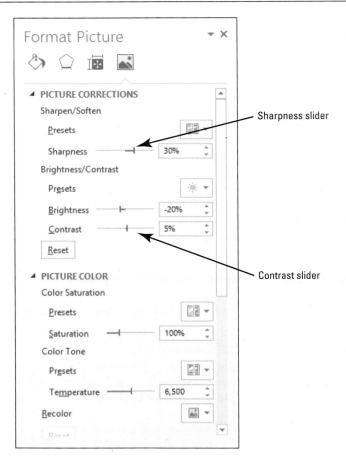

9. Close the task pane.
10. **SAVE** the presentation.

PAUSE. LEAVE the presentation open to use in the next exercise.

Applying Color Adjustments

Color adjustments enable you to correct minor exposure or color problems in an image without having to open it in a third-party photo editing program. You can improve the look of a picture by making subtle adjustments, or apply dramatic adjustments that distort the image for a special effect.

Each of the three sections on the Color button's palette controls a different aspect of the color. Color **Saturation** determines the intensity of the color, ranging from 0% (grayscale, no color) to 400% (extremely vivid color). Color **Tone** refers to the subtle tint of the image's color, ranging from warmer shades (more red) to cooler shades (more blue). **Recolor** enables you to select color wash to place over the image or to set it to grayscale, black and white, or washout. In this exercise, you will make some color corrections on a photo.

STEP BY STEP **Apply Color Adjustments**

USE the *Exhibits Final Version 2* presentation that is still open from the previous exercise.

1. Go to slide 5 and click the picture to select it.
2. Click the Picture Tools Format tab.
3. In the Adjust group, click Color. A palette of color choices appears (see Figure 8-19).

Figure 8-19

Select color correction presets
for the picture

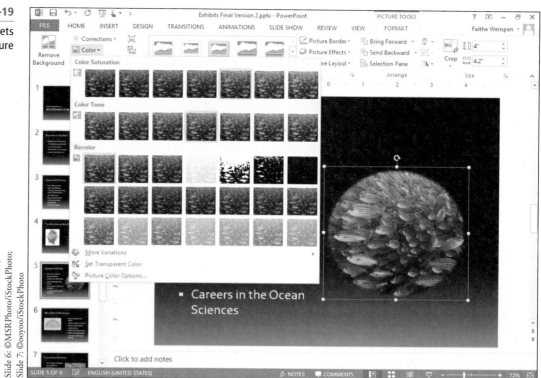

4. In the Color Saturation section, click Saturation 200%.

5. Click Color again to reopen the palette, point at More Variations, and in the Standard Colors group, point to Light Green to see a preview applied to the picture. Click away from the menu to close the menu without making a selection.

6. Click Color again to reopen the palette, and click Picture Color Options. The Format Picture task pane opens.

7. In the Picture Color section under Color Tone, set the Temperature value to 7,000 by typing 7,000 in the Temperature text box (see Figure 8-20).

8. Close the task pane.

9. **SAVE** the presentation.

Figure 8-20

Fine-tune color corrections from the Format Picture task pane

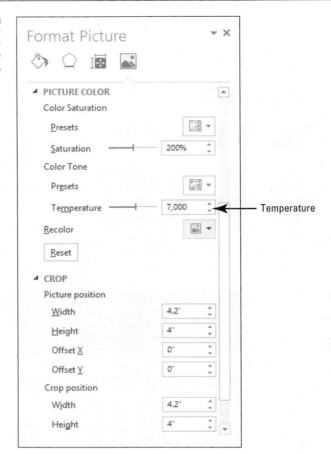

PAUSE. LEAVE the presentation open to use in the next exercise.

CERTIFICATION READY? 3.5.3

How do you apply effects to an image?

Adding Effects to an Image

There are two types of effects that you can apply to a picture: picture effects (such as Glow, Shadow, and Bevel), which affect the outer edges of the picture, and artistic effects (such as Chalk Sketch or Line Drawing), which affect the picture itself.

Adding Picture Effects

Picture effects apply to the edges of a picture, and not to the picture itself. For example, you can apply a beveled frame to a picture, or make its edges fuzzy. In the following exercise, you will apply a bevel and a glow effect.

STEP BY STEP   **Add Picture Effects to an Image**

USE the *Exhibits Final Version 2* presentation that is still open from the previous exercise.

1. Go to slide 4 and click the picture to select it.
2. Click the Picture Tools Format tab.
3. Click the Picture Effects button in the Picture Styles group, point to Preset in the drop-down menu that appears, and click Preset 2. A preset formatting effect is applied.
4. Click the Picture Effects button, point to Bevel, and click Art Deco. A different bevel is applied.
5. Click the Picture Effects button, point to Glow, and click Periwinkle, 8 point glow, Accent color 5. An 8-point periwinkle blue glow is placed around the picture.

6. Click away from the picture to deselect it so you can see it more clearly. The slide should look like Figure 8-21.

Figure 8-21

The slide after picture effects have been applied to the picture

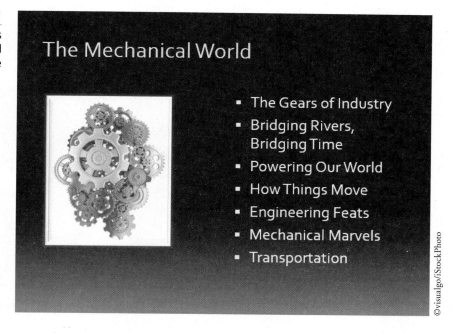

7. **SAVE** the presentation.

PAUSE. LEAVE the presentation open to use in the next exercise.

Adding Artistic Effects

Artistic effects enable you to transform the picture itself, not just the outer edges. Some of the effects, such as the Paint Strokes effect you apply in this exercise, can even make the picture look less like a photograph and more like a hand-drawn work of art.

STEP BY STEP   **Add Artistic Effects to an Image**

USE the *Exhibits Final Version 2* presentation that is still open from the previous exercise.

1. Go to slide 7 and click the picture to select it.
2. Click the Picture Tools Format tab.
3. Click Artistic Effects in the Adjust group to open the Artistic Effects gallery, and point to several different settings in the gallery. Observe their effect on the image behind the open palette.
4. Click Paint Strokes. (It is the second one in the second row.) Your slide should look similar to Figure 8-22.

Figure 8-22

Apply artistic effects
to an image

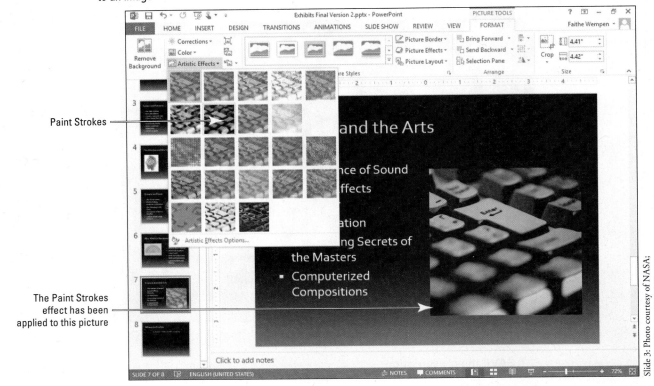

Paint Strokes

The Paint Strokes
effect has been
applied to this picture

5. **SAVE** the presentation.

PAUSE. LEAVE the presentation open to use in the next exercise.

Removing an Image's Background

Some graphic file formats allow a photo to have a transparent background, but most photos do not use transparency. If you want to make areas of a certain color transparent in the copy of the photo you use in your presentation, you can do so with the Remove Background command. You will learn how to use the Remove Background command in this exercise.

STEP BY STEP **Remove an Image Background**

USE the *Exhibits Final Version 2* presentation that is still open from the previous exercise.

1. Go to slide 3 and click the picture to select it.
2. On the Picture Tools Format tab, click Remove Background. The Background Removal tab appears on the Ribbon, and the picture turns purple except for one planet (see Figure 8-23). The purple areas are the parts that will be removed.

Figure 8-23

Tools for removing
a photo's background

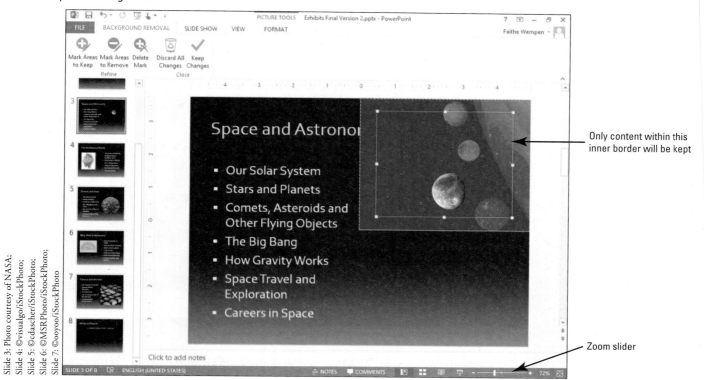

Only content within this
inner border will be kept

Zoom slider

3. Zoom in to 100% zoom using the Zoom slider in the bottom right corner of the PowerPoint window, and adjust the display so you can see the photo clearly.

4. Notice that inside the picture is a rectangular border with selection handles. Only content within this rectangle will be kept. Drag the corner selection handles of that rectangle so that the entire picture is inside that area.

5. On the Background Removal tab, click Mark Areas to Keep.

6. Click and drag to draw across one of the planets. If the entire planet does not turn back to its original color with a single click, continue clicking different parts of it until the entire planet appears in its original color. Zoom in further if needed to see what you are doing.

 Troubleshooting If you make a mistake and click too much, and the whole background turns black, press Ctrl+Z to undo your last action and try again.

7. Repeat step 6 until only the background is purple, and all planets appear in their original colors (see Figure 8-24).

Figure 8-24

Adjust the areas to keep

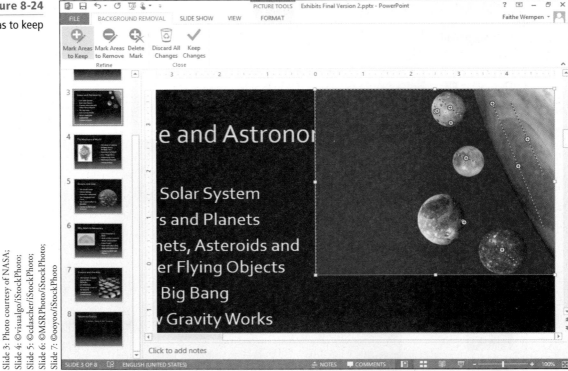

Slide 3: Photo courtesy of NASA;
Slide 4: ©visualgo/iStockPhoto;
Slide 5: ©cdascher/iStockPhoto;
Slide 6: ©MSRPhoto/iStockPhoto;
Slide 7: ©ooyoo/iStockPhoto

8. Click **Keep Changes** in the Close group of the Background Removal tab to finalize the background removal. Now that the background is removed, the slide title is no longer partly obscured.

9. Click **away from the image** to deselect it.

10. Click **Fit Slide to Current Window** in the status bar at the bottom of the PowerPoint window to reset the slide's zoom (see Figure 8-25).

Figure 8-25

The completed slide with background removed from the photo

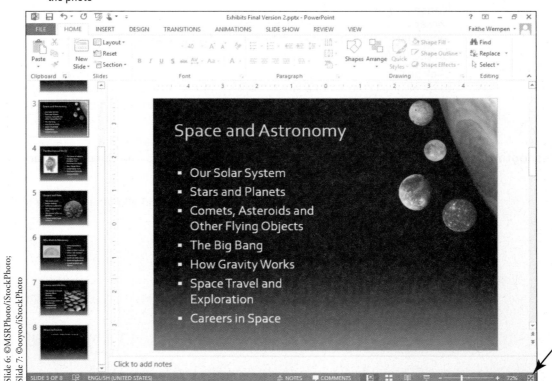

Slide 3: Photo courtesy of NASA;
Slide 4: ©visualgo/iStockPhoto;
Slide 5: ©cdascher/iStockPhoto;
Slide 6: ©MSRPhoto/iStockPhoto;
Slide 7: ©ooyoo/iStockPhoto

Fit Slide to Current Window button

11. **SAVE** the presentation.

PAUSE. LEAVE the presentation open to use in the next exercise.

The amount of effort required to remove a photo's background accurately depends on the individual photo and on the amount of contrast between the background and the foreground image. You may need to click several times on different parts of the image to mark them to keep. Other photos may be almost perfectly done with the default setting.

It is easy to make a mistake when marking areas for background removal. The Undo command (Ctrl+Z) easily reverses your last action and can be used when a particular marked area does not turn out as you expect. You can also use the Mark Areas to Remove command on the Background Removal tab to mark areas that have erroneously been marked for keeping.

Compressing the Images in a Presentation

When adding pictures to a presentation, you may need to consider the ultimate size of the presentation. Pictures will add considerably to the presentation's file size. This increased file size can make a large presentation difficult to store or work with. Compressing images reduces the file size of a presentation by reducing its resolution (dots per inch). This action can make the presentation easier to store and to email to others, and it speeds up display if you have to work on a slow projector or computer system.

STEP BY STEP **Compress the Images in a Presentation**

USE the *Exhibits Final Version 2* presentation that is still open from the previous exercise.

1. Click the **File** tab, and make a **note** of the file size under the **Properties** heading. Then press **Esc** to return to the presentation.
2. Click any picture in the presentation to select it, and then click the **Picture Tools Format** tab.
3. Click **Compress Pictures** in the Adjust group. The Compress Pictures dialog box opens.
4. Click the **Email (96 ppi)** option button.
5. Clear the **Apply only to this picture** check box (see Figure 8-26). If you wanted to compress only the selected picture, you would leave this option checked.

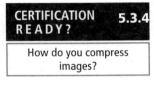

Figure 8-26

Compress the pictures in the presentation

Compress Pictures button

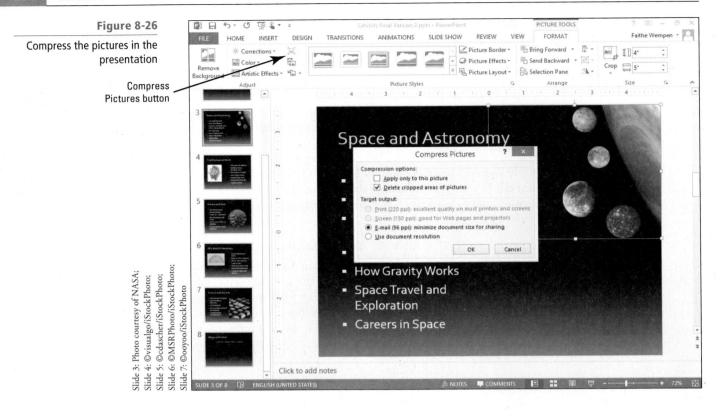

Slide 3: Photo courtesy of NASA;
Slide 4: ©visualgo/iStockPhoto;
Slide 5: ©cdascher/iStockPhoto;
Slide 6: ©MSRPhoto/iStockPhoto;
Slide 7: ©ooyoo/iStockPhoto

CERTIFICATION READY? 5.3.4

How do you compress images?

6. Click **OK**.

7. SAVE the presentation. PowerPoint applies the compression settings you selected.

8. Repeat **step 1** to recheck the presentation's file size.

PAUSE. LEAVE the presentation open to use in the next exercise.

Cross Ref

You will learn more about sharing a presentation in Lesson 10.

The compression utility allows you to choose several options that can reduce file size. You can choose to delete the hidden portions of cropped pictures, for example. You can also choose a target output setting. If you know your slides will be presented on the web or projected on a monitor, you can choose the lowest dpi (dots per inch) setting. Presentations to be shown on a screen do not have to have the same quality as materials that might be printed because the monitor screen itself is limited in the quality it can display. You can compress pictures individually, or apply the same setting to all pictures in the presentation.

ADDING SHAPES TO SLIDES

The Bottom Line

PowerPoint offers drawing tools that enable you to create both basic and complex drawings. Use line tools and shapes to construct the drawing. You can easily add text to shapes to identify them and format the drawing using familiar fill, outline, and effects options.

Drawing Lines

PowerPoint supplies a number of different line tools so you can draw horizontal, vertical, diagonal, or free-form lines.

To draw a line, you select the Line tool, click where you want to begin the line, hold down the mouse button, and drag to make the shape the desired size.

You can use the Shift key to **constrain** some shapes to a specific appearance. For example, you can hold down Shift while drawing a line to constrain it to a vertical, horizontal, or 45-degree diagonal orientation.

STEP BY STEP   **Draw Lines**

USE the *Exhibits Final Version 2* presentation that is still open from the previous exercise, and save it as *Exhibits Final Version 3*.

1. Go to slide 8. You will create a map on this slide to show potential visitors how to get to the museum. As you work, refer to Figure 8-27 for position of objects.

Figure 8-27

The streets and street names have been added

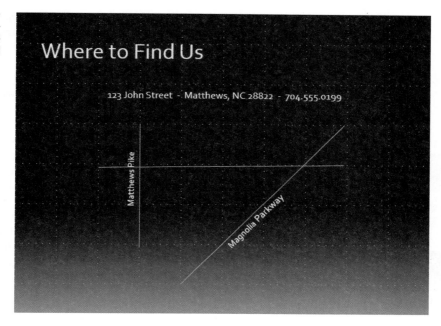

2. Click the View tab, and then click Gridlines to turn gridlines on.
3. Create the first street for the map as follows:
   a. Click the Home tab, and then click the Shapes button to display the gallery of drawing shapes.
   b. Click Line in the Lines group. The pointer takes the shape of a crosshair.
   c. Locate the intersection of vertical and horizontal gridlines below the letter *n* in *John*, click at the intersection, and drag downward to create a vertical line three "blocks" long.

Take Note   You can also access the Shapes gallery on the Drawing Tools Format tab.

4. Add the street name as follows:
   a. Click Text Box on the Insert tab, click anywhere on the slide, and type the text Matthews Pike.
   b. Click the outer border of the text box to select all content within the text box, and change the font size to 16.
   c. On the Drawing Tools Format tab, click Rotate, and click Rotate Left 90°.
   d. Move the rotated street name just to the left of the vertical line (see Figure 8-27).
5. Select the Line tool again, hold down Shift, and draw the diagonal line shown in Figure 8-27.

Take Note   Holding down the Shift key constrains the line to be exactly 45 degrees or exactly vertical or horizontal as you drag.

6. Select the Line tool again and draw the horizontal line shown in Figure 8-27.
7. Add the street name for the diagonal street as follows:
    a. Insert a text box anywhere on the slide, and type Magnolia Parkway.
    b. Change the font size to 16.
    c. With the text box still selected, click Arrange, point to Rotate, and click More Rotation Options. The Format Shape task pane opens.
    d. Type –45 in the Rotation box, and then close the task pane.
    e. Move the rotated text box to the right of the diagonal line (see Figure 8-27).
8. On the View tab, clear the Gridlines check box to turn off gridlines again.
9. **SAVE** the presentation.

PAUSE. LEAVE the presentation open to use in the next exercise.

Selected shapes have selection handles (also called sizing handles) that you can use to adjust the size of the object. Some complex shapes have yellow diamond adjustment handles that allow you to modify the shape. Drag a selected shape anywhere on a slide to reposition it.

Lines and other shapes take their color from the current theme. You can change the color, as well as change outline and other effects, at any time while creating a drawing.

Drawing and Resizing Shapes

PowerPoint's many shape tools allow you to create multisided, elliptical, and even freeform shapes. The Shapes gallery contains well over 100 different shapes. Just select a shape and then drag on the slide to draw it there, or click on the slide to create a shape with a default size and orientation.

CERTIFICATION READY? 2.2.3

How do you resize a shape?

CERTIFICATION READY? 2.2.4

How do you insert a shape?

When creating shapes, you can simply "eyeball" the size, use the rulers or gridlines to help you size, or use the Height and Width settings in the Size group on the Drawing Tools Format tab to scale the objects. Setting precise measurements can help you maintain the same proportions when creating objects of different shapes, for example, when creating circles and triangles that have to be the same height and width. You can also constrain a shape while drawing it by holding down the Shift key to maintain its aspect ratio. In the following exercise, you will draw some basic shapes.

STEP BY STEP   **Draw and Resize Shapes**

USE the *Exhibits Final Version 3* presentation that is still open from the previous exercise. As you work, refer to Figure 8-28 to help you position and size objects.

1. On the Home tab, click Shapes, and then click the Rectangle tool. Hold down the mouse button, and drag to create the taller rectangle above the horizontal line (see Figure 8-28).

Figure 8-28

Basic shapes have been added to the map

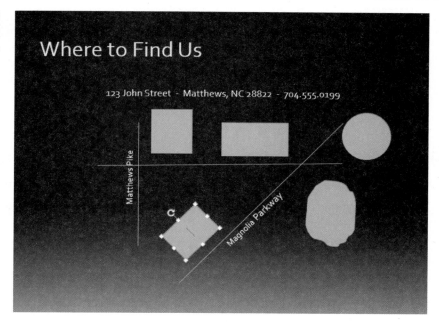

2. With the shape still selected, click the Drawing Tools Format tab. Note the measurements in the Size group. If necessary, adjust the size so the shape is **1 inch high** by **0.9 inches wide**.

3. Select the Rectangle tool again and use it to create the wider rectangle shown in Figure 8-28. This shape should be 0.7 inch high by 1.2 inches wide.

4. Select the Oval tool, hold down Shift, and draw the circle shown in Figure 8-28. This shape should be 1 inch high and wide.

5. Click the Rectangle tool and create a rectangle **0.7 inches high** by **1 inch wide** near the lower end of the diagonal street.

6. Click the shape's rotation handle and drag to the right to rotate the shape so its bottom side is parallel to the diagonal road (see in Figure 8-28).

7. Click the Freeform tool in the Lines section in the Shapes gallery. Near the bottom of the slide (so you can easily see the line you are drawing), draw an irregular oval shape to represent a lake. The shape should be about 1.4 inches high and 1.5 inches wide.

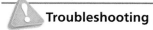 **Troubleshooting** When using the Freeform tool, if you return to the exact point at which you started drawing, PowerPoint will automatically close and fill the shape with color. If your shape does not fill, double-click to end it, click Undo, and start again.

8. Drag the lake shape to the right of the diagonal line (see Figure 8-28).

9. **SAVE** the presentation.

PAUSE. LEAVE the presentation open to use in the next exercise.

You can save yourself some time when drawing similar or identical shapes by copying shapes. Copy a selected shape, use Paste to paste a copy on the slide, then move or modify the copy as necessary. You can also select a shape, hold down the Ctrl key, and drag a copy of the shape to a new location.

If you are creating a drawing in which you want to show connections between objects, you can use connectors from the Lines group of the Shapes gallery. Connectors automatically snap to points on shape sides, so you can easily draw an arrow, for instance, from one shape to another. As you reposition objects, the connectors remain attached and adjust as necessary to maintain the links between shapes.

Adding Text to Shapes

You can often improve a drawing by labeling the shapes to state what they represent. In Power-Point, you can add text by simply clicking and typing the text. When you add text to a shape, the shape takes the function of a text box. PowerPoint automatically wraps text in the shape as in a text box; if the shape is not large enough to display the text, words will break up or the text will extend above and below the shape. You can solve this problem by resizing the shape or changing the text's size. You can use any text formatting options you like when adding text to shapes, just as when inserting text into a placeholder or text box. To select text in a shape to edit it, drag over it with the I-beam pointer. In the following exercise, you will add some text to shapes.

STEP BY STEP   **Add Text to Shapes**

USE the *Exhibits Final Version 3* presentation that is still open from the previous exercise.

1. While still on slide 8, click in the taller rectangle above the horizontal street, and then type West Bank Center.
2. Click in the wide rectangle shape, and then type Baldwin Museum.
3. Click in the circle shape, and then type Miller Arena.
4. Click in the rotated rectangle, and then type Holmes College. Note that the text is rotated as well.
5. Click in the freeform lake object, and then type Magnolia Lake.
6. Adjust the widths of any of the shapes as needed so that the text fits in them.
7. Drag over the Baldwin Museum text to select it, and then click the Bold button to boldface the text. Your map should look similar to Figure 8-29.

Figure 8-29

The map with text added to the shapes

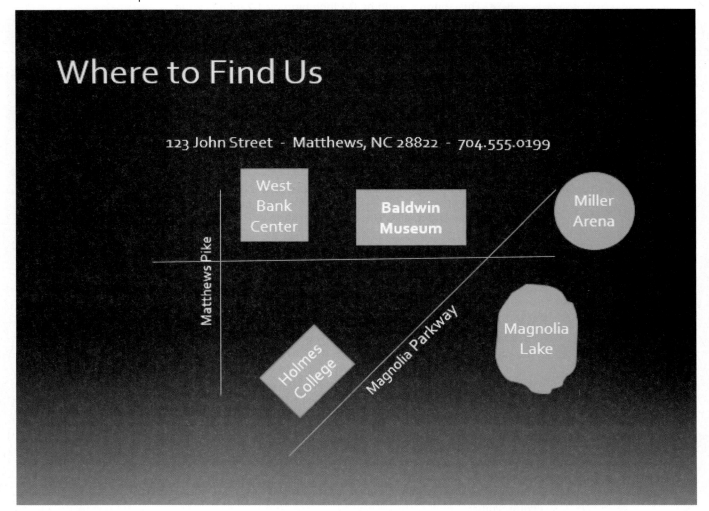

8. **SAVE** the presentation.

PAUSE. LEAVE the presentation open to use in the next exercise.

Take Note To adjust the way text appears in a shape, right-click the shape, click Format Shape, click Text Options, click the Textbox icon, and access the Text Box settings in the Format Shape task pane. For example, you can align the text vertically and horizontally within the shape.

Formatting Shapes

You can apply many of the same formatting effects to drawn lines and shapes that you apply to other objects in PowerPoint. For example, you can change the fill color or texture, add borders, and use effects such as shadows and bevels. You can also apply Shape Styles to save time by formatting a shape using a preset. In the following exercise, you will format shapes by changing their borders, fills, and effects and by applying Shape Styles.

STEP BY STEP   **Format Shapes**

USE the *Exhibits Final Version 3* presentation that is still open from the previous exercise.

1. On the drawing on slide 8, format the *Matthews Pike* line and label as follows:
   a. Click the vertical line that represents Matthews Pike.
   b. On the Drawing Tools Format tab, click the Shape Outline button, and then click the Gold, Accent 3 theme color.

Take Note You can use the Shape Outline button in the Drawing group on the Home tab or in the Shape Styles group on the Drawing Tools Format tab.

   c. Click the Shape Outline button again, point to Weight, and click 6 pt.
   d. Click the outside border of the Matthews Pike text box to select all content in the text box, and on the Home tab, click Font Color, and click Black, Background 1.
   e. With the text box still selected, click the Shape Fill button, and then click White, Text 1.
   f. Drag the text box to the left slightly if needed so that it does not overlap the vertical line.

2. Click the horizontal line and repeat steps 1a-1c to format the line with the White, Text 1, Darker 35% theme color and 6 pt. weight. (Do not worry if the street overlaps over the *Matthews Pike* text box. You will learn to fix this problem in a later exercise.)

3. Click the diagonal Magnolia Parkway line, click the Shape Outline button, point to Weight, and click 6 pt.

4. Format the Magnolia Parkway text box following steps 1d and 1e to change text to black and the fill to white.

5. Format the other shapes as follows:
   a. Click the West Bank Center shape above the horizontal street, hold down Shift, and click each additional filled shape until all are selected. (Do *not* click any of the lines or the street name text boxes.)
   b. Click Shape Outline, and then click No Outline. You have removed outlines from the selected shapes.
   c. Click the More button in the Shape Styles group, and click the Intense Effect - Black, Dark 1 effect (the first style in the last row).
   d. Click away from the shapes to deselect them all, and then click the Baldwin Museum shape to select it.
   e. On the Drawing Tools Format tab, click Shape Fill, and click Pink, Accent 2, Darker 25%.
   f. Click Shape Effects, point to Preset, and click Preset 1.

6. Apply a texture to the Magnolia Lake shape by doing the following:

   a. Click the Magnolia Lake shape.

   b. On the Drawing Tools Format tab, click Shape Fill, point to Texture, and click the Water Droplets texture.

   c. Click the Text Fill button's arrow to open its palette and click Black, Background 1.

7. Click away from the Magnolia Lake shape to deselect it. Your map should look similar to Figure 8-30.

Figure 8-30

The map has been formatted

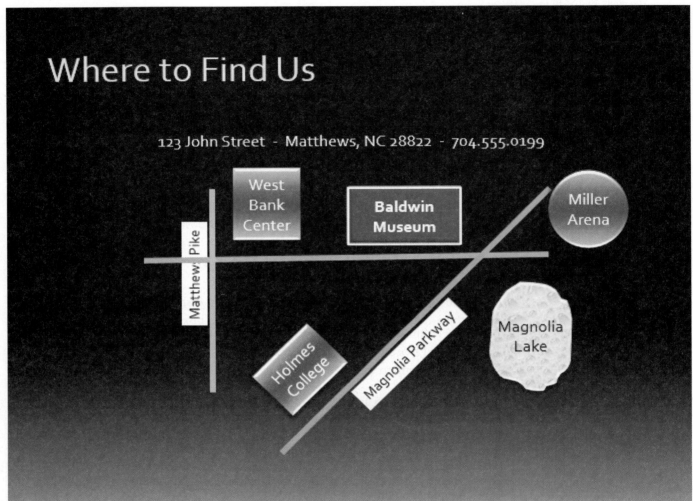

8. **SAVE** the presentation.

PAUSE. LEAVE the presentation open to use in the next exercise.

By now, you should be familiar with applying fills, outlines, and effects. You can format shapes using these options just as you formatted table cells, chart data markers, and SmartArt shapes in previous lessons.

Note that you can access fill, outline, and effect options from either the Home tab or the Drawing Tools Format tab. PowerPoint makes these options available on both tabs to minimize the amount of switching you have to do if you are also formatting text.

Save time when applying the same kinds of formats to a number of objects by selecting all the objects that need the same formatting. You can then apply the format only once to modify all the selected objects. To select several objects, you use the Shift-click method: click the first object you want to select, hold down the Shift key, and then click additional objects. If you select an object for your group by mistake, click it again to exclude it from the selection group.

Creating a Custom Shape

One of the most welcome new features in Office 2013 is the ability to combine multiple drawn lines and shapes together into more complex shapes. This feature makes the drawing tools in Office applications much more useful and flexible. You can overlap two or more shapes and then issue a command that combines them. There are several different commands for creating custom shapes, each of which produces a different combination effect. In this exercise you will combine several shapes to create a custom shape for use in a logo.

STEP BY STEP **Create a Custom Shape**

USE the *Exhibits Final Version 3* presentation that is still open from the previous exercise.

1. Go to slide 1, and on the Insert tab, click Shapes, and then click the 8-Point Star in the Stars and Banners section of the shape list.
2. Hold down the Shift key and drag on the slide, above the text, to draw a star that is approximately 2" in both height and width.
3. On the Insert tab, click Shapes, and then click the crescent moon shape. Drag to draw it over the 8-point star (see Figure 8-31).

Figure 8-31

Draw the crescent moon over the 8-point star

4. Click the 8-point star, hold down Shift, and click the crescent moon shape. Both are selected.
5. On the Drawing Tools Format tab, click the Merge Shapes button. A menu opens (see Figure 8-32).

Figure 8-32

Open the Merge Shapes menu

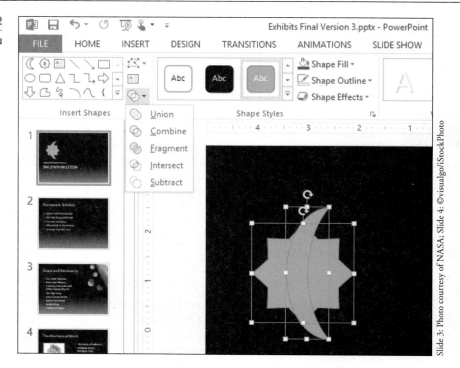

6. **Point** to each of the menu options to see that effect previewed on the shape.

7. Click **Combine**. The two shapes are combined such that the area where they overlapped is removed (see Figure 8-33).

Figure 8-33

The shapes have been combined using the Combine command

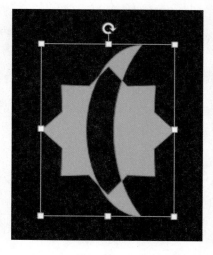

8. Select the **shape**, and on the Drawing Tools Format tab, click **Shape Fill** and click **Light Blue, Text 2, Darker 90%**.

9. Click **Shape Outline** and click **No Outline**.

10. **SAVE** the presentation.

PAUSE. LEAVE the presentation open to use in the next exercise.

As you saw in step 6, there are many options for merging shapes. These options are summarized in Table 8-1.

Operation	Description	Example
Union	Combines the areas of both shapes, and takes on the formatting of the top shape	
Combine	Includes areas where one of the two shapes appear, but excludes areas where both shapes overlap	
Fragment	Combines the areas of both shapes, but breaks the shapes into multiple pieces where overlap begins and ends	
Intersect	Includes only the areas where the top shape overlaps the bottom shape	
Subtract	Includes only the areas where the top shape did not overlap the bottom shape	

ORDERING AND GROUPING SHAPES

The Bottom Line

It is not uncommon to have to adjust the layout of objects you have added to slides. You may find that objects need to be reordered so they do not obscure other objects, or need to be aligned on the slide to present a neater appearance. You can also group objects together to make it easy to move or resize them all at once.

Setting Object Order

CERTIFICATION READY?   2.3.3

How do you align and group shapes?

Objects stack up on a slide in the **order** in which you created them, from bottom to top. If you insert a slide title on a slide, it will be the object at the bottom of the stack. The last item you create or add to the slide will be at the top of the stack. You can envision each object as an invisible layer in the stack. You can adjust the order in which objects stack on the slide by using Arrange commands or the Selection pane.

Some objects can obscure other objects because of the order in which you add them to the slide. You use the Order options to reposition objects in the stack:

- **Bring to Front:** the selected object to the front or top of the stack, on top of all other objects.
- **Bring Forward:** an object one layer toward the front or top of the stack. Use this option if you need to position an object above some objects but below others.
- **Send to Back:** an object all the way to the back or bottom of the stack, below all other objects.
- **Send Backward:** an object one layer toward the back or bottom of the stack.

In this exercise, you will arrange some objects by changing their stacking order.

STEP BY STEP   **Set Object Order**

USE the *Exhibits Final Version 3* presentation that is still open from the previous exercise.

1. Go to slide 1, and draw a new rectangle that covers the logo.
   a. On the Home tab, click **Shapes**, and click **Rectangle**.
   b. Drag to draw a square over the existing logo. Hold down **Shift** to constrain the rectangle to make it a square.
   c. On the Drawing Tools Format tab, adjust the **Height** and **Width** of the rectangle so that its height and width are equal and just large enough to cover the logo.
   d. Click **Shape Fill**, and click **Gold, Accent 3**.
   e. Click **Shape Effects**, point to **Bevel**, and click **Circle**.

2. On the Drawing Tools Format tab, click **Send Backward** (see Figure 8-34). The rectangle moves behind the star/moon shapes. Do not worry if they are not neatly aligned with one another; you will learn how to align them later in this lesson.

Figure 8-34

Move the rectangle behind the logo graphic

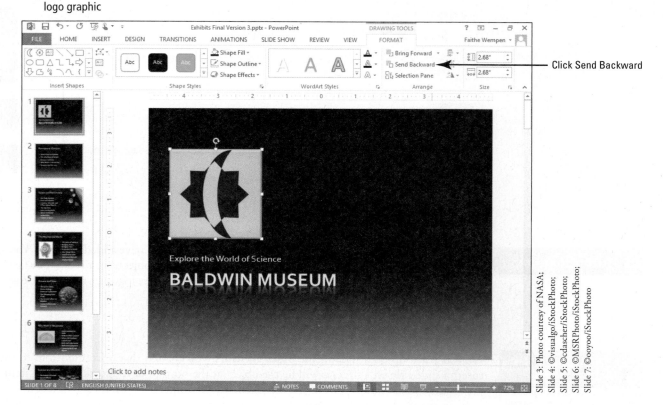

3. Go to **slide 8**. On the Home tab, click the **Arrange** button, and then click **Selection Pane**. The Selection task pane opens (see Figure 8-35), showing the current slide content in the order in which it was created, from bottom to top. This order is determined by the order in which the objects were added to the slide.

Figure 8-35

The Selection pane shows the current slide content

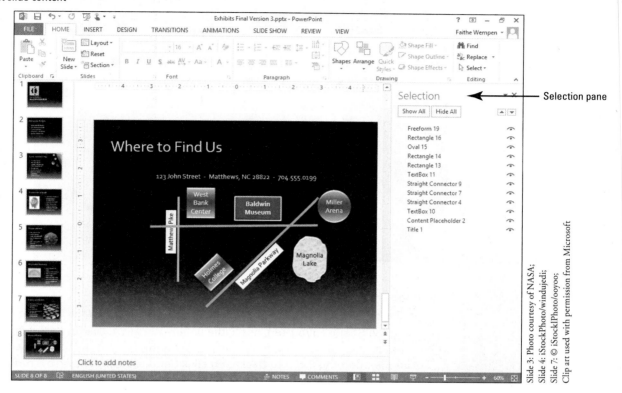

Slide 3: Photo courtesy of NASA;
Slide 4: iStockPhoto/windujedli;
Slide 7: © iStockIPhoto/ooyoo;
Clip art used with permission from Microsoft

Take Note The Arrange tools are available on both the Home tab and the Picture Tools Format tab.

 Troubleshooting Do not be concerned if the list in your Selection pane does not exactly match the one shown in Figure 8-35. The order and numbering of objects in the pane can be affected by many actions.

4. Click the gold Matthews Pike street line in the map to see how it is identified in the Selection pane—it will have a name such as *Straight Connector 7* (or some other number). Then click the horizontal street line to see its name.

 **Another Way**
You can also use the Bring Forward button on the Drawing Tools Format tab in step 6.

5. Click the Matthews Pike street line again to select it. If that line is not already on top of the horizontal street line, click the Bring Forward arrow (the up arrow button) in the Selection task pane until it is.

6. Click the Matthews Pike text box and click the Bring Forward arrow until the text box is on top of the horizontal gray line in the map if was not already so.

7. Click the Magnolia Parkway street line and click the Bring Forward arrow until the diagonal street is above the horizontal street in the map if it is not already so. Then close the task pane.

8. You have one more shape to add to the map: an arrow that labels the horizontal street as John Street and indicates that the street is one way. Click Shapes on the Home tab, click Right Arrow in the Block Arrows group, and draw a block arrow (see Figure 8-36). The arrow should be about 0.7 inches high and 5 inches wide.

Figure 8-36

Draw a block arrow

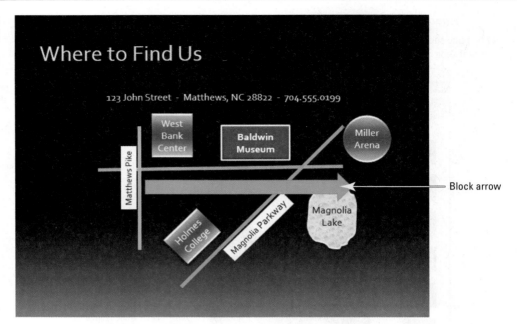

9. In the arrow, key John Street - ONE WAY.

10. On the Home tab, click Align Left to make the text align on the left side of the arrow.

11. Using the Shape Fill button, apply the Green, Accent 1, Darker 50% color to the arrow.

12. Right-click a blank area of the block arrow (to the right of the words *ONE WAY*, for example), point to Send to Back, and click Send to Back. The arrow moves behind all lines and shapes.

13. Click the Bring Forward button on the Drawing Tools Format tab until the arrow is in front of the diagonal line representing Magnolia Parkway but the behind Magnolia Lake shape. Figure 8-37 shows the completed map.

Figure 8-37

The completed map

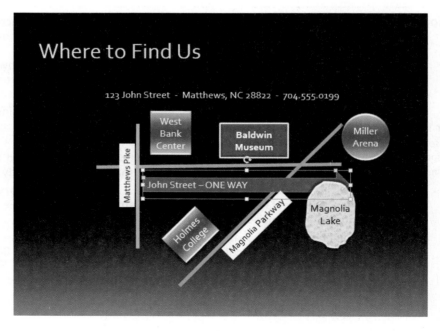

14. **SAVE** the presentation.

PAUSE. LEAVE the presentation open to use in the next exercise.

You can clearly see the stacking order of objects on a slide using the Selection pane. This pane is similar to the Layers palette in a program such as Illustrator or Photoshop. It allows you to easily move objects up or down in the stacking order. You can click the visibility "eye" to hide objects that might be in your way as you work on another object—a handy feature when creating a complex drawing.

If you do not want to use the Selection pane, you can use options on the Home tab's Arrange button menu to reorder objects, or you can use buttons on the Drawing Tools Format tab in the Arrange group. You can also access these options readily by right-clicking an object and selecting the appropriate command from the shortcut menu.

Take Note   Arrange options also display on other Format tabs, such as the Picture Tools Format and SmartArt Tools Format tabs.

Aligning Objects with Each Other

Your drawings will present a more pleasing appearance if similar items are aligned with each other or to the slide. Use PowerPoint's alignment options to position objects neatly.

PowerPoint's alignment options allow you to line up objects on a slide both horizontally and vertically:

- Use **Align Left**, **Align Center**, or **Align Right** to align objects horizontally so that their left edges, vertical centers, or right edges are lined up with each other.
- Use **Align Top**, **Align Middle**, or **Align Bottom** to align objects vertically so that their top edges, horizontal centers, or bottom edges are lined up with each other.

You can also use distribute options to space objects evenly, either vertically or horizontally. This feature can be a great time-saver when you have a number of objects that you want to spread out evenly across a slide.

PowerPoint allows you to align (or distribute) objects either to each other or to the slide. If you select Align Selected Objects on the Align menu, PowerPoint will adjust only the selected objects. If you select Align to Slide, PowerPoint will rearrange objects using the entire slide area.

STEP BY STEP   **Align Objects with Each Other**

USE the *Exhibits Final Version 3* presentation that is still open from the previous exercise.

1. On slide 8, click the West Bank Center shape, hold down Shift, and click the Baldwin Museum shape and the Miller Arena shape. These landmarks are all different distances from the John Street horizontal line but can be aligned for a neater appearance.
2. Click the Drawing Tools Format tab if necessary, and in the Arrange group, click Align Objects, and click Align Bottom (see Figure 8-38). The shapes are now aligned at the bottom so they are the same distance from the horizontal line.
3. SAVE the presentation.

PAUSE. LEAVE the presentation open to use in the next exercise.

Figure 8-38

Align the selected shapes at
their bottoms

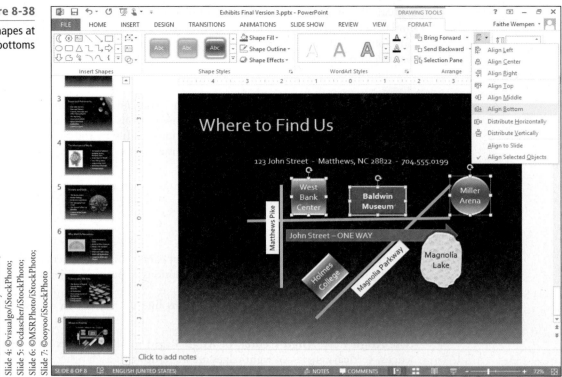

Slide 3: Photo courtesy of NASA;
Slide 4: ©visualgo/iStockPhoto;
Slide 5: ©cdascher/iStockPhoto;
Slide 6: ©MSRPhoto/iStockPhoto;
Slide 7: ©ooyoo/iStockPhoto

Grouping Objects

When a drawing consists of a number of objects, it can be tedious to move each one if you need to reposition the drawing. Grouping objects allows you to work with a number of objects as one unit. In the following exercise, you will group objects into a single unit.

STEP BY STEP   **Group Objects**

USE the *Exhibits Final Version 3* presentation that is still open from the previous exercise.

1. While still on slide 8, click **above and to the left of the map** (but below the line of text), and then hold down the **left mouse button** and drag downward and to the right until you have included the entire map in the selected area. This action is called **lassoing** the shapes.

2. Release the **mouse button**. All the shapes within the selection lasso are selected.

3. Click the **Drawing Tools Format** tab. Click the **Group Objects** button, and then click **Group** (see Figure 8-39). All objects are surrounded by a single selection border.

Figure 8-39

Use the Group command to
group the selected shapes

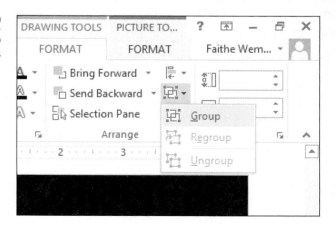

4. **SAVE** the presentation and **CLOSE** the file.

PAUSE. LEAVE PowerPoint open to use in the next exercise.

If a drawing contains a number of objects, it makes sense to group the objects when you are finished with the drawing. You can more easily reposition a grouped object, and you can also apply formatting changes to all objects in a group much more quickly than by applying formats to each individual object. To select a group, click any object in the group.

If you find that you need to work further with one object in a group, you can simply click it to activate it. It remains part of the group while you modify it. Most modifications are possible without ungrouping. (Exception: You cannot move the object separately from its group.) If you need to remove objects or make sweeping changes to a group, you can use the Ungroup option to release the group into its component parts. PowerPoint remembers the objects that are in the group so you can use Regroup if desired to restore the group.

If you are creating a very complex drawing, you can group portions of the drawing, and then group those groups. This makes it easy to reuse portions of a drawing—simply ungroup the entire drawing, copy the group you need elsewhere, and regroup the whole.

Take Note It is easy to miss an object when selecting parts of a complex drawing to create a group. To check that you have all objects selected, move the group. You will easily see if one or more objects do not move with the group. Undo the move, click the group, click any other objects that need to belong to the group, and issue the Group command again.

CREATING A PHOTO ALBUM PRESENTATION

The Bottom Line PowerPoint can create a special type of presentation for situations where the primary purpose is to display photos. Photo album presentations are easy to create and modify using a dialog box interface.

Creating a Photo Album Presentation

A photo album presentation is useful when you want to showcase multiple photographs. This special presentation type enables you to set up consistent formatting that will apply to every photo in the presentation automatically. You can also specify captions for the pictures and display them in color or black and white. In the following exercise, you will create a photo album presentation.

STEP BY STEP   **Create a Photo Album Presentation**

GET READY. Before you begin these steps, start PowerPoint. You do not have to start a new presentation, because you will create one as part of the exercise.

1. On the Insert tab, click **Photo Album**. The Photo Album dialog box opens.

Take Note Even though you are using the Insert tab, you are not actually inserting the photo album into the existing presentation; instead, you are creating a brand-new presentation file.

2. Click the **File/Disk** button. The Insert New Pictures dialog box opens.

3. Navigate to the **location** where the data files for this lesson are stored, and click *Astronomy.jpg*.

4. Hold down the **Ctrl** key and click the following files: *Biology.jpg, Chemistry.jpg, Circuit.jpg, Satellite.jpg, Shuttle.jpg*, and *Telescope.jpg* (see Figure 8-40).

Figure 8-40

Select multiple graphic files
for inclusion

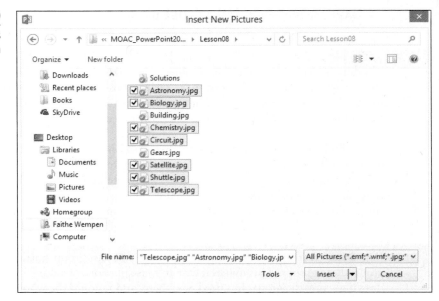

5. Click Insert. The Photo Album dialog box reappears, with all the selected pictures listed (see Figure 8-41).

Figure 8-41

The selected photos are now
listed in the Photo Album
dialog box

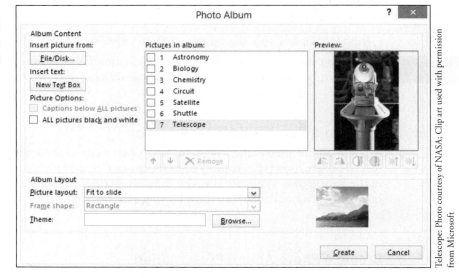

Telescope: Photo courtesy of NASA; Clip art used with permission from Microsoft

6. Click the check box for the Circuit.jpg graphic on the list, and then click the Move Up arrow three times to move it to the first position in the list. Then clear its check box.

7. Click New Text Box. A text box entry is inserted on the list of graphics between Circuit.jpg and Astronomy.jpg.

8. Click the check box for the Shuttle.jpg graphic, and then click the Rotate Right button to rotate it 90 degrees in a clockwise direction. Then clear its check box.

9. Click the check box for the Satellite.jpg graphic, and then click the Increase Brightness button twice to brighten the image. Then clear its check box.

10. Click the check box for the Biology.jpg graphic, and then click the Increase Contrast button to increase the image contrast. Then clear its check box.

11. Open the Picture Layout: drop-down list and click 1 Picture.

12. Open the Frame Shape: drop-down list and click Rounded Rectangle.
13. Click to mark the Captions below ALL pictures check box.
14. Click Create. The presentation is created.
15. Browse through the presentation to see what has been created. Notice that each picture has a caption under it that shows the file name (minus the file extension). Notice that the text box has been placed on its own separate slide, just as if it were a picture.
16. On the Insert tab, click the arrow next to the Photo Album button, and on the menu that appears, click Edit Photo Album. The Edit Photo Album dialog box opens. It is similar to the Photo Album dialog box in Figure 8-41.
17. Open the Picture Layout: drop-down list and click 2 Pictures.
18. Click the Browse button next to Themes. Click the Ion theme and click Select.
19. Click the ALL pictures black and white check box.
20. Click Update. The dialog box closes and the changes are reflected in the presentation.
21. Browse through the presentation to see what has been changed.
22. **SAVE** the presentation as *Photo Album Final*.

EXIT PowerPoint.

A photo album presentation is different from a regular presentation file. You could create the same end result using a regular presentation, but it would not be as easy to reformat and manipulate later. Using the Photo Album dialog box, you can easily reorder the pictures, choose whether or not to display captions, add text boxes, and more. You can also apply quick adjustments to photos, such as brightness and contrast changes and rotations.

You must create photo album presentations from scratch; an existing presentation cannot be converted to a photo album.

SKILL SUMMARY

In This Lesson, You Learned How To:	Exam Objective	Objective Number
Insert and Format Images	Display gridlines.	2.3.4
	Crop images.	3.5.2
	Resize images.	3.5.1
	Apply styles.	3.5.4
	Apply effects.	3.5.3
	Compress media.	5.3.4
Add Shapes to Slides	Resize shapes.	2.2.3
	Insert shapes.	2.2.4
	Apply borders to shapes.	2.2.2
	Apply styles to shapes.	2.2.6
	Create custom shapes.	2.2.5
Order and Group Shapes	Align and group shapes.	2.3.3
Create a Photo Album Presentation		

Knowledge Assessment

Matching

Match the term in Column 1 to its description in Column 2.

Column 1	Column 2
1. Order	a. Pre-drawn graphics you can use to illustrate a slide
2. Clip art	b. The relationship of width to height for a picture
3. Guides	c. A descriptive word or phrase you can use to search for specific types of objects
4. Constrain	d. Sizing to a percentage of the original size
5. Aspect ratio	e. A special type of presentation file designed to display images
6. Scaling	f. To force a drawing tool to create a shape such as a perfect square or circle
7. Keyword	g. A series of vertical and horizontal dotted lines that help you align objects on a slide
8. Crop	h. To move one object behind or in front of another
9. Photo Album	i. To remove portions of a picture you do not need
10. Gridlines	j. Non-printing lines that you can move or copy to help you position objects on a slide

True/False

Circle T if the statement is true or F if the statement is false.

T F 1. When adding clip art to a slide, you are limited to the pictures stored on your computer.

T F 2. When you use the Union option when merging shapes, only the area where the two shapes overlap is included in the merged shape.

T F 3. As you move the pointer, a short dotted line also moves on both rulers.

T F 4. The Recolor option lets you select colors in a picture and replace them with other colors.

T F 5. Compressing an image reduces the number of colors used.

T F 6. The color of a new shape is determined by the default shape formatting.

T F 7. To add text to a shape, select the shape and begin typing.

T F 8. If you want an object to be at the bottom of a stack of objects, you would use Send to Back.

T F 9. You can format a single object in a group without having to ungroup all objects.

T F 10. Any presentation can be converted to a photo album presentation.

Project 8-1: Get the Picture

You are a recruiter for Woodgrove Bank, and you have prepared a presentation to be delivered at a local job fair. You need to locate a picture to illustrate one of the presentation's slides. You can use Microsoft Office clip art files to find a suitable picture.

GET READY. LAUNCH PowerPoint if it is not already running.

1. **OPEN** the *Job Fair* presentation and save it as *Job Fair Final*.
2. Go to slide 5 and click the Online Pictures icon in the right-hand content placeholder.
3. Type business as the keyword in the Office.com Clip Art box and press Enter.
4. Review the results to find a photograph of a professionally dressed business person. Click the picture, and then click Insert to insert it into the placeholder.
5. Use the Size options on the Picture Tools Format tab to resize the picture to be 3 inches wide.
6. Click the View tab, and then click Gridlines. Use the gridlines to align the top of the picture with the top of the text in the left-hand placeholder.
7. Click the picture to select it, click Picture Effects on the Picture Tools Format tab, point to Shadow, and click the Offset Right shadow effect under the Outer heading.
8. Hide the gridlines.
9. **SAVE** the presentation.

LEAVE the presentation open for use in the next project.

Project 8-2: Final Touches

You have decided you need another picture in the Job Fair Final presentation. You have a picture file you think will work.

1. Go to slide 2 of *Job Fair Final* and click the Pictures icon in the right-hand content placeholder.
2. Navigate to the data files for this lesson, locate *Building.jpg*, click the file, and click Insert.
3. Right-click the picture and click Size and Position. In the Format Picture task pane, scale the picture to 90% of its current height and width.
4. Press Alt+F9 to display drawing guides. Click the slide title placeholder to display its border, and then drag the vertical guide to the right to align with the right border of the slide title text box.
5. Drag the horizontal guide up to align with the top of the capital letter *E* in the first bulleted item in the left-hand guide.
6. Reposition the picture so that its upper-right corner snaps to the intersection of the two guides. Press Alt+F9 to hide the guides.
7. Click the More button in the Picture Styles group on the Picture Tools Format tab, and then click the Drop Shadow Rectangle Quick Style.
8. Right-click the picture, click Format Picture, click the Picture icon, and under Picture Corrections, change Brightness to 5% and Contrast to 10%.
9. Click Compress Pictures in the Adjust group on the Picture Tools Format tab, and then click E-mail (96 ppi) and click OK.
10. **SAVE** the presentation and then **CLOSE** the file.

LEAVE PowerPoint open for use in the next project.

Proficiency Assessment

Project 8-3: **Go with the Flow**

You are a professional trainer teaching a class on basic computer skills. For your class today, you need to explain the systems development life cycle (SDLC) to a group of students. You can use PowerPoint's drawing tools to create a flow chart that shows the process.

1. Create a new, blank presentation.
2. Change the title slide to a Title Only slide, and type the slide title Systems Development Life Cycle (SDLC).
3. Draw five rectangles stacked vertically on the slide (or draw one and then copy it four times). You do not have to worry about alignment or distribution at this point.
4. Type Phase 1: Needs Analysis in the top rectangle.
5. Add text to the remaining rectangles as follows:
   Phase 2: System Design
   Phase 3: Development
   Phase 4: Implementation
   Phase 5: Maintenance
6. Resize the shapes as necessary so that text fits on a single line and all five rectangles fit on the slide with a small amount of space between each shape (see Figure 8-42).

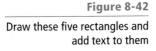

Figure 8-42

Draw these five rectangles and add text to them

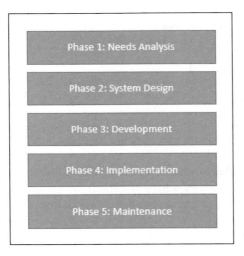

7. Set the width and height of all five rectangles to be identical if they are not already.
8. With all five rectangles selected, use the Align Left command to align them with one another.
9. Use the Distribute Vertically command to equalize the spacing between the rectangles.
10. Apply a different Shape Styles color to each rectangle. (Use the same effect for all rectangles, but vary the colors for each.)
11. Group all drawing objects.
12. Use the Align Center command to align the object horizontally in the center of the slide.
13. **SAVE** the presentation as *SDLC Final.pptx* and then **CLOSE** the file.

LEAVE PowerPoint open for the next project.

Project 8-4: Basic Logo with Stacked Shapes

You have been asked by the K-9 Agility Network to create a logo, which they will use as a marketing tool.

1. Start a new, blank presentation, and change the layout of the slide to Blank.
2. Draw a 3.5" five-pointed star on the slide. Hold down Shift as you draw it so its height and width are the same.
3. Apply a yellow fill to the star. Apply the Angle bevel to it from the Shape Effects menu.
4. Draw a 4" square over the star. Apply the Intense Effect - Blue, Accent 5 Shape Style to the square.
5. Send the square behind the star.
6. With both the square and the star selected, use Align Center and Align Middle to align the objects with each other both horizontally and vertically.
7. Lasso the two objects, and then group them.
8. **SAVE** the presentation as *Logo Final*, and then **CLOSE** the file.

LEAVE PowerPoint open for use in the next project.

Mastery Assessment

Project 8-5: Photo Flair

You are finalizing a presentation to introduce a speaker and want to do some work on the photo of the speaker you have included on a slide. You can use PowerPoint's picture tools to finalize the photo.

1. **OPEN** the *Speaker* presentation and save it as *Speaker Final*.
2. Go to slide 2 and select the picture.
3. Crop the picture to remove the coffee cup and newspaper at the right side of the picture.
4. Resize the photo so it is 4 inches high and align it with the top of the vertical line at the center of the slide.
5. Increase the contrast in the picture by 10%.
6. Draw a rectangle that exactly covers the picture. Remove the outline from the rectangle.
7. Click the down arrow key twice and the right arrow key twice to slightly offset the shape from the picture, and then send the shape behind the picture to act as a drop shadow.
8. Choose a new theme color for the rectangle shape that contrasts well with the picture but does not overwhelm it.
9. **SAVE** the presentation and then **CLOSE** the file.

LEAVE PowerPoint open for use in the next project.

Project 8-6: Merging Shapes

Your Consolidated Courier presentation needs a new logo. You can create one using the Drawing tools in PowerPoint.

1. Create a new, blank presentation.
2. Change the layout of the slide to Blank.
3. Draw the four shapes shown in Figure 8-43.

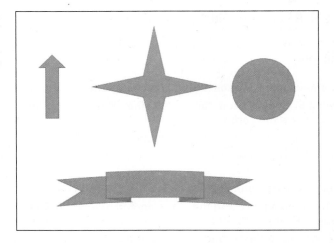

4. Place the arrow over the top point of the star (see Figure 8-44).

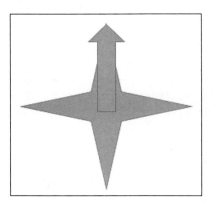

5. Use Merge Shapes, applying the Union effect, to combine the arrow and the star into a single shape.

6. Apply the dark red standard color to the new shape as a fill, and remove the shape's outline.

7. Select the banner shape, and fill it with the Dark Red standard color. Change its outline to the Orange standard color and set its Weight to 1/4 pt.

8. In the banner shape, type Consolidated Courier, pressing Enter between the words so each appears on its own line. Set the font to Arial Black. ("Black" is part of the font name, not a description of the color. The font color is white.)

9. Select the circle, and fill it with the Moderate Effect - Gold, Accent 4 Shape Style.

10. Arrange, align, and size the three shapes into the logo shown in Figure 8-45.

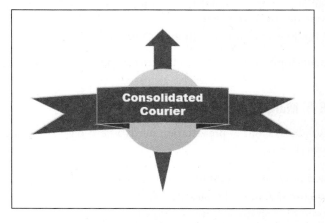

11. **SAVE** the presentation as *Consolidated Logo Final* and then **CLOSE** the file.

EXIT PowerPoint.

Using Animation and Multimedia 9

LESSON SKILL MATRIX

Skill	Exam Objective	Objective Number
Setting Up Slide Transitions	Insert transitions between slides.	4.1.1
	Modify transition effect options.	4.1.3
	Modify duration of effects.	4.3.1
	Manage multiple transitions.	4.1.2
Animating Slide Content	Apply animations to text strings.	4.2.2
	Add paths to animations.	4.2.3
	Modify animation options.	4.2.4
	Configure start and finish options.	4.3.2
	Apply animations to shapes.	4.2.1
	Demonstrate how to use the Animation pane.	4.3.4
	Reorder animations.	4.3.3
Adding Media Clips to a Presentation	Set media options.	3.6.4
	Trim timing on media clips.	3.6.2
	Set start/stop times.	3.6.3
	Adjust media window size.	3.6.1
	Compress media.	5.3.4

©CowboyRoy/iStockphoto

KEY TERMS
- After Previous
- animations
- Animation Painter
- Animation Pane
- audio
- delay
- duration
- emphasis effect
- entrance effects
- exit effect
- motion path
- On Click
- poster frame
- transitions
- video
- With Previous

321

©CowboyRoy/iStockphoto

In your role as director of promotions for the Baldwin Museum of Science, you are responsible for creating a multimedia presentation that will run on the video monitors in the museum's lobby. This self-running presentation should contain plenty of animation and movement to capture people's attention. The animation and multimedia capabilities of PowerPoint allow you to include transitions, animations, and audio and video clips to enliven your presentations.

SOFTWARE ORIENTATION

The Animation Pane

The **Animation Pane** (see Figure 9-1) enables you to manage all the animation effects on the active slide. Each object can have multiple animation effects, including entrance, exit, emphasis, and motion path effect types.

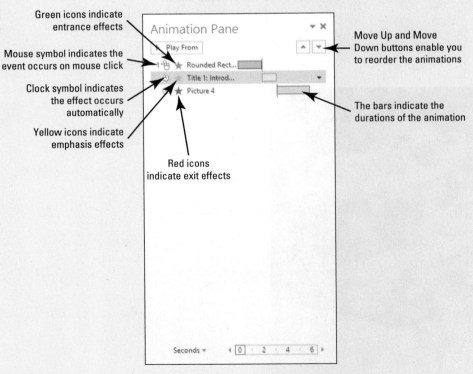

Figure 9-1
Animation Pane

PowerPoint professionals often use complex sequences of animation effects to add movement and interest to an otherwise static presentation. Animation effects applied to static images can be a cost-effective alternative to creating live motion video.

SETTING UP SLIDE TRANSITIONS

Transitions are animated effects that occur when you move from one slide to another. They differ from animations in that animations apply to individual items on a slide whereas transitions apply only to entire slides. You can control the effect, its speed, its sound effect (if any), and in some cases other options, such as direction.

Applying and Modifying a Transition Effect

By default, there are no transitions assigned to slides. When you advance to the next slide, it simply appears in place of the previous one. For more impressive-looking transitions, you can choose one of the preset transition effects that PowerPoint provides and then modify it as needed. In this exercise, you will apply and customize a transition effect.

You can apply any of the transition effects from the Transitions tab, and then modify the chosen transition's options. Some transitions have effect options you can choose from the Effect Options button; if you choose a transition that does not have any, that button is unavailable.

You can assign a sound to a transition if desired. You can select any of the PowerPoint preset sounds from the Sound menu, or choose Other Sound from the menu to open a dialog box from which you can browse for your own sounds.

The Duration setting for a transition is its speed of execution—that is, the number of seconds the effect takes to occur. Each transition has a default duration; increase the duration to slow it down, or decrease the duration to speed it up.

The Apply to All button copies the transition from the active slide to all other slides. To remove the transitions from all slides at once, first set one of the slides to have a transition of None, and then click Apply to All.

CERTIFICATION READY?　4.1.1

How do you insert transitions between slides?

CERTIFICATION READY?　4.1.3

How do you modify transition effect options?

CERTIFICATION READY?　4.3.1

How do you modify the duration of effects?

STEP BY STEP　　**Apply and Modify a Transition Effect**

GET READY. Before you begin these steps, make sure that your computer is on. Log on, if necessary.

1. **START** PowerPoint, if the program is not already running.
2. Locate and open the *Lobby* presentation and save it as *Lobby Final Version 1*.
3. Switch to Slide Sorter view, and select slide 2.
4. Click the Transitions tab, and then click the More button in the Transition to This Slide group. A palette of transition effects opens (see Figure 9-2).

Figure 9-2

The PowerPoint transition effects

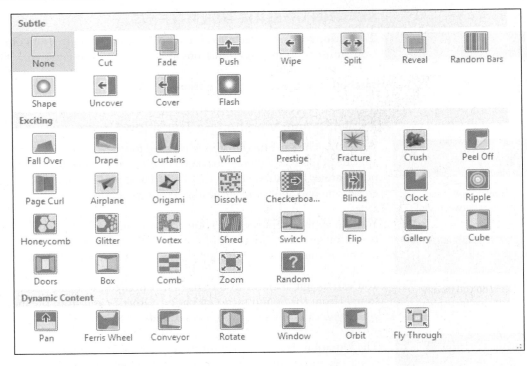

5. Click the Honeycomb effect. The effect is previewed immediately on slide 2.

Take Note   Notice that there is a small star below and to the right of slide 2. This indicates that a transition or animation has been applied to it.

6. On the Transitions tab, in the Timing group, set the Duration to 06.00. This action sets the transition to execute in 6 seconds.

7. Open the Sound drop-down list and click Camera, to add the sound of a camera shutter opening and closing at each transition (see Figure 9-3).

Figure 9-3

Set transition options

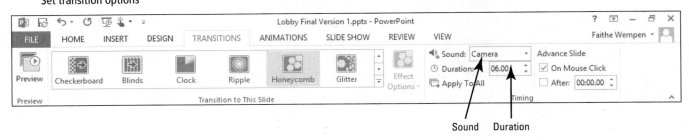

8. Click the Preview button in the Preview group, or click the small star icon below slide 2, to see the effect again at the new speed, including the newly assigned sound (see Figure 9-4).

Figure 9-4

The star indicates there is a transition or animation

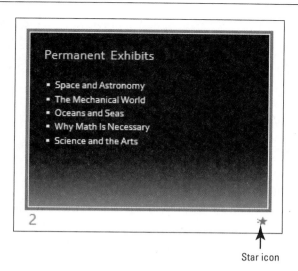

Star icon

Troubleshooting If you do not hear the sound, try previewing it again. If you still do not hear the sound, make sure your system's sound is not muted in Windows, and that the volume is turned up.

9. Click the More button again, and in the Subtle section, click Wipe to apply the Wipe transition to the selected slide.

Take Note Notice that the Duration setting is reset to the default for the newly chosen transition, but the sound (Camera) previously selected remains selected.

10. Click Effect Options. A menu of effect options opens (see Figure 9-5).

Figure 9-5

Select a transition option

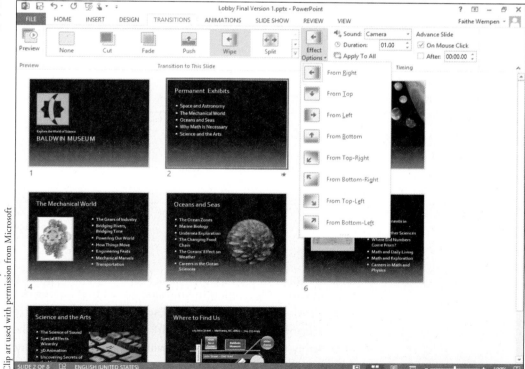

Slide 3: Photo courtesy of NASA;
Slide 4: iStockPhoto/windujedi;
Slide 7: © iStockIPhoto/ooyoo;
Clip art used with permission from Microsoft

11. Click **From Left**. The new effect option is previewed on the slide automatically.

12. Click **Apply to All**. The transition effect is copied to all the other slides in the presentation. Now all the slides have small star icons beneath them.

13. On the Slide Show tab, click **From Beginning**, and watch the whole presentation from beginning to end, clicking to move to the next slide. When finished, press **Esc** to return to **Slide Sorter** view.

14. **SAVE** the presentation.

PAUSE. LEAVE the presentation open to use in the next exercise.

CERTIFICATION READY? 4.1.2

How do you manage multiple transitions?

Determining How Slides Will Advance

By default, the presentation advances from one slide to the next when you click the mouse. Slides can be set to advance automatically after a certain amount of time, manually upon mouse click (or other signal, such as pressing the Enter key), or both. If both are selected, the slide will advance immediately if you click the mouse, otherwise advance will occur when the allotted time elapses. In this exercise, you learn how to set slides to advance automatically after a certain amount of time and to advance manually upon a mouse click.

STEP BY STEP   **Set Slides to Advance Manually or Automatically**

USE the *Lobby Final Version 1* presentation that is still open from the previous exercise.

1. In Slide Sorter view, click **slide 1** to select it.

2. On the Transitions tab in the Timing group, mark the **After** check box to indicate that the slide should advance manually after a certain amount of time has passed.

3. Click the **up increment arrow** in the **After** text box until it reads **00:10:00**, to set the amount of time to 10 seconds.

4. Clear the **On Mouse Click** check box (see Figure 9-6). Then click Apply to All.

Figure 9-6

Choose to advance automatically, but not on mouse click

Do not advance on mouse click

Advances automatically after 10 seconds

5. Click the **Slide Show** tab, then click **From Beginning**, and begin watching the **presentation**. Try clicking the **mouse**; notice that it does not advance to the next slide.

6. After viewing three slides, press **Esc** to return to Slide Sorter view.

7. On the Transitions tab, click to mark the **On Mouse Click** check box again.

8. Click **Apply to All**. Now all slides will advance automatically after 10 seconds, or earlier if the mouse is clicked.

9. **SAVE** the presentation.

PAUSE. LEAVE the presentation open to use in the next exercise.

When creating a self-running presentation, such as for a lobby display, it is important that nothing be set to happen only with a mouse click because the audience will have no access to a mouse.

ANIMATING SLIDE CONTENT

The Bottom Line

You can animate individual objects on a slide to give the presentation a more active and dynamic feel. Objects can be set to enter or exit the slide in an animated way. For example, a picture could fly onto the slide, stay on the screen for a few seconds, and then fly away again. Text can also be animated; it can be set to appear all at once or one bullet point at a time.

Animations are effects applied to placeholders or other content to move the content in unique ways on the slide. Animations can be roughly divided into four types: entrance, emphasis, exit, and motion paths. **Entrance effects** animate an object's entry onto the slide, separately from the entrance of the slide itself. If an object does not have an entrance effect, it enters at the same time as the slide. An **emphasis effect** modifies an object that is already on the slide, calling attention to it by moving it or changing its colors. An **exit effect** causes the object to leave the slide before the slide itself exits. A **motion path** effect moves the object from point A to point B, following along a path that you create for it.

Workplace *Ready* _____

USING ANIMATION EFFECTIVELY

Transitions and animation effects can actually do more harm than good in some business presentations. Flashy and dramatic effects can make the audience focus on the effects themselves rather than on the content you are delivering. PowerPoint and its capabilities are well-known to most business people, so they are not likely to be impressed by your transition and animation effects in and of themselves. They will be more interested in seeing that you have applied the effects intelligently to enhance the message you are delivering.

Here is an example of an effective use of PowerPoint animation. Suppose an attorney is creating a presentation to show that there are many more factors in favor of one outcome than another. He might use PowerPoint to show blocks being placed on a balance scale, with each block flying in individually onscreen as the text that explains that block appears. In such a slide, the message being presented is more effective because of the animation.

CERTIFICATION READY?   **4.2.2**

How do you apply animation to text?

Applying Animations

Many animation effects are available on the Animations tab for an object's entrance, emphasis, and exit. You can apply them to both graphic objects and text. After applying an animation, you can modify it by changing its options. In this exercise, you will apply an animation effect and then modify it for a custom effect.

STEP BY STEP   **Apply and Modify Animations**

USE the *Lobby Final Version 1* presentation that is still open from the previous exercise. Save the file as a new file named *Lobby Final Version 2*.

1. Switch to Normal view, and go to slide 2.
2. Click in the bulleted list to move the insertion point there.
3. On the Animations tab, click Add Animation. A menu of animation presets appears (see Figure 9-7).

Figure 9-7

Select an entrance animation preset

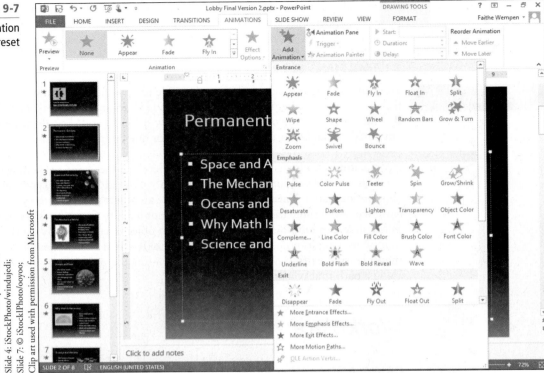

Slide 3: Photo courtesy of NASA;
Slide 4: iStockPhoto/windujedi;
Slide 7: © iStocklPhoto/ooyoo;
Clip art used with permission from Microsoft

4. Click **Fly In**. The animation is previewed on the slide.
5. Click the **Effect Options** button. A menu of options appears (see Figure 9-8).

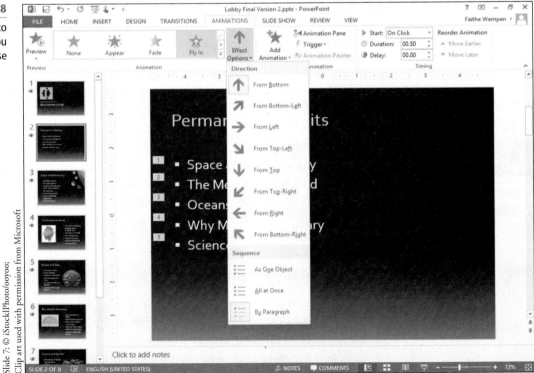

Slide 3: Photo courtesy of NASA;
Slide 4: iStockPhoto/windujedi;
Slide 7: © iStocklPhoto/ooyoo;
Clip art used with permission from Microsoft

6. Click **From Top-Left**. The effect is previewed. Notice that each bullet point flies in separately.
7. Click the **Effect Options** button again.
8. Click **All at Once**. The effect is previewed. Notice that all the bullets fly in at once.

Take Note   The text options like the one you selected in step 8 are available only when animating text, not graphics.

9. Go to **slide 3**, and select the **graphic** in the upper-right corner.
10. On the Animations tab, click the **Add Animation** button, and then click **More Emphasis Effects**.
11. In the Add Emphasis Effect dialog box, click **Pulse** (see Figure 9-9). The effect is previewed on the graphic.

Figure 9-9

Select an emphasis effect

12. Click **OK** to accept the new effect.
13. On the Animations tab, in the Duration box, click the **up increment arrow** until the setting is **04:00**.
14. Click the **Preview** button to preview the animation at its new duration setting.
15. **SAVE** the presentation.

PAUSE. LEAVE the presentation open to use in the next exercise.

The PowerPoint animations are very customizable, as you saw in the preceding exercise. You can adjust their direction, duration, text options, and more. Some animation effects have effect options you can select from the Effect Options button's menu. If the chosen animation has no options, the Effect Options button is unavailable.

When animating text, you have a choice of animating each paragraph individually or animating all the text at once. Keep in mind that each animation will be triggered (by default) by a mouse click, and think about whether you want to introduce each paragraph to the audience individually or not.

CERTIFICATION READY?   4.2.3

How do you add paths to animations?

Using Motion Path Animation

Motion paths enable you to set a graphic to move from one place to another. You can start with a preset, as you learn to do in this exercise, and then modify the path to fine-tune it. To modify the path, on the Animations tab, click Effect Options, and then click Edit Points. Then you can drag the individual points that comprise the path. In this exercise, you will apply a motion path animation to a graphic.

STEP BY STEP   **Use a Motion Path Animation**

USE the *Lobby Final Version 2* presentation that is still open from the previous exercise.

1. Go to **slide 5** and select the **graphic**.
2. On the Animations tab, click **Add Animation**, and then click **More Motion Paths**. The Add Motion Path dialog box appears.
3. In the Add Motion Path dialog box, scroll down to the **Special** section and click **Swoosh** (see Figure 9-10). The animation is previewed on the slide.

Figure 9-10

Select a motion path animation

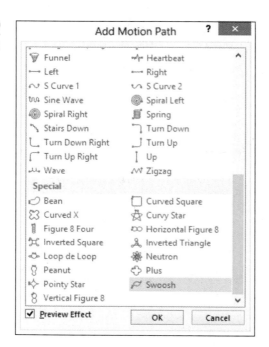

4. Click **OK** to apply the animation. A dotted line appears on the graphic, showing the motion path. This dotted line will not appear in Slide Show view.
5. Click **Effect Options**, and then click **Reverse Path Direction**. The Swoosh effect is previewed again, this time going in the opposite direction.
6. **SAVE** the presentation.

PAUSE. LEAVE the presentation open to use in the next exercise.

The start point is represented by an arrow (or in some motion paths, a circle). If the start and end point is the same spot, you see only that green arrow or circle; however, if the end point is different, it appears as a red arrow or circle. The motion path you applied in the preceding steps has the same starting and ending point, so only a green arrow appears.

CERTIFICATION READY?   **4.2.4**

How do you modify animation options?

Modifying an Animation's Start Options and Timing

Each animation has its own separate start, duration, and delay settings. The animation's **duration** determines how quickly it will execute. Each animation effect has a default duration, which you can adjust up or down. The **delay** is the amount of time to wait between the previous action and this animation. You might, for example, use a delay to give the audience a chance to read some text on the screen. By setting these properties, you can sequence multiple animation effects to produce the exact appearance you want.

CERTIFICATION READY? 4.3.2

How do you configure start and finish options?

CERTIFICATION READY? 4.2.1

How do you apply animation to a shape?

Each animation has its own start options and timing settings, separate from the slide itself. The start options available are On Click (the default), With Previous, and After Previous. **On Click** waits for a mouse click to start the animation; the slide show pauses until the click is received. **With Previous** starts the animation simultaneously with the start of the previous action. If it is the first animation on the slide, the previous action is the entrance of the slide itself; otherwise, the previous action is the previous animation on that slide. **After Previous** starts the animation after the previous action has completed. If the previous action is very quick, you may not notice any difference between With Previous and After Previous.

In this exercise, you will modify the start options and timing for an animation.

STEP BY STEP | **Modify Animation Start Options and Timing**

USE the *Lobby Final Version 2* presentation that is still open from the previous exercise.

1. Go to slide 6, and select the graphic.
2. On the Animations tab, click Add Animation, and click More Entrance Effects. The Add Entrance Effect dialog box opens.
3. In the Exciting section, click Pinwheel (see Figure 9-11).

Figure 9-11

Select an entrance effect

4. Click OK.
5. On the Animations tab, open the Start drop-down list and click After Previous.
6. In the Delay box, click the up increment arrow until the setting is 01:00.
7. In the Duration box, click the up increment arrow until the setting is 03:00. Figure 9-12 shows the settings on the Animations tab. This animation will start one second after the previous event and will last for three seconds.

Figure 9-12

Animation settings

8. Click the Preview button to check the new settings.

9. With the graphic still selected, click Add Animation, and click More Exit Effects. The Add Exit Effect dialog box opens.

10. Click Pinwheel, and click OK. Notice that there are 0 and 1 icons near the upper left corner of the graphic on the slide. The 0 represents the first animation effect (the entrance) and the 1 represents the second effect (the exit).

11. Click the 1 icon to make sure that the exit effect animation is selected.

12. On the Animations tab, in the Delay box, click the up increment arrow until the setting is 03:00.

13. Click the Preview button to watch the entire animation sequence.

14. Click in the bulleted list, and on the Animations tab, click Add Animation and then click Fade in the Entrance section. Notice that each bulleted item has a numbered icon to its left.

15. Click the 1 icon to the left of the graphic, and on the Animations tab, click Move Later. The exit effect moves to position 7 (after the bulleted list completes).

16. Click in the bulleted list again, and on the Animations tab, open the Start drop-down list and click With Previous. Then open the Effect Options button's drop-down list and click By Paragraph. The numbered icons on the slide should appear as in Figure 9-13.

Figure 9-13

The animation effects should be numbered as shown at this point

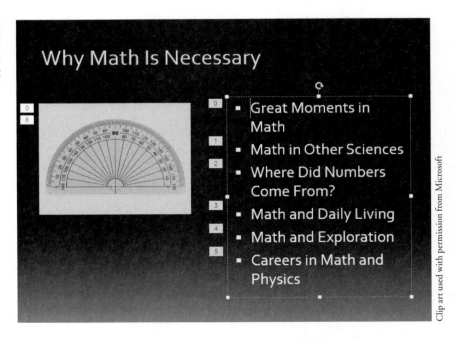

17. Click the Preview button to check the new settings.

18. **SAVE** the presentation.

PAUSE. LEAVE the presentation open to use in the next exercise.

Using the Animation Pane

When a slide has multiple animations on it, you might find the Animation Pane helpful in viewing and organizing the animations. The Animation Pane lists each of the animations associated with the active slide's content and enables you to make fine-tuning adjustments to them. From the Animation Pane you can reorder animations, adjust their settings, and see how they overlap and interact with one another. Within the Animation Pane, an animated object that consists of multiple paragraphs appears by default as a single item, so you can apply the same settings to all paragraphs. You can optionally expand that entry to a list of each individual paragraph, so you can animate them separately if you prefer. In this exercise, you use the Animation Pane to fine-tune the animation effects on a slide.

<table>
<tr><td>CERTIFICATION READY?</td><td>4.3.4</td></tr>
</table>

How do you use the animation pane?

In addition to using the controls on the Animations tab on the Ribbon, you can display a dialog box for each animation by opening the animation's menu in the Animation Pane and choosing Effect Options. The name of the dialog box depends on the animation type. Within this dialog box are settings that, among other things, let you associate a sound with an animation and let you reverse the order in which a list appears. To remove an animation from the slide, select the animation either in the Animation Pane or by clicking the numbered icon to the left of the object on the slide, and then press the Delete key on the keyboard.

STEP BY STEP   **Use the Animation Pane**

USE the *Lobby Final Version 2* presentation that is still open from the previous exercise.

1. On the Animations tab, click Animation Pane. The Animation Pane appears at the right. It lists the three animation items for slide 6 (see Figure 9-14).

Figure 9-14

The Animation Pane

2. Click the gray bar that separates the second and third animations. The list expands to show each bulleted list item as a separate animation event (see Figure 9-15).

Figure 9-15

The bulleted list animations
are expanded

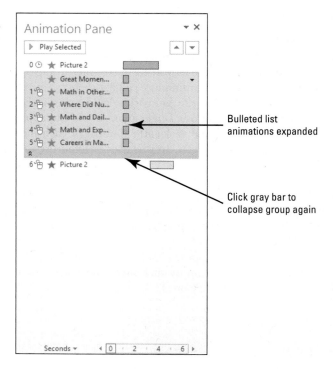

Take Note   When the list is expanded, each item is edited separately. If you want to change the settings for the entire list, you should collapse the list again before changing settings.

3. Click the **gray bar** again to collapse the animations for the bulleted list.

4. In the Animation Pane, click the **Content Placeholder** animation, and then click the **down arrow** to its right to open its menu. On the menu, click **Effect Options**. The Fade dialog box opens.

5. Click the **Text Animation** tab.

6. Click the **In reverse order** check box.

7. Mark the **Automatically after** check box, and click the **up increment arrow** to set the number of seconds to 3. Figure 9-16 shows the dialog box settings.

Figure 9-16

Fine-tune the animation in this
dialog box

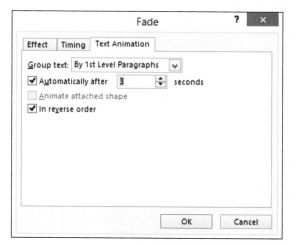

8. Click **OK**. Notice that the Start setting on the Animations tab has changed to After Previous.

9. If the animation does not preview automatically, click **Preview** to watch the animation for this slide.

10. Go to **slide 1**, and press **Ctrl+A** to select all objects on the slide.

11. On the Animations tab, click **Add Animation**, and then in the Entrance section, click **Float In**. The same animation effect is applied to all objects.

12. On the Animations tab, open the Start drop-down list and click With Previous.

13. In the Animation Pane, select the animation for the title (Title 1) and press the Delete key to remove the animation for that object.

CERTIFICATION READY? 4.3.3

How do you reorder animations?

14. Select only the slide's title text box and then click Add Animation, and in the Emphasis section, click Wave.

15. In the Animation Pane, confirm that the Title object's animation is already selected, and click the Move Up arrow (at the top of the task pane) three times to move the animation to the top of the list, so that it executes first.

16. Open the Start drop-down list and click After Previous, setting the wave animation to occur after the slide appears.

17. Click the arrow to the animation's right in the Animation Pane, opening its menu, and click Effect Options.

18. Open the Sound drop-down list, choose Arrow, and click OK.

19. Click the Preview button to preview the slide's animation.

20. **SAVE** the presentation.

PAUSE. LEAVE the presentation open to use in the next exercise.

Using Animation Painter

Animation Painter enables you to select an object that already has the animation you want, including the delay, duration, sound effects, and so on, and then copy that animation to another object. Animation Painter is very much like Format Painter, but it works for animation rather than for formatting. When you click Animation Painter, the mouse pointer becomes a paintbrush. You can then navigate to any other slide (or stay on the same slide) and click another object to receive the animation settings. If you double-click Animation Painter rather than single-clicking it, it stays on until you turn it off (by clicking it again, or by pressing Esc), so you can paint the same animation onto multiple objects. In this exercise, you will copy animation from one object to another.

STEP BY STEP   **Use Animation Painter**

USE the *Lobby Final Version 2* presentation that is still open from the previous exercise.

1. On slide 1, select the Explore the World of Science text box.

2. On the Animations tab, click Animation Painter.

3. Go to slide 8 and click Where to Find Us. The animation is copied to that text box.

4. Close the Animation Pane.

5. **SAVE** the presentation.

PAUSE. LEAVE the presentation open to use in the next exercise.

ADDING MEDIA CLIPS TO A PRESENTATION

The Bottom Line

Audio (sound) and **video** (moving picture) clips can add interest to a presentation by drawing the audience's attention more than a static show. You can include your own audio and video clips that you have recorded or acquired on disk, or select from clips you find on Office.com or via a Bing Video Search or YouTube search. You can also apply formatting styles to audio and video content, as you do for images.

Adding an Audio File to a Slide

Audio files can provide simple sound effects, music soundtracks, and/or prerecorded narration in a presentation. You can add audio from files on your own PC or from Office.com. You can specify when the sound will play, how loud it will be (in comparison to the overall sound level), and which user controls will be available onscreen.

You have a number of options for adding audio to a presentation:

- Use **Audio on My PC** if you have an audio file in a supported format that you want to insert. PowerPoint can handle AIFF, AU, MIDI, MP3, WAV, and WMA files.
- Use **Online Audio** to open the Insert Audio dialog box and search for an audio file in the same way you searched for clip art on Office.com.
- Use **Record Audio** if you want to record your own audio to play on the slide. You must have a microphone to record audio.

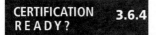

CERTIFICATION READY?   **3.6.4**

How do you set media options?

In this exercise, you will add an audio clip from Office.com to the presentation, delete it, and then add an audio clip from the data files provided for this exercise.

STEP BY STEP   **Add an Audio Clip to a Slide**

USE the *Lobby Final Version 2* presentation that is still open from the previous exercise. Save the file as a new file named *Lobby Final Version 3*.

1. Go to slide 1, and on the Insert tab, click the arrow under the Audio button. On the menu that appears, click Online Audio. The Insert Audio dialog box opens, showing a search box for Office.com Clip Art.
2. Type a keyword in the search box and press Enter. If you do not know what keyword to use, use sound to see an assortment of sound clips.
3. Click any of the clips that appear in the results and click Insert. A sound icon appears in the center of the slide (see Figure 9-17).

Figure 9-17

An audio clip inserted on a slide

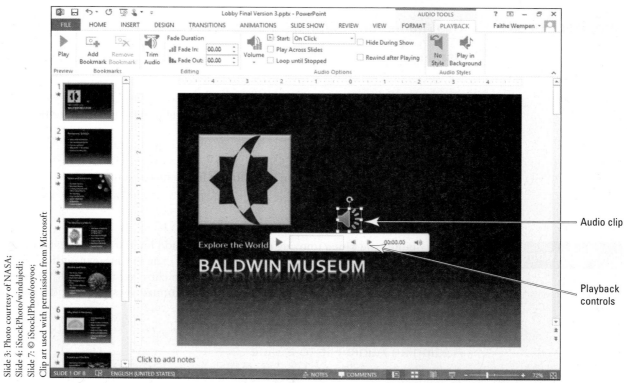

4. Press F5 to switch to Slide Show view, and click the sound icon on the slide. The sound plays.

5. Press Esc to return to Normal view.

6. Select the sound icon on the slide and press Delete on the keyboard to remove it.

7. With slide 1 still displayed, on the Insert tab, click the arrow under the Audio button and click Audio on My PC. The Insert Audio dialog box opens.

8. Navigate to the data files for this lesson, click *Beethoven's Ninth*, and click Insert. An icon appears in the center of the slide.

9. On the Audio Tools Playback tab, open the Start drop-down list and click Automatically.

10. Mark the Hide During Show check box.

11. On the Audio Tools Playback tab, click the Volume button, and then click Medium. Figure 9-18 shows the settings on the Audio Tools Playback tab.

Figure 9-18

Adjust the sound clip's volume, start setting, and visibility

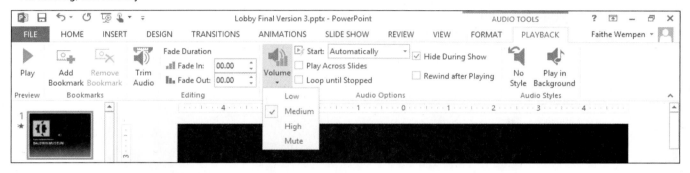

12. View the first two slides in Slide Show view. Notice that the sound quits after the first slide. The camera sound associated with the transitions is distracting from the music. Press Esc to return to Normal view.

13. On the Transitions tab, open the Sound drop-down list and click [No Sound]. Then click Apply to All.

14. Select the sound icon on slide 1.

15. On the Audio Tools Playback tab, click to mark the Play Across Slides check box.

16. Watch the first several slides in Slide Show view. This time notice that the sound continues as you move from slide 1 to slide 2. Then press Esc to return to Normal view.

17. **SAVE** the presentation.

PAUSE. LEAVE the presentation open to use in the next exercise.

Adding a Video to a Slide

You can insert videos from your own collection to add visual interest or information to a presentation. PowerPoint accepts Flash videos as well as many standard formats such as Windows Media, QuickTime, and MP4. You can insert video content using the Video button on the Insert tab, or using the Insert Video icon in a content placeholder.

In this exercise, you insert a video clip from a file, set it to play automatically, and set some playback options for it.

STEP BY STEP   **Add a Video to a Slide**

USE the *Lobby Final Version 3* presentation that is still open from the previous exercise.

1. Go to slide 9.
2. Click the Insert Video icon in the empty placeholder box (see Figure 9-19). The Insert Video dialog box opens.
3. Click the Browse button next to From a file. The Insert Video dialog box opens. (It is a different dialog box from the one in step 6, but it has the same name.)
4. Navigate to the folder containing the data files for this lesson and select *Sunspot.mp4*. Then, click Insert. The clip appears in the placeholder, with playback controls beneath it (see Figure 9-19).

Figure 9-19

The video clip appears on the slide

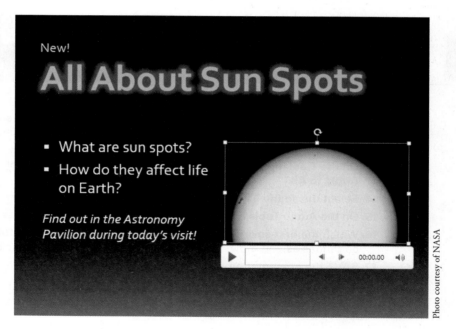

5. On the Animations tab, click Animation Pane. The Animation Pane opens. Notice that there is an animation event for the video clip already there (see Figure 9-20).

Figure 9-20

The video clip is part of the slide's animation sequence

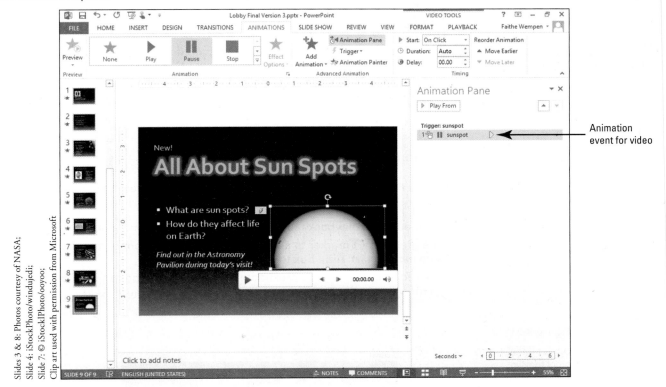

Animation event for video

Slides 3 & 8: Photos courtesy of NASA;
Slide 4: iStockPhoto/windujedi;
Slide 7: © iStockIPhoto/ooyoo;
Clip art used with permission from Microsoft

6. Close the **Animation Pane**.

7. On the Video Tools Playback tab, open the **Start drop-down list** and click **Automatically**.

8. Mark the **Loop until Stopped** check box. This action makes the clip continue to play until the slide advances.

9. Click the up **increment arrow button** on the **Fade In text box** until the value is **00.50** (one half a second). Do the same thing for the **Fade Out text box**.

10. On the Slide Show tab, click **From Current Slide** to watch this slide in Slide Show view.

11. **SAVE** the presentation.

PAUSE. LEAVE the presentation open to use in the next exercise.

As you saw in the preceding exercise, you can set a clip to start either automatically or on-click, and you can control its fade duration (both Fade In and Fade Out). Be careful when fading a clip in and out that do you not make it difficult for the audience to see something important that happens in the first or last second or two of the clip.

After inserting a video clip, you can use controls in the Video Options group on the Video Tools Playback tab to customize how it plays. The options available are:

- **Start:** Set to either Automatically or On Click.
- **Play Full Screen:** When the clip begins playing, it switches to full-screen mode.
- **Hide While Not Playing:** When the clip is not playing, it does not appear on the slide. Make sure that you set Start to Automatically if you use this option; otherwise, you will have no way of starting the clip.

**CERTIFICATION
READY?**   3.6.2

How do you trim timing on
media clips?

**CERTIFICATION
READY?**   3.6.3

How do you set start and
stop times?

• **Loop until Stopped:** The clip repeats over and over until the next slide appears.
• **Rewind after Playing:** When the clip is finished playing, the first frame of the clip reappears. (When this option is not selected, the last frame of the clip remains onscreen.)

Trimming a Video Clip

The raw video footage that you have on hand may need some cuts to be appropriate for your presentation. You can do this editing in a third-party video editing application, but if all you need is to trim some of the footage off the beginning and/or end of the clip, it may be easier to do that work in PowerPoint. In this exercise, you will trim 2 seconds off the beginning and end of a video.

STEP BY STEP   **Trim a Video Clip**

USE the *Lobby Final Version 3* presentation that is still open from the previous exercise.

1. Go to slide 9 and select the video clip.
2. On the Video Tools Playback tab, click Trim Video. The Trim Video dialog box opens.
3. Drag the green Start marker to approximately the 00:02 spot on the timeline, or change the value in the Start Time box to 00:02.00.
4. Drag the red End marker to approximately the 00:23.566 spot on the timeline, or change the value in the End Time box to 00:23.566 (see Figure 9-21).

Figure 9-21

Trim two seconds off the beginning and end of the clip

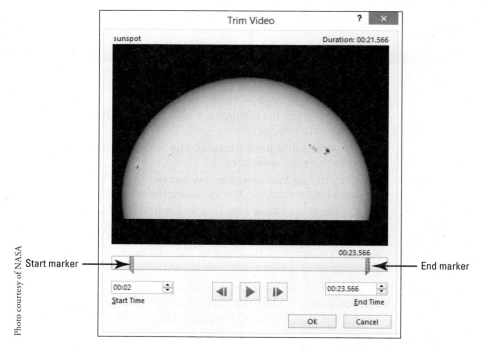

Photo courtesy of NASA

5. Click OK. The clip is now trimmed.

Formatting Video or Audio Content

Any video clip on a slide and any audio clip that has a visible icon on a slide can be formatted with the PowerPoint built-in styles. This works just like the style-based formatting for graphic objects: You select a style from a gallery. You can then customize it as desired by applying formatting. You can also choose a frame of the video clip that will appear on the slide whenever the video clip is not playing.

Choosing a Poster Frame   A **poster frame** is an image that displays on the slide when the video clip is not actively playing. You can use an outside image, but it is often easier to select a frame from the video clip itself. Poster frames are useful because often the first frame of the video clip is not an image that is meaningful or recognizable. Instead of choosing Current Frame from the Poster Frame menu, as you will do in this exercise, you can choose Image from File to select your own image. To remove any poster frame so that the first frame of the video clip is once again the default image for the clip, choose Reset from the menu. In this exercise, you choose a poster frame to display for a video clip.

STEP BY STEP   **Choose a Poster Frame**

USE the *Lobby Final Version 3* presentation that is still open from the previous exercise.

1. On slide 9, click the video clip.

2. Click the Play button (the right-pointing triangle) below the video clip to begin its playback. When the image onscreen shows the sun spot (the dark spot) in the center, click the Pause button to pause it.

3. On the Video Tools Format tab, click Poster Frame and click Current Frame (see Figure 9-22).

Figure 9-22

Select a poster frame

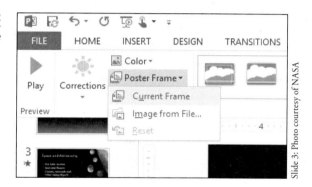

4. **SAVE** the presentation.

PAUSE. LEAVE the presentation open to use in the next exercise.

Applying a Video Style and Formatting   Whereas the tools on the Video Tools Playback tab control the clip's motion effects, the tools on the Video Tools Format tab control its static appearance, including its borders, effects, and any color or contrast corrections. The tools here are very similar to those for graphic images, which you learned about in Lesson 8. In this exercise, you will apply a video style and some picture corrections.

STEP BY STEP   **Apply a Video Style and Formatting**

USE the *Lobby Final Version 3* presentation that is still open from the previous exercise.

1. On slide 9, click the video clip.

2. On the Video Tools Format tab, click the More button in the Video Styles group, opening the Video Styles gallery (see Figure 9-23).

Slides 3 & 8: Photos courtesy of NASA;
Slide 4: iStockPhoto/windujedi;
Slide 7: © iStockIPhoto/ooyoo;
Clip art used with permission from Microsoft

Figure 9-23

The Video Styles gallery

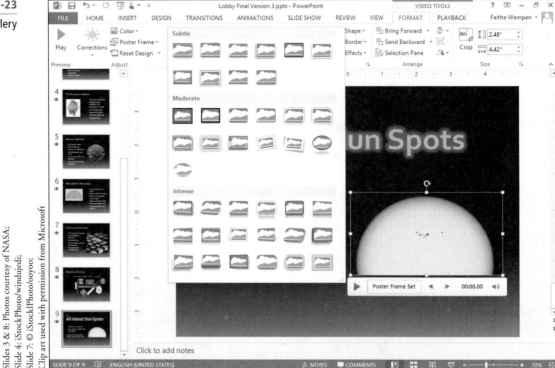

3. In the Subtle section, click the **Simple Frame**, **White** style. The frame of the video clip changes.

4. Click the **Video Shape** button, and on the Shapes palette that appears, click the **Rounded Rectangle**. The shape of the video clip's frame changes.

5. Click the **Video Border** button, and on the palette of colors that appears, click **Periwinkle**, **Accent 5**, **Darker 50%**.

6. Click the **Video Effects** button, point to **Glow**, and click **Periwinkle, 5 pt glow, Accent color 5**.

7. Click the **Video Effects** button, point to **Shadow**, and in the Perspective section, click **Perspective Diagonal Upper Right**. Figure 9-24 shows the completed formatting.

Figure 9-24

The formatted clip

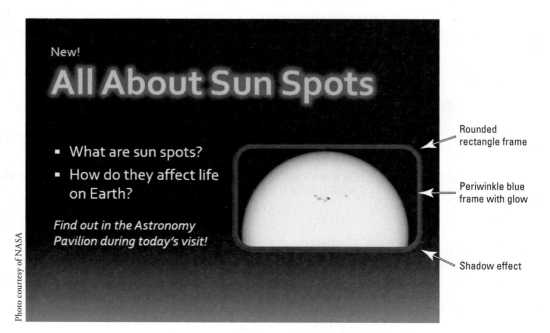

Photo courtesy of NASA

8. On the Video Tools Format tab, click the Corrections button, and click Brightness: 0% (Normal), Contrast +20%.

9. On the Slide Show tab, clear the Show Media Controls check box. This action prevents the media controls under the video clip from appearing in Slide Show view.

10. SAVE the presentation.

PAUSE. LEAVE the presentation open to use in the next exercise.

Take Note Part of the clip's appearance is the media control bar, or the thick gray bar that appears beneath the clip. If the presentation is self-running, you might prefer to hide that from the audience. To do so, clear the Show Media Controls check box on the Slide Show tab.

Sizing and Arranging Video or Audio Content

CERTIFICATION READY? **3.6.1**

How do you adjust the media window size?

Video clips (and audio clips that have a visible icon) can be sized and arranged like any other content on a slide. You can drag them to move or resize them or specify exact measurements. You can also align them with other content using the Align tools, which you learned about in Lesson 8 when working with drawn shapes. In this exercise, you change the size of a video clip and align it on the slide using guides.

STEP BY STEP **Size and Arrange a Video Clip**

USE the *Lobby Final Version 3* presentation that is still open from the previous exercise.

1. On slide 9, select the video clip.

2. On the Video Tools Format tab, type 2.4 in the Height box and then click away from it. The value in the Width box changes proportionally.

3. Click the video clip again to select it, if necessary.

4. On the View tab, click the Guides check box to turn on the guides. Drag the horizontal guide down so it aligns with the 1" mark on the vertical ruler above the midpoint.

5. Move the text box containing the bullets up so its upper-left corner aligns with the intersection of the guides at the left side of the slide.

6. Move the video clip so its upper-right corner aligns with the intersection of the guides at the right side of the slide (see Figure 9-25). Then turn off the guides by clearing the Guides check box on the View tab.

Figure 9-25

Use the guides to arrange the slide content

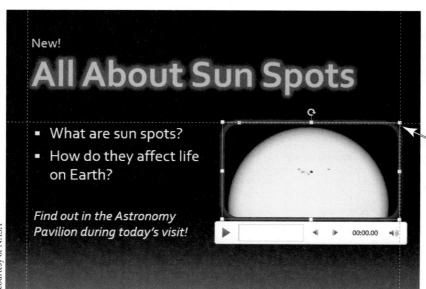

Place video clip at the intersection of the guides

New!

All About Sun Spots

- What are sun spots?
- How do they affect life on Earth?

Find out in the Astronomy Pavilion during today's visit!

Photo courtesy of NASA

Take Note Because there is a glow around the clip's border, it may not appear to align precisely with the guides. The glow may hang slightly over the lines.

    7. SAVE the presentation.

    PAUSE. LEAVE the presentation open to use in the next exercise.

There are many ways to size and arrange audio and video clips in PowerPoint. To size a clip, you can drag one of its selection handles, enter precise measurements in the Height and Width boxes on the Video Tools Format tab, or right-click the clip and choose Size and Position to open the size controls in the Format Video task pane.

To move (arrange) a clip, you can drag it where you want it, with or without the Guides and/or Gridlines to help you. You can also specify a precise position in the Position settings of the Format Video task pane, or use the Align command on the Video Tools Format tab to align the clip with other clips or with the slide itself.

Take Note The Align command works only if you are aligning similar objects. In the preceding exercise, you could not have aligned the text box and the video clip with one another using the Align command because when you select both objects, the Video Tools Format tab is no longer available, and that is where the Align command resides.

Compressing Media

CERTIFICATION READY? 5.3.4

How do you compress media?

If you plan on sharing a presentation that contains audio and video clips, you may want to compress the media in the presentation to make the overall file size smaller. This mode of compression is similar to the Compress Pictures command for graphics, but it works with video and audio files. You can choose high, medium, or low quality, depending on how you plan to use the presentation file. In the following exercise, you will compress media in a presentation.

STEP BY STEP   **Compress Media**

USE the *Lobby Final Version 3* presentation that is still open from the previous exercise.

    1. Click the **File** tab.
    2. Click **Compress Media**. A menu opens showing three choices for media quality (see Figure 9-26).

Figure 9-26

Compress media according to the usage you intend

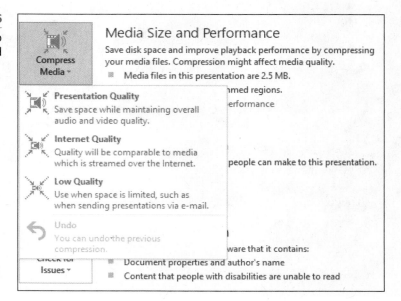

3. Click Internet Quality. The Compress Media dialog box opens, showing the progress of compressing each clip.

4. When each clip shows Complete, click Close.

EXIT PowerPoint, saving your changes.

SKILL SUMMARY

In This Lesson, You Learned How To:	Exam Objective	Objective Number
Set Up Slide Transitions	Insert transitions between slides.	4.1.1
	Modify transition effect options.	4.1.3
	Modify duration of effects.	4.3.1
	Manage multiple transitions.	4.1.2
Animate Slide Content	Apply animations to text strings.	4.2.2
	Add paths to animations.	4.2.3
	Modify animation options.	4.2.4
	Configure start and finish options.	4.3.2
	Apply animations to shapes.	4.2.1
	Demonstrate how to use the Animation pane.	4.3.4
	Reorder animations.	4.3.3
Add Media Clips to a Presentation	Set media options.	3.6.4
	Trim timing on media clips.	3.6.2
	Set start/stop times.	3.6.3
	Adjust media window size.	3.6.1
	Compress media.	5.3.4

Knowledge Assessment

Matching

Match the term in Column 1 to its description in Column 2.

Column 1	Column 2
1. Exit effect	a. Feature that enables you to copy animation effects
2. Emphasis effect	b. A sound clip
3. Motion path	c. The time between the previous and the current animation event
4. Transition	d. The time that an animation event takes to execute
5. Delay	e. An animation effect that moves an object along a predefined path that you create for it
6. Duration	f. An entrance effect that applies to an entire slide
7. Animations	g. The Ribbon tab from which you apply motion effects to individual objects

8. Entrance effect

9. Animation Painter

10. Audio

h. An animation effect that determines how an object appears on a slide

i. An animation effect that determines how an object exits a slide

j. An animation effect that draws attention to an object on a slide that is neither entering nor exiting the slide

True/False

Circle T if the statement is true or F if the statement is false.

T F 1. A transition can be applied to a specific object on a slide.

T F 2. You can assign your own sound clips to slide transitions.

T F 3. You can set up both transitions and animations from the Animations tab.

T F 4. Not all transition and animation effects have Effect Options you can set.

T F 5. An emphasis effect is a good way to draw audience attention to an object as it exits the slide.

T F 6. To reverse the order of text animation in a text box, click Effect Options and click Reverse Path Direction.

T F 7. An animation set to With Previous begins executing at the same time as the previous animation effect begins.

T F 8. To slow down the speed of an animation effect, increase its Duration setting.

T F 9. If you double-click the Animation Painter button, the feature stays on until you turn it off.

T F 10. You can insert audio and video clips from the Clip Art task pane.

Competency Assessment

Project 9-1: Make It Self-Running

You have been asked by Woodgrove Bank to modify a presentation that was originally designed to be used with a live speaker to a self-running presentation in which no user interaction is required. To accomplish this, you need to set all the slide transitions to occur automatically. You should also set up a more interesting transition effect than the default.

GET READY. LAUNCH PowerPoint if it is not already running.

1. **OPEN** the *Jobs* presentation and save it as *Jobs Final*.
2. On the Transitions tab, mark the After check box.
3. Click the up increment arrow for the After box until the value is 00:08.00.
4. In the Transition to This Slide group, select the Push transition. You might need to click the More button to locate it.
5. Click Effect Options, and click From Left.
6. Click the down increment arrow for the Duration box twice to set the duration to 00.50.
7. Click Apply to All.
8. On the Slide Show tab, click From Beginning, and watch the entire slide show by clicking the mouse to advance through each slide.
9. **SAVE** the presentation.

LEAVE the presentation open for use in the next project.

Project 9-2: Animate It

You have decided to add some object animations to the Woodgrove Bank presentation to make it more eye-catching.

1. **USE** the *Jobs Final* presentation from the last exercise, or OPEN the *Jobs 2* presentation and **SAVE** it as *Jobs Final*.
2. Go to slide 1, and select the subtitle (Central City Job Fair).
3. On the Animations tab, click Add Animation, and in the Entrance section, click Swivel.
4. Go to slide 2, and select the photo.
5. Click Add Animation, and in the Emphasis section, click Pulse.
6. Open the Start drop-down list and click After Previous.
7. Click the up increment arrow on the Duration box until the duration is 02.00.
8. Select the text box containing the bulleted list.
9. Click Add Animation, and click More Entrance Effects.
10. In the Subtle section, click Expand, and click OK.
11. Open the Start drop-down list on the Animations tab and click After Previous.
12. Click Move Earlier.
13. Click Preview to preview the slide's animation.
14. **SAVE** the presentation and **CLOSE** it.

LEAVE PowerPoint open for the next project.

Proficiency Assessment

Project 9-3: Adding Sound and Animation

You are teaching a computer basics class and have developed a slide that explains the Systems Development Life Cycle. Now you want to animate it and add some sound effects, to make it more interesting.

1. **OPEN** the *Life Cycle* presentation and save it as *Life Cycle Final*.
2. Select all five rectangles.
3. On the Animations tab, click Add Animation, and select the Grow & Turn entrance effect.
4. Open the Start drop-down list and choose On Click.
5. Display the Animation Pane.
6. Make sure all five animations are selected in the Animation Pane, right-click any of them, and then choose Effect Options from the shortcut menu.
7. In the Grow & Turn dialog box, open the Sound drop-down list and choose the Click sound, and then click OK.

8. On the Insert tab, click Audio, and then click Audio on My PC. In the Insert Audio dialog box, select *soundtrack.wav* from the data files for this lesson, and click Insert.
9. With the new sound's icon selected, on the Audio Tools Playback tab, mark the Hide During Show check box.
10. Open the Start drop-down list and choose Automatically.
11. Click the Volume button, and click Low.
12. In the Animation Pane, click the Move Up button until the audio clip is at the top of the list.
13. Switch to Slide Show view and click to move through the animations to check them.
14. **SAVE** the presentation and then **CLOSE** the file.

LEAVE PowerPoint open for the next project.

Project 9-4: Enhancing Video

You have been asked by the K-9 Agility Network to add a video clip of a dog agility performance to their marketing presentation. The video provided is not the best quality, but you can do some things in PowerPoint to make it better.

1. **OPEN** the *Agility* presentation and save it as *Agility Final*.
2. Go to slide 8, and click the Insert Video icon in the placeholder.
3. In the Insert Video dialog box, click Browse next to From a file. Navigate to the location of the data files for this lesson, select *AgilityRun.wmv*, and click Insert.

4. On the Video Tools Format tab, click Crop, and then drag the top and bottom selection handles on the clip to crop out the black bars at the top and bottom. Click away from the video to finalize the cropping when finished.
5. Click in the Height box on the Video Tools Format tab and set the height to 4.5". Let the Width setting adjust itself automatically.
6. Drag the video clip up or down on the slide to center it between the slide title and the bottom of the slide.
7. Click the Align button, and click Align Center to center the video clip on the slide.
8. Click the More button in the Video Styles group and click Beveled Rounded Rectangle in the Moderate section.
9. Click the Corrections button, and click Brightness: +20% Contrast: +40%.
10. On the Slide Show tab, clear the Show Media Controls check box.
11. Click From Current Slide, and then click the clip to start it playing. Watch the clip, and then press Esc to return to Normal view.
12. **SAVE** the presentation and then **CLOSE** the file.

LEAVE PowerPoint open for the next project.

Mastery Assessment

Project 9-5: Animating a Drawing

You are a professional trainer teaching a class on basic computer skills. You want to make the conceptual drawings and clip art images in your presentation more interesting and fun to view. You can use the PowerPoint animation tools to achieve this.

GET READY. LAUNCH PowerPoint if it is not already running.

1. **OPEN** the *Monitor* presentation and save it as *Monitor Final*.
2. Select the spray can graphic, and on the Animations tab, click Add Animation and in the Entrance section, click Fly In.
3. Click Effect Options, and click From Right.
4. Open the Start drop-down list and choose After Previous.
5. Click the spray can graphic again, then click Add Animation, and click More Motion Paths.
6. Click the Arc Down effect and click OK.
7. Open the Start drop-down list and choose After Previous.
8. Click Effect Options, and click Reverse Path Direction.
9. On the slide, drag the motion path to the left so that the green arrow (the start position) sits where the end position (the red arrow) previously was, where the spray can and the red circle meet (see Figure 9-29).

Figure 9-29

Move the motion path so the start arrow is over the spray can

Clip art used with permission from Microsoft

10. Click the red circle shape, and click Add Animation. In the Entrance section, click Fade.
11. Open the Start drop-down list and choose After Previous.
12. Click the up increment arrow on the Delay box to set the delay to 02.00.
13. Click Preview to preview the animation.
14. **SAVE** the presentation and then **CLOSE** the file.

LEAVE PowerPoint open for the next project.

Project 9-6: Animating SmartArt

Northwind Paper has a presentation about how paper is made, and the presentation includes a SmartArt diagram. You will apply transitions to each slide and animate the SmartArt diagram so that each part of the diagram appears on a separate mouse click.

GET READY. LAUNCH PowerPoint if it is not already running.

1. **OPEN** the *Paper Making* presentation and save it as *Paper Making Final*.
2. From the Transitions tab, apply the Box transition effect to all slides with a duration of 02.00.
3. Go to slide 4, and from the Animations tab, apply the Fade entrance effect to the SmartArt object.
4. Click Effect Options, and choose One by One.
5. Display the Animation Pane if it is not already displayed.

Take Note   Notice that there are more animation effects listed than there are boxes on the diagram; that is because the arrows that connect each box are animated along with the box to which they correspond.

6. Add an Object Color emphasis effect to the entire SmartArt diagram, and set its Start setting to After Previous.
7. Delete the color-changing emphasis effect for the Paper box (the last emphasis effect on the list).
8. Click Preview to preview the slide's animation.
9. Delete the color-changing emphasis effects for each of the three arrows.
10. Watch the slide's animation in Slide Show view to check the animation.
11. **SAVE** the presentation and then **CLOSE** the file.

EXIT PowerPoint.

Circling Back 2

You are a managing editor at Lucerne Publishing. You are preparing for an important meeting with the senior management team, and you are producing a presentation that should serve two purposes: to show how you intend to grow the publishing plan for the coming year and to convince senior management to let you hire several new editors. You can use PowerPoint tools to focus attention on these two goals.

Project 1: Basic Formatting and Tables

In this project, you will open your draft presentation, apply a theme, and add both a table and an Excel worksheet to present data.

GET READY. LAUNCH PowerPoint if it is not already running.

1. **OPEN** the *Opportunities* presentation and save it as *Opportunities Final*.
2. Apply the Slice theme. Apply the orange variant. Change the theme fonts to Gill Sans MT.
3. In the header and footer, insert a date that updates automatically, and the footer Editorial Opportunities. Apply to all slides except the title slide.

   Tip: To apply to all slides except the title slide, select all slides except the title slide before opening the Header and Footer dialog box or mark the Don't show on title slide check box on the Header and Footer dialog box.
4. Display the Slide Master and make these changes to the slide master (the top master, not one of the individual layout masters):

   a. Boldface the slide titles.
   b. Change the color of the first-level bullet character to Orange, Background 2, Darker 50%. (Hint: Just change the bullet character, not the text. You can do this from the Bullets and Numbering dialog box.)
   c. Close Slide Master view.
5. Go to slide 4 and create a table that has three columns and six rows. Type the following data in the table:

Division	Current Year	Next Year
History	23	27
Science Fiction	19	23
Literature	12	16
Nonfiction	26	31
Lifestyle	38	43
6. Format the table with the Light Style 3—Accent 1 Table Style.
7. Turn off banded rows. Select the column heading cells, and fill them with Orange, Background 2.
8. Center all entries in the center and right columns. Click the Table Tools Layout contextual tab, and in the Table Size group, change the table width to 8".
9. Go to slide 3 and format the existing table to match the one you inserted on slide 4. Be sure to also change column alignment and table size.
10. Go to slide 5 and insert an Excel spreadsheet. Enlarge the object so you can see at least 7 rows and at least 3 columns. Then, starting in cell A1, type the following data in the worksheet:

Division	Current Year	Next Year
History	4.65	4.89
Science Fiction	3.77	4.01
Literature	8.92	9.15
Nonfiction	4.41	4.79
Lifestyle	3.59	3.95

11. In cell A7 of the worksheet, type Average. In cell B7, type the formula =AVERAGE(B2:B6).

12. Copy the formula in cell B7 to cell C7.

13. Format the values in cells B2:C7 as currency with two decimal places.

14. Format the worksheet as follows:

   a. Apply the Wisp theme in Excel (you will find the themes on the Page Layout tab in Excel).
   b. Select the column headers in row 1, click the Cell Styles button in the Styles group on the Excel Home tab, and select Accent2.
   c. Boldface the column headings.
   d. Center all entries in the center and right columns.
   e. Change the font of the worksheet cells to Gill Sans MT to match the text in the presentation. Change the font size to 18 pt.
   f. Adjust columns to a width of 25.
   g. Use the Borders button (in the Font group on the Home tab) to apply All Borders in the range A1:C7. Use the default color and weight.

15. Adjust the size of the worksheet's hatched selection border to hide any empty rows or columns. Click outside the worksheet to deselect it.

16. Display the drawing guides and adjust them so the vertical guide aligns with the 4.5" mark on the ruler on the left side of the slide, and the horizontal guide aligns with the 2" marker on the vertical ruler at the top of the slide.

17. On slides 3, 4, and 5, reposition the tables so that their upper-left corners align with the intersection of the guides. Then turn off the guides.

18. SAVE the presentation.

PAUSE. LEAVE PowerPoint and your presentation open for the next project.

Project 2: Charting the Data

You are now ready to create a chart that shows the editorial workload for the current year and your projections for the next year. The chart will make it easy for your audience to compare the numbers.

USE the presentation that is open from the previous project.

1. Go to slide 6, and change the layout of the slide to Title and Content.

2. Click the Insert Chart icon in the content placeholder to begin a new chart. Select the 3-D Clustered Bar chart.

3. Insert the following data in the chart worksheet:

Division	Current Year	Next Year
History	5.8	6.8
Science Fiction	6.3	7.6
Literature	4	5.3
Nonfiction	4.3	5.2
Lifestyle	5.4	6.1

4. Delete the unneeded sample data in column D and make sure the range border surrounds only the data you need for your chart. Close the worksheet.

5. Change the chart type to a 3-D Clustered Column chart.

6. Format the chart as follows:

   a. Apply Layout 4 and the Style 9 Chart Style.
   b. Change the font size of the horizontal axis labels to 16 pt.
   c. Display the primary major vertical axis gridlines.
   d. Turn off the data labels for both data series.

7. Drag the chart frame's bottom selection handle downward about one-half inch, to the 1.5" mark on the vertical ruler, to enlarge the chart.

8. Draw a text box below the chart slide title and type the text *Books per editor, based on current staffing.

9. If necessary, resize the text box so that all text is on one line, and then apply the **Intense Effect—Dark Yellow, Accent 2 Shape Style** to the text box.

10. **SAVE** the presentation.

PAUSE. LEAVE PowerPoint and your presentation open for the next project.

Project 3: **Add Diagrams**

You are ready to add SmartArt diagrams to display additional information about your organization and your department's work processes.

USE the presentation that is open from the previous project.

1. Go to slide 7 and click the **Insert a SmartArt Graphic** icon in the content placeholder to start a new SmartArt graphic.

2. Choose to create a **hierarchy diagram** that uses the **Organization Chart** design, and add text to the chart as follows:
   a. In the top-level box, type the name **Bill Bowen**, press **Enter**, and type the title **Managing Editor**.
   b. In the assistant box, type **Eva Corets**, press **Enter**, and type **Chief Editorial Assistant**.
   c. In the second-level boxes, type the following names, titles, and departments:

Jo Berry	Dan Bacon	Jun Cao
Sr. Editor	Sr. Editor	Sr. Editor
History	Science Fiction	Literature

3. Add a new shape after Jun Cao's shape, type the name **Aaron Con**, the title **Sr. Editor**, and the department **Nonfiction**. Then add a new shape after Aaron Con's shape, type the name **Debra Core**, the title **Sr. Editor**, and the department **Lifestyle**.

4. Apply the **Inset SmartArt Style** and the **Colorful Range—Accent Colors 2 to 3** color scheme in the **Colorful** category.

5. Delete **Debra Core's shape**, and then change the division information for Aaron Con's shape to **Nonfiction & Lifestyle**.

6. Boldface the text in the **top-level shape**.

7. Go to slide 8, and convert the bulleted list to a **Vertical Bullet List SmartArt graphic**.

8. Apply the **Inset SmartArt style** and a **color scheme** that matches the one you used on slide 7.

9. Change the diagram layout to the **Vertical Box List layout**.

10. Click in the Notes pane for the slide and type:
    We are rolling the production preparation phase into the copyedit phase to save production time and costs.

11. Edit the Copyedit text to read **Copyedit and Production**, and then **delete the Production item** from the graphic.

12. **SAVE** the presentation.

PAUSE. LEAVE PowerPoint and your presentation open for the next project.

Project 4: **Insert and Format a Picture**

Now insert additional visual interest in the form of a picture. You will format the picture to improve its appearance.

USE the presentation that is open from the previous project.

1. Go to slide 2, and click the **Online Pictures** icon in the content placeholder to open the Insert Pictures dialog box.

2. Use the keyword **award** to search for a photograph of a **trophy**. If you do not find a silver trophy on a white background in your results, insert the picture *Award.jpg* in the placeholder.

3. Adjust the picture's **brightness to +10%** and **contrast to +20%**.

4. Apply the Perspective Shadow, White Picture Style, and then click Picture Border and select Green, Accent 4, Lighter 40%.

5. Move the picture to the right so that its right edge aligns with the left 0.5" mark on the horizontal ruler. (Use a guide to help you. If you cannot get the picture to align precisely with the guide, try holding down the Alt key as you drag it.)

6. Compress pictures in the presentation to the Screen setting.

7. **SAVE** the presentation.

PAUSE. LEAVE PowerPoint and your presentation open for the next project.

Project 5: Add a Drawing and Finalize the Presentation

You have been asked to suggest a new office layout to reorganize departments on the production floor. You can create a simple drawing to show the areas where each department, supporting personnel, and production will be placed.

USE the presentation that is open from the previous project.

1. Add a new slide after slide 7 with the Title Only layout. Type the slide title Revised Office Layout.

2. Create the drawing objects shown in Figure 1. You can choose your own sizes for objects, but they should be similar in scale to the ones shown.

Figure 1

Create these shapes

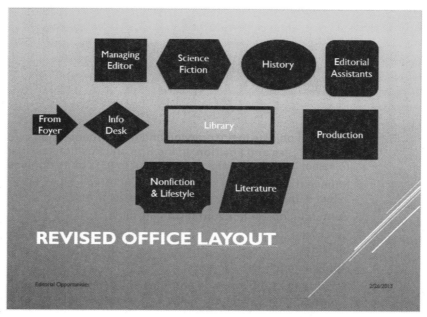

3. Modify your drawing as follows:

   a. Make all the department objects—the shapes for Nonfiction & Lifestyle, Literature, Science Fiction, and History—the same dimensions, even though they are different shapes; that is, they should all be the same height and width. For example, the ones in Figure 1 are 1.25" high and 1.8" wide. Make sure all text displays without breaking after resizing.

   b. Align the Info Desk and Library shapes to the middle of the block arrow. These three shapes will create a central area for the layout and should all be aligned middle with one another.

   c. Rotate the Editorial Assistants shape 90 degrees to the right. The text is now rotated, too.

   d. Use the Text Direction tool on the Home tab to rotate the text 270 degrees so it is once again running in its normal direction. Widen the shape slightly if needed to make the word Assistants fit on one line.

e. Align the Managing Editor, Science Fiction, History, and Editorial Assistants shapes by their tops. Align the Nonfiction & Lifestyle and Literature shapes by their bottoms. Align the Editorial Assistants and Production shapes by their right sides.

f. Distribute the top four shapes horizontally.

g. Make any other adjustments you think necessary to improve the look of the layout.

4. Apply colors and effects or Shape Styles to the shapes as desired to improve its appearance. Give each shape a unique look. Figure 2 shows one possible result.

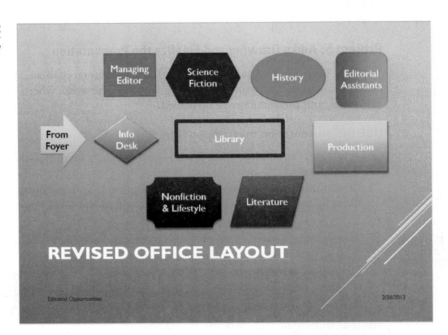

Figure 2

Format each shape differently

5. Select all objects in the drawing and group them. Right-click any shape in the group and click Size and Position. In the Size and Position task pane, click Lock aspect ratio to select it, and scale the group object to 95% of its original size.

6. If the text in any of the shapes runs over after scaling, click the shape in the group to select it and slightly widen the shape size or reduce the font size to fit the text.

7. Center the object horizontally on the slide.

8. Select the Curtains slide transition, choose 01.50 as the Duration, and apply it to all slides.

9. Apply animations as follows:

a. On slide 2, apply a Fade entrance animation to display the bullet items by first-level paragraphs. Then modify the first bullet's animation to occur After Previous. (The other bullets should remain set to On Click.) Set the duration to 01.00 for each bullet point's entrance.

b. Animate the organization chart on slide 7 to use a Fade entrance effect starting After Previous. Use the Effect Options dialog box to specify that the graphic displays by Level One by One.

c. Click the group on slide 8 to select it, and then apply the Diamond entrance animation starting After Previous.

d. Apply a Darken emphasis effect to the Books per editor text box at the bottom of slide 6. Set it to occur After Previous, and set the Duration to 02.00.

10. Run the presentation in Slide Show view. Then return to Normal view and make any corrections you think necessary to the animations.

11. PRINT the presentation as handouts in grayscale mode.

12. SAVE and CLOSE the presentation.

EXIT PowerPoint.

Securing and Sharing a Presentation 10

LESSON SKILL MATRIX

Skill	Exam Objective	Objective Number
Working with Comments	Manage comments.	5.2.4
Incorporating Reviewer Changes	Merge multiple presentations.	5.1.1
	Use the Reviewing/Revisions Pane.	5.2.1
	Compare revisions.	5.2.2
	Manage changes.	5.2.3
Protecting a Presentation	Encrypt presentations with a password.	5.3.1
	Restrict permissions.	5.3.6
	Mark as final.	5.3.3
Preparing a Presentation for Distribution	Maintain backward compatibility.	1.4.7
	Check for compatibility issues.	5.3.9
	Check for accessibility issues.	5.3.8
	Modify presentation properties.	1.3.4
	Remove presentation metadata.	5.3.7
Saving a Presentation in Different Formats	Save Presentations as XML.	1.4.4

KEY TERMS

- accessible
- comment
- encrypting
- MPEG-4 Video (mp4)
- Mark as Final
- Markup
- metadata
- null string
- OpenDocument
- password
- PDF
- picture presentation
- platform-independent
- PowerPoint Show
- Rich Text Format (rtf)
- Windows Media Video (wmv)
- XPS
- XPS Viewer

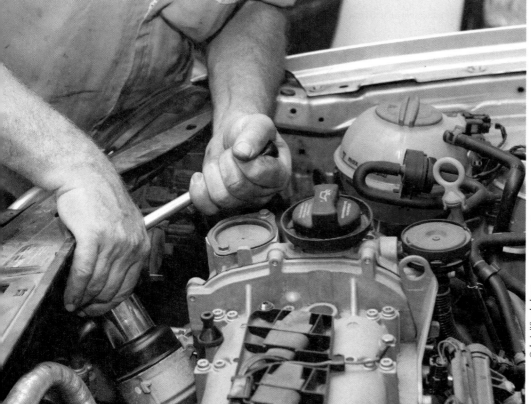
©choja/iStockphoto

©choja/iStockphoto

You are the Human Resources Director for Contoso, Ltd., a large company that manufactures automotive parts. You must give a 30-minute presentation to senior management and prominent shareholders during the company's annual operations review. You have asked a colleague to give you some feedback, and she has inserted comments that you need to address. You will add some comments of your own before finalizing the presentation and sharing them with the Vice President for Operations, who has promised to look over the slides before you present them. You can use PowerPoint to handle chores such as viewing and working with comments, password-protecting a file, comparing and combining versions, and saving the presentation in different formats for the various audiences that will be reviewing it, including a video format for people who might not have PowerPoint at all.

SOFTWARE ORIENTATION

The PowerPoint Review Tab

Tools on the Review tab make it easy for you to add comments to a slide. Figure 10-1 shows the Review tab.

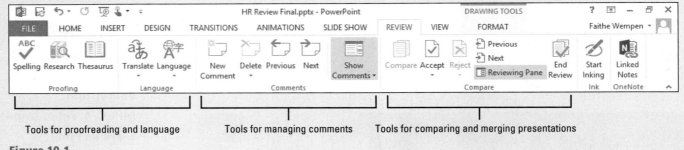

Tools for proofreading and language   Tools for managing comments   Tools for comparing and merging presentations

Figure 10-1
The Review tab

Besides allowing you to add comments, the Review tab lets you check spelling, access references such as encyclopedias, use a thesaurus, translate a word or phrase, or set the current language.

WORKING WITH COMMENTS

The Bottom Line

A **comment** is a note you insert on a slide. You can insert comments on slides to suggest content changes, add reminders, or solicit feedback. Use comments on your own presentations or on presentations you are reviewing for others. You can also let other people review your presentations and add comments addressed to you. The PowerPoint Review tab makes it easy to view, insert, edit, and delete comments.

Viewing Comments

Use the Show Comments button on the Review tab to show or hide comments. Clicking the button itself shows or hides the Comments task pane; clicking the arrow beneath the button opens a menu. On that menu you can select Show Markup to show or hide the comment balloons in the presentation itself, regardless whether the Comments pane is displayed or not. (**Markup** refers to both comments and marked changes in the file, but in this section we deal only with comments.) The Next and Previous buttons make it easy to jump from comment to comment in a presentation. In this exercise, you view the comments in a presentation.

STEP BY STEP	**View Comments**

GET READY. Before you begin these steps, make sure that your computer is on. Log on, if necessary.

1. **START** PowerPoint, if the program is not already running.
2. Locate and open the *HR Review* presentation and save it as *HR Review Final Version 1*.
3. Note the small balloon icon in the upper-left corner of slide 1 (see Figure 10-2).

Figure 10-2

A comment balloon indicates a comment on the slide

Comment balloon ➞

4. Click the Review tab, click the down arrow below Show Comments, and then click Show Markup. The comment balloon is hidden.
5. Repeat step 4 to redisplay the comment balloon.
6. Click the Show Comments button (the button face, not the arrow below it). The Comments pane appears.
7. Read the comment in the Comments pane (see Figure 10-3).

Another Way
Another way to display the Comments pane is to click a comment balloon. You can also click the word *Comments* in the status bar.

Figure 10-3

View comments in the
Comments pane

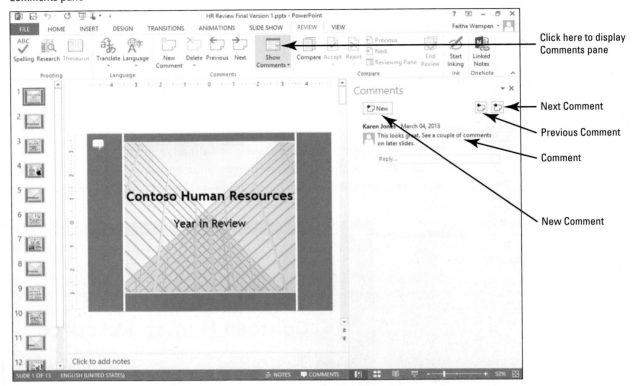

Click here to display
Comments pane

Next Comment

Previous Comment

Comment

New Comment

Another Way
You can also go to
the next comment by clicking
the Next button at the top of
the Comments pane.

8. On the Review tab, in the Comments group, click Next. The next comment appears, which is on slide 9. In this comment, Karen Jones suggests adjusting the diagram.

9. Click the SmartArt graphic, click the SmartArt Tools Design tab, click the More button in the SmartArt Styles group, and then click Metallic Scene. Click Change Colors, and click Gradient Loop-Accent 6. The diagram now has the "pop" Ms. Jones suggested (see Figure 10-4).

Figure 10-4

The revised diagram

10. Select the comment in the Comments pane, and then click the Next button at the top of the Comments pane to go to the next comment.
11. Click the Previous button twice to return to the first comment on slide 1.
12. Close the Comments pane. To do so, either click the Close button on the Comments pane or click the Show Comments button on the Review tab.
13. **SAVE** the presentation.

PAUSE. LEAVE the presentation open to use in the next exercise.

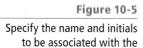

CERTIFICATION READY? 5.2.4

How do you manage comments?

The full name of the person who inserted the comment displays in the Comments pane, along with the date on which the comment was inserted (unless the comment was inserted today, in which case it shows the time that has elapsed since the comment was made).

Inserting a Comment

To add a comment to a slide, use the New Comment button on the Review tab. Comment markers are color-coded, so that if more than one reviewer adds comments, it is easy for you to identify the commenter simply by color. Comments are numbered consecutively as they are inserted, regardless of the order of slides. If you insert your first comment on slide 5, it will be numbered 1. If you insert your second comment on slide 1, it will be numbered 2. In this exercise, you will insert a comment in a presentation.

STEP BY STEP   **Insert a Comment**

USE the *HR Review Final Version 1* presentation that is still open from the previous exercise. You are now ready to add your own comments to the presentation, which you are going to send to the Vice President for Operations.

1. Click the File tab, and click Options. The PowerPoint Options dialog box opens.
2. Enter your own name and initials in the User Name and Initials boxes (see Figure 10-5). Then click OK to accept them.

Figure 10-5

Specify the name and initials to be associated with the comments you will enter

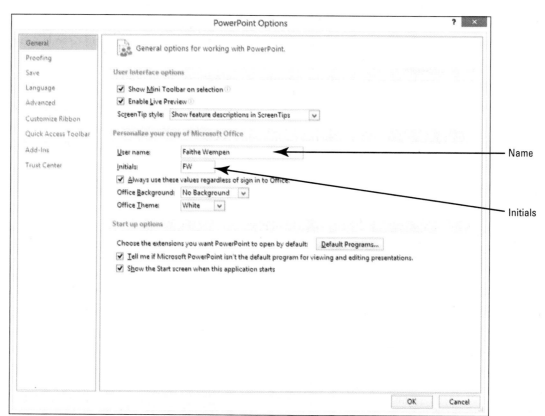

Figure 10-6

A new comment box ready for you to type a comment

3. With slide 1 displayed, click the New Comment button on the Review tab. The Comments task pane appears and a new comment text box opens there (see Figure 10-6).

You can drag the icon to reposition it on slide   New Comment buttons

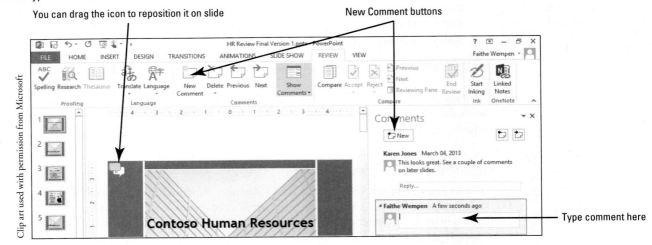

Type comment here

Clip art used with permission from Microsoft

4. Type the following text in the comment box:

Peter, I have already received feedback from Karen Jones. Please suggest any further changes you think necessary to make this a dynamite presentation.

5. Click outside the comment box. Your comment marker displays in the upper left corner of the slide, slightly overlapping the other comment marker.

6. Go to slide 10, and select the text 6 weeks in the third bullet.

Take Note   If you select text or an object on a slide before creating a new comment, the comment balloon appears adjacent to the selection. If you do not select anything beforehand, the comment balloon appears in the upper left corner of the slide.

7. Click the New button on the Comments task pane.

Another Way
You can use the New Comment button on the Review tab instead of the New button in the Comments pane if you prefer.

8. Type the following text in the comment box:

Peter, please see Karen's comment on this slide. I don't have access to the Design department schedule. Can you confirm the lag time is now only 4 to 5 weeks?

9. Click outside the comment box to see the entire comment.

10. Drag the comment balloon to move it so it slightly overlaps the other comment balloon on this slide. Moving a comment marker allows you to associate the comment with a specific area of the slide, such as a picture or a bullet item, or to place it in a general location.

11. Close the Comments pane.

12. **SAVE** the presentation.

PAUSE. LEAVE the presentation open to use in the next exercise.

Editing a Comment

Like any other text in a presentation, comment text should be clear and concise. If you find upon review that your comments do not convey the information they should, you can reword, insert, or delete text in the comment box. Use the Edit Comment button to open a comment box so you can modify the text. In this exercise, you edit a comment.

STEP BY STEP   **Edit a Comment**

USE the *HR Review Final Version 1* presentation that is still open from the previous exercise.

1. Go to slide 1 and click one of the comment balloons. The Comments pane reopens.

2. Click in the comment you typed in the previous exercise, select the text *to make this a dynamite presentation* at the end of the second sentence, and then press Delete. You have removed text from the comment. Figure 10-7 shows the edited comment.

Figure 10-7

Edit the comment

3. **SAVE** the presentation.

PAUSE. LEAVE the presentation open to use in the next exercise.

Deleting a Comment

You can easily remove comments from slides when they are no longer needed. If you point to a comment in the Comments pane, a Delete icon (X) appears in its upper right corner. You can click that X to remove the individual comment. You can also use the Delete button on the Review tab to remove a comment. To quickly remove all comments, click the down arrow under the Delete button to open a menu from which you can quickly delete all comments on this slide or in this entire presentation. In this exercise, you will delete a comment.

STEP BY STEP   **Delete a Comment**

USE the *HR Review Final Version 1* presentation that is still open from the previous exercise.

1. With slide 1 displayed, click Karen Jones's first comment in the Comments pane, then click the Delete icon in the upper right corner of the comment. The comment is removed from the slide, leaving only your first comment.

2. Go to slide 9 and click the comment in the task pane.

3. Click the Delete button on the Review tab. The comment is removed from the slide.

4. Close the Comments pane.

5. **SAVE** the presentation.

PAUSE. LEAVE the presentation open to use in the next exercise.

INCORPORATING CHANGES FROM REVIEWERS

The Bottom Line

PowerPoint does not have a Track Changes feature like the one in Word, but you can receive comments and feedback from reviewers by first saving your presentation to your computer, and then posting a second copy to a shared location such as SkyDrive or SharePoint, or distributing copies to reviewers via email. You can ask people to make changes and add comments to the shared copy. Once they are done, you can compare and merge the shared copy with the original one saved to your computer.

Comparing and Combining Multiple Presentations

Comparing presentations enables you to see the differences between two similar presentation files. You can easily identify the changes that have been made to a copy of a presentation. The Compare feature merges two presentation files. You then can use the Revisions pane and the Compare group on the Review tab to see what differences exist between the merged versions and either accept or reject each revision. When you mark a revision for acceptance or rejection, the change is not applied immediately; changes occur only when you click End Review. In this exercise, you compare and combine two presentations.

STEP BY STEP **Compare and Combine Presentations**

USE the *HR Review Final Version 1* presentation that is still open from the previous exercise. Save the file as a new file named *HR Review Final Version 2*.

1. On the Review tab, click **Compare**. The Choose File to Merge with Current Presentation dialog box opens.
2. Navigate to the **folder containing the data files** for this lesson and select *HR Summary* (see Figure 10-8).

Figure 10-8

Select the presentation to merge with the current one

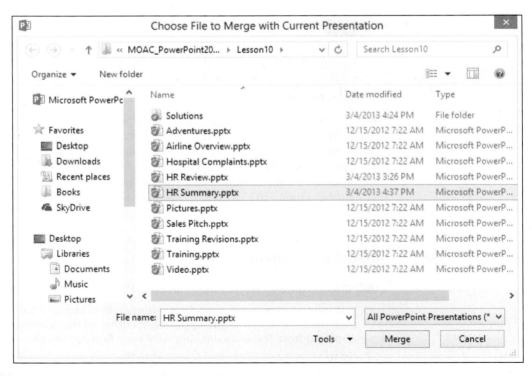

CERTIFICATION READY? **5.1.1**

How do you merge multiple presentations?

3. Click **Merge**. The presentation opens, and the Comments and the Revisions task panes open. Tip: To toggle the Revisions task pane on and off, you can click the Reviewing Pane button on the Review tab of the Ribbon.

Figure 10-9

Review the changes made to this slide

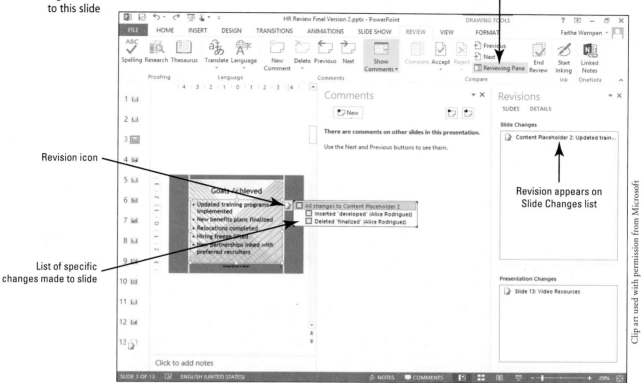

Display/hide the Revisions pane by clicking the Reviewing Pane button

Revision icon

Revision appears on Slide Changes list

List of specific changes made to slide

4. Go to slide 3 and click the revision icon on the slide. A balloon appears showing the changes to that slide (see Figure 10-9).

5. On the Review tab, click the Accept button. The changes on slide 3 are accepted. The revision icon changes to show a check mark.

6. Click the Next button in the Compare group. The next revision appears. It is a change from 12% to 10% on slide 6.

Take Note Do not confuse the Next button in the Compare group with the Next button in the Comments group.

CERTIFICATION READY? 5.2.1

How do you use the Reviewing/Revisions pane?

7. Click the Accept button, and then click Next. The next revision appears. The changes made to the SmartArt appear.

8. Click the Accept button, and then click Next. The next revision appears. It is a deletion of a bullet point. Click Accept, and then click Reject to change your mind.

9. Click Next. A message appears that you have reached the end of the changes. Click Cancel.

10. On the Review tab, click End Review. A confirmation box appears; click Yes.

CERTIFICATION READY? 5.2.2

How do you compare revisions?

11. Browse through the presentation to confirm that the changes were made. The revisions you accepted were finalized, and the revision you rejected was discarded. The comments are still there; they were not affected by the review.

12. On the Review tab, click the down arrow under the Delete button and click Delete All Comments and Ink in This Presentation.

13. Click Yes to confirm. All remaining comments are removed.

14. Close the Comments pane.

CERTIFICATION READY? 5.2.3

How do you manage changes?

15. SAVE the presentation.

PAUSE. LEAVE the presentation open to use in the next exercise.

PROTECTING A PRESENTATION

The Bottom Line

Password-protecting a presentation file ensures that unauthorized users cannot view or make changes to it. You can set, change, and remove passwords from a file. You can also mark a presentation as final, which does not provide much security, but can prevent accidental changes.

Encrypting Presentations with a Password

A **password** is a word or phrase that you, the user, must enter in order to get access to a file. Adding a password to a presentation prevents anyone from opening the presentation who does not know the password. Passwords are case-sensitive. You will assign a password to a presentation in this exercise.

STEP BY STEP	**Set a Password**

USE the *HR Review Final Version 2* presentation that is still open from the previous exercise. Save the presentation as a new file named *HR Review Final Version 3*.

1. Click the **File** tab, and click **Protect Presentation**. A menu appears.
2. Click **Encrypt with Password**. The Encrypt Document dialog box opens.
3. In the Password box, type **ProtectMe**. Black circles appear in place of the actual characters you type (see Figure 10-10).

Take Note   The password used for this exercise is not a very strong password. It would not be that difficult to guess, because it consists only of letters. When creating your own passwords, try to include a combination of uppercase letters, lowercase letters, numbers, symbols, and spaces.

Figure 10-10

The Encrypt Document dialog box

4. Click **OK**. Another dialog box appears asking you to confirm the password; type **ProtectMe** again and click **OK** again.
5. Click the **File** tab if needed to reopen Backstage view, and click **Close**. When prompted to save your changes, click **Save**.
6. Click the **File** tab, click **Open**, and on the Recent Presentations list, click the **HR Review Final Version 3.pptx** document. A Password dialog box opens.
7. In the Password box, type **ProtectMe** and click **OK** (see Figure 10-11).

Figure 10-11

The Password dialog box

Password	?	×
Enter password to open file		
HR Review Final Version 3.pptx		
Password: ********		
	OK	Cancel

8. **SAVE** the presentation.

PAUSE. LEAVE the presentation open to use in the next exercise.

CERTIFICATION READY?   **5.3.1**
How do you encrypt a presentation with a password?

Password-protecting a file is a type of **encrypting**, which prevents a file from being read by unauthorized users. Password-protection might be useful on a presentation that contains sensitive data, such as human resources or medical information. If a user does not know the password, he or she cannot open the file.

Another Way

If you want to prevent a file from being changed, but you do not mind it being opened by anyone, you can set the password in a different way. Click the File tab and click Save As. Click Browse to open the Save As dialog box, and then at the bottom of the dialog box, click Tools to open a menu, and click General Options. In the dialog box that appears, there are boxes for Password to Open (which is the same as the password you learned to set in the preceding steps) and Password to Modify. If you set a Password to Modify here, and there is no Password to Open assigned, anyone will be able to open the file, but only those who know the password will be able to make and save changes.

When choosing a password, try to think of one that is easy for you to remember but difficult for others to guess. For example, you might use the name of a family pet with a number substituted for one or more of the characters or a combination of the street name and ZIP code you had as a child.

CERTIFICATION READY? 5.3.6

How do you restrict permissions?

For more control over who views your presentation and what they can do with it, you may choose to use the Restrict Access command. Click the File tab, click Protect Presentation, point to Restrict Access, and then click Connect to Rights Management Servers and Get Templates. To use this feature you must have Windows Rights Management access. Contact your employer's IT department to find out if you have access to this feature.

Changing or Removing a Password

You can change a password in much the same way as you created it. To remove a password entirely, use the same process as for changing it, but change it to a **null string** (blank, no characters, not even spaces). In this exercise, you will remove a password from a presentation.

STEP BY STEP | **Change or Remove a Password**

USE the *HR Review Final Version 3* presentation that is still open from the previous exercise.

1. Click the File tab, and click Protect Presentation. A menu appears.
2. Click Encrypt with Password. The Encrypt Document dialog box opens. The password previously assigned is already filled in.
3. Double-click the current password and press the Delete key on the keyboard to clear it.

Take Note In step 3, you could have entered a different password instead of removing the password entirely.

4. Click OK. The password has been removed.
5. Close the presentation and reopen it to confirm that no password prompt appears.

PAUSE. LEAVE the presentation open to use in the next exercise.

Marking a Presentation as Final

When you have completed all work on a presentation, you can mark it as final to prevent any further editing. When you use the **Mark as Final** command in a presentation, you can open the presentation and read it, but you can no longer edit it or add comments. You are also restricted in other activities, such as encrypting the document. For this reason, marking a presentation as final should be one of your last tasks when finalizing a presentation. In this exercise, you mark a presentation as final.

STEP BY STEP | **Mark a Presentation as Final**

USE the *HR Review Final Version 3* presentation that is still open from the previous exercise.

CERTIFICATION READY? 5.3.3

How do you mark a presentation as final?

1. Click the File tab, click Protect Presentation, and click Mark as Final. A confirmation box appears that it will be marked as final and then saved.
2. Click OK to continue. A confirmation box appears that it has been marked as final.
3. Click OK to close the confirmation box. Notice that the Ribbon is hidden; an information bar appears with a message that the file is Marked as Final (see Figure 10-12).

Figure 10-12

The presentation has been
marked as final

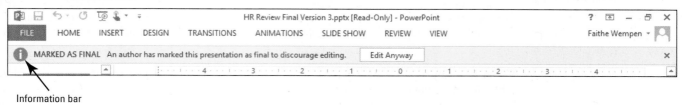

Information bar

4. Click **Edit Anyway**. The editing commands on the Ribbon are displayed again.

5. **SAVE** the presentation.

PAUSE. LEAVE the presentation open to use in the next exercise.

Marking a presentation as final does not prevent you from ever making additional changes to a presentation. You can reverse the Mark as Final command by clicking Edit Anyway on the information bar. All features are then available to you again.

PREPARING A PRESENTATION FOR DISTRIBUTION

The Bottom Line

As you are preparing to distribute your presentation to other people, there are some issues to consider. For example, if the person working with your presentation uses a different version of PowerPoint than you have, will he or she still have access to all the content? Will personal information from your computer be stored in the data file's properties? In the following sections you will learn how to control these and other factors.

Checking for Compatibility Issues and Optimizing Media Compatibility

If you need to share your presentation file with someone who uses PowerPoint 2003 or earlier, save it in PowerPoint 97-2003 format from the Save As dialog box, as you learned to do in "Choosing a Different File Format" in Lesson 2. The file format is the same for PowerPoint versions 2007, 2010, and 2013, so if you need to share your work with people who use one of those versions, no special translation is usually required for the user to open and view the presentation.

CERTIFICATION READY? 1.4.7

How do you maintain backward compatibility?

There are some minor compatibility issues among PowerPoint 2007, 2010, and 2013, however, and these issues may not be obvious until a user tries to use your file and encounters an error or a feature that does not work as it should. For example, PowerPoint 2013 supports more video formats than PowerPoint 2007 and 2010 did, so if the presentation includes one of the formats that their version of PowerPoint cannot use, you may have a problem. To minimize the impact of such compatibility issues, you may want to check the file for compatibility problems prior to distributing it. The Compatibility Checker will recommend fixes that will help you minimize the impact of any compatibility issues.

CERTIFICATION READY? 5.3.9

How do you check for compatibility issues?

In this exercise, you will check a presentation for compatibility issues, and then save it in PowerPoint 97-2003 format. This exercise uses not only the HR Review Final presentation that you have been working with, but also a presentation file that you worked with in Lesson 9, which has a video clip in it, so you can see how to optimize media compatibility as well as overall compatibility.

STEP BY STEP   **Check for Compatibility Issues and Optimize Media Compatibility**

USE the *HR Review Final Version 3* presentation that is still open from the previous exercise. Save the file as a new file named *HR Review Final Version 4*.

1. Click the File tab, and then click Check for Issues. A menu appears.

2. Click Check Compatibility. The Microsoft PowerPoint Compatibility Checker dialog box opens. It has found one potential issue (see Figure 10-13).

Figure 10-13

The Compatibility Checker has noted that SmartArt cannot be edited in Office versions earlier than 2007

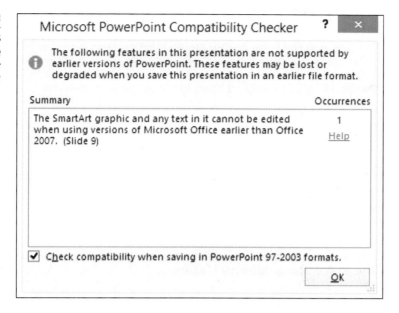

3. Click OK. The dialog box closes.

4. Click the video on slide 13 and press the Delete key to remove it.

5. Save the presentation file. Leave it open to use in the next exercise.

6. Open the file *Agility Media* from the data files provided for this lesson, and save it as *Agility Media Final*.

7. Click the File tab. Notice that the Optimize Compatibility button appears, and is available. That is because this presentation contains an actual embedded video clip, not just a link to an online clip.

8. Click Optimize Compatibility. The Optimize Media Compatibility dialog box opens and immediately begins processing the video clip in the presentation to improve its compatibility. Figure 10-14 shows this processing in progress.

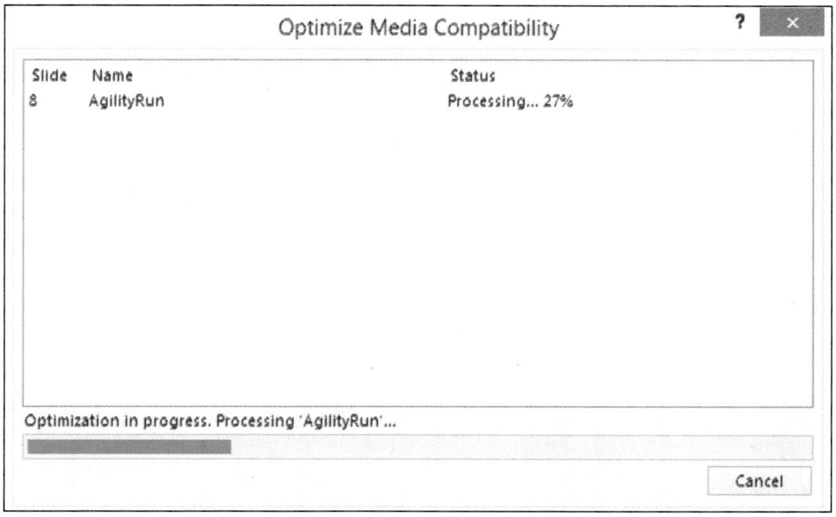

Figure 10-14

The media clip is automatically optimized

Optimize Media Compatibility

Slide	Name	Status
8	AgilityRun	Processing... 27%

Optimization in progress. Processing 'AgilityRun'...

Cancel

9. When the optimization is complete, click Close.

10. If necessary, click the File tab, click Check for Issues, and click Check Compatibility. The Microsoft PowerPoint Compatibility Checker dialog box opens.

11. Note the compatibility issue that the checker found: that the media clips will be saved as pictures.

12. Click OK to close the dialog box.

13. Save and close the Agility Media Final presentation. Leave the HR Review Final Version 4 file open.

PAUSE. LEAVE PowerPoint open to use in the next exercise.

Checking for Accessibility Issues

An **accessible** presentation is one that can be viewed by a wide variety of computer users, including those who may have disabilities that require them to use adaptive technologies such as screen reading programs. PowerPoint includes a command that checks the accessibility of your work and offers suggestions for improving it. In this exercise, you will check a presentation for accessibility issues and make corrections to it.

STEP BY STEP **Check for Accessibility Issues**

USE the *HR Review Final Version 4* presentation that is still open from the previous exercise.

1. Click the File tab, click Check for Issues, and click Check Accessibility. The Accessibility Checker pane opens (see Figure 10-15).

Figure 10-15

Accessibility issues were found

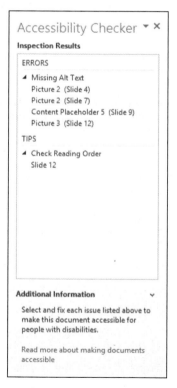

2. In the Accessibility Checker task pane, click Picture 2 (Slide 4). Slide 4 appears and the picture is selected.

Take Note You can scroll down in the Additional Information area of the task pane to find steps for fixing the problem.

3. Do the following to add alt text to the picture:
   a. **Right-click** the picture and choose **Format Picture**.
   b. Click the **Size & Properties** icon at the top of the Format Picture task pane.
   c. If needed, click **Alt Text** to expand that heading's options.
   d. In the Title box, type **Smiling businessman**.
4. Repeat **steps 2-3** for Picture 2 on slide 7. (You can skip steps 3a through 3c because the Format Shape task pane is already open.) For its alt text, type **Balance scale**.
5. Repeat **steps 2-3** for Picture 3 on slide 12. (You can skip steps 3a through 3c because the Format Shape task pane is already open.) For its alt text, type **Woman writing**.
6. Do the following to add alt text to the SmartArt graphic on slide 9:
   a. In the Accessibility Checker task pane, click **Content Placeholder 5 (Slide 9)** to jump to slide 9.
   b. In the Format Shape task pane, in the Alt Text section's Title box, type **SmartArt graphic of key positions to fill**.
   c. On the SmartArt Tools Design tab, click **Text Pane** to display the text pane for the SmartArt.
   d. Select **all the text** in the text pane (**Ctrl+A**) and press **Ctrl+C** to copy it.
   e. Close the **SmartArt** text pane.
   f. Reselect the **outer frame** of the SmartArt graphic, and in the Format Shape task pane, click in the **Description** box under the Alt Text heading and press **Ctrl+V** to paste the copied text. The Format Shape task pane should resemble Figure 10-16 at this point.

Figure 10-16

Add alt text both as a title and as a description for the SmartArt object

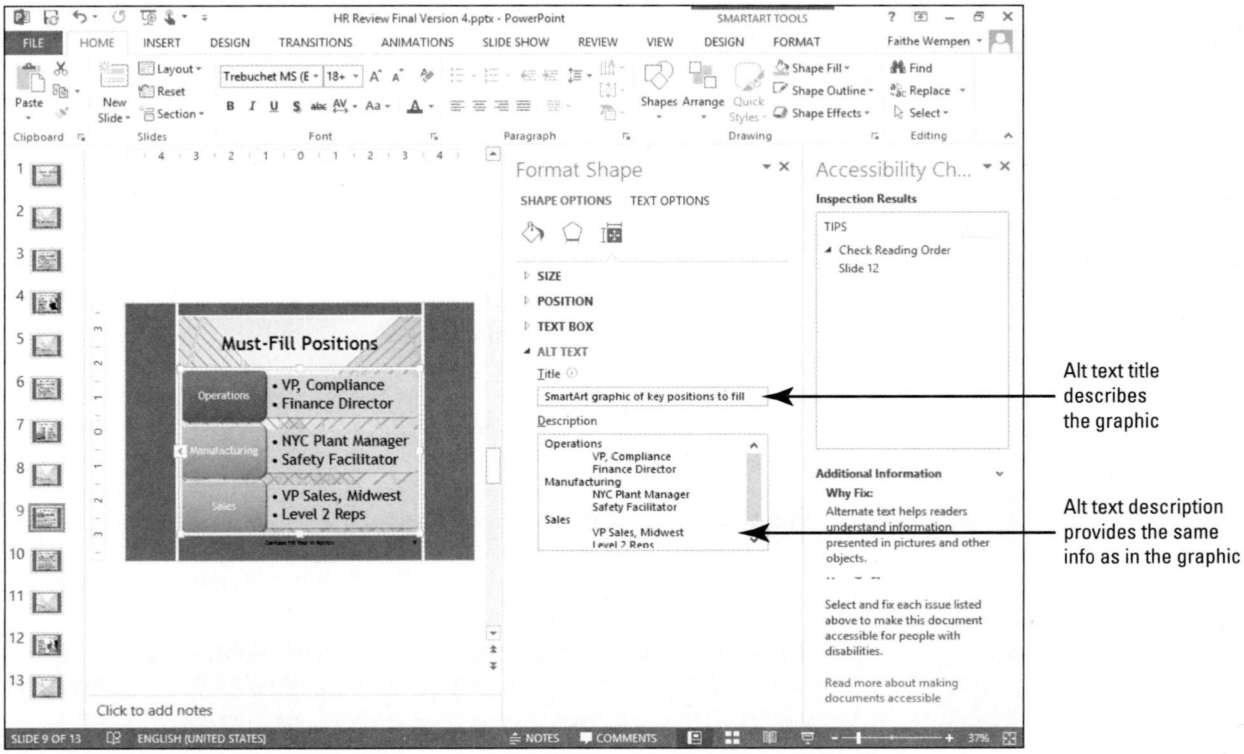

Clip art used with permission from Microsoft

7. Close the Format Shape task pane.

8. In the Accessibility Checker task pane, click Slide 12 under the Check Reading Order heading.

9. Follow the instructions in the Additional Information section of the task pane to check the reading order. Note that the slide's content is set to appear before its title.

10. On the Home tab, click the Select button, and on the menu that appears, click Selection Pane.

11. In the Selection pane, click Title 8, and then click the Bring Forward button (the up arrow button) twice so that Title 8 appears at the top of the list of objects (see Figure 10-17).

Figure 10-17

Move the slide objects in the selection task pane

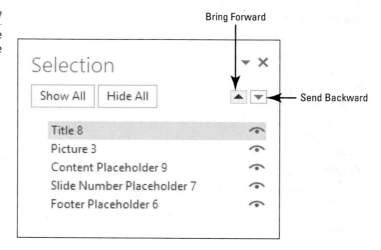

12. Close the Selection task pane, and close the Accessibility Checker task pane.

13. Save the presentation.

PAUSE. LEAVE the presentation open to use in the next exercise.

Modifying Properties and Removing Metadata

A file's *properties* provide information about the file, such as the date and time it was created or last modified, the file size, whether or not the file is read-only, and so on. The properties also include **metadata** (which literally means "data about data") such as the author's name (taken from the name you are logged into Office or Windows with), the subject, and any keywords you may have assigned to it. You can modify a presentation's properties to provide information to the people who will later receive the presentation file, such as your co-authors or your audience members. In some cases you may want to remove your personal information from the file for privacy reasons, and PowerPoint provides a command that enables you to do so. In this exercise, you will change the properties for a presentation file and remove your personal information from it.

STEP BY STEP **Modify Properties and Remove Metadata**

USE the *HR Review Final Version 4* presentation that is still open from the previous exercise.

1. Click the File tab, click the Properties heading on the right, and click Show Document Panel. The Document Properties panel appears below the Ribbon (see Figure 10-18).

Figure 10-18

Display the Document
Properties panel

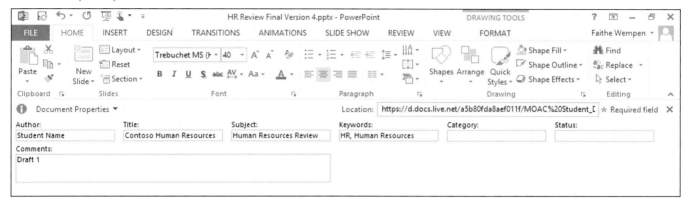

2. Click in the **Author** text box and type *your own name*, replacing the generic Student Name there.

3. Click in the **Status** text box and type **Final**.

4. Delete the text from the **Comments** text box.

5. Click the **Document Properties** heading in the upper left corner of the document panel, opening a menu, and click **Advanced Properties**. A Properties dialog box opens for the file.

6. Click the **Summary** tab. Note that the same properties appear here as in the Document Properties panel. Click the **Statistics** and **Contents** tabs and note the information that appears on each of those tabs.

7. Click the **Custom** tab.

8. In the list of properties at the top, click **Language**. Then in the **Value** text box, type **English**, and click **Add** (see Figure 10-19).

Figure 10-19

Add a custom property

9. Click **OK** to close the dialog box.

10. Click the **File** tab, click **Check for Issues**, and click **Inspect Document**. At the confirmation box, click **Yes** to save your changes. The Document Inspector dialog box opens.

11. Click Inspect. A report appears showing what the inspection found (see Figure 10-20).

Figure 10-20

The inspection report

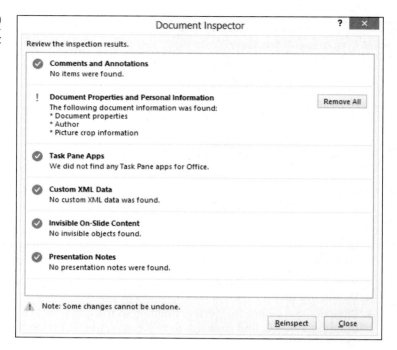

12. Click the Remove All button next to Document Properties and Personal Information.
13. Click Close.
14. Examine the Document Properties panel. Note that most of the information has been removed from its text boxes.
15. Click the Close (X) button in the upper right corner of the Document Properties panel to close it.
16. Save the presentation.

PAUSE. LEAVE the presentation open to use in the next exercise.

SAVING A PRESENTATION IN DIFFERENT FORMATS

The Bottom Line

There are many formats available for sharing your PowerPoint work with others who may not have PowerPoint, or who may prefer to view your presentation in another format. Each format is suited for a different usage; you choose the best one for your situation.

Saving a Presentation as XML

CERTIFICATION READY? 1.4.4

How do you save a presentation as XML?

Extensible Markup Language (XML) is a structured markup language that makes it easier to exchange data files across various types of computers, operating systems, and applications. When you save a file in XML format, it does not seem obviously different from a normal PowerPoint presentation file, but internally the way the data is stored is different. PowerPoint 2013 supports two different XML formats: PowerPoint XML Presentation (*.xml) and Strict Open XML Presentation (*.pptx). The former allows files to contain some Office-specific encoding that was used in earlier versions of Office for XML files; the latter translates the file into a fully independent file format that does not rely on anything Microsoft-specific. Depending on the program that you are exchanging files with, one of those formats may be more useful than the other; you might even want to save in both of those formats and send the recipient both files, so they can see which works best for them. In this exercise, you save in Strict Open XML format.

STEP BY STEP   **Save in XML Format**

USE the *HR Review Final Version 4* presentation that is still open from the previous exercise.

1. Click the File tab, and click Save As.
2. Click Browse and navigate to the location where you are saving files for this lesson.
3. Open the Save as type drop-down list and click Strict Open XML Presentation.
4. In the File name box, type HR Review Open XML.
5. Click Save.
6. Close the file.

PAUSE. LEAVE PowerPoint open to use in the next exercise.

Saving As a Picture Presentation

A **picture presentation** looks, on the surface, the same as any other PowerPoint presentation. When you save as a picture presentation, however, PowerPoint saves each slide as a graphic, and then replaces the slide's content with that graphic. This tool can be useful in cases where you want to copy individual slides into other applications as graphics, for example. In this exercise, you save a presentation as a picture presentation.

STEP BY STEP   **Save As a Picture Presentation**

OPEN the *HR Review Final Version 4* presentation that you created earlier in the lesson.

1. Click the File tab, click Export, and click Change File Type.
2. In the Change File Type list, type PowerPoint Picture Presentation.
3. Scroll down to the bottom of the list and click the Save As button. The Save As dialog box opens.
4. In the File Name box, type HR Review Pictures, and then click Save. A message appears that a copy has been saved.
5. Click OK. Notice that the original file is still open; your newly saved version is not.
6. Open *HR Review Pictures.pptx*.

7. Click the background of slide 1. Notice that the entire slide appears with selection handles around it.
8. Drag one of the corner selection handles inward, decreasing the size of the image. Notice that all the slide's content is a graphic placed on a blank slide (see Figure 10-21).

Figure 10-21

In a picture presentation, each slide is a graphic on a plain slide background

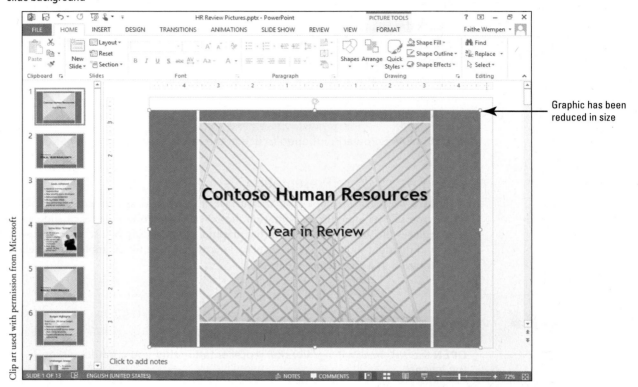

Graphic has been reduced in size

Clip art used with permission from Microsoft

9. **CLOSE** *HR Review Pictures.pptx* without saving the changes to it.

PAUSE. LEAVE *HR Review Final Version 4.pptx* open to use in the next exercise.

Another Way
You can also save each slide individually as a graphic in a number of formats. To do this, choose File, Save As and then set the file type to one of the graphic formats available, such as JPEG, GIF, TIF, Device Independent Bitmap, or Windows Metafile.

Saving a Presentation in PDF or XPS Format

Portable Document Format (PDF) and XML Paper Specification (XPS) are page layout formats. They each create **platform-independent** files that can be displayed on any computer system that has a reader for the format, and the files will display and print exactly the same way on any system or any printer. Page layout formats like XPS and PDF are great for situations in which you want the content to be uneditable. People can see the content exactly as you designed it, but cannot modify it. These formats also work well for situations in which you are not sure which applications your audience may have installed, or even what platform (Windows, Macintosh, etc.) they might be using. In this exercise, you save a presentation as an XPS file.

STEP BY STEP   **Save a Presentation as an XPS File**

USE the *HR Review Final Version 4* presentation that is still open from the previous exercise.

1. Click the **File** tab, click **Export**, and click the **Create PDF/XPS** button on the right side. The Publish as PDF or XPS dialog box opens.
2. Navigate to the **folder** where you store files for this lesson.
3. In the File name box, type **HRXPS**.
4. Open the **Save as type drop-down list** and click **XPS Document** (see Figure 10-22).

Figure 10-22

Choose to create a PDF
or XPS document

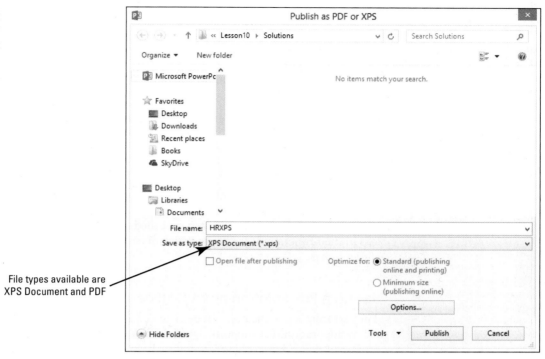

Figure 10-22

Choose to create a PDF
or XPS document

File types available are
XPS Document and PDF

5. If the Open file after publishing check box is marked, click to clear it.
6. Click Options. The Options dialog box opens (see Figure 10-23).

Figure 10-23

The Options dialog box

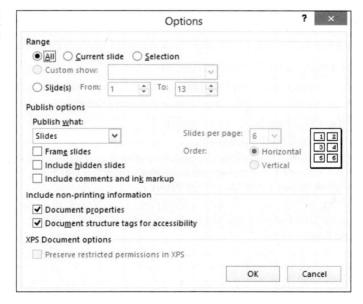

7. Mark the Frame slides check box to add an outline frame around each picture.
8. Clear the Document properties check box so that the XPS file does not include the document properties.
9. Click OK. You return to the Publish as PDF or XPS dialog box.
10. Click Publish.
11. In Windows, navigate to the location containing the XPS file you just saved and double-click it to open it in the XPS Viewer utility in Windows.

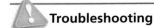

⚠️ **Troubleshooting** The XPS Viewer is not available in Windows XP and earlier versions of Windows. If you distribute your XPS version to someone who does not have the viewer, he or she can download it free from Microsoft.com.

12. Scroll through the presentation in the XPS Viewer, and then **CLOSE** the XPS Viewer window.

PAUSE. LEAVE the *HR Review Final Version 4* presentation file open to use in the next exercise.

XPS is a Microsoft page layout format, and XPS documents can only be viewed using the **XPS Viewer** utility. This utility comes free with Windows Vista and later, and is available for free download from Microsoft for other operating systems. **PDF** is an Adobe page layout format, and can be viewed using a free utility called Adobe Reader (available for most operating systems) or a full-featured commercial program called Adobe Acrobat. PDF and XPS are roughly equivalent in their functionality; choose which one to use based on what software you think your target audience has.

Saving a Presentation as an Outline

The text from a presentation can be exported as a text-only outline that you can open in Word, or in any application that supports the **Rich Text Format (rtf)** file type. Rich text format is a generic file format that is compatible with almost all word-processing programs. Exporting text as an outline can be useful if you need to repurpose the text from a presentation for a different situation, say using the headings from a presentation as the basis for a report. In this exercise, you save a presentation as an outline.

STEP BY STEP **Save a Presentation as an Outline**

USE the *HR Review Final Version 4* presentation that is still open from the previous exercise.

1. Click the File tab, and click Save As.
2. Click Browse, and then navigate to the location where you want to save.
3. Open the Save as type drop-down list and click Outline/RTF.
4. In the File name box, type Outline.
5. Click Save. The file is saved.
6. In Windows, navigate to the location where you saved the Outline.rtf file, and double-click it to open it in the application set as the default for RTF files on your system. (This location is probably Microsoft Word.)
7. Switch to Outline view in the application. (In Word, the command is View, Outline.) Figure 10-24 shows the file opened in Word and displayed in Outline view with the Zoom set to 40%.

Figure 10-24

The exported outline opened in Word 2013

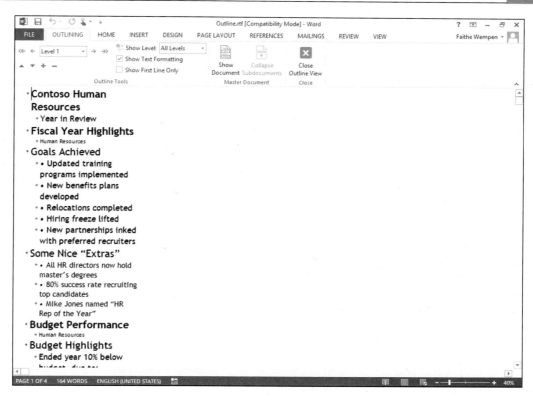

Figure 10-24

The exported outline opened in Word 2013

8. Scroll through the outline to review how it was exported. Then close the application.

PAUSE. LEAVE the presentation file open to use in the next exercise.

Another way to export an outline to Word is to click the File tab, click Export, click Create Handouts, and then click the Create Handouts button. Then in the Send to Microsoft Word dialog box shown in Figure 10-25, click Outline Only and click OK.

Figure 10-25

Send to Microsoft Word is another way of exporting text as an outline

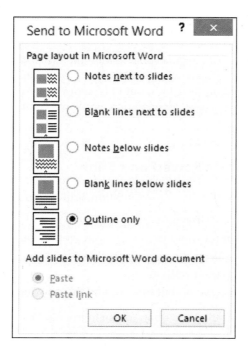

Text exported as an outline from PowerPoint does not include text in manually-placed text boxes or text typed into shapes. Therefore, be careful not to lose essential content when exporting as an outline. You may need to edit the outline afterwards in Word or another word processing program to add important text back in.

Saving a Presentation as an OpenDocument Presentation

OpenDocument is a standard format that many applications, including free Office suites online such as OpenOffice, use to ensure compatibility between programs. If you are going to share PowerPoint files with others who may use one of these applications, you may want to save your work in OpenDocument format. Some of the features of PowerPoint 2013 may not translate to the OpenDocument version, such as certain transitions and object types. In most cases, special object types will be converted to regular graphics when saved in OpenDocument format, such as SmartArt. In this exercise, you save a presentation in OpenDocument format.

STEP BY STEP   **Save a Presentation in OpenDocument Format**

USE the *HR Review Final Version 4* presentation that is still open from the previous exercise.

1. Click the File tab, and click Save As.
2. Click Browse, and then navigate to the location where you want to save.
3. Open the Save as type drop-down list and click OpenDocument Presentation.
4. In the File name box, type HR Open.
5. Click Save. A warning appears, stating that the file may contain features that are not compatible with this format.
6. Click Yes to confirm. The file is saved.

PAUSE. CLOSE the presentation file.

After completing this exercise, if time permits, you may want to experiment with opening the file in different open-source applications such as Google docs (www.google.com/goodle-d-s/presentations) or Open Office (www.openoffice.org).

Saving a Presentation as a PowerPoint Show

A **PowerPoint Show** file is just a regular presentation file except that it opens in Slide Show view by default. You may want to distribute a presentation in this format if you expect your recipients to have PowerPoint installed on their PCs, but to be more interested in viewing the show than in editing it. In this exercise, you save a presentation as a PowerPoint Show.

STEP BY STEP   **Save a Presentation as a PowerPoint Show**

OPEN the *HR Review Final Version 4* presentation, which you created earlier in this lesson.

1. Click the File tab, and click Save As.
2. Click Browse, and then navigate to the location where you want to save.
3. Open the Save as type drop-down list and click PowerPoint Show.
4. In the File name box, type HR Show.
5. Click Save. The file is saved in that format, and the new file is open in PowerPoint.

PAUSE. LEAVE the presentation file open to use in the next exercise.

When you save as a PowerPoint Show, nothing changes about the presentation except its file extension: instead of .pptx, it is .ppsx. This differing extension prompts PowerPoint to open the file in Slide Show view, rather than Normal view.

Saving a Slide or Object as a Picture

You can export individual slides or objects as pictures. In the case of a slide, the entire slide becomes a graphic, which you can then use in any application that accepts graphics. In the case of an object, that individual object is saved as a graphic in any of a variety of formats you choose. In this exercise, you save a slide as a picture.

STEP BY STEP	**Save a Slide or Object as a Picture**

USE the *HR Show* presentation that is still open from the previous exercise.

1. Go to slide 3.
2. Click the File tab, and click Save As.
3. Click Browse, and then navigate to the location where you want to save.
4. Open the Save as type drop-down list and click JPEG File Interchange Format.
5. In the File name box, type Goals Achieved.
6. Click Save. A dialog box prompts you to choose whether to save every slide or only the current slide (see Figure 10-26).

Figure 10-26

Choose to export the current slide or all slides as graphics

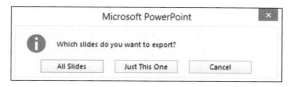

7. Click Just This One. The current slide is saved as a graphic with the name you specified.
8. Go to slide 4.
9. Right-click the photo and click Save as Picture. The Save As Picture dialog box opens.
10. Navigate to the location where you want to save.
11. In the File name box, type Businessman.
12. Click Save. That photo is saved as a separate graphic.

Another Way
You can also copy and paste photos from PowerPoint into your favorite graphics program.

PAUSE. LEAVE the presentation file open to use in the next exercise.

Saving objects as graphics enables you to export specific content from PowerPoint for use in other applications. For example, you can use PowerPoint to store photos, and then export them as separate graphics whenever you need one of them.

Saving as a Video

Videos are a great way to distribute self-running presentations to people who do not have PowerPoint. PowerPoint creates videos in either **MPEG-4 Video (mp4)** or **Windows Media Video (wmv)** format, both common video formats that most applications support. You can distribute videos on websites, via email, or on CD-ROM. In this exercise, you will make a video from a presentation.

STEP BY STEP   **Create a Video**

USE the *HR Review Final Version 4* presentation that is still open from the previous exercise.

1. Click the File tab, click Export, and click Create a Video. The Create a Video controls appear in Backstage view (see Figure 10-28).

Figure 10-28

Set the options for creating a video

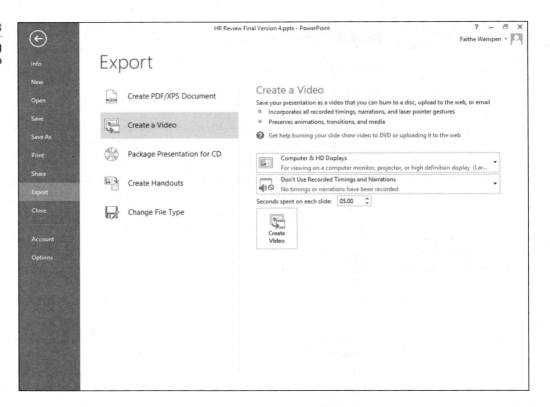

2. Click the up increment arrow on the Seconds spent on each slide text box until the setting is 10.00.
3. Click Create Video. The Save As dialog box opens.
4. In the File name box, type HR Video. Ensure that the file type is set to MPEG-4 Video.
5. Navigate to the location where you are storing the files for this lesson.
6. Click Save. The video is created. A progress bar in the status bar shows the creation. Wait until the creation is complete before going on to the next step.
7. **CLOSE** PowerPoint, saving your changes to the presentation file.
8. In Windows, navigate to the folder containing the video and double-click the video clip to play it in your default application for video clips.

SKILL SUMMARY

In This Lesson, You Learned How To:	Exam Objective	Objective Number
Work with Comments	Manage comments.	5.2.4
Incorporate Reviewer Changes	Merge multiple presentations.	5.1.1
	Use the Reviewing/Revisions Pane.	5.2.1
	Compare revisions.	5.2.2
	Manage changes.	5.2.3
Protect a Presentation	Encrypt presentations with a password.	5.3.1
	Restrict permissions.	5.3.6
	Mark as final.	5.3.3
Prepare a Presentation for Distribution	Maintain backward compatibility.	1.4.7
	Check for compatibility issues.	5.3.9
	Check for accessibility issues.	5.3.8
	Modify presentation properties.	1.3.4
	Remove presentation metadata.	5.3.7
Save a Presentation in Different Formats	Save Presentations as XML.	1.4.4

Knowledge Assessment

Fill in the Blank

Fill in each blank with the term or phrase that best completes the statement.

1. A(n) _____ is a note you can insert directly on a slide.
2. When you compare and _____ presentations, you consolidate all changes into a single copy.
3. A(n) _____ protects a presentation file so that only authorized users can open it.
4. To make changes to a comment, click the comment marker to open the _____ pane and then make changes there.
5. A(n) _____ presentation converts each slide to a graphic and places the graphics on blank slide backgrounds.
6. PowerPoint saves in page layout formats including XPS and _____.
7. _____ Text Format is a common word processing format to which PowerPoint exports outlines.
8. To exchange files with someone who uses OpenOffice, save your presentation in _____ format.
9. If you save a presentation in PowerPoint Show format, it opens in _____ view by default.
10. When you create a video from a presentation, PowerPoint saves it in _____ format.

Multiple Choice

Circle the correct answer.

1. To see the presentation's properties,
   a. Click the File tab, click the Properties heading, and click Show Document Panel.
   b. Click the View tab and click Properties.
   c. Click the View tab, click Advanced, and click Show Document Panel.
   d. Click the File tab, click Share, and click Properties.

2. When you save a PowerPoint 2013 presentation in a file format that does not support SmartArt, those objects are:
   a. saved as uneditable pictures.
   b. deleted.
   c. preserved just as in the 2013 presentation.
   d. converted to shapes.

3. Which of these is an example of metadata that can be removed with the Inspect Document command?
   a. File size.
   b. File type.
   c. Creation date.
   d. Keyword.

4. How do you change the user name that will appear on each comment?
   a. Manually type your name into each comment.
   b. Click File > Options and type a different User Name and Initials.
   c. Click the Change User button on the Home tab.
   d. Click the Manage Comments button on the Review tab.

5. Which of these is an example of a strong password?
   a. password
   b. Mary
   c. 12345
   d. d9V9n9tY

6. How do you remove a password from a PowerPoint file?
   a. Change the password to a null string.
   b. Click Encrypt with Password, then click Decrypt.
   c. Click Encrypt with Password, then click Remove.
   d. Click the File tab, then click Unprotect.

7. Marking a presentation as final is:
   a. the same level of security as password protection.
   b. not as strong security as password protection.
   c. stronger security than password protection.
   d. Useful only when saving in Text Only format.

8. What is required in order for a user to read a PDF file?
   a. Adobe Reader or Adobe Acrobat.
   b. XPS Viewer.
   c. A Macintosh computer.
   d. Windows 95 or higher.

9. What happens to text that is typed inside shapes or manually created text boxes when you save a presentation as an outline?
   a. It is included in the outline.
   b. It is not included in the outline.
   c. You can specify whether you want it included in the outline.
   d. It is included as a separate graphic file.

10. To save a presentation as a video, start by clicking the File tab, then click:
    a. Export.
    b. Save.
    c. Print.
    d. Info.

Competency Assessment

Project 10-1: Messenger Messages

You are the new Marketing Manager for Consolidated Messenger. The company owner has given you a presentation to review with his comments already inserted and has asked you to add your own comments in response to his and describe any changes you would make.

GET READY. LAUNCH PowerPoint if it is not already running.

1. **OPEN** the *Sales Pitch* presentation and save it as *Sales Pitch Final*.
2. Click the Review tab, and then click the Next button to read the comment on slide 1.
3. Click Next, read the comment on slide 3, then click Next again to read the comment on slide 5.
4. Click the Previous button two times to return to the comment on slide 1.
5. Click the Delete button to delete the comment on slide 1.
6. Click the New Comment button and insert the following comment:
   I think the template is fine as is.
7. Go to slide 3 and insert the following comment:
   I will try to find a picture with color values more in line with the template.
8. Go to slide 5 and delete the comment.
9. **SAVE** the presentation and then **CLOSE** the file.

LEAVE PowerPoint open for use in the next project.

Project 10-2: **Travel Protection**

You are a travel agent working for Margie's Travel Agency. Blue Yonder Airlines has asked you to start pitching their services to corporate clients and has sent you a copy of their presentation. Your contact at Blue Yonder has asked you to share the presentation with other agents in your office, but she does not want anyone to change the presentation. You can use PowerPoint features to safeguard the presentation.

1. **OPEN** the *Airline Overview* presentation and save it as *Airline Overview Final*.
2. Click the comment on slide 1 to open the Comments pane, and then read the comment.
3. Delete the comment.
4. Click the File tab, click Protect Presentation, and click Mark as Final.
5. Click OK twice to save the presentation and mark it as the final version.
6. Close the presentation file.
7. Reopen *Airline Overview*, and save it as *Airline Overview Protected*.
8. Click the File tab, click Protect Presentation, and click Encrypt with Password.
9. In the Password box, type ProtectMe, and click OK.
10. In the Reenter password box, type ProtectMe, and click OK.
11. **CLOSE** the file, saving your changes if prompted.

LEAVE PowerPoint open for use in the next project.

Proficiency Assessment

Project 10-3: **Confidential Feedback**

You are the research director at Trey Research. You have just completed a confidential presentation for Center City Hospital regarding recent complaints from patients. You will save the file with a password, and create an XPS version of the presentation to distribute to upper management.

1. **OPEN** the *Hospital Complaints* presentation and save it as *Hospital Complaints Final*.
2. Click the File tab and click Export.
3. Click Create PDF/XPS Document.
4. Click the Create PDF/XPS button.

5. In the Publish as PDF or XPS dialog box, change the name in the File name text box to Hospital Complaints Distribution.

6. Open the Save as type drop-down list and click XPS Document if it is not already selected.

7. Click Publish.

8. Click the File tab and click Protect Presentation, then click Encrypt with Password.

9. In the Password box, type ProtectMe and click OK.

10. Type ProtectMe again and click OK.

11. Press Esc to exit from Backstage view.

12. CLOSE the file, saving changes to it if prompted.

LEAVE PowerPoint open for use in the next project.

Project 10-4: Adventure Review

You are the owner of Adventure Works, a company that offers outdoor adventures for groups of young people. The marketing manager has created a presentation to show to some local civic organizations and wants your feedback on it. You can share your ideas using comments.

1. OPEN the *Adventures* presentation and save it as *Adventures Final*.

2. Read the comment on slide 1.

3. Go to slide 2 and add the following comment:
   Don't forget our new Horseback Trekking adventure.

4. Go to slide 4 and add the following comment:
   Can we replace this picture with a more youth-oriented one?

5. Drag the comment marker closer to the picture.

6. Go to slide 5 and add the following comment:
   Good job, Marie. I like the clean, modern look of this theme.

7. Go to slide 1 and delete Marie's comment.

8. Go back to slide 4 and change your comment to read:
   I like this picture, but can we replace it with a more youth-oriented one?

9. Hide all comments.

10. SAVE the presentation and then CLOSE the file.

LEAVE PowerPoint open for use in the next project.

Mastery Assessment

Project 10-5: Training Day

You are the Training Manager for Northwind Traders. You have just finished a presentation for your trainers to use in training new cashiers, and a draft has been reviewed by one of your coworkers. You will merge the coworker's changes with your own copy of the presentation. Then you will save the presentation as a Picture presentation, and then save one of the picture presentation's slides as a separate PNG graphic.

1. OPEN the *Training* presentation and save it as *Training Final*.

2. Use the Compare feature to merge this presentation with *Training Revisions*.

3. Reject the changes on slide 1, and accept the changes on all other slides. End the review.

4. Save the presentation as a Picture presentation. Name the file *Training Pictures*.

5. Close the *Training Final* presentation, and open *Training Pictures*.

6. Right-click slide 5, and choose Save as Picture.

7. Change the Save as type to PNG Portable Network Graphics Format.

8. Save the picture as *Training Common Questions* in the folder where you are storing the files for this lesson.

9. **SAVE** and **CLOSE** the presentation.

LEAVE PowerPoint open for the next project.

Project 10-6: Video Production

You are the owner of Southridge Video. You want to share a presentation you have created with a potential vendor, but he does not have PowerPoint. You will make a video of the presentation that you can share with him, and you will export an outline of the text in the presentation.

1. **OPEN** the *Video* presentation.

2. Click the File tab, click Export, and click Create a Video.

3. Set the Seconds Spent on Each Slide setting to 12 seconds.

4. Save the video as *Southridge.wmv*. (Make sure the Save as type is set to Windows Media Video (*.wmv).)

5. Click the File tab, click Export, click Create Handouts, and then click the Create Handouts button.

6. Create Outline Only handouts in Word.

7. Save the Word document as *Southridge Outline.docx* and close it. Exit Word.

8. **CLOSE** the presentation file. Do not save changes to it if prompted to do so.

EXIT PowerPoint.

11 Delivering a Presentation

LESSON SKILL MATRIX

Skill	Exam Objective	Objective Number
Adjusting Slide Orientation and Size	Change page setup options. Configure slideshow resolution.	1.3.1 1.5.4
Customizing Audience Handouts	Set handout print options.	1.4.1
Choosing Slides to Display	Hide slides. Create custom slideshows.	2.1.3 1.5.1
Rehearsing and Recording a Slide Show	Rehearse timings.	1.5.3
Setting Up a Slide Show	Configure slideshow options.	1.5.2
Working with Presentation Tools	Navigate within slideshows. Use Presenter View. Annotate slideshows.	1.5.6 1.5.5 1.5.7
Packaging a Presentation for CD Delivery	Package presentations for CD.	1.4.3

KEY TERMS

- annotate
- aspect ratio
- custom shows
- Handout Master
- ink
- landscape orientation
- orientation
- portrait orientation
- presentation tools
- resolution
- slide size
- timings

©graemenicholson / iStockphoto

©graemenicholson / iStockphoto

You are an engineer for A. Datum Corporation, a contractor specializing in pile-driving and heavy concrete construction. Your team has put together a bid on a large bridge construction project for the town of Center City, and you must present the bid package to the client. You will present a slide show for the client before reviewing the bid in detail. Your presentation will introduce your company and provide an overview of the bid itself. PowerPoint provides a number of tools that can help you set up your presentation, rehearse it, and then package it to use in the final presentation.

ADJUSTING SLIDE ORIENTATION AND SIZE

The Bottom Line

Orientation refers to the direction material appears on a page when printed. A page printed in **landscape orientation** is wider than it is tall, like a landscape picture that shows a broad panoramic view. A page printed in **portrait orientation** is taller than it is wide, like a portrait picture that focuses on a single, upright figure. **Slide size** is expressed as a ratio of height to width, also called **aspect ratio**. You can choose Standard (4:3) or Widescreen (16:9) or you can set up a custom slide size with your choice of ratios.

Take Note   Do not confuse slide size with resolution. **Resolution** refers to the number of pixels that makes up a slide display on the monitor and is applicable only in Slide Show view. Resolution is configured in the Set Up Show dialog box, covered later in this lesson.

Selecting Slide Orientation

CERTIFICATION READY?   1.3.1

How do you change page setup options?

By default, slides are displayed so they are wider than they are tall (landscape orientation). You may want to change the orientation of a presentation for a special case, such as to accommodate large graphics that have a portrait orientation or to print slides at the same orientation as other materials. You can easily change this orientation by using the Slide Size dialog box or a Ribbon command. In this exercise, you will practice changing slide orientation.

CERTIFICATION READY?   1.5.4

How do you configure slide show resolution?

You cannot mix landscape and portrait orientations in a single presentation the way you can in a word processing document. All slides in a presentation must have the same orientation. However, if you need to display one or more slides in a different orientation, you can create a secondary presentation with the different orientation and then provide links between the main presentation and the secondary one. You can easily click the link during the slide show to jump to the secondary presentation, and then click another link to return to your main presentation.

Presentation materials such as notes pages and handouts print in portrait orientation by default because this orientation allows the most efficient placement of slide images and text on the page. Adjusting orientation for these materials allows you to fit more information across the longest axis of the page—a plus if you have a great many notes for each slide.

STEP BY STEP   Select Slide Size and Orientation

GET READY. Before you begin these steps, make sure that your computer is on. Log on, if necessary.

1. **START** PowerPoint, if it is not already running.
2. Locate and open the *Bid* presentation and save it as *Bid Final*.
3. Click the Design tab, and then click the Slide Size button. A menu opens.
4. Click Widescreen. The height/width ratio for all slides in the presentation changes to widescreen (16:9).

5. Click the Slide Size button again, and click Custom Slide Size. The Slide Size dialog box opens (see Figure 11-1). Note the current width and height measurements at the left side of the dialog box.

Take Note   The measurements for Width and Height in the Slide Size dialog box are in inches, but an inch on a monitor can look different depending on the monitor's size and display resolution. The main concern is the ratio between the height and the width here. For example, the ratio of 13.333" by 7.5" expressed as a fraction is 16/9, the standard for widescreen.

Figure 11-1

Slide Size dialog box

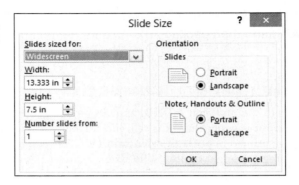

6. Open the Slides Sized For drop-down list and examine the available options for slide sizes. Click 35mm Slides, and note the width and height settings.

7. Click Portrait in the Slides area.

8. Click OK. A dialog box opens asking whether you want to maximize the size of your content or scale it down.

9. Click Ensure Fit. The slide's orientation and aspect ratio has changed (see Figure 11-2).

Figure 11-2

The slides display in portrait orientation

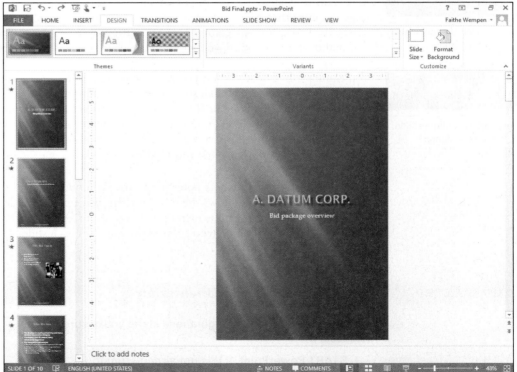

Clip art used with permission from Microsoft

10. Reopen the Slide Size drop-down list and click Standard (4:3).

11. When prompted whether you want to maximize or ensure fit of the content, click Maximize. The slides return to their original 4:3 dimensions. The content has been somewhat distorted in size due to your choices of Ensure Fit and Maximize in steps 9 and 11 respectively.

12. **CLOSE** *Bid Final* without saving your changes to it.

PAUSE. LEAVE PowerPoint open to use in the next exercise.

If you do not find a suitable size for a specific need, you can create a custom slide size. Adjust the width and height as desired in the Slide Size dialog box to create the custom slide size.

Besides allowing you to set slide size and orientation, the Slide Size dialog box lets you choose the starting number for slides in a presentation. This option is useful if you are combining several separate presentations into one comprehensive slide show.

CUSTOMIZING AUDIENCE HANDOUTS

The Bottom Line

You can help your audience follow a presentation by giving them handouts, which show small versions of the slides arranged in various ways on a page. Handout layouts are controlled by a **Handout Master**, as slide appearance is controlled by the Slide Master. You can customize the Handout Master to create your own handout layout. You can also export handouts to Microsoft Word, where you can customize them further.

CERTIFICATION READY?   1.4.1

How do you set handout print options?

Customizing the Handout Master

You can customize the layout of the Handout Master, which controls how handouts are formatted in PowerPoint. You can add text boxes to it, enable or disable certain placeholders, and format those placeholders. In this exercise, you customize the Handout Master in several ways.

You can create handouts that show one, two, three, four, six, or nine slides on a page. If you make changes to any of these layouts, the changes are reflected on all other layouts.

You cannot adjust the position or size of the slide placeholders in the Handout Master. (You can do that in Word, though, which you will learn about in the next exercise.) You can, however, adjust both size and position of the Header, Date, Footer, and Page Number placeholders. You can also choose to hide some or all of these placeholders by deselecting their check boxes in the Placeholders group on the Handout Master tab.

The Handout Master tab allows you to change both slide orientation and handout orientation, using buttons in the Page Setup group. To further modify the appearance of handouts, you can change theme colors and fonts (but not the current theme) and apply a different background style. You can format the Header, Date, Footer, and Page Number placeholders like any text box or placeholder using Quick Styles, fills, or outlines.

Note that you can also customize the Notes Master in many of the same ways that you customize the Handout Master. Click the Notes Master button on the View tab to display the Notes Master tab. The Notes Master allows you to adjust the size and position of the slide image as well as other placeholders on the page.

STEP BY STEP   **Customize the Handout Master**

REOPEN the *Bid Final* presentation that you created at the beginning of the previous exercise.

1. Click the Insert tab, click Header & Footer, and click the Notes and Handouts tab.
2. Set up headers and footers as follows:
   a. Click to mark the Date and time check box, and make sure the Update automatically option is selected.
   b. Click to mark the Header check box, and type the header A. Datum Corporation.
   c. Click to mark the Footer check box, and type the footer No Job Is Too Big for A. Datum.
   d. Click Apply to All.
3. Click the Design tab, click Slide Size, and then click Custom Slide Size.
4. Under the Notes, Handouts & Outline heading, click Landscape, and click OK.
5. Click the View tab, and then click the Handout Master button in the Master Views group. The Handout Master view opens (see Figure 11-3) with the header and footer you supplied in step 2.

Figure 11-3

Handout Master view

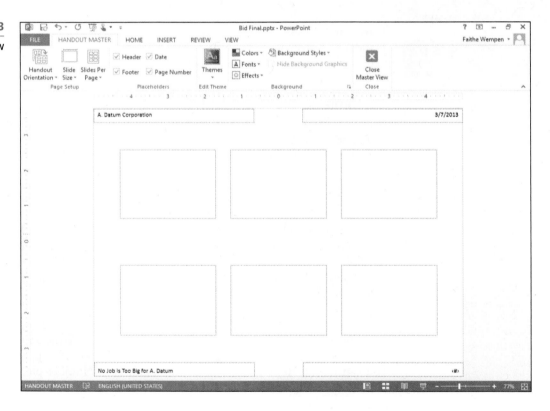

Take Note   If the file is stored on a server, you may see a message about edits made in this view being lost when saved to the server. Click Check Out to continue.

6. Click the Slides Per Page button in the Page Setup group, then click 3 Slides. The Handout Master displays the layout used to show three slides across the width of the page.

Figure 11-4

Add a text box to the
Handout Master

7. Click the Insert tab, click Text Box, and draw a text box above the center slide placeholder of the same width as the placeholder (see Figure 11-4).

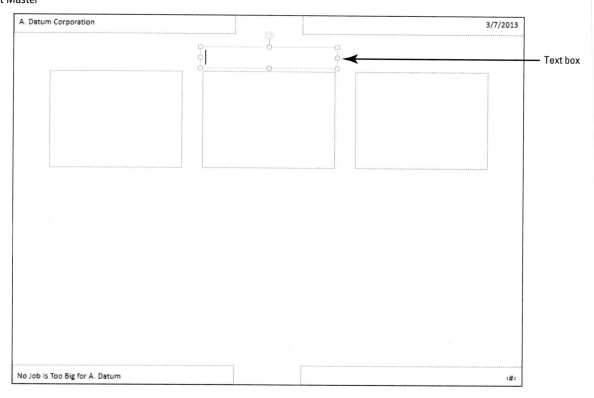

Text box

8. Type Center City Bridge Project in the text box.

9. Change the font size of the text box text to 16, apply bold formatting, change the color to Dark Blue, Text 2, and center the text. Adjust the size of the text box as necessary to display the text on one line.

10. Click the outside border of the header placeholder in the upper-left corner of the master, hold down Shift, and click the date, footer, and page number placeholders.

11. Change the font size to 14 pt, apply bold formatting, and change the color to Dark Blue, Text 2.

12. Click the Handout Master tab, and then click the Close Master View button to exit Handout Master view.

13. Click the File tab and click Print. Open the Full Page Slides button's list and click 3 Slides. Your customized handout master should resemble the one previewed in Figure 11-5.

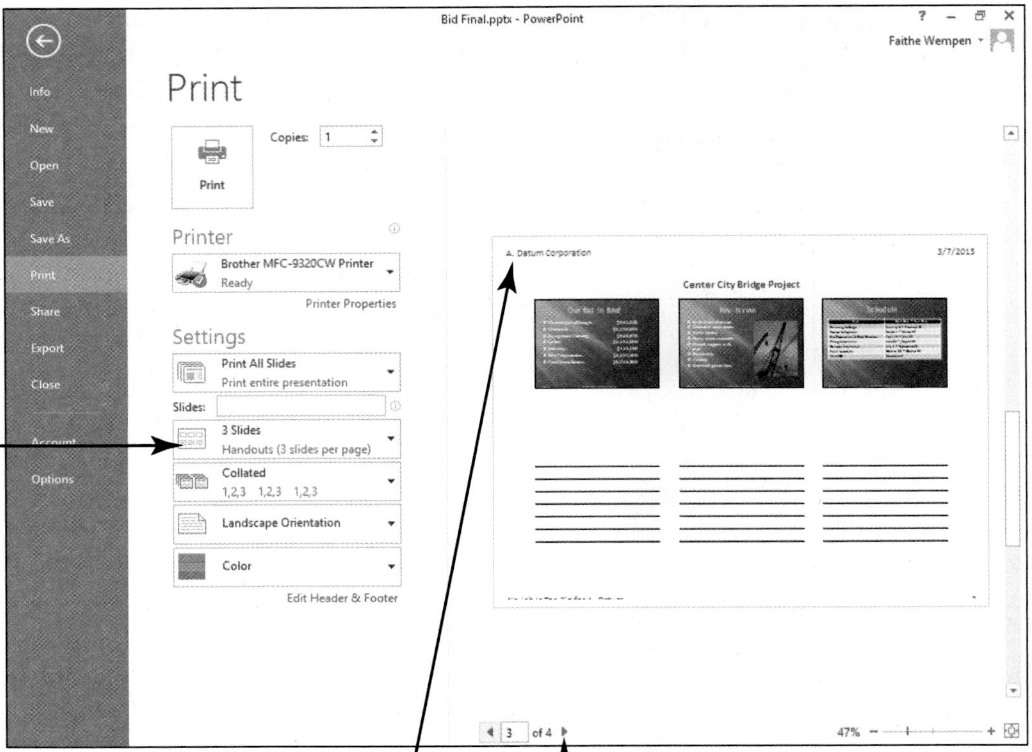

Clip art used with permission from Microsoft

Figure 11-5

Preview of the customized handout

Select the 3 Slides handout here

Company Name   Next Page

14. Click the Next Page arrow to see that the text box you added displays on each page of the handouts.

15. Click the Print button to print the handouts.

Take Note   In some classrooms, printing is limited or unavailable. Check with your instructor as needed to make sure it is okay to print a multiple-page document in your classroom.

16. **SAVE** the presentation.

PAUSE. LEAVE the presentation open to use in the next exercise.

Exporting Handouts to Word

As you saw in the preceding exercise, there is a limit to what you can do with handout layouts in PowerPoint. For maximum control over handouts, including the ability to resize the slide images, you must export handouts to Word. In this exercise, you export handouts to Word.

STEP BY STEP   **Export Handouts to Word**

USE the *Bid Final* presentation that is still open from the previous exercise.

1. Click the File tab, click Export, click Create Handouts, and then click the Create Handouts button (see Figure 11-6). The Send to Microsoft Word dialog box opens.

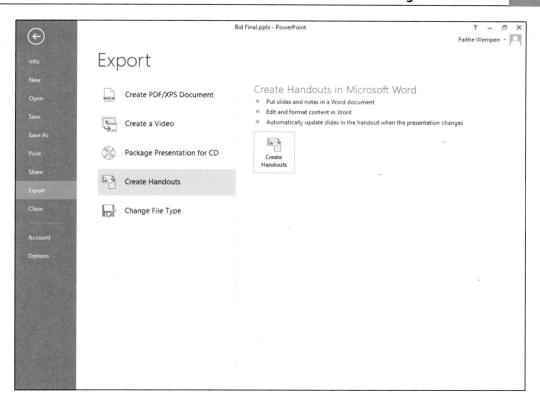

Figure 11-6

Choose to create handouts
from Backstage view

2. Click Blank lines next to slides (see Figure 11-7). Then click OK. Microsoft Word opens
and a new document is created containing the handouts.

Figure 11-7

Choose which handout
format you want

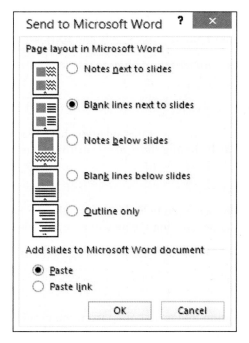

3. Click the first slide's image, and drag its lower-right corner selection handle to
decrease the image's size by about 0.25", so it fits in the cell.
4. Drag across the horizontal lines in the first row to select them.

Figure 11-8

Change graphic size and
spacing between lines

5. On the Home tab, click the Line and Paragraph Spacing button, and click Remove Space After Paragraph. The spacing between lines tightens up (see Figure 11-8).

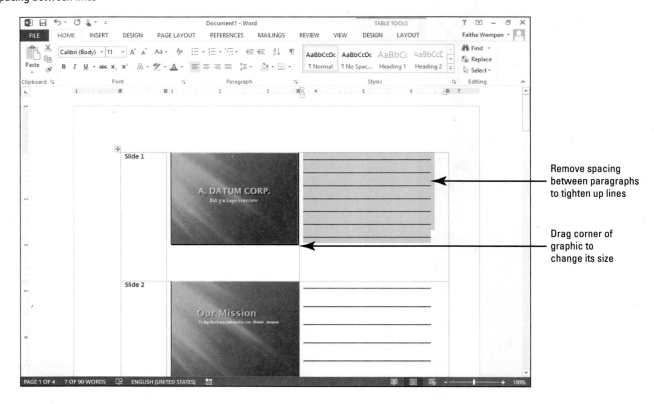

6. Repeat the changes from steps 3–5 for each slide.
7. SAVE the Word document as *Handouts.docx* and EXIT Word.

PAUSE. LEAVE the *Bid Final* presentation open to use in the next exercise.

CHOOSING SLIDES TO DISPLAY

The Bottom Line

You may want to present only a portion of the slides you have prepared on a specific subject. You can select the slides to display by hiding slides or by creating a custom slide show.

CERTIFICATION READY? 2.1.3

How do you hide slides?

Hiding Selected Slides

You can omit slides from a presentation by hiding them. Use the Hide Slide button or command to hide a slide so it will not appear during the presentation. In this exercise, you hide a slide.

STEP BY STEP | **Hide a Slide**

USE the *Bid Final* presentation that is still open from the previous exercise.

1. Go to slide 2, and then click the Slide Show tab.
2. Click the Hide Slide button in the Set Up group. The slide is shaded in the Slides pane at the left (see Figure 11-9), and the slide number is surrounded by a box with a diagonal bar across it.

Figure 11-9

A hidden slide is shaded in the Slides pane

The hidden slide is shaded and its number is crossed out on the Slides pane

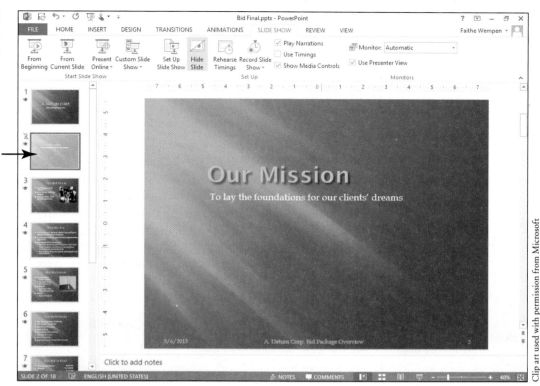

Clip art used with permission from Microsoft

Another Way
Right-click a slide in the Slides pane or in Slide Sorter view, and click Hide Slide on the shortcut menu.

3. Press F5 to start the presentation from slide 1.
4. Click the mouse button and notice that slide 2, *Our Mission*, does not display—you go directly to slide 3, *The Bid Team*.
5. Press Esc to stop the slide show.

PAUSE. LEAVE the presentation open to use in the next exercise.

When you hide a slide, you can still see it in Normal view and Slide Sorter view. It is hidden only in Slide Show view, when you present the slides. You can unhide a slide using the same procedure you used to hide it.

Another Way
Set a range of slides to show in the Set Up Show dialog box, covered later in this lesson.

If you find that you want to display a hidden slide during the presentation, you can show it using PowerPoint's presentation tools. You will learn more about controlling a presentation with these tools later in this lesson.

Creating a Custom Show

Here we look at how to create **custom shows** to customize presentations for different groups using slides from a single presentation. A comprehensive year-end corporate review presentation, for example, might include information on the company as a whole as well as on the operations of each department. You could show all of the slides to the board of directors and use custom shows to present to each department the general company statistics and the information specific to that department. Custom shows allow you to focus attention on the material most relevant to a specific audience. In this exercise, you will create a custom show that contains a subset of the slides in the main presentation.

CERTIFICATION READY? **1.5.1**

How do you create custom slide shows?

You can create any number of custom shows in a presentation. When you set up a presentation for showing, you can specify that only the custom show slides will be presented. You can also choose to run the show while you are in Slide Show view.

You select the slides for a custom show in the Define Custom Show dialog box. Add slide titles from the main presentation to the custom presentation. You can adjust the order in which the slides display in the custom show: Use the up and down arrows to the right of the Slides in custom show list to move a selected title up or down in the list.

STEP BY STEP   **Create a Custom Show**

USE the *Bid Final* presentation that is still open from the previous exercise.

1. Click the Slide Show tab, if necessary, and then click the Custom Slide Show button in the Start Slide Show group.
2. Click Custom Shows. The Custom Shows dialog box opens.
3. Click the New button. The Define Custom Show dialog box opens.
4. In the Slide Show Name box, type Corporate Information.
5. Click the check box for slide 2 in the *Slides in presentation* list, and then click the Add button to place this slide in the *Slides in custom show* list.
6. Add slides 4, 5, and 6 to the custom show list. Your dialog box should look like Figure 11-10.

Figure 11-10

Four slides have been added to the custom show

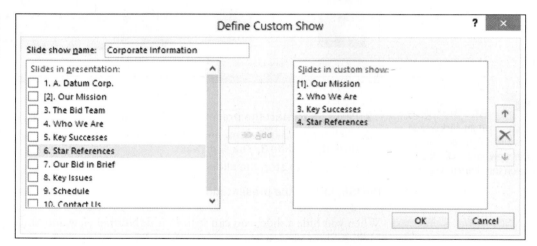

Take Note   The brackets around slide 2's number indicate it is a hidden slide.

7. Click OK, and then click Show. The custom show starts with the second slide you added (the first slide, slide 2, is still hidden). If you were to unhide slide 2, it would also be unhidden in this custom show.
8. Click the mouse button to proceed through the slides of the custom show until the show ends.
9. **SAVE** the presentation.

PAUSE. LEAVE the presentation open to use in the next exercise.

Take Note   When you add slides to the Slides in custom show list, they are renumbered in the list, but the slide numbers on the slides do not change.

After you create a custom show, its name appears in the Custom Slide Show button's drop-down list, as well as in the Custom Shows dialog box. You can run the custom show from either list. You can also select the custom show in the Custom Shows dialog box and choose to edit the show, remove it, or copy it.

REHEARSING AND RECORDING A SLIDE SHOW

The Bottom Line

To make sure that your audience will have enough time to read and absorb the content on your slides, you can rehearse your delivery. When you rehearse a presentation, you read it just as if you were a member of the audience viewing the slides for the first time. Look at pictures, charts, and diagrams to read any information they supply. After you rehearse, you have the option of saving your timings to use during your presentation.

You cannot only record timings, but also narration (recorded audio commentary), annotations, and other features. If you cannot reach an audience in real time with your presentation, recording the presentation for later playback is an attractive option. As with timings, you can record the presentation from start to finish or re-record individual slides.

Rehearsing Timings

Rehearsing a presentation can help you set the **timings** for it. Slide timings are particularly important if you intend to show the slides as a self-running presentation that viewers cannot control. You should allow plenty of time for viewers to read and understand the content on each slide. (You will learn more about self-running presentations in the next section.) When you rehearse, you read the text on the slide out loud (or silently to yourself) to see how long each slide should appear onscreen. You can then choose to keep those timings after the rehearsal or discard them. In this exercise, you will rehearse timings for a presentation and record the timings for later use.

CERTIFICATION READY?   **1.5.3**

How do you rehearse slide timings?

The Rehearsal toolbar that displays when you rehearse slides shows you how much time you have spent reading the current slide as well as the elapsed time for the entire presentation. You can pause the rehearsal if necessary and then resume it when you are ready to continue. You can also choose to start the time again for a particular slide.

Note that saving your rehearsed times applies timings to the slide that allow PowerPoint to control the slides for you. The presentation can run automatically without your having to click buttons to advance slides. If you have applied animations to slide objects, rehearsing will set the proper timing for those objects to display.

You do not have to save the slide timings after rehearsal if you do not want PowerPoint to control the slides for you. You can tell PowerPoint not to save the timings, or you can deselect Use Timings in the Set Up group on the Slide Show tab to remove slide timings.

STEP BY STEP   **Rehearse and Record Timings**

USE the *Bid Final* presentation that is still open from the previous exercise.

1. On the Slide Show tab, click the Rehearse Timings button. The slide show starts from slide 1 and the Rehearsal toolbar appears in the upper-left corner of the screen (see Figure 11-11).

Figure 11-11

The Rehearsal toolbar appears in Slide Show view

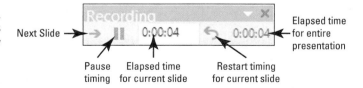

Next Slide →

Pause timing   Elapsed time for current slide   Restart timing for current slide   Elapsed time for entire presentation

2. Read all the content on each slide, clicking the mouse button to display bullet items and advance slides. As you read, the timer is recording the time you spend. If you get interrupted, you can click the Pause button on the toolbar to pause.

3. When asked if you want to save the slide timings, click Yes.
4. Switch to Slide Sorter view. The presentation appears with the timing for each slide displayed below it (see Figure 11-12).

Figure 11-12

Slide timings appear beneath each slide

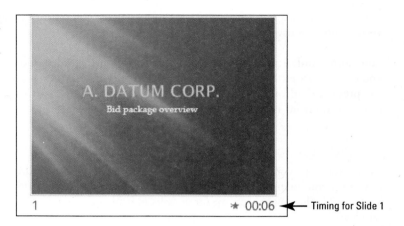

A. DATUM CORP.
Bid package overview

1   ✳ 00:06 ◄—— Timing for Slide 1

5. On the Slide Show tab, mark the Use Timings check box if it is not already marked.
6. Press F5 to start the slide show again from slide 1. This time, let PowerPoint control the slides according to the rehearsal times you set.
7. After three or four slides have displayed, press Esc to end the slide show.
8. **SAVE** the presentation.

PAUSE. LEAVE the presentation open to use in the next exercise.

Adjusting Timing for an Individual Slide

After recording the timings for a presentation, you may decide that you need more or less time for a particular slide. You can change the timing on the Transitions tab. In the following exercise, you change the timing for an individual slide.

STEP BY STEP   **Adjust a Slide's Timing**

USE the presentation that is still open from the previous exercise.

1. Click the Transitions tab.
2. Select the slide for which you want to change the timing.
3. Click the up or down arrows in the After box in the Timing group, to incrementally adjust the number of seconds up or down (see Figure 11-13).

Figure 11-13

Change the timing for a slide on the Transitions tab

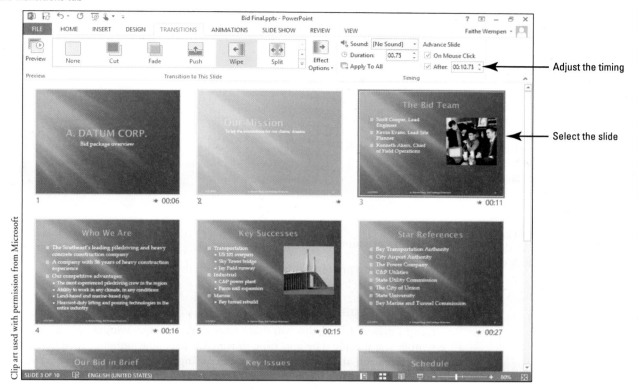

Clip art used with permission from Microsoft

PAUSE. LEAVE the presentation open to use in the next exercise.

Clearing Timings

If you decide not to use automatic timings, you can easily clear all the timings from all slides at once. The following exercise shows how to clear the timings for all slides.

STEP BY STEP   **Clear Slide Timings**

USE the presentation that is still open from the previous exercise.

1. Click the Slide Show tab.

2. Click the arrow below the Record Slide Show button to open a menu, point to Clear, and click Clear Timings on All Slides (see Figure 11-14).

Figure 11-14

Clear all slide timings from the Slide Show tab

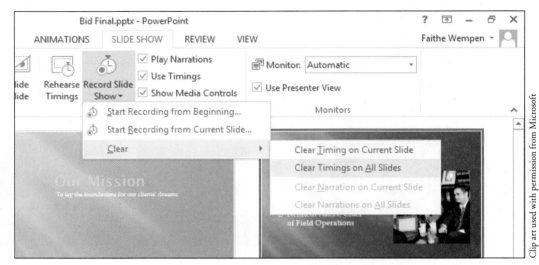

Another Way

You can also turn off all the automatic transitions by clearing the After check box on the Transitions tab and then clicking Apply to All, or by deselecting the Use Timings check box on the Slide Show tab. However, this does not remove the timings; it just disables their ability to execute automatically. You could later re-enable timings for all slides and have your previously set timings back.

3. **SAVE** the presentation.

PAUSE. LEAVE the presentation open to use in the next exercise.

Recording an Entire Presentation

Recording a presentation helps you share your work remotely with people who may not be able to all assemble at a specific date and time to watch it live. The audience members can view your recorded presentation at their convenience. Recording a presentation saves narration, annotations, and timings. It does not create a separate file as a recording; all those settings are saved in the regular PowerPoint file. In the following exercise, you record a presentation from start to finish.

Take Note   If you want to save a separate file for distribution, consider making a video of the presentation, a topic covered in Lesson 10.

Take Note   In order to record narration, you will need a computer that has sound support and a microphone. You should set up and test the microphone ahead of time in Windows. In Windows 7, click Start, type microphone, and then click the Set Up a Microphone link at the top of the Start menu. Follow the prompts to prepare the microphone for recording. In Windows 8, from the Start screen, type microphone, and then click Settings. On the list of search results, click Set Up a Microphone, and then follow the prompts.

STEP BY STEP   **Record a Presentation from the Beginning**

USE the presentation that is still open from the previous exercise.

1. On the Slide Show tab, click the Record Slide Show button. The Record Slide Show dialog box opens (see Figure 11-15).

Figure 11-15

The Record Slide Show dialog box

2. Make sure your microphone is ready.
3. Click Start Recording to begin the recording.

4. Click through the presentation, reading the text of the slides into the microphone at a moderate pace. The Rehearsal toolbar appears as you work through the presentation, the same as when rehearsing timings.

Take Note   If you flub the narration when recording, keep going. You can re-record individual slides after you are finished.

5. When you reach the end of the presentation, click one more time to return to Normal view.

PAUSE. LEAVE the presentation open to use in the next exercise.

Re-Recording an Individual Slide

If you make a mistake in recording a certain slide, you can re-record it. In the following exercise, you re-record a single slide.

STEP BY STEP   **Record a Presentation from the Current Slide**

USE the presentation that is still open from the previous exercise.

1. Display slide 8.
2. On the Slide Show tab, click the arrow under the Record Slide Show button and click Start Recording from Current Slide. The Record Slide Show dialog box opens.
3. Click Start Recording.
4. Click to advance the bullet points on slide 8 at a moderate speed, while reading the text for slide 8 into the microphone.
5. Instead of advancing to the next slide, press Esc to quit recording. PowerPoint returns to Normal view.
6. **SAVE** the presentation file.

PAUSE. LEAVE the presentation open to use in the next exercise.

SETTING UP A SLIDE SHOW

The Bottom Line

The Set Up Show dialog box allows you to make a number of decisions about how slides display during a presentation.

CERTIFICATION READY?   **1.5.2**

How do you configure slide show options?

Setting Up a Slide Show

The following exercise walks you through the settings in the Set Up Show dialog box. Not all of these settings are applicable to the presentation being used for the example, but all are useful to know about because of the variety of presentations you may create in the future. In this exercise, you configure various settings that govern how a slide show runs in Slide Show view.

STEP BY STEP   **Set Up a Slide Show**

USE the *Bid Final* presentation that is still open from the previous exercise.

1. **SAVE** the presentation as *Bid Kiosk*.
2. On the Slide Show tab, click Set Up Slide Show. The Set Up Show dialog box opens.
3. Examine the settings in the Show type section, but do not make a change yet.
4. In the Show Options section, mark the Loop continuously until 'Esc' check box.

Take Note   This setting is turned on automatically if you choose Browsed at a kiosk (full screen) as the show type.

5. Click to mark the **Show without narration** check box.

 Cross Ref   Narrations are recorded when you record a presentation, which is covered earlier in this lesson.

6. Click to mark the **Show without animation** check box.

7. Click the **Pen Color** button, and click the **purple standard color**.

Take Note   The pen color is not important for this presentation because it will be self-running, but it is useful for future reference to know how to change it.

8. In the Advance Slides section, click the **Use timings, if present** option button.

9. In the Show Type section, click **Browsed at a kiosk (full screen)**. Several settings become unavailable when you choose this option, including Loop Continuously Until 'Esc' (which becomes permanently on) and Pen Color. That is why this exercise does not change the show type until after you have tried out those settings.

10. In the Show Slides section, click the **Custom show** option button.

Take Note   The Corporate Information custom show is automatically selected because it is the only custom show in the presentation.

11. In the Multiple Monitors section, open the **Slide show monitor** drop-down list and click **Primary Monitor**. The Resolution drop-down list becomes available.

12. Open the **Resolution drop-down list** and click **800 x 600**. The dialog box should look like Figure 11-16 at this point.

Figure 11-16

The Set Up Show dialog box with custom settings applied

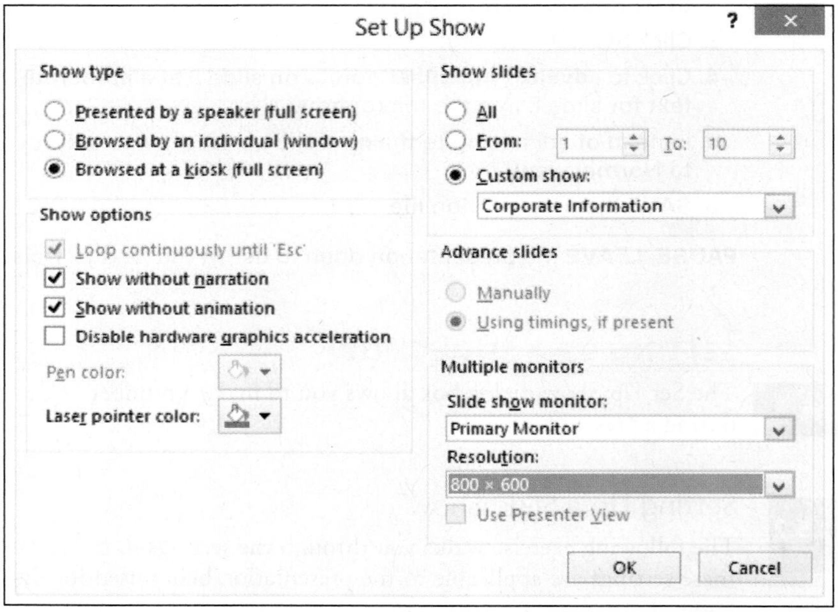

Set Up Show   ?   ×

Show type

○ Presented by a speaker (full screen)
○ Browsed by an individual (window)
● Browsed at a kiosk (full screen)

Show options

☑ Loop continuously until 'Esc'
☑ Show without narration
☑ Show without animation
☐ Disable hardware graphics acceleration

Pen color:
Laser pointer color:

Show slides

○ All
○ From: 1 To: 10
● Custom show:
  Corporate Information

Advance slides

○ Manually
● Using timings, if present

Multiple monitors

Slide show monitor:
Primary Monitor

Resolution:
800 × 600

☐ Use Presenter View

OK   Cancel

Take Note   If you have multiple monitors, the controls in the Multiple Monitors section will be available. (They are not available in Figure 11-17.) With multiple monitors, you can mark the Use Presenter View check box, so that one monitor displays presenter controls (including speaker notes) and the other monitor displays the slides in full-screen mode.

13. Click **OK**. The dialog box closes.

14. Examine the **check boxes** in the Set Up group on the Slide Show tab. Notice that the **Play Narrations** check box is cleared because of the check box you marked in step 5. Notice that the **Use Timings** check box is marked because of the option button you chose in step 8.

15. Clear the **Show Media Controls** check box. This setting is not directly applicable to this presentation. However, knowing how to turn on/off the onscreen controls for such clips is useful for future reference. This setting was also covered in Lesson 9.

16. SAVE the presentation and close it.

PAUSE. LEAVE PowerPoint open to use in the next exercise.

When setting up a slide show, you have the option of choosing a Show Type. The choices are:

- **Presented by a speaker (full screen)** is the option to choose if the slides will be presented by a moderator (you or some other person) to a live audience. The slides will display at full screen size.
- **Browsed by an individual (window)** is the option to choose if you are preparing the presentation for a viewer to review on his or her own computer. The slides display within a window that contains a title bar with size/close controls. You can also choose to display a scrollbar to make it easy for the individual to scroll through the slides.
- **Browsed at a kiosk (full screen)** is the option to choose if you intend to have the presentation run unattended, with no moderator. This option is a standard choice for trade shows or other venues where the slides can loop indefinitely for viewers to watch as long as they desire.

You can also configure the slide resolution for a specific monitor. (The default monitor is Automatic, which adjusts the resolution based on the monitor in use.) To set a specific resolution, select a monitor from the Slide Show Monitor drop-down list, and then choose a resolution from the Resolution drop-down list.

SOFTWARE ORIENTATION

Presentation Tools in Slide Show View

When in Slide Show view, presentation tools appear in the bottom left corner of the screen. They are faint until you point at them; then they become bright icons that you can click to open menus. In Figure 11-17 the Menu button is active and its menu is open.

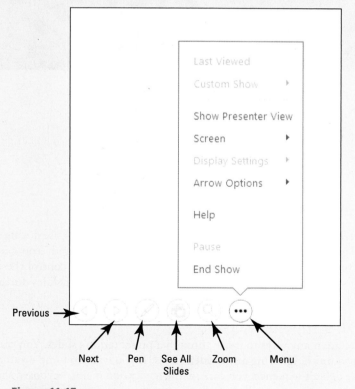

Figure 11-17
The presentation tools

You can also display a navigation menu by right-clicking anywhere on the slide. The right-click menu contains an additional command, Pointer Options, which opens the same menu as the Pen button in the presentation tools.

If you have a second monitor available, you can optionally choose to display Presenter View on the monitor that the audience does not see. Presenter View contains many tools for controlling the presentation behind-the-scenes, and provides a quick look at any speaker notes you may have included in the presentation file (see Figure 11-18).

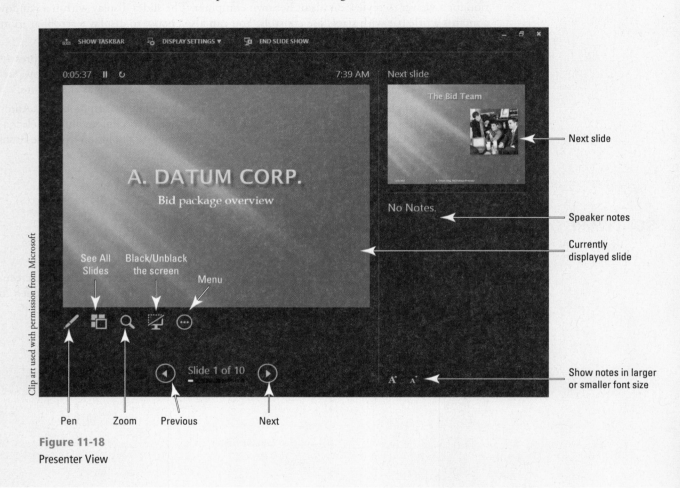

Figure 11-18
Presenter View

WORKING WITH PRESENTATION TOOLS

The Bottom Line

PowerPoint offers a number of **presentation tools** you can use during a presentation to control the display of slides and mark directly on the slides if desired. You can use keyboard commands, mouse clicks, presentation tools, or menu commands to control the presentation. You can select from several marking options and colors to annotate your slides during the presentation.

CERTIFICATION READY? 1.5.6

How do you navigate within a slide show?

Moving Through a Presentation

There are many ways to move through a presentation's slides. You can simply click to move from start to finish, ignoring any hidden slides. If you want to jump around to other slides that are not in the default sequence, you can use the navigation menu, keyboard shortcuts, or other techniques. In this exercise, you will practice moving through a presentation.

PowerPoint provides many methods so that you can use the tools that are most comfortable for you to go forward, backward, or to a specific slide. Table 11-1 summarizes the most popular navigation options in Slide Show view.

Table 11-1

Navigation Options in Slide
Show View

Action	Keyboard	Mouse	Right-click menu	Presentation tools
Show the next slide or animation	N Enter Spacebar Page down Right arrow	Left mouse button.	Right-click, then click Next.	Next button.
Show the previous slide or animation	P Page up Backspace Left arrow	n/a	Right-click, then click Previous.	Previous button.
Go to the next slide if hidden	H	n/a	n/a	n/a
Go to the last slide viewed	n/a	n/a	Right-click, then click Last Viewed.	Menu button, then click Last Viewed.
Go to a specific slide	Press G and use the arrow keys to move the highlight to the desired slide, and then press Enter to display it. OR Press Ctrl+S for the All Slides dialog box, click the desired slide, and click Go To. OR Type the slide number and press Enter.	n/a	Right-click, then click See All Slides, then click the desired thumbnail.	See All Slides button, then click the desired thumbnail.
End show	Esc	n/a	Right-click, then click End Show.	Menu button, then click End Show.
Zoom in on a part of the current slide	+ to zoom in (press again to zoom in more) - to zoom out (press again to zoom out more)	Right-click to return to regular viewing after zooming in.	Right-click, then click Zoom In. Click an area of the slide to zoom in on. Drag to move the zoomed area.	Zoom button. Click an area of the slide to zoom in on. Drag to move the zoomed area.
Get Help (command summary)	n/a	n/a	Right-click, then click Help.	Menu button, then click Help.

If you have chosen the *Browsed by an individual (window)* show type in the Set Up Show dialog box, the presentation tools at the lower-left corner of the screen do not display and you cannot use the mouse button to go to the next slide. You can use the keyboard options to go to the next or previous slide, or you can right-click the slide and select Next to move forward or Previous to move backward through slides.

STEP BY STEP   **Move through a Presentation**

REOPEN the *Bid Final* presentation you worked with earlier in this lesson.

Take Note   An easy way to reopen Bid Final is: click the File tab, click Open, and click the *Bid Final* file at the top of the list of recent files.

1. Make the following changes to the presentation's setup so that it is configured to be used by a live speaker:

   a. Click the Slide Show tab, click the down arrow under the Record Slide Show button, point to Clear, and click Clear Timings on All Slides.

   b. Click the down arrow under the Record Slide Show button, point to Clear, and click Clear Narrations on All Slides.

   c. Click the Set Up Slide Show button, and in the Show Slides section, make sure All is selected (not Custom Show).

   d. In the Show Type section, click Presented by a speaker (full screen).

   e. Open the Slide show monitor drop-down list and click Automatic.

   f. Click OK.

2. Click the From Beginning button to start the presentation from slide 1.

3. Move the pointer on the slide until you can see the presentation tools in the lower-left corner of the screen (see Figure 11-17).

4. Click the Next button (the right-pointing arrow). The next slide displays.

5. Click the Previous button (the left-pointing arrow at the far left of the tools). Slide 1 redisplays.

6. Right-click anywhere on the slide to display the presentation shortcut menu, and click See All Slides. Thumbnail images of the slides appear. Notice that slide 2 is darker than the others because it is hidden (see Figure 11-19).

Another Way

You can also start the presentation from the beginning by pressing F5.

Figure 11-19

After choosing See All Slides, click the slide to jump to

Clip art used with permission from Microsoft

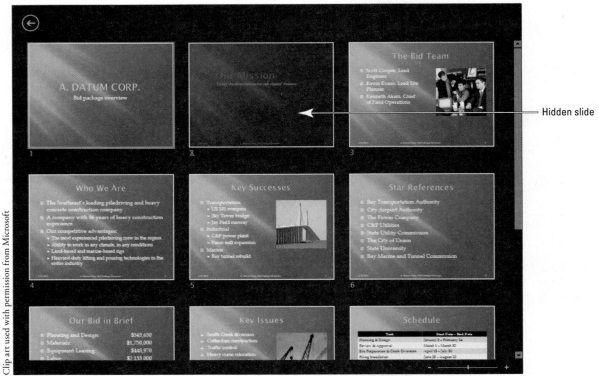

Hidden slide

Another Way

To go to the next slide if it is hidden, you can press H.

7. Click the Back arrow in the upper left corner to return to the slide shown, and then press Page Down to display the next slide.

8. Move the mouse pointer to display the presentation tools, and then click the Zoom button (looks like a magnifying glass). A large rectangular shaded area appears, attached to the mouse pointer.

9. Move the mouse pointer so the shaded area is over the photo and then click to zoom in on the photo. After looking at the photo, right-click to zoom out again.

10. Click the Menu button in the presentation tools (the rightmost button) to display a menu (see Figure 11-17), and then click Last Viewed. The slide you previously viewed (slide 1) displays.

Another Way
You can also end the show by pressing Esc.

11. **Right-click** the screen again, then click **End Show** on the presentation shortcut menu to end the presentation.

PAUSE. LEAVE the presentation open to use in the next exercise.

As you work with PowerPoint, you will find that you develop a feel for the navigation tools that you find easiest to use. It is often more efficient, for example, to use keyboard options because they can be quicker than right-clicking and selecting options from shortcut menus.

Using Presenter View

Presenter view, as you saw in Figure 11-18, provides an interface for controlling a live show. You can use it on another monitor as your slides display in Slide Show view on the monitor or projector that the audience sees. New in PowerPoint 2013, you can display Presenter view even if you do not have two monitors. This gives you a chance to practice working with Presenter view in advance of your presentation, regardless of the hardware you have to practice with. In this exercise you will enter Presenter view and learn about some of its tools and features.

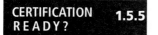

CERTIFICATION READY?   **1.5.5**

How do you use Presenter View?

STEP BY STEP   **Use Presenter View**

USE the presentation that is still open from the previous exercise.

1. On the Slide Show tab, click **From Beginning** to start the presentation from slide 1.
2. **Right-click** anywhere on the slide and click **Show Presenter View** on the menu. Presenter view appears (see Figure 11-20). The current slide appears in the large pane on the left. Beneath it are icons that represent some of the same presenter tools as in Slide Show view. These icons were pointed out in Figure 11-18. The next slide appears in the smaller pane on the right. If this slide contained any speaker notes, they would appear in the lower right corner.

Figure 11-20

Presenter view

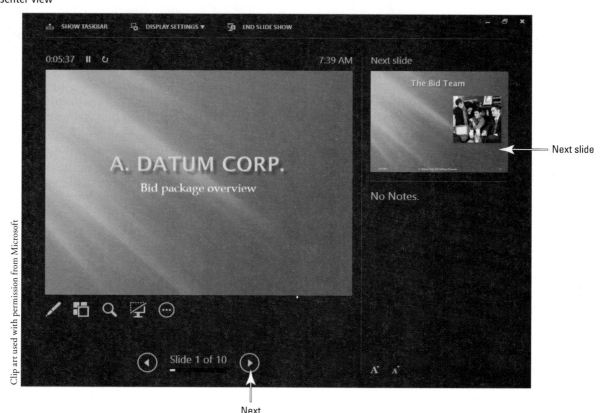

Next

3. Click the Next arrow (right-pointing arrow) at the bottom of the screen. The presentation advances to the next slide.

4. Below the notes pane, click the Make the text smaller button. The note text appears smaller (see Figure 11-21).

Figure 11-21

Use the buttons below the notes pane to make note text larger or smaller

Show Taskbar

Elapsed time

Pause the timer

Restart the timer

Black or Unblack
Slide Show

Make the Text
Larger button

Make the Text
Smaller button

5. Above the current slide, note the timer, which has been recording how much time the presentation has been running. Click the Pause the timer button next to it. The timer stops, and the button turns to a Resume the Timer button (right pointing arrow).

6. Click the Restart the timer button (the button to the right of the Resume the Timer button). The timer resets, and the timer resumes counting.

7. Click Show Taskbar. The taskbar appears at the bottom of the screen. Click Show Taskbar again to turn it off. Showing the taskbar during a presentation can be useful because it enables you to jump out to some other application temporarily.

8. Click the Black or unblack slide show button below the current slide. The image of the current slide appears black, and appears that way on the audience's screen too.

9. Click the Black or unblack slide show button again to restore the current slide's image to the audience's screen.

10. Click End Slide Show to end the presentation.

Another Way
You can also black or unblack the screen by pressing B. If you prefer white, use the W key instead.

PAUSE. LEAVE the presentation open to use in the next exercise.

Annotating Slides with the Pen or Highlighter

As you proceed through a presentation, you may want to pause to emphasize certain points. You can **annotate** (write) directly on a slide with the annotation tools in PowerPoint. You can control these tools, including setting the color and width of the onscreen pen, via the Pen menu in the presentation tools. Various pen types, thicknesses, and colors are available. In the following exercise, you create ink annotations during a slide show.

PowerPoint offers three different annotation pen options: Laser Pointer, Pen, and Highlighter. The Laser Pointer does not leave marks on the slide at all. The Pen leaves marks where you drag it, about the same thickness as an ink pen. The Highlighter leaves a colored swath where you drag it that is semi-transparent, so it does not obscure content. You can change the ink color for any of these pen types.

The Black Screen and White Screen options allow you to replace the current slide with a black or white screen that you can use for annotations or to cover the current material if you want to keep it under wraps while you are discussing some other issue.

CERTIFICATION READY? **1.5.7**

How do you annotate slide shows?

STEP BY STEP   **Annotate Slides**

USE the *Bid Final* presentation that is still open from the previous exercise.

1. Press F5 to start the presentation from slide 1, type 7, and press Enter. Slide 7 appears.
2. Move the mouse to display the presenter tools, click the Pen icon, and Pen (see Figure 11-22). The pointer changes to a small, round pen pointer.

Figure 11-22

Choose the Pen pointer

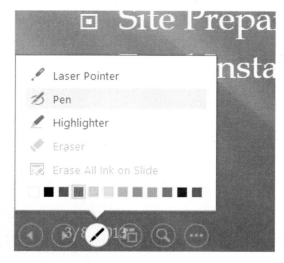

Another Way
You can also right-click, click Show All Slides, and select slide 7. This lesson uses a variety of navigation methods, for practice.

3. Right-click the slide, point to Pointer Options, and click Ink Color. Then click Orange in the Standard Colors palette.
4. Press the space bar until the site preparation bullet point appears, and then use the pen pointer to circle the value for site preparation, $1,125,500 (see Figure 11-23).

Figure 11-23

Make an annotation on a slide

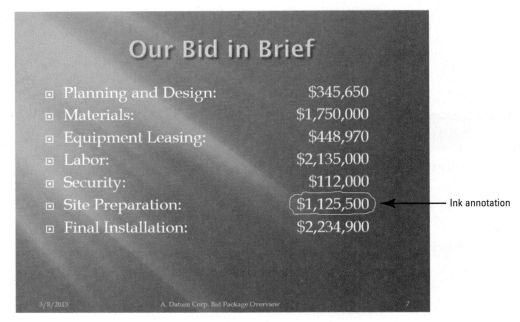

Ink annotation

5. Press the **B key** on the keyboard. The screen is blacked out so you can annotate without the distraction of the slide material.

6. Use the **pen pointer** to draw a large U.S. currency symbol ($) in the middle of the slide.

Take Note While a pen pointer is active, you cannot use the mouse button to advance slides.

7. Press the **B key** again. The slide background is restored and the annotation disappears.

8. Press **Esc** on the keyboard. The arrow pointer is restored.

9. Click or press **Enter** to go to slide 8.

10. Press the space bar until the Weather and Overhead power lines bullet points appear, and then click the **Pen** button in the presentation tools, and then click **Highlighter**. Drag the **highlighter pointer** across the **Weather** bullet item to highlight it (see Figure 11-24).

Figure 11-24

Highlighting text on a slide

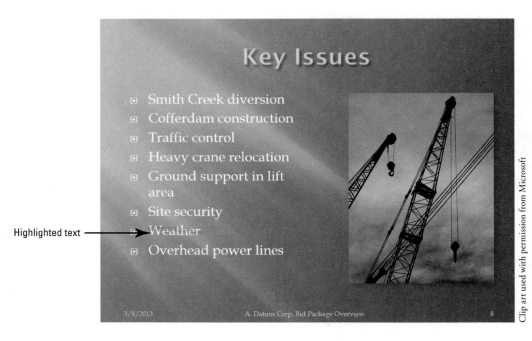

Highlighted text

Clip art used with permission from Microsoft

Another Way
You can also press E to remove all annotations on a slide.

11. Click the **Pen** button, and then click **Erase All Ink on Slide**. The highlight you added is removed.

12. End the slide show. When asked if you want to keep your annotations, click Keep.
13. **SAVE** the presentation.

PAUSE. LEAVE the presentation open to use in the next exercise.

When you reach the end of the presentation (or end it early), if you have created any annotations, you are prompted to either save or discard them. If you save them, they are saved on the slide as **ink**, which is similar to a drawing you might do with the Shapes tool.

Editing Ink Annotations

You can move and delete individual annotations on slides as you would any other graphics, and you can also manage ink with the Ink Tools Pens tab. In the following exercise, you edit an ink annotation in Normal view and add a new annotation there.

STEP BY STEP **Edit Ink Annotations**

USE the *Bid Final* presentation that is still open from the previous exercise.

Figure 11-25

Ink Tools Pens tab on the Ribbon

1. In Normal view, display slide 7 and click the orange circle you drew as an annotation.
2. Click the Ink Tools Pens tab to examine the options available (see Figure 11-25).

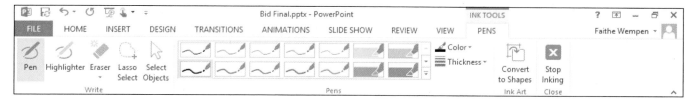

3. Click the Color button to open its palette, and click Light Green. The selected annotation changes color.
4. Click the Thickness button to open its menu, and click 3 pt. The selected annotation increases in thickness.
5. Click the More button in the Pens group to open a gallery of pen styles (see Figure 11-26).

Figure 11-26

Gallery of pen styles

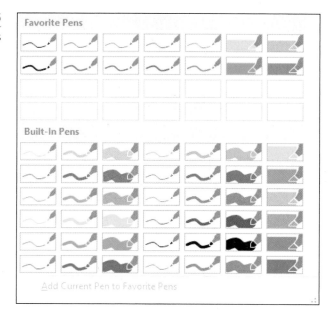

6. In the Built-In Pens section, click **Red Pen (1.0 mm)**. Notice that the selected annotation does not change. These pen styles are for creating new annotations, not editing existing ones.

7. Drag to draw an **underline** beneath Site Preparation.

8. On the Ink Tools Pens tab, click the **Select Objects** button to return to using the arrow pointer again.

9. **SAVE** the presentation.

PAUSE. LEAVE the presentation open to use in the next exercise.

Presenting Online

Presenting online (also called broadcasting a presentation) makes it possible for people to see the presentation who may not be able to attend in person. An online presentation is still a live show with a live speaker, but is delivered remotely.

You control the sequence and timing of the slides from your PC, and you can optionally speak into your microphone to add live voice narration. You can also use the ink annotation tools, pause or resume the show, and use the Black Screen or White Screen options or any other Slide Show view feature. In this exercise, you broadcast a presentation online.

STEP BY STEP   **Present Online**

USE the *Bid Final* presentation that is still open from the previous exercise.

1. If you do not have a Microsoft ID, go to **www.live.com** and get one.

2. In PowerPoint, on the Slide Show tab, click the bottom part of the **Present Online** button to open its menu, and click Office Presentation Service. The Present Online dialog box opens.

Take Note   You must have a Windows Live ID to broadcast a presentation using the Online Presentation Service. Depending on what other services you have installed, Online Presentation Service may be the only option on the menu.

3. Click **Connect**. If prompted to sign in with your Microsoft ID, do so. After a short wait, a link appears that you can share with audience members (see Figure 11-27). The link you receive will be different from the one shown.

Figure 11-27

Share the link with audience members

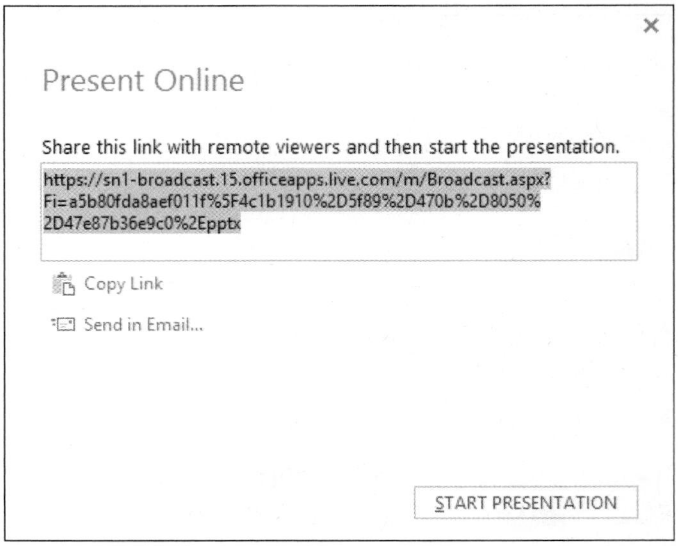

Present Online

×

Share this link with remote viewers and then start the presentation.

https://sn1-broadcast.15.officeapps.live.com/m/Broadcast.aspx?Fi=a5b80fda8aef011f%5F4c1b1910%2D5f89%2D470b%2D8050%2D47e87b36e9c0%2Epptx

📋 Copy Link

📧 Send in Email...

START PRESENTATION

4. (Optional) If you know people who want to see your broadcast, give them the link.

You can do this by clicking Send in Email and emailing them the link, or by distributing the link in some other method, such as manually writing it down on paper. You do not have to have any audience members in order to practice broadcasting, however.

Take Note   To see how a broadcast presentation looks when viewed remotely, team up with a classmate and take turns watching each other's shows.

5. Click Start Presentation. The slide show opens in Slide Show view. You are now broadcasting.

6. Move through the presentation as you normally would. You can optionally use your microphone to comment on the slide content or read it aloud as you go.

7. When you reach the last slide, click one more time to exit, returning to Normal view.

8. On the Present Online tab, click End Online Presentation. Then in the dialog box that appears, click End Online Presentation.

PAUSE. LEAVE the presentation open to use in the next exercise.

PACKAGING A PRESENTATION FOR CD DELIVERY

| **The Bottom Line** |

You may need to transport your presentation materials to another computer to run your slide show. The Package for CD feature streamlines the process of packing all the materials you need to show the presentation even if PowerPoint is not installed on the other computer.

| **CERTIFICATION READY?**   **1.4.3** |

How do you package a presentation for CD?

Packaging a Presentation for CD

The Package for CD feature makes short work of packing all the files you need to show your slides, no matter what kind of system you have to use to run the show. In this exercise, you create a version of your presentation on a CD that you can distribute to others.

Take Note   Some earlier versions of PowerPoint packaged presentations to CD along with a PowerPoint Viewer utility. PowerPoint 2013, however, takes a different approach; it packages presentations with a Web page on the CD. On this Web page is a link for downloading the PowerPoint Viewer if it is needed. If you plan on showing the presentation somewhere that does not have Internet access, make sure you download the PowerPoint Viewer ahead of time on the computer you will be working with if it does not have a full version of PowerPoint on it.

STEP BY STEP   **Package a Presentation for CD**

Take Note   You must have a writeable CD drive inserted in your system to complete this exercise. If you do not, or if you do not have a blank writeable CD disc available, skip this exercise.

USE the *Bid Final* presentation that is still open from the previous exercise.

1. Insert a blank writeable CD disc in your writeable CD drive. If an AutoPlay box pops up, close it.

2. Click the File tab, click Export, click Package Presentation for CD, and click Package for CD. The Package for CD dialog box opens.

3. In the Name the CD box, type Bid, replacing the default name (see Figure 11-28).

Figure 11-28

Package for CD dialog box

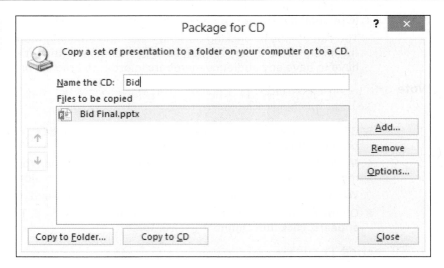

Take Note You can optionally add other presentations onto the same CD to avoid using a separate CD for each presentation. To add other presentations, you would click Add and select the presentations to include. You could then reorder them with the up and down arrow buttons in the dialog box. This exercise packages only one presentation on CD, so it does not include these actions.

4. Click the Options button. The Options dialog box opens. Note that linked files are marked to be included, and TrueType fonts will be embedded. Note that you can also optionally specify passwords to control access to the presentation(s) (see Figure 11-29).

Figure 11-29

The Options dialog box for packaging a presentation

5. Click OK to accept the default settings and close the Options dialog box.
6. In the Package for CD dialog box, click Copy to CD.
7. A dialog box asks if you want to include linked files in your package. Click Yes.
8. A message appears that the presentation contains comments or annotations, stating that these will not be included. Click Continue.
9. Wait for the presentation to be written to the CD. It may take several minutes. The CD ejects when finished.
10. In PowerPoint, a message appears stating that the files were successfully copied to CD and offering to copy the same files to another CD. Click No.
11. Click Close to close the Package for CD dialog box.
12. To test your new CD, reinsert the CD into your computer. If an AutoPlay box opens, click Run PresentationPackage.html. If no box opens, open File Explorer (or Windows Explorer if using Windows 7), click Computer, and double-click the CD drive.
13. A Web page displays, showing a page that lists the presentations on the CD. (There is only one in this case.) See Figure 11-30. A link also appears for downloading the PowerPoint Viewer. You do not need it on your PC since you have the full version of PowerPoint.

Take Note   Note that the name might appear as Bid%20Final, as in Figure 11.30, because the space between the two words is treated as a non-breaking space in HTML.

Figure 11-30

This web page has been generated

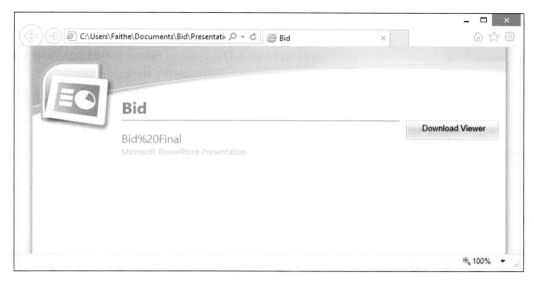

14. Click the name of the presentation. Respond to any security warnings you might see in your Web browser. The presentation opens in PowerPoint, in Read-Only mode.

15. Click the File tab and click Close to close the copy of the presentation that originated from the CD. (The original *Bid Final* presentation is still open.)

PAUSE. LEAVE the presentation open to use in the next exercise.

To make the process of storing files on a CD more efficient, you can choose to copy more than one presentation to the same CD. Click the Add Files button to open additional presentations. This feature can reduce the amount of wasted space that results if you copy a single presentation to a CD.

The Options dialog box that you can access from the Package for CD dialog box gives you additional choices for the packaging process:

- Linked files, such as large movie and sound files, are included automatically, and you will normally want to retain this setting. You can, however, save the package without linked files if desired by deselecting this option.
- Embedding TrueType fonts is a good idea if you are not sure what fonts you might have access to on the system where you will run the presentation. Embedding fonts will add to file size but ensure the quality of your presentation's font appearance.
- You can specify a password to open or modify the presentation, and you can prompt PowerPoint to inspect the presentation for hidden or personal data you do not want to share.

Take Note   Package for CD works only with CDs, not DVDs. If you want to store a presentation on a DVD, you can save materials in a folder as described in the following section, and then use your system's DVD burning tools to copy the files to the DVD.

Packaging a Presentation to a Folder

In addition to using Package for CD to create materials to transport a presentation, you can use this feature to archive presentations onto a CD or into folders for storage. The packaging process pulls together all the files you need for a presentation, so your stored presentation provides an excellent long-term backup for your work. In this exercise, you package a presentation to a folder.

STEP BY STEP | **Package a Presentation to a Folder**

USE the *Bid Final* presentation that is still open from the previous exercise.

1. Click the File tab, click Export, click Package Presentation for CD, and click Package for CD. The Package for CD dialog box opens.
2. Click Copy to Folder. The Copy to Folder dialog box opens.
3. In the Folder name box, change the default name to *Bid*.
4. In the Location box, change the path to the location where you store files for this lesson (see Figure 11-31).

Figure 11-31

Specify a folder and location for the packaged presentation

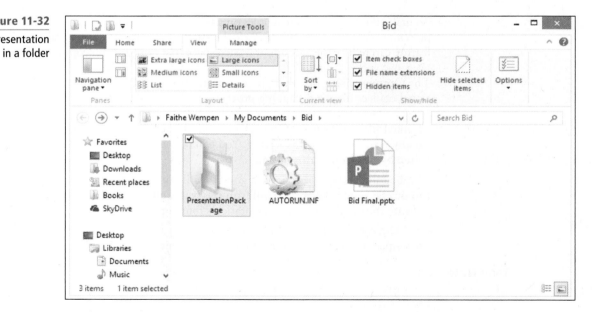

9. In the folder window, double-click the PresentationPackage folder to see what is inside it. The folder contains some graphics and support files that are needed to show the Web page.
10. Close the folder window and return to PowerPoint. The Package for CD dialog box is still open.
11. Click Close to close the dialog box.
12. **SAVE** the presentation and then **CLOSE** the file.

EXIT PowerPoint.

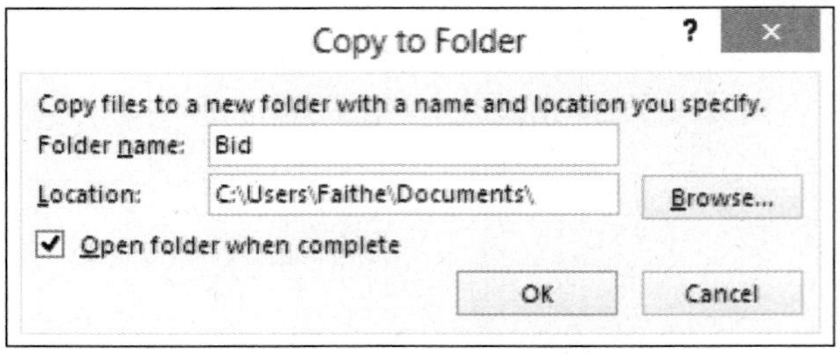

5. Click OK.
6. A message appears asking if you want to include linked files in your package. Click Yes.
7. A message appears that the presentation contains comments or annotations, and that these will not be included. Click Continue.
8. Wait for the presentation to be written to the new folder. It should occur almost instantaneously (unlike when making a CD). The folder opens in Windows when it is finished (see Figure 11-32).

Figure 11-32

The packaged presentation in a folder

SKILL SUMMARY

In This Lesson, You Learned How To:	Exam Objective	Objective Number
Adjust Slide Orientation and Size	Change page setup options.	1.3.1
	Configure slideshow resolution.	1.5.4
Customize Audience Handouts	Set handout print options.	1.4.1
Choose Slides to Display	Hide slides.	2.1.3
	Create custom slideshows.	1.5.1
Rehearse and Record a Slide Show	Rehearse timings.	1.5.3
Set Up a Slide Show	Configure slideshow options.	1.5.2
Work with Presentation Tools	Navigate within slideshows.	1.5.6
	Use Presenter View.	1.5.5
	Annotate slideshows.	1.5.7
Package a Presentation for CD Delivery	Package presentations for CD.	1.4.3

Knowledge Assessment

Fill in the Blank

Fill in each blank with the term or phrase that best completes the statement.

1. Use the _____ dialog box to change to a non-standard slide size.
2. You can set up a presentation to loop continuously until you press the _____ key.
3. Use the _____ toolbar to view timings as you rehearse a presentation.
4. For more control over handouts, you can export them to _____.
5. To display a hidden slide during a presentation, click _____ on the shortcut menu and then click the hidden slide.
6. If the computer on which you will present your slides does not have PowerPoint, you can use the _____ to show the presentation.
7. Customize the _____ to create your own handout layouts.
8. If you have two monitors, you can use _____ to control the presentation on one screen while your audience looks at the other screen.
9. When you _____ slides, you use the pointer to draw or write.
10. Use the _____ feature to deliver a presentation in real time over the Internet.

Multiple Choice

Circle the correct answer.

1. A slide that is wider than it is tall is displayed in:
   a. portrait orientation.
   b. column orientation.
   c. picture orientation.
   d. landscape orientation.
2. If you need to show slides on a wide-screen monitor, you might set their size to:
   a. Onscreen Show (16:9).
   b. Onscreen Show (3:4).

    c. 35 mm Slides.

    d. Ledger Paper (11×17 in).

3. Which of these is not one of the standard placeholders on the Handout Master?
   a. Date
   b. Header
   c. Page Number
   d. Author

4. To prevent a slide from displaying during a presentation, select it and then choose:
   a. Delete Slide.
   b. Hide Slide.
   c. Show/Hide Slide.
   d. Conceal Slide.

5. If you want to show only a selected series of slides from a presentation, the most efficient option is to:
   a. hide each slide you do not want to use.
   b. create an entirely new presentation and copy into it the slides you want to use.
   c. create a custom show of the slides you want to show.
   d. copy the presentation and then delete the slides you do not want to use.

6. When you rehearse timings, you should:
   a. skim over the content of each slide.
   b. read the entire content of each slide and look carefully at pictures and diagrams.
   c. allow yourself a set amount of time to view each slide regardless of its content.
   d. look only at the slide titles.

7. If you set up a slide show to be browsed by an individual, the slides display:
   a. using the full screen.
   b. in a virtual kiosk.
   c. in a window with a title bar.
   d. within the PowerPoint window.

8. Which of the following is *not* a way to advance to the next slide during a presentation?
   a. Press Home
   b. Press the spacebar
   c. Click the left mouse button
   d. Press Page Down

9. A quick way to restore the arrow pointer after you have used it for drawing is to:
   a. press End.
   b. double-click the screen.
   c. click the arrow pointer button in the presenter tools.
   d. press Esc.

10. Package for CD can also package a presentation to
   a. a Web address.
   b. a printer.
   c. a folder on your hard disk.
   d. None of the above

Competency Assessment

Project 11-1: Preparing to Fly

You are nearly ready to present the slide show for Blue Yonder Airlines. Use the tools you have learned about in this lesson to finalize the presentation and create handouts.

GET READY. Launch PowerPoint if it is not already running.

Online

The *Airline* file is available on the book companion website or in WileyPLUS.

1. **OPEN** the *Airline* presentation and save it as *Airline Final*.

2. Click the **Design** tab, click the **Slide Size** button, and click **Standard (4:3)**. When prompted to scale the content, click **Ensure Fit**.

3. Click the Slide Show tab, and then click the Set Up Slide Show button.

4. Choose the Presented by a speaker option and choose to have slides advance Manually. Choose Blue as the pen color. Click OK to accept the new settings.

5. Click the Insert tab, click Header & Footer, and on the Notes and Handouts tab, choose to display the date (update automatically), the header *Blue Yonder Airlines*, and page numbers. Click Apply to All to apply the setting to all slides.

6. Click the View tab, and then click Handout Master to open Handout Master view.

7. Center the header text and date in their placeholders, and right-align the page number in its placeholder. Close Handout Master view.

8. Hide the last slide in the presentation.

9. Click the File tab, click Print, and set the following print options:

   a. Choose to print handouts with four slides per page, in vertical order.

   b. In the Slides settings, deselect the Frame Slides option.

   c. In the Print All Slides settings, deselect the Print Hidden Slides option.

10. Print the handouts.

11. **SAVE** the presentation and **CLOSE** the file.

LEAVE PowerPoint open for use in the next project.

Project 11-2: Twin Cities Crawl

You are ready to finalize the presentation you created to publicize the Twin Cities Gallery Crawl. You need to rehearse and set up the show and then package the presentation for delivery.

Online

The *Galleries* file is available on the book companion website or in WileyPLUS.

1. **OPEN** the *Galleries* presentation and save it as *Galleries Final*.

2. Click the Slide Show tab, and then click the Rehearse Timings button.

3. Read each slide. When the slide show ends, choose to save the rehearsed timings.

4. Click the Set Up Slide Show button, and set up the show to be browsed at a kiosk using the timings you saved to advance slides. Click OK to close the dialog box.

5. Click the File tab, click Export, click Package Presentation for CD, and click Package for CD.

6. Type the package name Galleries. If you can copy to a CD, click Copy to CD and complete the packaging process. If you cannot copy to a CD, click Copy to Folder, select the folder in which you are storing solutions for Lesson 11, and complete the packaging process. If prompted, include linked files.

7. Close the Package for CD dialog box.

8. **SAVE** the presentation and then **CLOSE** the file.

LEAVE PowerPoint open for the next project.

Proficiency Assessment

Project 11-3: Final Airline Check

You want to run through the Airline Final presentation before delivering it to make sure you are familiar with content and how to display it during the slide show.

1. **OPEN** the *Airline Final* presentation you created in Project 11-1.

2. Hide slide 7.

3. Press F5 to view the presentation from slide 1.

4. Use the Next button in the presentation tools to move to slide 3.

5. Use the Previous button in the presentation tools to go backward to slide 1.

6. Right-click the slide to display the shortcut menu, and use See All Slides to jump to slide 4.

7. Right-click the slide, click Pointer Options, and select Highlighter.

8. Highlight the bullet items *Caribbean* and *Scuba*.

9. Restore the arrow pointer and press Esc to end the show. Choose to keep your annotations.

10. Rehearse timings for the presentation. When the presentation ends, save the slide timings.

11. Set up the slide show to use the slide timings you saved.

12. **SAVE** the presentation as *Airline Final Check* and then **CLOSE** the file.

LEAVE PowerPoint open for use in the next project.

Project 11-4: Year-End Review

You are ready to do the final tweaking of the year-end review for Contoso's Human Resources department. You will create a custom show to send to Contoso's president and CEO, customize handouts for the year-end review meeting, and adjust slide size for printing.

1. **OPEN** the *Review* presentation and save it as *Review Custom*.

2. Create a custom show named Review Summary. Include in the custom show slides 1, 3, 4, 6, 7, 9, 10, and 12.

3. Change the slide size to Letter Paper (8.5x11 in).

4. Display a date that updates, the header *Contoso HR Year in Review*, and page numbers for all handouts and notes pages.

5. Display the handout master, and show the 3 Slides layout.

6. Select the Header and Date placeholders, center the text in these placeholders, and adjust the vertical alignment in these placeholders to Middle. (Hint: Use Align Text on the Home tab to set Middle alignment.)

7. Reduce the width of each placeholder (both at the top and the bottom of the handout layout) to 2.5 inches wide. (Hint: Use the Width box on the Drawing Tools Format tab.)

8. Move the Header and Date placeholders down about a quarter of an inch from the top of the page.

9. Center the Header placeholder over the slide image column, and center the Date placeholder over the empty column where the lines will appear to the right of the slide images. (You can check placement by displaying the handouts in Print Preview.)

10. Apply the Colored Outline, Blue, Accent 1 shape style (from the Drawing Tools Format tab) to the Header and Date placeholders. Figure 11-33 shows the completed layout.

Figure 11-33

The modified handout layout

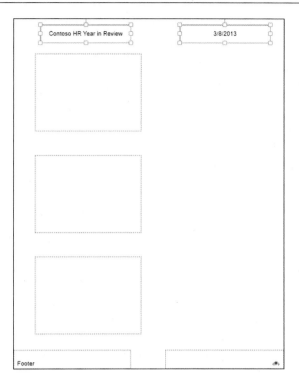

11. Print handouts with three slides per page.
12. **SAVE** the presentation.

LEAVE the presentation open for use in the next project.

Mastery Assessment

Project 11-5: Review Final

You need to complete your preparation of the Review Custom presentation and test it before you send it to the HR executive staff.

1. **USE** the file from the previous exercise, and **SAVE** the presentation as *Review Final*.
2. Set the slides for Widescreen 16:9 display.
3. Set up the slide show to display only the Review Summary custom show for an individual. Turn on the Show without animation option, and choose to advance slides manually.
4. Start the slide show from slide 1 and view the slides in the custom show, using keyboard options to advance slides.
5. **SAVE** the presentation and then **CLOSE** the file.

LEAVE PowerPoint open for use in the next project.

Project 11-6: Museum Online Presentation

You have been asked to broadcast the Museum presentation over the Internet to some students at a middle school as part of their science and technology class project. You will prepare the presentation and then broadcast it.

1. **OPEN** the *Museum* presentation. **SAVE** the presentation as *Museum Final*.
2. On the Slide Show tab, turn off Use Timings.
3. In the Set Up Show dialog box, set the Show Type to Presented by a speaker (full screen) and mark the Show without animation check box.
4. Begin an online presentation, logging into Windows Live when prompted. When the link appears to share, send it to your instructor in an email message.
5. Begin the broadcast. Move through the entire presentation, and then end the broadcast.
6. **CLOSE** *Museum Final*.

EXIT PowerPoint.

Circling Back 3

You are a project manager at Trey Research. You must give a report to your managers on the status of a major project you are running. Use PowerPoint tools and features you have learned about throughout this course to create, format, and finalize a presentation that you can use to report your project status.

Project 1: Create the Presentation

In this project, you will create your presentation and insert a slide from another presentation. You will also create and format a chart and insert headers and footers for slides and handouts.

GET READY. LAUNCH PowerPoint if it is not already running.

1. Create a new blank presentation.
2. **SAVE** the presentation as *Report*.
3. Type the slide title Trey Research and the slide subtitle Woodgrove Bank Customer Survey.
4. Insert slide 2 from the *Update* presentation into the current presentation using the Reuse Slides option on the New Slide drop-down list.
5. Apply the Facet theme.
6. Go to slide 1 and boldface the slide title. Increase the font size of the subtitle to 20 pt.
7. Add a new slide at the end of the presentation with the Title and Content layout. Type the title Customer Types.
8. Insert a 3D pie chart on the slide using the following data:

	Customers
Main office	23
Branches	49
Online	16
Telephone	12

9. Remove the chart title and add data labels at the inside end of the pie slices.
10. Apply the Style 4 chart style to the chart.
11. Select the data labels and click the Increase Font Size button on the Home tab until the size is 20 points.
12. Insert the date (updating automatically), slide numbers, and the footer Woodgrove Bank Customer Survey on all slides except the title slide, and the same footer and page numbers on notes and handouts. Add the header Trey Research for notes and handouts.
13. **SAVE** the presentation.

PAUSE. LEAVE PowerPoint and your presentation open for the next project.

Project 2: Add Research Data

You are now ready to add a slide to show the data you have collected in your project. Some of the data is still in an Excel worksheet, so you will add an action button link to the worksheet.

USE the presentation that is open from the previous project.

1. Add a new slide at the end of the *Report* presentation with the Title and Content layout, and type the slide title Overall Responses.
2. Insert a new table with four columns and eight rows. Type the following data in the table:

Experience	Positive	Negative	No Response
Customer Service: Overall	91%	8%	1%
Customer Service: Tellers	86%	12.5%	1.5%
Customer Service: Managers	75%	23%	2%
Transaction Handling	80%	20%	0%
Wait Times	41%	58%	1%
Convenience of Facilities	89%	9%	2%
Sense of Security	84%	15%	1%

3. Format the table with the Medium Style 2 – Accent 1 table style.

4. Adjust column widths so that all text in the first column appears on a single line and the other three columns are the same width as one another.

5. Add a shadow effect to the table.

6. Insert a text box above the table, to the right of the slide title, and insert the following text:
   For detailed results, visit www.treyresearch.net, log in with your password, and click the Woodgrove Survey link.

7. Check the URL to make sure the hyperlink is to http://www.treyresearch.net.

8. Format the text box to be 4" wide, and apply a Shape Style to the text box that coordinates well with the table.

9. Draw an Information action button in the bottom right corner of the slide, and link the button to the *Woodgrove Results* Excel file.

10. Apply the same Shape Style to the action button that you applied to the text box.

11. **SAVE** the presentation.

PAUSE. LEAVE PowerPoint and your presentation open for the next project.

Project 3: **Add Graphic Interest**

You need to add some graphic interest to the presentation. You will use a clip art picture to illustrate one of the slides. You also need to insert a diagram to show the process required to change customer interaction behavior.

USE the presentation that is open from the previous project.

1. Add a new slide at the end of the *Report* presentation with the Title and Content layout. Type the title Change Process.

2. Insert the Staggered Process SmartArt diagram in the content placeholder.

3. Display the Text pane if necessary and insert the following text:

   1. Data collection
   2. Present to management
   3. Revise policies and procedures
   4. Management/HR training
   5. Staff training

4. Apply a different SmartArt style to the diagram, such as the Cartoon style, and change colors to one in the Colorful range.

5. Go to slide 1. Click the Online Pictures button on the Insert tab to open the Insert Pictures dialog box.

6. Using Office.com Clip Art, find and insert a photo that could represent a businessperson talking to a customer.

7. Size and format the picture so it looks attractive in the area to the left of the title and subtitle.

8. Apply the Beveled Oval, Black picture style. Change the picture's border to Dark Green, Accent 2.

9. **SAVE** the presentation.

PAUSE. LEAVE PowerPoint and your presentation open for the next project.

Project 4: **Prepare for Delivery**

You are ready to apply transitions and animations to add interest during the presentation. It is also time to prepare handouts that your audience can use to follow the presentation as you deliver it.

USE the presentation that is open from the previous project.

1. Apply the Wipe transition with the From Top option at a speed of 01.50 for all slides.
2. Go to slide 2 and apply the Fade animation effect to the text in the content placeholder.
3. Insert a comment on slide 2:
   Should we also evaluate the customer service provided by support staff?
4. Export handouts to Microsoft Word, using the blank lines next to slides layout.
5. Save the handouts as a Word document named *Handouts.docx*. Close Word.
6. In PowerPoint, print the handouts with the Six Slides Horizontal layout.
7. **SAVE** the presentation.

PAUSE. LEAVE PowerPoint and your presentation open for the next project.

Project 5: **Final Touches**

You are ready to test your presentation. You will review the show, test the annotation options, rehearse timings, and set up the show for its final delivery. Finally, you will package the show so you can transport it easily on the day of the presentation.

USE the presentation that is open from the previous project.

1. Start the slide show from slide 1 and use any combination of keyboard shortcuts, menu commands, or mouse clicks to advance slides until you reach slide 4.
2. On slide 4 (Overall Responses), change the pointer to the Pen and circle the URL in the text box.
3. Restore the arrow pointer and test the action button. Close Excel after you have looked at the data and return to the slide show.
4. Continue with the remaining slide and end the show. Save the annotation.
5. Run the show again to rehearse timings of slides. Save your slide timings.
6. Open the Set Up Show dialog box and make sure the Advance Slides option is set to Using timings, if present.
7. Package the presentation to a folder named Trey Report. Choose to include linked content in the package.
8. **SAVE** and **CLOSE** the presentation.

EXIT PowerPoint.

Microsoft Office Specialist (MOS) Skills for PowerPoint 2013: Exam 77-422

Matrix Skill	Objective Number	Lesson Number
Create and Manage Presentations	**1**	
Create a Presentation.	1.1	
Create blank presentations.	1.1.1	1, 2
Create presentations using templates.	1.1.2	1, 2
Import text files into presentations.	1.1.3	1, 2
Open Word document outlines into presentations.	1.1.4	1, 2
Format a Presentation Using Slide Masters.	1.2	
Apply a slide master.	1.2.1	4
Add new layouts.	1.2.2	4
Modify existing layouts.	1.2.3	4
Add background images.	1.2.4	4
Control slide numbers.	1.2.5	4
Insert headers and footers.	1.2.6	4
Modify presentation themes.	1.2.7	4
Customize Presentation Options and Views.	1.3	
Change page setup options.	1.3.1	11
Change to view in color/grayscale.	1.3.2	1
Demonstrate how to use views to navigate through presentations.	1.3.3	1
Modify presentation properties.	1.3.4	10
Configure Presentations to Print or Save.	1.4	
Set handout print options.	1.4.1	11
Print selections from presentations.	1.4.2	1, 2
Package presentations for CD.	1.4.3	11
Save presentations as XML.	1.4.4	10
Print presentations in grayscale.	1.4.5	1, 2
Print speaker notes.	1.4.6	1, 2
Maintain backward compatibility.	1.4.7	10

Matrix Skill	Objective Number	Lesson Number
Configure and Present Slideshows.	1.5	
Create custom slideshows.	1.5.1	11
Configure slideshow options.	1.5.2	11
Rehearse timing.	1.5.3	11
Configure slideshow resolution.	1.5.4	11
Demonstrate how to use presenter view.	1.5.5	11
Navigate within slideshows.	1.5.6	11
Annotate slideshows.	1.5.7	11
Insert and Format Shapes and Slides	**2.0**	
Insert and Format Slides.	2.1	
Add singular layouts.	2.1.1	4
Duplicate existing slides.	2.1.2	1, 2
Hide slides.	2.1.3	11
Delete slides.	2.1.4	1, 2
Modify slide backgrounds.	2.1.5	4
Apply styles to slides.	2.1.6	2
Insert and Format Shapes.	2.2	
Modify shape backgrounds.	2.2.1	3
Apply borders to shapes.	2.2.2	8
Resize shapes.	2.2.3	8
Insert shapes.	2.2.4	8
Create custom shapes.	2.2.5	8
Apply styles to shapes.	2.2.6	8
Order and Group Shapes and Slides.	2.3	
Insert section headers.	2.3.1	4
Modify slide order.	2.3.2	2
Align and group shapes.	2.3.3	8
Display gridlines.	2.3.4	8
Create Slide Content	**3.0**	
Insert and Format Text.	3.1	
Change text to WordArt.	3.1.1	3
Create multiple columns in a single shape.	3.1.2	3
Insert hyperlinks.	3.1.3	4

Matrix Skill	Objective Number	Lesson Number
Apply formatting and styles to text.	3.1.4	3
Create bulleted and numbered lists.	3.1.5	3
Insert and Format Tables.	3.2	
Create new tables.	3.2.1	5
Modify the number of rows and columns.	3.2.2	5
Apply table styles.	3.2.3	5
Import tables from external sources.	3.2.4	5
Insert and Format Charts.	3.3	
Create and modify chart styles.	3.3.1	6
Insert charts.	3.3.2	6
Modify chart type.	3.3.3	6
Add legends to charts.	3.3.4	6
Modify chart parameters.	3.3.5	6
Import charts from external sources.	3.3.6	6
Insert and Format SmartArt.	3.4	
Add shapes to SmartArt.	3.4.1	7
Change color of SmartArt.	3.4.2	7
Move text within SmartArt shapes.	3.4.3	7
Reverse direction.	3.4.4	7
Convert lists to SmartArt.	3.4.5	7
Insert and Format Images.	3.5	
Resize images.	3.5.1	8
Crop images.	3.5.2	8
Apply effects.	3.5.3	8
Apply styles.	3.5.4	8
Insert and Format Media.	3.6	
Adjust media window size.	3.6.1	9
Trim timing on media clips.	3.6.2	9
Set start/stop times.	3.6.3	9
Set media options.	3.6.4	9
Link to external media.	3.6.5	9
Apply Transitions and Animations	**4.0**	
Apply transitioning between slides.	4.1	

Matrix Skill	Objective Number	Lesson Number
Insert transitions between slides.	4.1.1	9
Manage multiple transitions.	4.1.2	9
Modify transition effect options.	4.1.3	9
Animate Slide Content.	4.2	
Apply animations to shapes.	4.2.1	9
Apply animations to text strings.	4.2.2	9
Add paths to animations.	4.2.3	9
Modify animation options.	4.2.4	9
Set Timing for Transitions and Animations.	4.3	
Modify duration of effects.	4.3.1	9
Configure start and finish options.	4.3.2	9
Reorder animations.	4.3.3	9
Demonstrate how to use the Animation Pane.	4.3.4	9
Manage Multiple Presentations	**5.0**	
Merge Content from Multiple Presentations.	5.1	
Merge multiple presentations.	5.1.1	10
Reuse slides from other presentations.	5.1.2	1, 2
View multiple presentations.	5.1.3	1
Review Changes.	5.2	
Use the Reviewing/Revisions Pane.	5.2.1	10
Compare revisions.	5.2.2	10
Manage changes.	5.2.3	10
Manage comments.	5.2.4	10
Protect and Share Presentations.	5.3	
Encrypt presentations with a password.	5.3.1	10
Proof presentations.	5.3.2	3
Mark as final.	5.3.3	10
Compress media.	5.3.4	8
Embed fonts.	5.3.5	1, 2
Restrict permissions.	5.3.6	10
Remove presentation metadata.	5.3.7	10
Check for accessibility issues.	5.3.8	10
Check for compatibility issues.	5.3.9	10

PowerPoint 2013
Glossary

A

Accessible   A type of presentation that can be viewed by a wide variety of computer users, including those who may have disabilities that require them to use adaptive technologies such as screen reading programs.

action   A button or text block programmed to perform a specific action, such as jumping to a slide or starting a program.

action button   A graphic that serves as a hyperlink to jump to a location or perform an action.

After Previous   An animation sequencing setting that causes the animation to trigger after the previous event has finished. Compare to *With Previous*.

animations   An effect you apply to placeholders or other content to move the content in unique ways on the slide.

Animation Painter   A feature that copies animation settings from one object to another.

Animation Pane   A pane that enables you to manage all the animation effects on the active slide.

annotate   To write or draw on a slide during a presentation.

aspect ratio   The relationship of width to height in a picture or shape.

assistant   In an organization chart, a person who reports directly to a superior.

audio   A sound or music clip.

B

Backstage view   The view that opens when you click the File tab, containing commands for managing files, setting program options, and printing.

Bulleted list   Groups of items or phrases that present related ideas.

C

caption   A few descriptive words providing readers with information regarding a figure, table, or equation.

cells   The rectangles that are formed when rows and columns intersect.

chart area   The entire area inside the chart container that holds background as well as plotted data.

chart element   A feature that helps a user clarify the data in a chart.

charts   Visual representations of numerical data.

clip art   A collection of media files available to insert in Microsoft Office documents that can include illustrations, photographs, video, or audio content.

columns   Vertical blocks of text in which text flows from the bottom of one column to the top of the next.

Command   An instruction users give Word by clicking a button or entering information into a command box.

comment   A note a user inserts on a slide while reviewing.

constrain   To force a drawing object into a particular shape or alignment.

contiguous
contiguous   Adjacent to one another. For example, slides 1 and 2 are contiguous.

crop   The process of trimming the horizontal or vertical edges of a picture to get rid of unwanted areas.

custom show   A group of slides in a presentation that can be shown separately from the entire presentation.

D

data marker   A single column, pie slice, or point from a data series.

data series   All the data points for a particular category of plotted information.

delay   An animation setting that specifies how long the effect should pause before it begins.

demote   To make an item subordinate to another item.

dialog box   A box that prompts the user for additional information when executing a command.

dialog box launcher   In some command groups on the Ribbon, a small icon that opens a dialog box related to that group.

drop-down arrow   A small, downward-pointing arrow next to some tools on the ribbon.

drop-down list   A list that appears once a drop-down arrow is clicked, allowing you to choose from available options.

duration   An animation setting that determines how long an animation effect should take to execute.

E

embedded   Data that has been placed in a destination application so that it can be edited with the tools of its original source applications.

emphasis effect   An animation effect that causes an object to move, change color, or otherwise call attention to itself when it is neither entering nor exiting the slide.

encrypting   The process of transforming data into a nonreadable form for security purposes.

entrance effect   An animation effect that occurs when an object is entering the slide.

entrance effect   An animation effect that occurs when an object is entering the slide.

exit effect   An animation effect that occurs when an object is exiting the slide.

F

file tab   The tab on the Ribbon that opens Backstage view.

fonts   Typefaces that are used to display characters, numbers, and symbols in your PowerPoint presentation.

font theme   A combination of two fonts to be applied to headings and text as part of a theme.

footer   Text that appears on the bottom of a page.

formatting   The shape, shape, and general characteristics of a presentation.

Format painter   A tool to copy character and format painting.

G

gridlines A tool that provides a grid of vertical and horizontal lines that help you align graphics and other objects on a slide.

groups A set of related tools on the ribbon.

guides Nonprinting vertical and horizontal lines that a user can move or copy to align objects on a slide.

H

handout A printed copy of a presentation.

Handout master The master that controls the layout and elements of a handout.

header Information such as a date, slide number, or text phrase that appears at the top of each page of a presentation's handouts.

hyperlink An address that refers to another location, such as a website, a different slide, or an external file.

I

I-beam pointer The mouse pointer, when over a text box or editable text area, appearing as a curly capital I. If a user clicks when the I-beam pointer is displayed, the insertion point moves to that spot.

Indent level The distance of a paragraph of text from the placeholders left border.

ink The annotations created with the pen and highlighter tools during a slide show.

K

KeyTips A letter or number that appears next to an onscreen tool when the Alt key is pressed; keying that letter or number activates the associated tool.

keyword A word or phrase that describes a subject or category on which you can search.

L

landscape orientation A page orientation that is wider than it is tall.

lassoing To drag an imaginary box around a group of objects to select them.

layout A predefined arrangement of placeholders for text or objects (such as charts or pictures).

layout master The slide master for a particular slide layout.

legend The key to a chart that explains what each data series represents.

line spacing The amount of vertical space between paragraphs.

linked Data that has been placed in a destination application so that it maintains a link with its source file; changes to the source file are also made in the linked object.

Live Preview A feature that allows a user to preview how a change to a slide object will look before accepting or declining the change.

M

Mark as Final A setting that prevents changes from being made to a presentation unless the user chooses to acknowledge the warning and edit it anyway; does not provide security.

markup The changes identified between two versions of a presentation when using Compare.

metadata Information about data.

mini toolbar A small toolbar that appears when the mouse pointer is placed on a selected text object; provides commands for working with the text.

motion path An animation effect that moves an object along a specified path.

N

non-contiguous Not adjacent to one another.

Normal view The default PowerPoint view, suited for editing individual slides; includes the slide pane, Notes pane, and Slides/Outline pane.

note Additional information associated with a slide.

Notes Page view A view that displays a single slide and its associated notes.

null string Blank, with no characters or spaces.

numbered list A group of steps, procedures, or actions that are listed in numerical order.

O

On-click A trigger for an animation or transition that occurs when the mouse is clicked.

OpenDocument A standard format that many applications, including free Office suites online such as OpenOffice, use to ensure compatibility between programs.

Order The way in which objects stack up on a slide as a user creates them.

Organizational chart A diagram that shows the relationships between personnel or departments in an organization.

Orientation The direction that material appears on a page when printed.

P

password A word or phrase that a user must enter in order to get access to a file.

PDF Portable Document Format; one of the page description languages to which PowerPoint can export; requires Adobe Reader or Adobe Acrobat to read.

picture presentation A presentation that consists of a series of full-screen graphics of slide content, placed on blank slide backgrounds.

Placeholder On a slide, a box that holds a specific type of content, such as text.

platform-independent Able to be used on a variety of operating systems.

plot area The area in the chart container that shows the data series compared to the chart's gridlines.

portrait orientation A page orientation that is taller than it is wide.

Poster frame An image that displays on a slide when a video clip is not actively playing.

PowerPoint Show A presentation that opens by default in Slide Show view.

Presentation tools The tools and commands that are active during Slide Show view.

Presenter View A viewing mode that allows the presenter to see notes on one screen while the audience views slides on another screen.

Promote To make an item superior to another item.

Q

Quick Access Toolbar Toolbar on the upper-left corner of the PowerPoint window that provides easy access to tools you use frequently, such as Save and Undo.

Quick Style Built-in formatting for text, graphics, SmartArt diagrams, charts, WordArt, pictures, tables, and shapes.

R

Reading view   Displays a slide show presentation in a window rather than filling the entire screen, enabling a user to work in other windows at the same time.

Recolor   A feature that enables a user to select color wash to place over an image or to set it to grayscale, black and white, or washout.

reset   To restore a picture or other formatted object to its default settings.

Ribbon   A strip of icons that appears across the top of the PowerPoint window; divided into tabs, each of which contains groups of related tools.

Rich text Format (RTF)   A text file format that most word processing programs can open and save as.

rows   Horizontal lines in which information and text can be typed.

rulers   Horizontal and vertical measures that help you position objects on a slide.

S

saturation

ScreenTip   A pop-up box that gives a command's name when you point at its button on the Ribbon.

section   A grouping of contiguous slides.

shortcut menu   A menu that appears when you right-click an area or object.

slide library   An organized database of slides.

slide master   A slide that stores information about the formats applied in a presentation, such as theme, fonts, layouts, and colors.

Slide Show view   A view that allows the user to preview a presentation on the screen as it will appear to the audience.

slide size   The dimensions of a slide, which can be altered in the design tab.

Slide Sorter view   A view that displays all of a presentations slides in a single window suited for reorganizing slides.

Smart Guides   Dashed lines that help a user with alignment as shapes are moved around a slide.

SmartArt layout   A particular arrangement of shapes that a SmartArt graphic can have.

subordinates   In an organization chart, persons or departments who are subordinate to another person or department.

ScreenTip   A tool that provides more information about commands.

shortcut menu   A menu that contains a list of useful commands.

SmartArt graphics   Graphical illustrations available within Word from a list of various categories, including List diagrams, process diagrams, Cycle diagrams, Hierarchy diagrams, Relationship diagrams, Matrix diagrams, and Pyramid diagrams.

T

tab   A labeled section of the Ribbon, contains a group of related tools.

table   An arrangement of columns and rows used to organize information.

target   The page, file, or slide that opens when a user clicks a link.

template   A predesigned presentation.

text box   A container that holds text on a slide.

text pane   The fly-out pane that allows you to type information for a SmartArt diagram.

texture   A graphic that repeats to fill an image, creating the appearance that the surface is a certain material, such as marble, wood, or paper.

themes   Schemes of complementing colors.

thumbnails   A small picture of a slide.

timings   The amount of time assigned to each slide before it automatically advances to the next slide.

tone   The subtle tint of an image's color, ranging from warmer shades (more red) to cooler shades (more blue).

top-level shape   In an organization chart, the person or department at the head of the organization.

transitions   The movement from one slide to the next.

V

video   A movie, animated graphic, or motion video clip.

views   The ways in which presentation content can be displayed onscreen, such as Normal view, Slide Sorter view, or Slide Show view.

W

With Previous   An animation setting that causes the animation to begin executing simultaneously with the previous animation or event.

Windows Movie Video (WMV)   The format that PowerPoint saves to when creating videos from presentation files.

worksheet   An excel document used to organize numerical data that can then be analyzed or otherwise manipulated.

workbook   A spreadsheet file containing three pages or worksheets.

WordArt   A feature used to turn text into a formatted graphic.

X

XPS   XML Paper Specifications; one of the page description languages to which PowerPoint can export; requires an XPS Viewer utility to view; this utility comes with Windows Vista and higher, and can be downloaded free from Microsoft for other Windows versions.

XPS Viewer   A utility that views XPS document. This utility comes with Windows Vista and higher, and can be downloaded free from Microsoft for other Windows versions.

Z

zoom   The amount of magnification used to show content onscreen; the higher the zoom, the larger the content.

Index